Media Cleansing: Dirty Reporting
Journalism and Tragedy in Yugoslavia

Peter Brock

Foreword By David Binder

GMBooks
Los Angeles

Library of Congress Cataloging-in-Publication Data

Brock, Peter.

Media Cleansing: Dirty Reporting
Journalism and Tragedy in Yugoslavia
Peter Brock.

Some of the material appearing in this book was published in
Foreign Policy, Number 93/Winter 1993-94, "Dateline Yugoslavia: The Partisan Press"
Mediterranean Quarterly, Volume 6 Number 1, Winter 1995,
"'Greater' Serbia Vs. The Greater Western Media"
Mediterranean Quarterly, Volume 7 Number 4, Fall 1996,
"The Hague: Experiment in Orwellian Justice"
Excerpts from *A Witness to Genocide* reprinted with the permission of Scribner,
an imprint of Simon & Schuster Adult Publishing Group, from *A WITNESS
TO GENOCIDE* by Roy Gutman. Copyright © 1993 by Roy Gutman.

Graphics Management Press
10520 Ohio Avenue
Los Angeles, CA 90024
(310) 475-2988 Fax (310) 475-9486
www.gmbooks.com

ISBN Number 1882383-30-3

1. Media 2. Yugoslavia 3. War correspondents.
4. Journalism. 5. Former Yugoslav republics.
6. Balkan civil wars. 7. Ethnic cleansing.
8. International Criminal Tribunal for Yugoslavia.

Author's web: www.mediacleansing.com

2 4 6 8 9 7 5 3 1

FIRST EDITION

Cover & Book Design by William Dorich

Printed in the United States of America

• 200,000 Bosnian Muslims killed...

• 60,000 Bosnian Muslims raped...

• Serbs had superior weapons while the Bosnian Muslims were virtually "unarmed" and peace-loving "victims."

• Croats, Slovenes, and Bosnians abandoned the Yugoslav federation to avoid "Serb domination."

• 8,000 Muslims killed in Srebrenica massacre...

• 100,000 Muslims slaughtered in Kosovo...

• Tens of thousands of Serb war criminals...

• White House denies violating Bosnian weapons embargo...

• Only Serbs committed atrocities, violated truces, maintained concentration camps, and destroyed shrines and historic sites...

"If you tell a lie big enough and keep repeating it people will eventually come to believe it."

—Paul Joseph Goebbels,
Third Reich Minister of Propaganda
(attributed, circa 1942)

• Dubrovnik destroyed...

• Bosnian government denies blame for Sarajevo breadline, market bombings...

• Serbs "occupied" land belonging to Croats and Muslims...

• Bosnian, Croat hospitals overflow with babies born to Muslim rape victims...

• No mujahedin or al Qa'eda mercenaries fighting in Bosnia...

• Starving villagers resort to cannibalism in eastern Bosnia...

• Bosnian prime minister says 70,000 killed in Bihac...

• Only Serbs had "concentration," and "rape camps"

• Bodies of slaughtered Albanian Muslims dissolved in mining acid pits...

• No massacre of Serbs by Bosnian government troops before Srebrenica attack...

Contents

I

Foreword

By

David Binder

Peter Brock comes from Texas and in this work I detect something of the Lone Ranger in him. He has cantered far and wide seeking out notorious badmen—and some badwomen—in what he accurately describes as "the self-adulating profession of American journalism." His aim: to bring them to a kind of justice.

His context is the decade of civil wars that befell the former Yugoslavia at the end of the 20th century. The timing of these events is important in the evolution of contemporary journalism because they occurred just before the massive reporting-editing scandals that shook such institutions as *The New York Times, CBS, USA Today* and others at the beginning of the 21st century. Those scandals, arising from abuses similar to and as flagrant as those chronicled here, served to enlarge corrective mechanisms throughout the media, enhancing the role of ombudsmen. They also predated the appearance and pell-mell spread of Internet blogs, which also seem to have developed some corrective powers.

The question left hanging is how there could be such a hullabaloo over phony reporting in the new century and virtually none just before. The answer I believe lies partly in the relative safety conferred by the distance of the Balkan conflicts in contrast to the greater likelihood of exposure deriving from the proximity of the later abuses. Another factor might have been the phenomenon of "pack journalism" first identified in 1973 during an American political campaign and appearing abroad for the first time centered at the media hostelry, Sarajevo's Holiday Inn, in the summer of 1992. A technological reason may also have played a role: the satellite uplink for direct television broadcasting was located in the Bosnian capital.

Others (including *BBC's* Nick Gowing and myself) addressed the issue of media bias during the Balkan conflicts at one time or another. But Peter Brock is the first to undertake a full scale investigation: the repulsive, even odious task of charting transgressions by correspondents covering the three-sided 1992-1995 Bosnian conflict as well as the Slovenia and Croatia wars that preceded it plus the Kosovo fighting that followed. These include outright fabrications, widespread use of dubious secondhand sources and blatantly one-sided accounts of strife involving at least two and sometimes three sets of combatants.

Their common denominator was the characterization of Serbs as the principal perpetrators of "ethnic cleansing," mass murder, mass rape and "war crimes" up to and including genocide.

In the category of fabrication he has dissected several articles that led to the award of the parallel 1993 Pulitzer prizes for international reporting: first, the "confession" of thirty-five murders and sixteen rapes in Sarajevo by Borislav Herak, a Bosnian Serb, in a 3,500-word story by John F. Burns for The New York Times and, second, the stories by Roy Gutman of Newsday alleging the creation by Serbs of Nazi-style "concentration camps" for thousands of Bosnian Muslim prisoners, some of whom were slaughtered. Gutman went so far as to evoke Auschwitz.

Brock painstakingly establishes that Herak's "confession" had been tortured out of him by his Bosnian Muslim captors. Separately he determines that Gutman's stories, far from representing on-the-scene reporting, were based on scantily identified sources who never surfaced as real people.

Then he goes further, seeking in "repeated attempts" to confront Burns with his findings. Burns dodges, as do his editors, and never responds. But Brock does finally manage to beard Gutman in Germany more than eighteen months after his "concentration camp" stories. Gutman refuses to discuss his work. Regardless, Brock gives him and others who come under his magnifying glass more than ample space quoting their articles and public commentaries.

One of the themes that runs like an obbligato through this study involves numbers—how many displaced? How many killed? How many raped? The author establishes that all at once in 1993 the number of Bosnian Muslims estimated to have been killed rose astronomically from 20,000 to 200,000. Burns of The Times amplified this at one point to 300,000! Brock then recounts how George Kenney, a Foreign Service officer who quit the State Department in disillusionment over United States passivity toward the Bosnia fighting subsequently became vocally skeptical about the ballooning death numbers. After a lot of research he put the toll at 70,000 to 90,000 and was immediately blackballed by the pro-Bosnian establishment. Not incidentally, the total for ALL SIDES killed in the Bosnia fighting was estimated in mid-2005 by Muslim researchers to be under 150,000.

The author details an almost identical numbers game played by the media and various government officials regarding the number of women raped in Bosnia. Here Roy Gutman again played a central role using dubious sources. Others pouncing on the allegations of "up to 60,000 rapes" of Muslim women by Serb soldiers included *Newsweek's* Charles Lane and colleagues for a cover story and the *Philadelphia Inquirer's* Judy Bachrach for a magazine piece. Conspicuously ignored then and later, as Brock points out, were the 800 cases of raped Serbian women copiously documented for the United Nations. (As with Borislav Herak, whom the International Criminal Tribunal in The Hague refused to indict after the story fell apart, so the court declined to accept as a witness one of Gutman's principal rape accusers who turned out to be using five aliases.)

At the end of the Bosnia fighting in 1995 there were the killings of Muslim males at Srebrenica with numbers climbing from several thousand initially to 8,000 and even 10,000—depending on who was doing the guessing.

It soon became "the worst massacre in Europe since the Holocaust." What we have witnessed with Srebrenica and with the other cases of escalating numbers is a kind of ghoulish rhetorical calculation concocted by the media in conjunction with nongovernmental organizations and various government agencies. The unspoken calculation evidently arises from the perception that one cannot have an accusation of "genocide" or a concomitant indictment by the prosecution at The Hague unless certain levels of "thousands" are involved. The same rationale applied in the Kosovo crisis of 1999, with U.S. Government officials asserting at one point that Serbs had killed "100,000" Albanians.

Other media travesties catalogued here involve such past notables of *The New York Times* as the correspondent, Roger Cohen, and the columnists William Safire and Anthony Lewis. Brock also nails the late Peter Jennings of *ABC News*, Tom

Gjelten of *National Public Radio*, Christiane Amanpour of *CNN*, *Christian Science Monitor's* David Rohde and Mary Battiata of *The Washington Post*.

The Associated Press and *Reuters* also come in for some knocks.

When *USA Today's* Jack Kelley was belatedly (five years after the events) exposed in 2004 as a serial fabricator including his phony Kosovo stories, Brock noted "the eerie hush from other Balkan correspondents" about this affair and writes that the "obvious question went unasked, profession-wide: Was Kelley alone?"

Brock's focus is the American press during the Balkan wars, but he indicates other nationalities were guilty at best of extreme bias and at worst of outright fabrication, He names the *BBC's* Martin Bell and *The Guardian's* Ed Vulliamy as two who openly and proudly boasted of abjuring objectivity.

That reminded me of George Orwell's 1944 condemnation of a phase of extreme bias in the British press (pro-Soviet, anti-Polish at the time of the Warsaw Uprising), coupled with his warning, "Do remember that dishonesty and cowardice always have to be paid for," and his conclusion, "Once a whore, always a whore."

Throbbing like a muffled drumbeat throughout this study is the contention that in the Balkan conflicts the media served as a "co-belligerent"—clearly taking one side. One need only pause an instant to determine whether the media has done the same again by accepting the "invitation" to embed itself with the coalition forces that invaded and occupied Iraq.

David Binder was a member of the Washington Bureau of *The New York Times* from June 1973 to his retirement in 1996. He continued reporting until 2004, specializing in coverage of Central and Eastern European affairs and producing numerous outstanding articles that afforded unique insights into foreign policy and the Yugoslav breakup, differing from the routine slant by most war correspondents. His assignments for *The Times*, including posts in Germany, Belgrade (as East European correspondent) and in Washington as diplomatic correspondent. He reported on the building and fall of the Berlin wall and the collapse of Communist systems in East Germany, Romania, Bulgaria, Albania and Yugoslavia. He graduated from Harvard University and was a Fulbright scholar at the University of Cologne. He has lectured and published articles in Germany, Austria, the former Yugoslavia, Albania, Macedonia, Romania, Hungary, Finland, Japan, Canada and the United States.

He is the author of *Berlin East and West* (1962) and *The Other German—The Life and Times of Willy Brandt* (1976); and a co-author of *New York Times* books on *Project Apollo*, the *Fall of Communism* and *Scientists at Work*.

He lives in suburban Maryland just outside of Washington, D.C.

Preface

There are times when a reporter must sit on his story—and wait. He must wait to see if his original perceptions and information are correct and complete enough, or if there will be new and better information.

Also, he must determine whether later information, though voluminous, might only blur the picture.

It is often an uncomfortable period because friends, colleagues and collaborators expected results sooner. Others are unsympathetic, but equally impatient. They are nervous about what might be written.

Certainly, publishers and editors grow less interested as timeliness is diminished. After all, potentially interested readers cannot be expected to wait forever. The news, as those of us in the business are fond of saying, is highly perishable.

Meanwhile, plenty of other books are churned out by former correspondents who covered parts of events that occurred during the Yugoslav civil wars in the last decade of the 20th Century. Some of the volumes, though necessarily limited in focus and time, are quite sincere and even useful memoirs. Some are not. Some attempted to bolster the toppling façade of biased reporting connected to those wars. And, anyone who claimed they presented the whole "truth" about the latest Balkan upheaval is a liar.

Journalists are poor political scientists and worse foreign policy analysts. Diplomacy is not their game; selling newspapers is. Their job is to factually report what they see and hear, and to ask questions—lots of them. Above all, they are supposed to personally stay out of the story, and not get involved.

The greatest failure of what was published about Yugoslavia during the 1990s is that the Western and chiefly American media's role as a co-belligerent in the sadistic wars that erupted—wars that were certainly preventable—was minimized. Certainly, if the institutional propaganda was modulated, the killing would have diminished.

That is the job of this book, which belatedly attempts to deal with some of the key events and information, but certainly does not presume to be the whole truth about what happened in Yugoslavia. It does describe recurring trends, circumstances and conclusions about what was and what was not written that very probably explain the hazy portrayal of the available "truth" then and now.

It turns out that the "new" information is less abundant although repetitive. And, the "better" information tends to support the grounds for the original inquiries about whether there was, as we in the trade used to caution ourselves before writing, another side to the story.

At a minimum, what follows is a studied examination—though not by any means comprehensive—behind the pattern of what most American daily news consumers could have read and watched for more than a decade concerning the criminal destruction of a sovereign nation. Adding to the abundant volumes with apologetic and clever revisionist themes by the reporters themselves at the end of the decade and the century, here is yet another voice crying out from the wilderness din of the Western media.

After my first trip to Yugoslavia in 1976, I returned to the local library with the typical and intrigued perplexity to find out where I had been. There were only a handful of books on the subject. Today, there are two-shelves full. You'd think Yugoslavia was discovered—and destroyed!—in the 1990s.

For seventy-eight straight days in early 1999, the United States—with token assistance from its puppet partners in NATO—bombed and re-bombed the independent, sovereign republic of Serbia. All agree that relatively few military targets were hit and that massive damage was inflicted instead upon innocent civilian populations in a punitive campaign where cruise missiles were launched and smart bombs were dropped by orders from intelligent generals in Brussels. But the expensive ordnance was lured to hit large wood or metal profiles of tanks and other military vehicles. Attached microwave ovens were used to attract aircraft weapons sensors, said some. Or, NATO pilots who couldn't find new prey simply blew up wreckage from previous attacks. Farm tractors towing wagons full of refugees and trains carrying other civilians were also destroyed in the frenzy. Only later was it realized that the environment is seriously polluted with depleted uranium used in NATO armaments. Plagues of cancer and birth defects are anticipated in the region.

Eventually, even the media became bored with the senseless air show. It was not the video-game successor to the earlier air siege of Baghdad in 1991, as NATO generals hoped. The air attacks ended. Occupation troops—Americans leading the way—settled perhaps permanently in Kosovo.

Except for a handful of highly visible, non-American NATO troops, everybody else wearily went home.

To the few who cared, the international reporting did not improve in coverage of the trickle of returning refugees and the sporadic, inevitable "blood-revenge" between Albanian Muslims and Serbs.

The press infrequently made half-hearted attempts to verify the echoes of what it thought had happened during the decade of Yugoslav fratricide, generally using the war crimes trials at The Hague to trot out the frayed, tiresomely re-inflated statistics.

On November 30, 1999, the *Associated Press* reported tediously from Amsterdam that 8,000 Muslims were massacred in Srebrenica in 1995—four years after the original episode. A day later, *Reuters* reported that the Red Cross estimated that it was 7,300 who were killed in the small eastern Bosnian town that was not listed on most maps. There is no question that several thousand people were killed—some by fellow combatants—in a murderous orgy.

What the International Committee of the Red Cross originally said on September 13, 1995, and again on February 8, 1996, was that 5,000 mostly Muslim troops and civilians fled from Srebrenica into other areas of Bosnia before and during the Serb attacks.

Some reports indicate that many were discreetly assigned to other Bosnian Army units. Some managed to join up with paramilitary groups. Others hid in forests.

Limited exhumations of supposed mass graves near Srebrenica resulted in identifying only some of the "missing" thousands of Muslim corpses—later categorized as civilian non-combatants—the largest number of which were taken to a warehouse at Tuzla. In fact, the Srebrenica region also contains intermittently re-discovered—and, reluctantly reported—mass graves of hundreds of Serb victims murdered during atrocities before 1995. An understandable, even reasonable provocation for subsequent retaliation, some may assert!

The questions about Srebrenica will never be fully answered, and all of the bodies—whether Serb and Muslim fighters and/or civilians—will never be found.

Thus, part of the role of this volume is to consider the many questions that went unasked by the Western media when they should have been asked about the Srebrenica incident in 1995, as well as about other episodes throughout the entire maelstrom. More curious is what happened when the questions—along with others throughout the wars—were asked and answers were ignored or withheld.

There are a few of us who are still wondering.

Introduction

Vukovar, Eastern Slavonia—July 1998

What started in Vukovar in 1991 did not end in Kosovo. Some would say that someday it will all ...end. It will all end in the Balkans, the bloody, bloody Balkans ...despite confidences in interims of enforced "peace." But the "domino theory" in the Balkans still has a long way to go. And the "domino theory" was always the correct theory, the predictable theory, and the only reliable theory to cover up a catastrophic sequence of American and European foreign policy blunders.

When Kosovo re-ignites, the long-awaited tumult could spread to the adjacent Sandjak region, a heavily Muslim area in southwestern Serbia. Would Bosnia explode again? The answer to *when* Bosnia will erupt is probably a generation away—but maybe sooner. Warnings of earlier resumptions of fratricidal chaos accompany fears that American troops under NATO would be involved. Then, Macedonia erupts at some point, and that spillover inflames the jittery Greeks. American troops initially forayed into Macedonia long before the start of KFOR occupation of Kosovo in 1999, when the U.S. government refused to say how many body bags accompanied the "peacekeepers" into the Balkans.

And, if Greece, then Bulgaria and Turkey? Maybe Vojvodina in northern Serbia will destruct, too. And, who knows when Croatia would implode again?

Strange names of strange places, most of these.

Part of the New World Disorder in which the United States is perfecting its most devastating genocidal weapon to date against any sovereign upstart that defies its global *diktat*. The Serbian model began with economic sanctions, then political and social dismemberment and, ultimately, military attack and occupation.

Such is the fate of the former Yugoslavia. And, in 1998, the falling domino was Kosovo. And, the politicians and "war reporters" never could or would get the names and numbers right. Forget sorting out the names. Kosovo-Serbs? Muslim-Kosovars? Even after a blood-soaked decade, the journalists couldn't get it right. Why?

For instance, a reporter for *Reuters* who covered the Yugoslav wars for several years wrote about a man named "Zarko Spasic" who disappeared near the village of Sipovac in Kosovo,[1] one of two "autonomous provinces" in Serbia. Finally, in the eleventh paragraph of the report, readers could figure out that Zarko Spasic was a Serb who was kidnapped and murdered by Albanian Muslims in the Kosovo Liberation Army (KLA).

"Zarko" and "Spasic" are recognizably *enough* Serbian names. But, most people who read the article, including American news editors, did not speak Serbo-Croatian and could not make any distinction. And, chances are that readers never found out because rarely did such a story include explanations that were readily "edited" or "chopped." Most newspapers were "tight on space," and "readers have short attention spans." Besides, it was like every second, third or hundredth story that came out of "the war."

---

1. Kurt Schork, *Reuters*, May 18, 1998.

But, the reporter *knew* what he was writing.

Maddeningly, journalists used this method of allowing presumption and mistaken inference to occur until deep into the narratives of thousands of such accounts—and long after copy editors had excised the most critical information—throughout the war reporting of the 1990s!

And, the Kosovo "liberation army"?! An embarrassment for democratic apologists in the West that such an obsolete "communist" term self-identified a rabble of Islamic terrorist/secessionists propped up by the international press as freedom-fighting, democracy-loving "patriots."

The same reporter wrote another story a month later on June 26, 1998:

> "(H)undreds of people have been killed since February when the police killed more than 80 people, including 25 Albanian women and children, in assaults on suspected strongholds of armed insurgents of the Kosovo Liberation Army."

The numbers *do* say something. Supposedly, fifty-five Albanian Muslim rebels made up the balance, it could be calculated. Then, who were the rest of the "hundreds of people"? Who were these other "people"? The reporter did not or would not say.

But two days later, a report by the *Associated Press* described "a Serb police offensive against secessionist ethnic Albanian militants" who in March had "killed 300 people."[2] So, there were at least 220 other "people" who were killed! Who were they?

Obviously, they were Serbs. Does it matter?

That's the way the Yugoslav wars were reported for most of the decade.

There were originally two million or so Muslims—of Albanian ancestry, supposedly—in Kosovo. They were portrayed as an "oppressed minority" by the media. There were less than 200,000 resident Serbs there characterized as their oppressors.

Maybe someone would sit down in the cold ashes and dusty rubble when it was all over and try to figure out the numbers.

Which numbers? The right numbers, that is. It should matter.

They ought to try to figure it all out from the numbers. Because the words and pictures didn't get the job done, and nothing else will matter except that sickening Balkan rottenness of death by the numbers.

Does it really matter where it officially started or who started it and who kept it going, officially? And, why would somebody write a book about it?

Vukovar is as good a place as any to begin. It was one of the most over-reported though factually disjointed and most damning stories about the dismantling of Yugoslavia.

Preposterously, some of the more romantic sensationalists in the Western press in 1991 tried to call the three-month shelling of Vukovar the modern-day successor to the infamous two-year siege of Stalingrad. That's because they were never at Stalingrad a half-century earlier or they never read the history of Stalingrad where hundreds of thousands of Russians and German troops perished in World War II. However, "Stalingrad" looked surrealistically good in headlines about Vukovar—which few in the West ever knew existed.

Actually, Kosovo was the predictable sequel to the previous seven years of tragedy and catastrophe which began at, among other places, Vukovar.

It doesn't matter after the long years of American-coerced economic sanctions by the United Nations that inflicted Third World poverty and resurrected medieval

---

2. Adam Brown, *Associated Press*, June 28, 1998.

suffering for millions of innocent victims in Serbia and Kosovo—Serb and Muslim alike.

Thus, a "new" global totalitarianism in the guise of NATO and thousands of occupying troops instituted an international police state, aided and abetted organized crime and black-marketeering, manipulated outlawed shipments of sophisticated weapons (with chemical and biological capabilities), and incited religious and civil war, revolution, terrorism and genocide in the Balkans—which until recent years had existed in relative peace and slowly emerging prosperity.

That all ended when the so-called "peace agreements" of the extorted Dayton Accords in 1995 guaranteed further bloody outbreaks and carnage—throughout future generations, as well—in what was called too glibly the "former Yugoslavia."

To most Western politicians and journalists, who a decade earlier had no competent understanding of the region and its people, the self-fulfilling ends justified the criminal means that were instigated far from the bloody battlefields, the refugee collection centers, vile detention camps, mass graves, and the ruthless and cruel displacement of civilians.

The civilized hypocrisy of war crimes trials, so-called, at The Hague is itself an illegal exercise of selective prosecution to demonize, generally, one group of belligerents, while the political masterminds, international corporate and diplomatic mercenaries, their slavish media operatives and strategists in Washington, D.C., New York City, Bonn, London, Paris and the Vatican—war criminals all—are untouched and concealed from an uninterested public.

Ever so rare was that lone and outraged voice of journalistic conscience:

> "The 'international community' has prolonged the war, has added to the number of deaths by the thousands. And, if there were ever any real celestial war crimes trials, then people like Chancellor Kohl of Germany, the then-foreign minister Hans Dietrich Genscher of Germany, who pushed for the recognition of Slovenia and Croatia all through the summer and fall of 1991, should be in the dock as war criminals. And I think you'd have George Bush and James Baker in there as war criminals for recognizing Bosnia-Herzegovina …(T)hey are at least as guilty for the deaths of hundreds of thousands of Muslims, Serbs and Croats."[3]

The "beginnings" of this fratricide were especially vexing for Western journalists and media.

Especially, to American memories, Pearl Harbor or the more recent "wars" in the Persian Gulf and other expeditions for partial conquest had, apparently, emphatic enough beginnings. Americans believed that they "won" World War II, and assumed "victory" against Iraq under George Bush Sr.[4]

But wars are never really won; they are only ended by exhaustion, depletion and the temporary amnesia for recalling why and how it all started, or why it should go on. Americans "won" their last war too long ago. They will not "win" future wars.

---

3. Veteran *New York Times* Balkan correspondent David Binder, interviewed in the documentary film, "Dr. Dove: International Involvement in the Balkan Conflict," directed/produced by Milka Stanisic, 1997.

4 Conflicts in Afghanistan and the second Iraqi war under President George W. Bush remained inconclusive through mid-2005.

Nobody will. Most prophetic were the Korean and Vietnam wars, which were emphatically lost. True enough, mainland cities of the United States never were climactically overrun nor decimated by foreign attackers (until September 11, 2001). During Vietnam, American cities did burn at the hands of their own citizens, but there were no dramatic surrenders. There was only humiliating withdrawal and abandonment of Southeast Asia.

In Yugoslavia, although the numbers of soldiers and civilians killed, wounded and missing—and the refugees and victims seemed important enough to magnify as the horrific events themselves were occurring—the numbers seemed less compelling, even when echoed by war crimes prosecutors at The Hague.

Surrealistically (the use of the word cannot be excessive when used to describe the war reporting in Yugoslavia), scores of thousands of lives were too routinely eliminated by rounding off a decimal point by the journalists or their editors. So, expunged citizens became faceless. They had never laughed nor wept. They had never struggled nor sweat, nor had families, celebrated marriages nor had children. They never suffered anguish, remorse, hatred. They never buried the dead. For that matter, they never had died because, being numberless, they had never lived.

Such thoughts echoed randomly while I drove through the deserted and exploded remains of the Serb village of Grubisno Polje—formerly a small town with a mostly Serbian population in northern Croatia—on a hot day in early 1992.

The Slovenian "war" ended after just ten days during the previous summer. The subsequent Croatian war ended after six months. The Bosnian war was starting and would continue for three and a half years. Kosovo? Who knew?

Except for the flapping of curtains and broken windows, or breezes ruffling clothes that still hung in exposed second-story closets where the sides of houses were blown away, there was no movement. No people. Not even soldiers from the Croatian army were left behind to guard—what? Ruins? Piles of broken plaster, burned bricks and beams?

Only the roses remained. Gangly, unpruned, top-heavy stems loaded with blooms of all colors, swaying, mourning and leaning out from walls, dangling trellises and lattices now smashed and splintered.

An occasional house appeared with no damage at all. Red, pink and white geraniums overflowed their boxes beneath unbroken windows. Shutters were not torn from their hinges. It was as though a visitor could walk up to the front door and knock and be asked inside for coffee and pose stupid questions to dazed but polite hosts. What happened here? How many people were killed? Where are the rest? When did it begin? Who was responsible? What else do I need to ask? What should I ask?

But taking a few steps around the side of the unscratched front, the back of the house came startlingly into view—scorched, collapsed and splotched from sprays of bullets and shrapnel gouges.

I spotted a wool cap half buried in the dirt and walked over to pull it up. A few feet away was an unexploded artillery round. And, mines! I stepped into my footsteps back to the road, angry at my carelessness. Driving away from the edge of the ghostly ruins, I noticed a small house in the middle of a barren field. I saw an old man and woman sitting on their front stoop, motionless, wearing smudged, dark clothes. They didn't move. With their patient peasant gazes, they sat and stared. But, were they the ones who had never lived because they had never died?

People should be careful with numbers and decimal points. They can be dangerous. In Yugoslavia, the Western press was not careful with numbers or words or pictures.

But, why would somebody write about it—now? And, what was it about the "numbers"—and Vukovar? Remember?

In the beginning of 1991, there were 600,000 or more Serbs living in pockets of the boomerang-shaped republic of Croatia. In a five-day period between January 25 and January 29, the international news services variously reported the population of Croatia at 4.6 million, 4.7 million, 5 million, 5.4 million, even up to 5.8 million. Sometimes it counted Croats alone, and sometimes it included Serbs. Sometimes it didn't say at all. But, moving the decimal point either way erased or added at least 100,000 people. True, the official numbers differed from Zagreb and Belgrade, but getting sloppy about the numbers was the beginning of bad habits by the Western press on the eve of the war.

The 1981 federal census reported the population of Vukovar, once prided by communists as an ideal industrial city beside the Danube River in Croatia's eastern Slavonia, was 82,375. The ethnic breakdown of Vukovar's population gave the Croats an apparent thirty-seven percent majority, while Serbs accounted for thirty-one percent, "Yugoslavs" twenty-two percent, and "others" ten percent. The latter comprises sizable numbers of Hungarians, Slovaks, Ruthenians and Ukrainians.[5]

However, an important distinction cannot be casually bypassed. Vukovar was populated mostly by Serbs from ancient times up until the beginning of World War II when forced mass conversions, killings and displacements of Serbs by the Croat Ustashe were carried out. In the post-war period through 1990, the Croatian government manipulated subtle changes in the character of Vukovar with its Serb majority. Sensing Croat designs for an ethnically pure state, many Serbs concealed their identities and instead officially designated themselves as "Yugoslavs" for census purposes.

By 1990, the nationalist movement among Croats—expressed the loudest by the Croatian Democratic Union (HDZ) political party—was openly promoting Croatian independence, secession from Yugoslavia and inciting anti-Serb hostility. Formation of a Serbian national party was disallowed just before the 1990 multi-party elections (April 22 and May 6), leaving Serb "Yugoslavs" no option but to support the League of Communists of Croatia/Party of Democratic Changes (SKH-SDP).

The HDZ was solidly defeated, while the SKH-SDP won four out of Vukovar's allotted five seats to the Croatian Parliament. The fifth seat went to a so-called "Independent" candidate. Also, the HDV won only twenty-six of the 116 positions in the Vukovar Municipal Assembly—the HDV representatives coming only from areas with absolute Croatian majorities. The election losses in Vukovar set the stage for the HDV's plan to suspend the rule of local government through incitement of Croat-Serb antagonisms and the eventual appointment of a Zagreb-appointed "commissioner." On July 17, 1990, the Vukovar Municipal Assembly voted against ratification of the revamped Croatian constitution, which radically reflected Croatian supremacy and substantially excluded provisions for equality and protection of minorities.

The next year saw a series of orchestrated murders, night arrests, random shootings into darkened Serb houses, café bombings, residential explosions and the circulation of bogus "liquidation lists" naming Vukovar Serbs. It eventually realized the strategically planned exodus or "cleansing" of 14,000 out of the city's 18,000 remaining Serbs before August 1, 1991, according to documents filed later at The Hague—which were remarkably ignored by the Western media. Sporadic though predictable incidents of Serb retaliation played into the plan, receiving exaggerated outrage in Zagreb.

The Hague documents describe in detail numerous grisly episodes of kidnapping, torture, sensational allegations of forced donations of blood from Serb prisoners at the Vukovar hospital and executions on the banks of the Danube River that became

---

5. Ethnic Comparison of Population in SFR Yugoslavia, Vol. 1,
Data by Communities and Municipalities, Belgrade, 1981.

the dumping ground for Serb corpses. The Danube, it was historically proven with Ustashe atrocities in World War II, rarely gives up its dead and can be counted upon as a faithful accomplice, a reliable mass grave that can never be exhumed. One recovered body, according to Croatian police records on July 11, 1991, was identified as forty-six-year-old Slobodan Vuckovic, who had been beaten and shot in the head. The "epidermis (was) removed from the entire body," and his throat was cut.

Tanks and armored vehicles from the Yugoslav Peoples Army (JNA) garrison in Vukovar finally clashed with Croatian troops and militia after a truck bombing near the village of Borovo Selo where one JNA private was killed and four were wounded. At about the same time, local Serbs had ambushed and killed several Croat police at Borovo Selo. The "siege of Vukovar," as Croatian secessionists had hoped and planned would captivate international headlines and television reports, was deliberately allowed to rage until late November.

But, was it all planned in advance, as documents on file at The Hague suggested? It was claimed that several large "nuclear fallout" shelters in Vukovar were constructed, capable of holding 10,000 persons. The shelters were supposedly constructed during the previous ten years, using revenues from a three-percent tax collected on all local construction. By mid-October 1991, Serbs were being herded into supposed "shelters" which were used as detention locations, according to files at The Hague. Many Serb and some Croat civilians, who chose to remain in their sturdy cellars (built routinely throughout the bountiful wine producing region), were searched out, seized and killed just before the "fall of Vukovar"—and, as possible witnesses to Croat war crimes, were disposed of into the insatiable Danube and other rivers and ponds.

As late as April 9, 1991, Vukovar's Serbian mayor Slavko Dokmanovic pleaded with Croatian President Franjo Tudjman to act to prevent chaos and tragedy, and "demanded measures that would prevent the outbreak of armed conflicts." The plea was ignored.

When Vukovar was emptied of most of its Serb citizens, and the remainder would not or could not leave, Tudjman arrived on July 24, 1991, when every government function, especially local law enforcement, was broken down. According to documents at The Hague, Tudjman hypocritically chastised Serbs who had barricaded themselves outside town in a half-dozen small villages for being voluntarily "detached from other parts of the municipality."

"...(T)he law and constitution should be allowed to function and institutions of the system to discharge their duties throughout the entire territory of the Vukovar municipality," said Tudjman,[6] knowing full well that "cleansing" of Serbs and Croat spouses of Serbs was openly occurring at the hands of some Croat police and members of his own party's "militia."

In late June 1998 after his trial ended at The Hague and just days before the Tribunal justices would announce their verdict,[7] Dokmanovic supposedly hanged himself at midnight in his cell, though "under close surveillance for his psychological condition." Although lights were ordered kept on at all times in his cell, his body was found hanging in the dark. A cord from somewhere outside the cell was used.

He had been arrested and charged with complicity in the alleged murders of 200 Vukovar hospital patients after the city fell to the JNA. It was the same hospital where injured and wounded Serbs were brought and were frequently denied treatment, say documents at The Hague, adding that forced Serb blood donors were held in the hospital cellar where their blood was extracted at gunpoint!

---

6. *Vukovarske Novine*, July 27, 1991.
7. *Reuters*, June 29, 1998.

"There was no reaction from chief prosecutor Louise Arbour (about Dokmanovic's death) to this latest setback to the Tribunal's work, which took the shine off the Dutch government's recent announcement that The Hague would play host to a permanent international court," said a *Reuters* report cynically. The former Vukovar mayor had insisted he was innocent throughout his six-month trial.

There would be no verdict for the dead man nor any official resolution of the charge of conspiracy in the 200 alleged murders at the Vukovar hospital. The international media did not get the headline it planned for, and Dokmanovic's "suicide" became as forgotten as the 220 Serbs—or "other people"—killed seven years later in Kosovo where, like Vukovar, it was just the beginning.

Chapter 1

Yugoslavia and
'The Despair Of Tidy Minds'

"A bad beginning makes for a bad ending."[1]
—Aeolus

"Hear the other side."[2]
—Saint Augustine

Joe Suponcic joined the Army in 1991 a few days after he graduated from Jersey Shore High School. Nobody was surprised. It was the customary ticket out of small-town monotony for countless Pennsylvania youngsters.

Only a tiny ten-day-old civil war was hiccupping to an end in the far-away Yugoslav republic of Slovenia. Nobody was worried.

Ironically, Suponcic had distant Slovenian ancestors. But Jersey Shore only had about 5,000 people and was not one of those huge Slavic-American melting pots like Pittsburgh. In small towns people got along.

One look at the local plastics manufacturing plant and nearby steel mill inspired vows to leave town as soon as possible. It was, after all, a big world out there. So, the eighteen-year-old Suponcic and a few others joined up.

Jersey Shore is not a beach front town. Two-hundred miles or so inland from New Jersey and the Atlantic Ocean, Jersey Shore sits on the west bank of the Susquehanna River that curls south and then slides westward a few miles later. Supposedly, the original inhabitants were from New Jersey, as one story has it. So, when folks on the east bank of the river said they were going to visit friends on the west side, they said they were going to the Jersey shore.

Another story about how the town got its name was that a farmer used to let his Jersey cows wander down the far side of the river to graze near the site of the future town. Joe's mother, Patty, disagrees that the cows were founders of Jersey Shore.

No surprise, then, that journalists and television crews never showed any interest in Jersey Shore, which seemed to be just another one of those oddly-named central Pennsylvania communities. When Joe Suponcic left town, it had three traffic lights; one blinked red continuously.

---

1. Fragment 32
2. From *De Daubus Animabus*, XIV, 2.

"It's so quiet around here in winter," said one resident, "you can hear the snow fall."

But the reporters swarmed noisily into town just a few days after Patty Suponcic sent off her twenty-six-year-old son's Christmas package. It seemed she had just left the Jersey Shore post office, when the Army solemnly informed the family he was being brought home.

Staff Sgt. Joe Suponcic's casket arrived two days before Christmas beneath an American flag.

On the day of the funeral, the sun was brilliant, dodging past clouds. The air was crisp and cold. The wind was raw and, eventually, snow flurries swirled haphazardly. A packed crowd turned out for the funeral. Among them was a sprinkling of uniformed young men who formed the honor guard.

The weather was the same in far-away Kosovo.

That's where Joe Suponcic, a Green Beret, died when an anti-tank mine exploded on a road supposedly cleared of explosives. Suponcic was riding in the Humvee as it bumped along on patrol just outside of Kosovska Kamenica.

Until Suponcic died, nobody in Jersey Shore had ever heard of Kosovska Kamenica. Few remembered it moments after it was first mentioned.

"He went to serve his country and an unfortunate thing happened," said a neighbor, sounding somewhat vexed and struggling to explain why the young man died.

The Army admitted, reluctantly, he was the first U.S. soldier killed—technically as a combatant—in Kosovo, although at least seven others died in vehicle accidents, from electrocution, parachuting mishaps and suicide.

Suponcic's C Company, 3rd Battalion, of the 10th Special Forces, was attached to the North Atlantic Treaty Organization's (NATO) Kosovo Force, or KFOR. Acronyms don't answer questions about why young men die.

Suponcic's commanding officer, a lieutenant colonel, gave the eulogy. His most memorable statement to mourners, according to one reporter, was that Suponcic was the honor graduate of his class at the Army's Ranger School. Nobody uttered "martyr."

Just before he was sent to Kosovo in October 1999, Suponcic learned basic Serbo-Croatian—politically corrected and cleansed by the Army as only "Croatian." With slightly different dialects, it also is the historically common language of Slovenia, Serbia, Bosnia, Montenegro, Macedonia, and Kosovo.

He was proud of the accomplishment and spoke it enthusiastically for the Albanian population in Kosovo, newly called "Kosovars." The Slav-featured kids followed him around, calling him "Joey Blue Eyes."

On December 16, 1999, the American flags outside the little Pennsylvania post office and other buildings were lowered to half-mast to honor Suponcic. Nobody in Jersey Shore seemed to know exactly when to raise them again.

Despite the flag-waving and patriotic sentiments of Jersey Shore's veterans of past wars, Suponcic died nobly for an increasingly questionable cause.

"We have no regrets," said Patty Suponcic later. Joe was her eldest son, ahead of a younger brother and sister.

Joe Suponcic was buried at Arlington National Cemetery.

Exactly four years later, former NATO commander Wesley Clark, in panting pursuit of the Democratic presidential nomination and anxious to polish up his checkered Kosovo record, would advertise that "he led a multinational force that stopped a campaign of terror, liberated a people and brought peace without the loss of a single American soldier," according to *The Washington Post* (December 17, 2003). The newspaper's war memory was equally short.

Clark's boast was not received well in Jersey Shore.

Borovo Selo, Eastern Slavonia (Croatia)—May 1991

Vukasin Soskocanin, pronounced (VOO-kah-sheen shosh-KO-cha-neen), comes to mind again. It is January 13, 1994. I practiced saying it since I first heard it in the summer of 1991, and then it was forgotten. I am surprised to hear it echoing in my mind three years later as I drive off from Gnadenthal in the hilly Taunus region of western Germany.

Soskocanin was dead, and one story was as believable as the next about how he died in early May 1991 while crossing the Danube River to Borovo Selo, a tiny village at the edge of eastern Croatia just north of Vukovar. Borovo Selo, inhabited mostly by Serbs, was where Croat police and armed Serb civilians one day "officially" opened fire on each other, killing several on both sides.

Supposedly, a Serb "who fired the first shot" was quickly given sanctuary in England, according to Croatian television reports. But, it wasn't Soskocanin.

Soskocanin made an earlier night crossing over the huge river along with others in a group of mercenaries with members of a small group of Serb militia. Depending on the storyteller, Soskocanin was not a Serb and instead was believed to be Rumanian. He was reportedly shot by sniper fire from the Croatian riverbank. He died before toppling into the water or drowned. Either way, his bulletproof vest quickly dragged him under. He was found later and his body was kept for burial—for three weeks! Serbs hailed him as a martyr; Croats claimed he was drunk when he fell into the Danube and died not from a bullet but because he did not know how to swim.

After three weeks of eulogies and ridicule in the humid summer heat, his rapidly decaying body was finally buried to the relief of mourners and scoffers alike. His name escaped mention in most of the news reports. It wasn't likely he would be mentioned prominently, if at all, when books were written about the war.

Books would assemble the "facts" according to dates, travels, places, events, personal anecdotes and so on.

Western news articles and wire services often included such chronologies first in the Slovenian war, then the Croatian and subsequent Bosnian and Kosovo wars. But the chronologies omitted or oversimplified much important information. The routine recitations and references to "ancient" hostilities were left out gradually as the events appeared to be self-fulfilling—likewise with the battles, the diplomatic charade, the sieges, the refugees, the atrocities and the dead.

Chronology has its place, especially in the Balkans and certainly in Yugoslavia where the past is always palpably present. But the chronology is not finished. There is no "last word" about the destruction of Yugoslavia or the demise of the Western media that manipulated the cruel tragedy.

Especially in Yugoslavia, there is always at least one more side to any story.

Torine, Vojvodina (Serbia)—October 7, 1988

The probability of war in Yugoslavia is worrisome even on this beautiful morning. But it is unthinkable to speculate aloud. Instead, I turn over in my mind the vexation about when it will start, where it will start.

Certainly, not here, above the glistening Danube River on hills garnished with the deep hues and pungent aromas of fall. The abundant Pannonian harvest is gathered. Orchards are ablaze with leaves daubed in gold, red and maroon, ignited in a final flourishing radiance before the year-end. The frost-softened ground heaves up its loamy, death-sweet, incense-like respirations.

Beginnings derive, after all, from such endings. Or, in the case of Yugoslavia, endings aborted by official pronouncements four decades earlier that World War II —and the Yugoslav civil war it concealed—had "ended." It wasn't that simple. Such wars become devoutly internalized, nurtured, and then are resurrected in vile, self-damning fury.

There are many such beginnings, fewer endings. Or, at least, this is how it seems to be. Who can know when a thing really begins? Especially, if it is a war—or several wars imploding on each other?

It seems useless speculation. It is easier not to think about what will happen to the people who try to live peaceably between them. For them the worries are ever present, resonating with the thud of a spade at the base of a plum tree, a surprisingly clear call from a neighbor far up the side of the hill, or a piercing note from a bird somewhere high in the cloudless morning sky.

Paul Ceric's voice penetrates my dull musings. He talks incessantly as we trudge up the path, hauling the huge tub of fermented fruit between us.

He draws long breaths of crisp October air, exhaling smoky vapors that curl behind him as we climb the dew-slicked embankment. The handful of small summer-houses and gardens below Paul's orchards form the tiny hamlet of Torine.

The sun has not yet touched the dusky yellow grass on the west slope of the hill. Behind us and below, the Danube catches the first beams of light. To the west and north are the outskirts of Novi Sad, the largest city in Vojvodina of northern Serbia. Further up river is Vukovar, a less known and smaller city on the great trans-European river.

"Isn't it wonderful here?" He exults, his free hand sweeping over his acreage, the river and sky all at once. It is all a spoil won in Paul's own desperately personal conflict.

About twenty-five years earlier, Paul and his wife lugged two suitcases along the railroad tracks to the train station at Novi Sad, having finally received official permission to emigrate from communist Yugoslavia. Paul, a physician, and his wife, a dentist, had tickets for a train to the Hungarian border and just enough money for airfare to the United States. They chose to stumble over the rail ties in the dark rather than walk along the road because Paul feared they would be shot by police agents who might be waiting along the main road. They were leaving their families behind, maybe forever.

And now, decades later, Paul has recently left his wife and their two American-born teenage daughters with their ample home and swimming pool in New Jersey, vowing to pay for their schooling and other needs as best he could. In America, he started out pumping gas and working at odd jobs until he joined the medical research staff at a hospital and started, he hoped, a fulfilling career. The house was eventually paid for. His wife had a good job as a dental assistant. In fact, she was a better dentist than her boss, he boasts. He loves his family, but he did not expect them to come with him or even to completely understand why he was uprooting and returning to Yugoslavia when the Balkan nation was on the eve of disintegration and a series of wars.

"Life in the States is empty and lonely," he often said. "You cannot have a few friends come over to sit in front of your house, tell some stories and have a few drinks. Not like here. You go to help friends with a roof or to prune their trees. Then, they come to help you. Everyone is friendly. In America, you don't even know your neighbor who lives in the next house. You see him go to work and come home, and maybe you wave sometime. But it is not like here. America is a cold place."

4

He made two trips back since arriving the year before, returning with large shipping containers filled with equipment and supplies for construction of his new house down the hill and across a large orchard from Dusan Stanar, the patriarch of Torine. Old Dusko, a famous World War II partisan, helped Paul build his new house that, unlike his neighbors' dwellings, featured plenty of double-pane storm windows, plumbing, gadgets, American touches.

We lug the first of two containers into a small shed in front of Dusko's plain two-story farmhouse. It is not even seven o'clock, but Dusko has the fire burned down to coals beneath his shining copper still. The three of us pour the mash into it, and the national ritual of homemade *slivovitsa* commences, requiring a series of tests from a small cup filled from a spigot under the coils. First, the white-headed Dusko takes a sample, smacking his lips in mock expression of the serious connoisseur. Then it is Paul's turn, as I realized that I am to join in as the morning's entertainment for the two more experienced enthusiasts of brandy at sunrise.

I hold my own quite impressively, I think, until an hour later I announce that I will just step outside for some fresh air. The light is blinding, and the air has become warm, almost stifling. A little exercise seems like a good idea, and I begin to walk toward the nearby farmhouse, using a fence to steady my strangely uncertain steps. I don't even notice that I am groping my way along the top strand of barbed wire. Dusko's white farmhouse looms ahead like an iceberg. I spot a large stuffed chair just inside an open door. I don't remember sitting or even falling toward it.

Hours later, my eyes open and begin to focus on the large round moon. But, instead it gradually becomes an old woman's face, blinking and smiling behind the steam from a cup of Turkish coffee. It is Dusko's wife, trying to coax me back to consciousness. I can hear Paul and Dusko talking at a table just outside the door. I sip the Turkish coffee, watching the old lady carry out plates of bread, pork and huge scallions. It is early afternoon. Surprisingly, I can stand, waiting for my knees to buckle. Several deep breaths later, I steady myself and walk outside.

"Well, did you have a good nap?" asks Paul behind a teasing smile. Dusko points to an empty chair. His speech is unintelligible to me, but Paul translates.

"He says you are now an official partisan." Everyone laughs, including a third younger man with darker Illyrian features. His name is Ibrahim, and his huge hand swallows mine as we are introduced. He is barefoot and has walked over to see Dusko.

"Ibrahim is genuine Albanian," says Paul. "He came here with his family from Kosovo because of all of that trouble. Dusko let him have some of his land, and he is building a new house."

Dusko growled something.

"Dusko says the nationalism is all bad and that it is right for all Yugoslavs to help each other."

Again, Dusko's gruff voice interrupts.

"He says there is only Yugoslavia. The ones who are trying to break it up should all be shot."

And he means it. Paul goes on to tell a story about how Dusko, a partisan sapper who blew up bridges while fighting the Germans forty years before, came back to Novi Sad after the war. The old decorated war hero sits with one lanky leg crossed over the other, leaning on the blue table and puffing on a cigarette stub.

"Once, he was in a kafana with his friends and this drunk guy began insulting communists and Yugoslavia and the partisans. The guy went to the toilet, and Dusko got up and went after him. They found the guy later. He was shot dead."

The old partisan was arrested for murder, but he was later released without a trial.

Dusko takes the bottle of his homemade wine and tops off my glass with the dark red vintage, passing it next to Paul.

"He is famous, you know," says Paul. "He was one of the partisans who blew up the bridge over the Neretva River in the war. His name is in a book."

I ask Paul to tell more about the famous episode on the Bosnian river that cut off huge numbers of German troops and armor. Paul shrugs, saying he cannot remember much. I suspect the *slivovitsa* and wine is blurring his memory. It has been a successful day with a good yield from Dusko's distillery.

We say goodbye and leave in Paul's car for his native village about forty kilometers north of Novi Sad.

"We'll stay there tonight because there is no stove yet at my house," he says.

As we drive along, he points out several landmarks, giving short histories about an event or a person he remembers from his boyhood. He becomes more serious as his recollections came closer to the present.

"I don't know what will happen, but I think it is incredible that these people in Slovenia and Croatia want to pull out of Yugoslavia," he laments angrily. "Everywhere in Europe, the walls and borders are coming down. They are going to be using one currency. But in Slovenia and Croatia they want to put in borders and use different money. They're crazy to stir all this up. And Bosnia, too. It could be very bad there. And Kosovo, you know. Where Ibrahim and his family came from. Do you know? They came here with *nothing*!"

"Did Dusko really just give this man, a stranger, a piece of his land?" I ask.

"Of course, but he will pay Dusko something later. Now, the two of them will work together, both of them."

Paul becomes silent, lost in thought behind the same worried expression I had seen on the faces of most of my friends in Serbia, Croatia, Bosnia, Slovenia, and now in Vojvodina.

He brightens a moment later. "But here in Vojvodina, we are very lucky. Things are peaceful. It will not happen here. It will not start here."

By "it" he means more than one war, maybe several wars simultaneously. Slovenia, he says, should secede.

"There are very few Serbs there. But in Croatia there are more than 600,000 Serbs, and more than one million in Bosnia!"

It is dark by the time we arrive in Zabalj, and supper is waiting for us at the flat of a childhood friend he is re-acquainted with.

As we eat, the words echo beneath the warmth of the conversation. If...when... where... But we do not talk about it again that night, or the next morning.

Vinkovci, Eastern Croatia – June 1991

I sit with a friend and his family I've known for fifteen years here in Vinkovci. We watch Secretary of State James Baker say on Belgrade television that the United States favors a continued unity of the Yugoslav republics. I need no interpreter, listening to Baker's own words as the commentator translates. My hosts are silent. Baker is visibly nervous. He knows the Balkan volcano is primed.

I drove over from Belgrade, the Serb and Yugoslav capital, a few days earlier. While there, I sensed the epidemic tension, becoming finally listless, sitting in my room at the Park Hotel near the teeming Slavija Circle. Slumped in a chair, I watched the evening haze change the color of the blotched plaster and mottled exteriors of adjacent apartment buildings. Occasionally, someone moved past a lighted window or hung a cloth on the railing of a tiny balcony.

Huge swarms of blackbirds flew south over the city.

I brought no good news back to Vinkovci, only desperate optimism from Belgrade friends.

I was reassured in Osijek, also in Croatia, a day or so later when another longtime acquaintance Peter Kuzmic smiled and announced, "There will be no war. We Yugoslavs are very good at improvising at the last minute."

I wanted to believe him, but went back to nearby Vinkovci to say goodbye to my longtime friend.

After the uncomfortable, too euphoric sharing of departure wishes with his family, I drove off, planning to visit another friend, Gregor, a physician in the federal Yugoslav army now stationed at Zagreb. Gregor is a Serb from Nis.

A few hours later, Gregor and I walk quickly up into the old town district above Zagreb's crowded main square. He is in civilian clothes and very edgy, fearful he would be recognized as a Serb. We choose a small restaurant in Tkalciceva Street and order beer and pizza. We chat for a while at a corner table about anything but politics or thoughts about how the "situation," as he calls it, worsens each hour. He looks up anxiously each time the door opens, as though expecting something or someone. It is late afternoon when we walk grimly back to his quarters in a large hotel-like barracks just off Zagreb's main square. He said he'll be glad when he returns home in a few days.

I return to the main square, called *Trg Republike*, and the swarms of pedestrian commuters. It is quitting time and thousands are going home to watch television news programs for the rest of the night. People stare with paralyzed expressions at the headlines of *Vjesnik* and other newspapers they buy mechanically, never seeing the hand that takes their money. Some take a few steps and then stop to read entire articles before continuing on to the tram stops. Others fold their papers and hurry off.

The sun is just above the rim of the buildings at the west end of the large square. I don't feel like eating or returning to my small room at the Hotel Dalmatia just off the square. Instead, I spot an empty table outside of a restaurant at the far end where I watch the flow of people. Another beer might cure the dreary echoes of my depressing reunion and conversation with Gregor. I plan to leave for Ljubljana in Slovenia the next day and try to absorb a last impression of Zagreb.

I understand the Croats least of all. My closest friends in Yugoslavia are Croats, but I have not read too deeply into their literature, politics or their Austro-Hungarian, Slavic history. "The Croats are always in search of their next master," said a young, urbane Zagreb architect.

Unlike Slovenia, Croatia contained hundreds of thousands of Serbs who lived there for generations, or had lately descended from transplanted populations before and after World War II. As with huge relocations of Albanians to Kosovo, the communists went too far in tampering with people and soil. The whimsical imposition of administrative borders after World War II was naively utopian. Now, it seemed criminal. Slovenia and Croatia were always sentimentally if not practically joined to the Austro-Hungarian empire and Germany.

Most people in Croatia, Serbia and Slovenia are terrified that war was coming. They fear most what will happen in Bosnia-Herzegovina. Conflict would come to Croatia and Slovenia; it is only a question of severity. But madness would visit Bosnia. It would be Serbs fighting "Serbs" who centuries earlier converted to Islam to survive the half-millennium of occupation by the Ottoman Turks.

Catholic Slovenia and Croatia are no less reconcilable with Orthodox Serbia.

Serbs would fight fellow Slavs in Croatia and probably Slovenia. Then Serbian

Slavs, joining Bosnian Serbs would fight converted Islamic "Serbs," derisively called "Turks," in Bosnia in the bloodiest of feuds between brothers, proclaiming sovereignty of borders, independence, democracy, idealized wishes for harmonious plurality or adamant separation—whatever is dictated by Bonn or Paris, London or Washington. It all masked the terrors that were threatening survival. And well-intending outsiders, as in every such case of fratricide, would only make matters worse by interfering or intervening. As with all deadly feuds between brothers, neighbors should stay indoors, close their windows—or else have their own murderous natures exposed.

The West, partly in order to legitimize its own poised opportunism, pronounced Yugoslavia was descending into violent psychosis. Extreme enforcement, extreme restraint would be required as an illusion of remedy.

Meanwhile, the media is already cultivating the chaos, eager to harvest the morbid melodrama of victims and aggressors, concocting a simplistic explanation about the self-devouring enmity that always plagues the Yugoslav soul.

I conclude that there will be a schizophrenic, three-sided war, at least. Serbs, Croats, Muslims.

British novelist Evelyn Waugh, who spent time in the region during World War II, comes to mind with the threefold psychosis portrayed in one of his characters:

> "He had aroused three irreconcilable feuds in Capri; he had practiced black art in Cefalu; he had been cured of drug taking in California and of an Oedipus complex in Vienna."[3]

The Western media's own personality is splitting. What is it—professionally neutral, objective, analytical? Or co-combatant? Co-conspirator? Provocateur?

How obscenely rational to be here casually pondering such bloodless themes while looking at faces already agonizing, waiting for mayhem to descend.

The sun slips into a gap between rooftops and floods the *Trg* with the last warm moments of light. It feels good, and the beery moroseness dissolves. My mood becomes agreeable and relaxed. I think again about Gregor and his nervous reclusiveness. He looks guilty. For what? I have a feeling I know what he's planning with his Croatian wife and their children: When the war arrives, they won't be here.

A young, thin man and his wife ask if they can sit in the two vacant seats at the table. I nod and they sit down, quietly ordering a beer and coffee from the waiter.

I notice the silence of the crowds swarming through the square. There is only the grind and urgent bells of the trams, the electrical snapping of wires above the tracks, whisking movements of overcoats and shopping bags in all directions and the rattle of bicycles between somber tolls from the cathedral on the quarter hour. But nothing else. Nobody speaks.

Most noticeable of all is the solitude of the man and his wife. They exchange a quiet word between sips from their cup and glass, and then recede into deep thoughts. I think that I might attempt some conversation about the weather. Or, I can be an interesting American with an optimistic outlook, maybe imitating Peter Kuzmic's optimism that there will be no war. After all, the Yugoslavs always improvise at the last minute.

No, I have no right to intrude. Their faces show fear, sadness, worry, desperation, confusion, resolve—all of the ingredients being worked into the crucible of the crisis as they prepare to suffer and survive. It is intensely private between them. They do not notice or care that I sit nearby.

---

3. *Brideshead Revisited*, Book I, Ch. 2.

He spots their tram approaching across the square, sets down his glass and stands, reaching for their shopping bag and umbrella. They smile cordially and walk away. I watch them until they disappear. I should have said something to them.

The sun lowers further, and I sit in the shadows. The abandoned coffee cup and the unfinished glass of beer seem like orphans. People begin to leave from under the restaurant's outdoor awnings.

Gnadenthal, Germany – January 1994

Instead of veering into the village, I wheel the car up the soggy tractor ruts, stopping beside a stand of trees above a bare field.

Thoughts and memories drift up from the past. I swing the car back around toward the road below and switch off the engine.

Silence.

The late afternoon sun hangs like a dirty ten-watt light bulb behind gray German sky. A cold wind kicks up pieces of wheat stubble that scratch across the windshield. The warmth of the engine won't give off much heat if I spend the night here.

Three weeks before in Belgrade, several days in Vienna, and now Germany—searching for information, answers. My mood is reclusive, and a hotel room too confining. The woods are already dark. No chance for a walk to go over it all again.

How different from that bright autumn day six years before with Paul, Dusko and Ibrahim, who tried like all brave Yugoslavs to believe that war could be avoided. But the shooting and dying started anyway, and now it seems it will never end.

I pop open a beer. The rain starts again as the blind eye above the valley fades. It will be completely dark in a few minutes.

My friends at Gnadenthal are expecting me, but I'm not in the mood for a long night of conversation. They are good souls, but they are nonetheless Germans who after three years have their minds made up about the Yugoslav wars only a few hundred miles away. The idea of more than one war is perplexing, too disorderly. I do not want to explain again all the details and the background of the past unraveling of Yugoslavia. They listened to be me before, frowning because it was not the same story they were getting from their German newspapers, television and the politicians.

It is the same back in America. After all, Yugoslavia is a mystery for this generation, a distant place in a distant galaxy.

True, Germans always liked the tourist spots on the warm Adriatic beaches of Dalmatia, but they rarely detoured from their summer holiday destinations to visit the inland regions to the east. They noticed the road signs to Belgrade, Zagreb and Sarajevo, but they were uneasy about venturing away from the Adriatic coast. After all, recent decades had not dimmed the bitter memories toward Germans and two world wars brought by them to Yugoslav soil. Better to stick close to the tourist zones and dark-featured hoteliers, waiters and merchants who smiled at Germans with money. That's how Germans pay for the sins of past generations—grudgingly tolerating the employment of hordes of Yugoslav guest workers, the hated, swarthy *gasterbeiters* who drive little beat-up Zastava clunkers to Hamburg, Munich, Dusseldorf and Frankfurt. Later, they went back to Yugoslavia—somebody started calling it "ex-Yugoslavia" in 1991—driving sleek Mercedes with trunks full of Levi's and pockets full of *deutschmarks*.

One was a hard-working Croatian fellow from tiny Tordinci, twenty kilometers east of Vinkovci (eastern Croatia), who worked in Germany for nearly two decades, gradually bringing home a complete inventory of machinery from western Europe for his small farm with its large barn. On my previous visit three years ago, his short, plump wife glided between the huge oak-veneer cabinets, dining table and chairs from Austria, Hungary and Germany, serving coffee and cakes on brightly colored Swiss dishes. His comfortable home in Tordinci seemed safely distant from the conflict about to vomit across the rolling fields of maize and sugar beets.

He stood nervously at the head of the table while a mutual friend and I sat and listened to him speak in great agitated bursts about the political crisis, waving his arms impotently. His nineteen-year-old son jumped up, bleary-eyed and still intoxicated from the previous night, announcing that all will be settled and that he and others in the local Croat militia are ready to take on those "Serb bastards" and the entire Yugoslav People's Army.

The boy lunged from the room and out the door toward the barn as his haggard father slumped into a chair. His wife smiled sadly and offered more coffee and cakes, admiring her delicate cups and saucers. The farmer said that his son had a new automatic rifle wrapped in oilcloth and hid somewhere in the barn.

Three years later, the family was living as refugees in Vinkovci. Their farm was obliterated along with Tordinci's treasured 230-year-old church. The ex-guest worker saved a few pieces of furniture and moved into a small house, which until recently belonged to a Serb family that fled from Vinkovci before the advancing Serbs and the JNA abruptly stopped outside Vinkovci. Another nearby house had also belonged to fleeing Serbs. Once they were gone, it was dynamited by unknown Croat "patriots" into a heap of broken bricks, blackened beams and planks. The Tordinci farmer quickly sloshed "Tordinci Croat" in large letters on the front and sides of the house when he moved in, not wanting to be mistaken as relatives of the original Serb occupants.

He sat at a small table, again presiding over coffee while his wife served sweets on plain chipped crockery, retelling with wild-eyed grimaces how his son had attempted to use his vintage machine gun against a JNA tank before being dragged to cover during the mauling of the Croatian militia at Tordinci. No longer a defiant nationalist, the son and his young wife now lived passively with his parents in Vinkovci and infant daughter. The farmer's wife tried not to think about happier days in her old house or what had happened to her prized furniture and dishes. She focused instead on the baby.

Next to me, as before in Tordinci, was my long-time friend, Matije Toth, who translated in resonant English and always seemed out of place among rural peasants and the townspeople of eastern Croatia. He listened attentively. Rational, polished, intellectual and always ready to use his sense of humor, he remained balanced, calm and detached during my frequent visits in the late 1980s when post-Titoist Yugoslavia began falling apart and tensions and local suspicions were epidemic. He was a thorn in the side of the communists for over thirty years. Matije listened patiently, inquiring about details in the conversation and passing a few words on to me.

When the vicious shelling of Vinkovci started in the summer of 1991, Matije moved his family west to Zagreb, where he later learned that his home was destroyed by a mortar fired from the nearby Serb-held village of Mirkovci about six kilometers away. Or, he alternately insisted, it was hit by a bomb from Serb aircraft. He never knew for sure.

After our visit with the Tordinci farmer, we went to Matije's demolished house across town, the scene of many joyful reunions since our meeting fifteen years before. We stared through the blown out windows into his study. Rubble from the destroyed roof was piled next to the most damaged side of the structure. It was the darkest end of the house and the most concealed from the street. I noticed that other houses in the residential neighborhood were only superficially damaged.

I never contradicted his theory, though I doubted a Serb pilot had picked out such an unimportant target or that fate guided the trajectory of a single mortar shell fired by Serbs—from 6,000 yards away! He would not accept that he had for many years been a voice of conscience and tolerance. And, he was a critic of blind, destructive, Croat and Serb "patriotism" alike.

The large Catholic church in the center of Vinkovci was slightly damaged during the worst days of the fighting in late 1991. But the town's Serbian Orthodox church a few hundred meters away, and pointed out as being closer to Serb mortars in Mirkovci, was completely destroyed. I said it seemed more probable because of the position of the debris that an explosion was detonated inside the church and caused a fire that charred the posts and timbers.

"Isn't it interesting that the great Catholic Christian Constantine was born in the Serbian heartland at Nis?" he asked. It was another of his droll, strategically humorous attempts to change the subject and break the gray mood around the destruction. "Ah, the ironies of history. You know, he must have had some ancient premonition."

I remembered the sudden appearances of swastikas and the Ustashe "U" painted on walls and town monuments just before the war. It contradicted the rhetoric about ethnic and religious tolerance coming from the Croatian capital of Zagreb.

Matije now lived as a refugee himself in a town many kilometers west of Vinkovci where, several days later, we were walking down Vlatka Maceka Street and discussing the great Fourth Century Roman emperor and pontiff, wondering about the cruel taunts of history and the inveterate hatred between Croat Catholics and Orthodox Serbs incarnate in Constantine.

It was cheerfully sunny and warm.

Two soldiers approached us. One was wearing a dark green military uniform, but the other slightly taller and younger man was in black, identifying him as a member of the HOS ultra-nationalists. His buckles glinted and the sleek polished leather duty belt gleamed on his waist and down across his chest. I didn't notice the nervous look on Matije's face until we passed. He hissed at me not to look back at them.

"I've never seen that uniform being worn on the street in the daylight," he said in a low whisper. We were walking beside an empty, burned out structure in the middle of other undamaged houses along the street.

The war, after all, reached this town, too. Scrawled by a drunken hand in large letters on the front of the house was the warning *"Ovako svakom srbjino."* I asked Matije to translate.

"It means 'the same for every Serb'," he said irritably. Beside it was the crude drawing of the blue and white checkerboard Croat crest and a large Ustashe "U."

On our last day together, his modulated temperament was taken over by angry accounts of Serb atrocities he knew about.

It was useless to mention the destroyed Serb church in Vinkovci or to try to tell him that I saw bodies of executed Serb civilians exhumed from mass graves at Zvornik with their hands bound by wire loops and nooses around their necks.

He would not speak about claims of atrocities committed against Serbs while being disgusted that Croat postal censors had opened his mail from one of his Serb colleagues in Belgrade. A few weeks before, his telephone clicked several times when I called him from America. I asked him if his calls were still monitored.

"No," he answered calmly, adding with cryptic sarcasm, "I record all my calls so that I have a complete record of all my telephone conversations."

He often repeated his amazement about the absence of any "voice of reason from the Belgrade intellectuals."

Lately, he resisted any mention about conscientious Serbs: "It is safe to say before a Serb even opens his mouth—that it is a lie!"

He was more tired, exasperated and angry than when I visited him on the eve of the short war in Slovenia in 1991. Now, he spoke slowly from exhaustion, trying to again tell a joke about a Bosnian peasant. But there was none of his past enthusiastic humor. The fighting in Yugoslavia now engulfed Bosnia's population of Serbs, Croats and Muslims. He half-heartedly responded to my selfish request to tell again about the rich Bosnian peasant whose wife was customarily obliged to walk behind him in public until a neighbor noticed his habit had changed. The neighbor said he was surprised, and that it was gratifyingly civilized.

"And now, he makes her walk thirty paces in front of him. The neighbor asked why, and the Bosnian fellow answered, 'So he will know if there are any land mines ahead'!" Matije's once hearty baritone laugh was gone. He ended the story with only a smile and a sigh. The first time I heard the joke, it was innocent—to Croats—black humor.

The Bosnian border was only twenty kilometers south, and Serbs still occupied Mirkovci. Somebody drunkenly triggered off a burst of automatic rifle fire some-where in the dark.

"The end of a matter is better than its beginning." So goes the optimistic saying I had tried to end with on our last evening together.

I repeat it to myself now hundreds of miles away, sitting in the dark, listening to voices—all of them mine. But, it could not get worse, after three years of this war. I seem to be part of the black gloom on that German hillside, recalling the startling gunfire and the resigned smile on Matije's fading face, as the reverie evaporate and there is only the rain on the roof of the car.

"Why," he once asked, "is there no voice of reason from the Belgrade intellectuals?"

Somewhere in my notes and documents strewn around the backseat is an essay that Filip, who lives in Banovci Dunav, a few kilometers northwest from Belgrade, translated and read to me before I made Matije read what was written by a well-known Serb mathematician.

"This is being circulated now among Belgrade 'intelligentsia'," I told Matije, who read the title slowly. "Monotonous Barbarism."

"These words are hard, condemning. Maybe it's over-emphasized, but we have to declare the truth that we are living in monotonous barbarism. "Every evening we fearfully turn on the television in certain fear of the news. This presidency did or did not have a meeting. Or some new victims were killed. Or some new conflicts have occurred. Once again, they have condemned us, and once again we have energetically rejected the condemnation. There is no lightness in life. There is no vision. There is no good will. And, there is no sign of friendship. How long? And all these presidencies, all these political parties, all these coalitions, all these republics, all these remains of the Federation should be, ought to be protecting the roofs above the people, of the families of the nations. Where have all these words fled, all these words about brotherhood? Where are all these people from past decades who got their decorations because of 'brother-hood and unity'? What happened to all these people who were repeating to us that nothing could surprise us?

"The great majority of our people today, here and on the other side, feel the need for renewed life. They cannot accept life in 'monotonous barbarism,' a life of every-day hatred, scowling, angry, fear-filled faces. Can it be that with so many victims during and after the war, only a sad melancholy remains?

"Are there no people with the strength to say 'enough—no more!' and to show the way to the new fountains and springs of life? for life in truth and dignity? I am convinced that there are such people. There must be. Because life would be a very sad dream if there are no such people. But it seems that there are such moments in human life and in the society where soberness and what is wise and good retreats before the swarming events of unreasonableness and evil, there must be enough strength and courage to gather to stand in the face of that which manipulates life at its root. It seems to me we are now at that moment.

"All those black beetles of evil, all those caterpillars which want to become butterflies, all the scorpions, all the parasites from the lowest level of society that crawled out from beneath the great rock of despotism that was pressing down upon us and insisting their time had come ...they now yell and weep and growl and threaten and think that it will be the same forever. But it will not. All the people with some memory know that this happened in the past as well, as long as the Almighty was looking the other way from all the noise and chaos. And that's the reason this underworld is now afraid because He has seen what is happening. And, we believe in His power and goodness because the lowest level of human society is only the lowest level."

Such gloom had three years later eroded deeply into the lives of the Serb intelligentsia in Belgrade. The economic sanctions by the West had frayed whatever was left of reasonable optimism, they said. After reading the essay, Filip had gathered up his young sons for bedtime. His wife, Mira, always an image of strength and radiance, busied herself in the small kitchen.

Filip reappeared, attempting to resume the discussion and remarked that he, too, was hopeful, noting that there were many automobiles in Belgrade with Croatian and Slovenian license plates. But he doubted if any Serb plates could be seen in Zagreb and Ljubljana.

A few days later in eastern Croatia, Matije seemed unimpressed with the essay.

A gust of wind sends leaves cart wheeling across the hood. Lights glimmer in the windows across the valley of Gnadenthal...

In Vienna, I listened to his deliberately modulated, somber voice over the phone. Matije said he had been sick. I was troubled by something he mentioned without any further explanation.

"Your Serb friends have turned on you," he said. I had the feeling he sensed other ears were listening and he was recording our words. "You take care of those who are not friendly to you, and you neglect those who are your friends. You see, I know about everything."

Of course, he was referring to my controversial article, "Dateline Yugoslavia: The Partisan Press" (*Foreign Policy* magazine, Number 93, Winter 1993-94), that exposed the Western media bias in the war reporting. But, I wanted to continue, there was no question that the bias existed. A forty-to-one ratio of stories written from Sarajevo.[4]

Comparing types of stories and articles–human interest, features, editorials, analyses—the ratio expanded even more. But nobody in the West had wanted to talk about it.

Sitting in the subdued lighting of my room at the Prinz Eugen Hotel, I heard the disappointment in his voice. A long and trusted friendship was ending. It wasn't the first.

It was raining harder. I was tired and hungry from the afternoon drive along the swollen Rhine River and up through the fog and woods of the German Taunus...

War stories—everyone had one. That was the trouble; there were just too many.

Gradually, I began to have doubts about the media and the war coverage. I was suspicious after reading thousands of articles and reports—and the patterns fell into place.

Again and again, I considered whether I jumped to conclusions. Had I mistaken legitimate consensus among the profession, supported by an appearance of over-whelming "facts," as bias? Who cared? It was war. People are dying!

The doubts were creeping out invisibly from the black groves and dripping thickets, and the wind and rain carried a faint unanimity of accusing voices.

There, in the darkened car, I thought through the whole position again. Is any of this professional introspection necessary or useful?

The Western media isn't actually pulling any triggers. Or, are they?

Who cares about these questions or any of this esoteric soul-searching, or cover-up crap?

But, the reporters and the correspondents themselves have the answers if some-one asks the questions. They'll talk alright. They're busting to talk.

Who are "they," anyway?

Like, *Newsday's* Roy Gutman in Bonn, *The New York Times'* John F. Burns and even *CNN's* Christiane Amanpour were not exactly household names. But they were the most prominent in the war reporting by westerners in Yugoslavia.

Gutman and Burns shared, with jealous resentment, the 1993 Pulitzer Prize for International Reporting. Amanpour's trademark scowls and sneers were the most recognizable in television scenes from Sarajevo.

There were also the *BBC's* Maggie O'Kane and Martin Bell, *Newsweek's* Tom Post and Charles Lane, *The New York Times'* David Binder, Roger Cohen, Chuck Sudetic, Anthony Lewis, William Safire, Abe Rosenthal, John Kifner, Michael Gordon and others. *The Washington Post's* Mary Battiata and Blaine Harden. Laura Silber of *The Financial Times of London. Der Spiegel's* Renate Flottau. Hanspeter Born of *Die Weltwoche* in Zurich. *National Public Radio's* Sylvia Poggioli, Tom Gjelton and others. Chris Rohde of *The Christian Science Monitor. Reuters'* Don Forbes and Kurt Schork. Bill Maynes of *Foreign Policy. The Toronto Globe's* Paul Koring. Mik Gowing of *ITN Channel Four News* in London. Tim Judah of *The Times of London.* Independents like Sean Gervasi, Joan Phillips, Misha Glenny, Thomas Deichmann, Gregory Copley, P.J. O'Rourke, Bella Stumbo and Paul Jenks. Yugoslav journalists like *Vreme's* Ljiljana Smajlovic, Duska Anastasijevic and Stojan Cerovic in Belgrade, Laslo Toth in Novi Sad, Lajus Engler in Zrenjanin and their counterparts in Zagreb and Ljubljana. Dusan Stojanovic, Julijana Mojselovic, Tony Smith, George Jahn, David Crary, Maud Beelman, Mark Porubcansky, Roland Prinz, Alison Smale, Nick Tatrow, Bill Ahearn and others with the *Associated Press.*

---

4. Author's sampling and tabulation of datelines, types of articles and authors from approximately 4,000 reports, analyses, editorials and features through November 1992.

Saints, for sure, liberally mixed with sinners. Some were dead.

What separated the few good journalists from the wave of world-class ambulance chasers, gossips and media mercenaries trooping into Yugoslavia to hover over the corpse?

Conscience, I supposed. Good journalists don't need them. Bad ones can't escape from them or keep them quiet—especially when they're coaxed away from the pack and talked to quietly.

They talked and talked. But, was it the truth? Could they tell the truth? What, after all, was the truth? Well, for starters, the numbers were being cooked. Some governmental officials lied; some were allowed to lie.

And what about criticizing the members of the media themselves? Wasn't that hypocritical during a war? Wasn't it abstract, absurd, lavish, obscene? Professional pretense?

Who else would look for these people? Or, at least some of them? They were all over the map.

Somebody had to try. Why shouldn't journalists, correspondents and editors answer questions? What did they have to hide? What did the silences mean?

And if the truth be told finally, what would be the responses from professional colleagues?

"They're going to come after you," warned one sympathetic editor.

So, I decided to confront as many journalists as I could, personally or in print. Let them answer questions face-to-face, or through what they had written in their own words. And let the silences speak for themselves.

I roll back down the muddy ruts and head for nearby Bad Camberg...

And what of my own foraging for truths beneath the deafening claims that a "new holocaust" was rampaging through Yugoslavia? In publicly stating that there was a bias in the war reporting that loomed as big as anything Goebbels' dreamed of and that it would suck the world into a Balkan maelstrom, I was accused of being not only pro-Serb and therefore an advocate for the horrors and alleged atrocities committed already. But, from those fearing exposure and bent on reprisal I was marked as a holocaust-denier!

Serbs themselves admitted there were criminals among them. But the Western media irrationally condemned all Serbs.

People died in Croatia and Slovenia and were dying again in Bosnia after the manner of traditional brutality seen just short decades ago and historically witnessed for centuries in the manner of grand European carnage. The varieties of infliction and cruelty connected to such killing and catastrophe are myriad. The victims of one or two past wars were dead and still alive, as the truths and lies about them still lived and were killed and resurrected again.

The journalists and correspondents too easily skimmed through the politics, the diplomatic theater, the military campaigns and the press briefings. They wrote their stories sometimes within hours after arriving from the U.S. or from European news bureaus before they could even speak enough of the language to ask directions to the toilet. They thought they could steer around the intimidating cultural and historical swamps and jungles. As they saw it—or wanted readers and viewers to see it—it was all about good guys and bad guys. Later, they wrote books, re-selecting and qualifying their original exaggerations and outrageous omissions with apologetic gloss...

At a Belgrade restaurant, I recently met a young American Serb and independent filmmaker. A few drinks warmed up the mood for the half-dozen or so academics, politicians and artists—intelligentsia—at the dinner who were laughing and momentarily forgetful. But this filmmaker, who said he was also a "journalist," was sullen and unsociable and was just returned from one of the Bosnian war zones. He stared down for most of the time until someone on the other side of the table boastfully reminded him that he had put aside his cameras a few days earlier and picked up an automatic rifle during a skirmish with Bosnian government troops.

"Isn't that right, Sasha?" chided the other. "Were you shooting because you wanted the experience for your films?" Everyone laughed. He looked up nervously and began to tell a story he heard from a Bosnian Serb officer about how Muslims and Serbs from the same areas often had trouble telling each other apart. Uniforms were rarely distinguishable and were no help.

"This officer said that different pieces of cloth were pinned or tied to a certain place on their clothes or uniforms for a few days, and that was the only way to identify each other. He was making coffee one night when he heard someone coming up and speaking to him. He didn't recognize the man, but he appeared to be from nearby because of the way he spoke. They had coffee and talked awhile. And then the officer calmly shot the guy dead. I asked him why he did it, and he told me the man was not wearing that small piece of colored cloth. He said it wasn't important to ask him why he wasn't wearing it. It didn't matter." The filmmaker drank his *slivovitsa* in silence for the rest of the night and was in a stupor when we left the restaurant at two o'clock in the morning.

It was an interesting story, but was it true? It was a good story worth repeating. But that's the trouble with filmmakers, journalists and too many stories in this war.

I wrote little about Yugoslavia during my first eighteen years of traveling off-and-on to the Balkans.

I resisted writing anything presumptuous. The country and its culture were too diverse. Its history and politics were too complex. Yugoslavia, summarized one respected Balkan scholar, is "the despair of tidy minds."[5] Yes, "despair" is the right word.

Instead, I read everything I could find. And I returned again and again to the Yugoslav republics where I walked the streets with the crowds or by myself, listened to friends and strangers, risked stupid questions to professors, journalists, peasants, physicians, theologians, doctors, students and children. And I listened to the noises and silences in the cities and villages. I went to weddings and funerals. More than once I slept on empty seats in railroad stations or walked along the streets all night if I could not find or afford a hotel room or was unable to locate friends.

I listened and watched and tasted, returning again to America, to read again, to sort it all out. I gradually became familiar with parts of the history, the difficult geography, peoples' names and places.

Washington, D.C. – February 11, 1997

Alex Dragnich and I meet on a Metro platform and take the escalator up to the street level on a frigid Washington morning. Chilly gusts bent us forward, unable to speak, quickly walking the short distance until reaching the warm lobby of the *Voice of America* offices.

Most of the audience for that morning's panel discussion was already seated, holding folded overcoats and sweaters in their laps. I heard several European accents and realized this would be another one of those shrill sessions where American and foreign journalists and correspondents banter at each other and try to sound authoritative about what they saw or heard, or what they were told was seen and

---

5. Historian Stella Alexander, *Church and State in Yugoslavia Since 1945*, Cambridge University Press, 1979, p. 292.

heard, or read about. "Questions" for panelists were preceded by lengthy discourses and the typical assumptions, cliche and oratory from the last decade in and around—where else?—Yugoslavia.

The billing for the get-together was "Freedom of the Press in the Balkans."

But it was immediately clear that the theme applied to native reporters in former Yugoslav republics—principally Croatia and Bosnia—and not any freedom for Western journalists to write and report what they would not or could not write and report about.

Empaneled were *National Public Radio's* Tom Gjelton, Kati Marton of Committee for the Protection of Journalists, the State Department's John Shattuck, and Jonathan Landay, of *The Christian Science Monitor*.

"The usual suspects?" I whispered to Dragnich, who smiled and nodded. The atmosphere was similar to the crowded international press centers in Belgrade and Zagreb a few years earlier.

I was hoping Roy Gutman would be there, among the rest of the familiar faces who liked to grandstand at these frequent Washington press get-togethers. But, nothing meaningful would occur this morning.

The wind had quieted somewhat as the respected Vanderbilt professor and I headed back to the Metro, and began our short subway ride to the faculty dining room at George Washington University across town where we met David Binder, newly forced into retirement by squeamish overlings at *The New York Times*.

Though they had not seen each other recently, Dragnich and Binder seemed to resume a conversation paused only moments before, mentioning last names rapidly along with inquiries about health and locations in a seeming roll call for anyone missing-in-action on news desks or in academia.

I reread parts of Dragnich's latest book the night before and wanted to ask him some questions about something that arrested my contemplations and concerns over the years about Yugoslavia. We were joined by an official from the Yugoslav Embassy, and so the questions would have been uncomfortable.

After the handshakes and good byes, Dragnich and I walked back to the Metro entrance.

"I think you gave me the key," I began, "to clarifying a lot of the disappointment and failed expectations about Yugoslavia that I see in antagonisms from the press."

He walked on further without responding, and I was about to repeat my words, thinking he did not hear me. But, Dragnich, though retired, was customarily allowing the student to think further about his own words.

"And, what is that?" he finally asked, smiling.

"Dreams," I said. "Yugoslavia was about dreams and myths. But, mostly dreams."

"Oh, that!" he replied, chuckling, since for him the idea was nothing new. At the entrance to the Metro station, we shook hands.

It was a long walk back to my office in the National Press Building, thinking over the passages in his book:

> "They had never lived together in one dwelling. They lived in diverse homes, often not their own, and under masters who had different codes of behavior. Although, in essence, they spoke the same language, they knew each other only distantly and incompletely. Most of them were adherents of Christianity, either Orthodox or Roman Catholic, but some of them were believers in Islam. They had often heard romanticized versions of how they were alike and why they should be together, but this had

seemed a distant dream. Then suddenly, while their masters were warring, they found themselves free to come together. In an atmosphere of mixed emotions, and with many idealistic expectations, they seized the moment and consummated a hasty union.

"Such was the situation of the South Slavs near the end of 1918, when they created the new state known as the Kingdom of the Serbs, Croats, and Slovenes...

"What can be learned from the tragedy of Yugoslavia? Perhaps the most obvious answer is: Those who contributed to the formation of Yugoslavia were motivated by expectations that were unrealistic. Yugoslavia may have been a dream that could not be realized, or, at best, could be only imperfectly attained. Contrary to the views of some historians, however, it was not an idle dream; nor was Yugoslavia an unnatural or artificial creation. It came about as the result of the reasoned thought and forceful action of a number of South Slav writers and politicians during the latter half of the nineteenth century and the first two decades of the twentieth.

"The formation of the state came about hurriedly, without concrete preparation. Romanticized visions and dreams smothered practical considerations...

"The haste with which the European Community, subsequently joined the United States, recognized the secessionist Yugoslav republics—first Slovenia and Croatia, later Bosnia-Hercegovina (can Macedonia be far behind?)—was purportedly to prevent, or at least minimize, bloodshed. Although the motive was laudable, the aim was not attained. As in other civil wars, atrocities, destruction of cultural monuments, and other untoward cruelties were committed by both sides. And truth became the first casualty."[6]

Yes, dreams, visions, myths, romantics, writers and poets.

Such were the legendary likes of Robert St. John, of *The Associated Press*, and Ray Brock, a *New York Times* correspondent, during and after World War II.

St. John wrote *From the Land of Silent People* soon after he fled Yugoslavia ahead of advancing Nazi divisions in 1941. In his escape, he saved his typewriter, but lost all of his notes. It was recalled on the eve of his 100th birthday in 2002 that writing his book in a room at the top of New York's Roosevelt Hotel, St. John used only his memory and a steady supply of scotch to resurrect his Balkan experiences. In a 1948 sequel, St. John wrote *The Silent People Speak* (Doubleday & Co., New York, 1948) after revisiting post-war Yugoslavia.

He included an unforgettable scene of a "brigade" of young men and women who were clawing out railroad track beds and tunnels with only their bare hands and basic tools. It was in wintry, bitter cold weather, and St. John described how their

---

6. Alex Dragnich, *Serbs and Croats: The Struggle in Yugoslavia*, New York: Harcourt Brace & Co., 1992, pp. 39, 174, 189.

ungloved hands stuck to the frigid iron when they moved rails onto wooden ties. But, he wrote, they were committed to the dream of an ideal and shared society. He said they smiled proudly at him and endured the pain because of the "vision" for Yugoslavia.

Louis Adamic, a native Slovenian and naturalized American, finished his excellent and passionate Yugoslav trilogy by mid-20th Century. Relatives in Ljubljana still believe his supposed pro-Tito views may have led to his suspicious "suicide" and arson when his rural New Jersey home was burned.

Rebecca West's classic *Black Lamb and Grey Falcon: A Journey through Yugoslavia* enjoyed continued popularity, and there were Ivo Andric's translated masterpieces. Dreamers, idealists, visionaries, romantics, writers of breadth and depth.

And, the communist dictator Josip Broz Tito, beloved and despised through the 40s, 50s, 60s and 70s, had thumbed his nose at the United States and the Soviet Union and manipulated them both. And, there was Tito's equally formidable and decadent ghost through the 80s and into the early 90s, as even those who hated him remembered the "good old days of Communism" compared to the mayhem of Yugoslavia's breakup.

And, in the 1990s, the Western press belatedly arrived, sensing angrily the "dream" was long ago betrayed.

By the time someone noticed the 21st Century had arrived, there were tens of thousands of American troops occupying areas of something called the "former Yugoslavia" at the largesse of American taxpayers and costing billions of U.S. tax-dollars.

Chapter 2

From Bias To Bombs To Body Bags

*"My solution to the problem would be to tell them frankly
that they've got to draw in their horns and stop their aggression,
or we're going to bomb them back into the Stone Age."*[1]
—General Curtis LeMay

*"And silence sounds no worse than cheers
After earth has stopped the ears."*[2]
—A.E. Housman

A long-awaited cheer went up from journalists when the bombs and cruise missiles finally slammed down onto Serb-controlled Bosnia for two weeks in late 1995.

Losses were minimal, and nobody argued that it was anything more than symbolic—or that it was the achievement of the media's own frantic campaign for military intervention throughout five years and five civil wars in the former Yugoslavia. Reporters and commentators chided and congratulated the international community and NATO for finally finding their conscience.

But it was the Western media—and especially the self-adulating profession of American journalism—that lost its objectivity!

Also lost was the fragile equilibrium of post-Cold War relations with the Russians who chafed at the wide-angle, laptop bashing of their South Slavic cousins:

> "The pounding NATO air strikes against Bosnian-Serb targets
> may reap an unintended effect: the end of Russia's friendship
> with the West."[3] "The war in the former Yugoslavia... has posed
> the greatest challenge to the U.S.-Russian relationship since
> the Soviet collapse four years ago. Russia ferociously opposes
> NATO air strikes."[4]

As they had done for a half-decade in avoiding detached and fair coverage in the Yugoslav wars, pack-journalists ignored meaningful discussion about the consequences of a peace agreement brokered by the U.S. during fifteen days of NATO bombings that August and September. It was later ceremonialized at Dayton in November 1995 and signed by all sides amid deteriorating pomp in Paris before Christmas.

---

1. Curtis LeMay, *Mission with LeMay: My Story*, autobiography
with MacKinlay Kantor, New York: Doubleday & Co., 1965.

2. A.E. Housman, *To an Athlete Dying Young.*

3. Chrystia Freeland, *The Financial Times of London*, September 14, 1995.

4. Deborah Seward, *Associated Press*, September 15, 1995.

Media Cleansing: Dirty Reporting

The fratricidal fighting in Bosnia had for the most part stopped anyway, as it had in previous Balkan winters when heavy snows, bitter cold and rugged terrain pacified even the most determined armies and their mercenary bands. From the times of the Ottoman hordes to Hitler, all Balkan conquests inevitably succumb to winter.

The lesson was about to be learned by occupying NATO troops and 20,000 or more American soldiers who dug into the snow to "robustly enforce," as American generals liked to tell gullible television panel moderators, "the peace."

Americans arrived in Bosnia where they were actually enforcing not peace but intervention—an apologetic for "occupation"—as well as reinforcing the all-or-nothing reelection gamble of Bill Clinton who sensed a win-win potential on the eve of the presidential primary voting in the spring of 1996. If winter could hold off a new round of hostilities and for as long as the "peace" lasted, Clinton could claim success in foreign policy. If American casualties were encountered, he could quickly withdraw the troops and declare he and the U.S. would not be dragged into another Vietnam-style quagmire.

The talk was tough. Debate in Congress and, predictably, the media was tentative:

> "The Americans would be heavily armed to deter violators of the peace. And they would have a green light to shoot—not just to punish but to defeat violators... President Clinton has said that if (peace) comes, the United States will provide up to half of a NATO peacekeeping force—up to 25,000 U.S. troops—that could stay for months *or years*."[5] (Italics added)

From its "moral high ground,"[6] the media generally saw nothing wrong in bombing the Bosnian Serbs to the peace table. Past incidents of casualties in shelling of Sarajevo—at times involving only two or three actual victims—received lavish coverage, while reporters preposterously conveyed the NATO bombings of Bosnian Serbs, including civilians of all ages, as nearly bloodless events.

NATO paraded its 1995 air show over Bosnia, deploying a thousand or more air sorties, $100,000 smart bombs and $1.3 million Tomahawk cruise missiles, while diplomats with their entourage of reporters and commentators shuttled breathlessly back and forth on the negotiations circuit. It was another spectacular example of media self-mesmerizing in the Balkan upheaval. But again, the major questions went unasked; the simplistic answers went unchallenged. The endless cheerleading by the Western media prevailed over objective scrutiny as the international community and the United States were dragged deeper into a widening Yugoslav and European catastrophe.

Since the episode ignited an outburst of Russian threats to drop the curtain on congeniality with the New World Order, it was unusual that reporters refrained from taking a harder look at what came nearest to triggering a dreadful century-ending sequel to the precedent assassination of an Austrian archduke in Sarajevo eighty years earlier.

---

5. Robert Burns, *Associated Press* News Service, September 16, 1995

6. Lisa Hoffman, *Scripps Howard News Service*, quoting military analyst Loren Thompson, of the Alexis de Tocqueville Institute, Virginia, September 13, 1995.

Who Pulled Nato's Trigger?

There is more than casual skepticism about the bizarre mortar attack that occurred in Sarajevo on August 28, 1995. There were immediate cynics who noticed the similar pattern of deliberate media omissions about accountability for the suspicious incident, which occurred less than a hundred yards from its bloody predecessor—also fired by Bosnian Muslims but blamed on Bosnian Serbs—at the *Markale* market on February 5, 1994. It was typical of the Balkan war coverage.

The August 1995 blast killed thirty-seven people—again just before an important diplomatic initiative—and touched off the huge NATO retaliation and political extortion:

> "The attack came just as a U.S. negotiating team, led by Assistant Secretary of State Richard Holbrooke, arrived today in Paris for talks intended to reactivate the peace process."[7]

> "Suspicion fell on Bosnian Serbs, who have besieged Sarajevo for 40 months *and rejected previous peace efforts*."[8] (Italics added)

Bosnian government negotiators threatened a walkout in Paris unless NATO immediately punished the Bosnian Serbs.

But a report from *Reuters*—distributed four days later and significantly re-edited and shortened when published by *The International Herald Tribune* on September 4—received little play in the American press and other major media. Around-the-clock bombings of Bosnian Serbs had commenced and drowned out the alarm sounded by a Russian colonel assigned to the United Nations Protection Force (UNPROFOR) in Sarajevo.

Colonel Andrei Demurenko, an artillery specialist, had performed his own investigation of the August 28 explosion and determined in "the startling break with U.N. findings" that Serbs were *not* responsible:

> "It is extremely rare for a U.N. officer, particularly one of Colonel Demurenko's rank, to publicly disagree on an issue of such importance. ...(He) said his own technical analysis had shown that a 120mm mortar bomb could not have come from Bosnian Serbian positions."[9]

In the original and longer version of the Reuters report, a U.N. spokesman said Demurenko's findings were among "several reports" which were contradictory to initial U.N. conclusions and were submitted to United Nations officials in New York.

Evidently, journalists could not be compelled to do any serious checking.

Contradictions were sidestepped, as were the repeated previous requests by Bosnian Serbs for peace negotiations, when Bosnian government troops carried out vicious sweeps the previous spring throughout Bosnia. These included the resumption of using U.N.-declared "safe havens" (Gorazde, Bihac, Tuzla, Srebrenica, etc.) as

---

7. Liam McDowall, *Associated Press*, August 28, 1995.

8. Srecko Latal, *Associated Press,* August 28, 1995.

9. "Russian Disputes UN Report on Shelling" from *Associated Press* and *Reuters* dispatches; *International Herald Tribune*, September 4, 1995.

launching pads for brutal ethnic cleansing of scores of Bosnian Serb towns and villages. At summer's end, the savage push through Sector West and Krajina resulted with reports minimizing the numbers of Serb civilians "fleeing" as "refugees" to Serbia or toward Serb-controlled Banja Luka in Bosnia from lands they had owned for more than three centuries!

The media, from its distant vantage in Zagreb, lapsed into hypocritical rhetoric about whether the episode should be labeled as "ethnic cleansing" by the Croatian government and army:

> "Croatia's offensive against secessionist Serbs...virtually emptied the Krajina region of its Serbian population...Was it another round of ethnic cleansing in the Balkans? No, says the U.S. ambassador to Croatia, Peter Galbraith. ...(But) 'a war that begins with civilian areas being shelled at 5 a.m. when women and children are asleep in their beds and ends with a massive exodus...is surely tantamount to ethnic cleansing,' said Chris Gunness, a United Nations spokesman."[10]

While international leaders and the media winked and scolded murderous rampages by Muslim and Croat forces, Ambassador Galbraith theatrically accompanied one convoy of Serb refugees as it made a humiliating trek toward Serbia amid beatings, insults, broken windshields, and being spat upon by rock- and mud-throwing Croat civilians in an orgy of hatred. Galbraith said his presence with the convoy was "an act of solidarity and a warning that the international community was watching."[11]

Rather than inquire too closely about the forced "cleansing" of hundreds of thousands of Serb civilians, Western correspondents covered the Croatian and Bosnian campaigns—and the Serb exodus—with apologetic tones and the insipid irony from one German reporter about the positive side of the Croatian army's bloody crusade:

> "Brisk efforts are underway to bring a semblance of normalcy to Okucani town (sic), just retaken by Croatian government troops from the separatist Krajina Serbs. You can telephone anywhere in Croatia from the post office, which is again under Croatian control. Soldiers queue before the card telephone to make calls. Nearby, two women scrub the windows of a reopened Zagreb Bank branch. Colorful posters outside the bank announce that MasterCard and EuroCard are accepted.
>
> ...Shortly after being retaken, the city was being disinfected and cleaned."[12]

With double-barreled hostilities launched by the Bosnian and Croat federation with Western approval that May and August, reporters appeared embarrassed as they were in early 1993 when the Muslim-dominated Bosnian army and Croats turned on each other, committing atrocities that rivaled their previous three years' worth of allegations of similar crimes by Serbs.

---

10. Raymond Bonner, *The New York Times*, August 12, 1995.
11. Bonner, *ibid.*
12. Gregor Mayer, *Deutsche Presse Agentur*, May 15, 1995.

As for the portrayal of Serbs rejecting peace proposals, it is hard to believe the vigorous White House press corps did not know about the series of letters from Bosnian Serb President Radovan Karadzic which sat on President Clinton's desk:

> "What we ask of you, Sir, is to call a 'Camp David' style conference, inviting all parties to the conflict as well as representatives of the international community. We can promise you that in a short time all problems can be settled, peace signed, and normal multinational cooperation established in the Balkans, leading eventually to the region becoming part of the European Union. We have been so many times close to a peace agreement that only questions of detail remain to be solved. *However, for nearly a year no one has talked to us.* ...If negotiations are not resumed, we are heading for a totally unnecessary war in which the United States will inevitably be involved."[13] (Italics added)

Reporters and editors relentlessly downplayed the exodus from the Krajina, insisting that "only" 100,000 Serb refugees were on the move.

Nearly two years later, referring to the episode, it was casually mentioned deep in a story by *The Washington Post* that 350,000 Serbs were ruthlessly ousted from their lands and homes in the Krajina,[14] which was never an "occupied" region by Serbs who had owned and held title to their properties in that area for many generations.

'The Unraveling Campaign Of Disinformation'

By August 1995, former President Jimmy Carter was attracting too much attention with his outspoken candor that ran counter to current obfuscation from the White House and its reporters:

> "'I think the Croats who are now forcing the Serbs out of Krajina are *equally* guilty of ethnic cleansing as were the Bosnian Serbs.'"[15]
> (Italics added)

Further, Carter denounced actions and statements by Ambassador Galbraith as "atrocious" and "biased" while Croat "shells slammed down on columns of Serb refugees" along escape routes into Bosnia and Serbia that became clogged to a standstill with Serb civilians. Croat air attacks against the fleeing Serbs were also reported, and artillery rounds fell on them as they huddled around the U.N. base at Topusko. Officials at the United Nations High Commission on Refugees (UNHCR) said civilian casualties "were believed to be high."[16]

A more effective maneuver to paint Serbs as the "bad guys" could not have been better choreographed than with the August 28 explosion in Sarajevo that spurred NATO's two-week bombing spree. It also turned out to be face-saving for the White House, which really preferred sanctions-leveraged negotiations with Serbian President Slobodan Milosevic and did not want to face some hard truths from Karadzic and the Bosnian Serb

---

13. Letter from Karadzic to Clinton, June 8, 1995.
14. *The Washington Post*, May 16, 1997.
15. *Associated Press*, August 11, 1995.
16. *Associated Press*, ibid.

leadership about the West's open violations of the international weapons embargo, marauding Bosnian Muslim and Croat government troops and their international manipulators. Disgusted with one-sided reporting, Karadzic had previously expelled several Western journalists, including *CNN* reporters in mid-1994.[17]

The Bosnian Serbs likely had some legitimate negotiating grounds, but there were worrisome memories that the media would compare discussions with the vilified Bosnian Serbs to conversations between Hitler and Chamberlain a half-century earlier. The press would be indignant about Clinton or others negotiating with Bosnian Serbs. An official quarantine was also needed to incarcerate Karadzic in Bosnia and away from the upcoming ceasefire negotiations at Dayton, Ohio.

The leprous stigma of "war criminal"—tailored for headlines and newscasts—was conveniently provided with indictments against Karadzic and others on July 25, 1995, even though a senior Tribunal prosecutor, Minna Schrag, had stated at a University of Virginia Law School conference the previous March that investigators at The Hague had "no evidence" to indict Bosnian Serb leaders! But only a month later on April 24, Karadzic and others were suddenly and officially named as war crimes suspects, preventing travel to sites of peace negotiations where arrests could occur at any moment. Journalists sniffed at the ploy but sidestepped "the legal maneuver that could further damage U.N. relief and truce efforts in Bosnia."[18]

Also, it was unreported by major news organizations at The Hague that Tribunal President Antonio Cassese was impatient with Prosecutor Richard Goldstone's methodical investigations. Cassese went public with a press release in February 1995, demanding indictments against "big fish" to satisfy the media clamor.[19]

The press' focus was distracted by claimed atrocities committed by Serbs in Srebrenica, diverting from the huge exodus of Serbs from Croatia and increased discovery of mass graves containing Serb civilians. U.S. spy satellites and unmanned Predator "drone" aircraft—with around-the-clock, night vision and infrared capabilities—had scanned Srebrenica for days, searching without convincing results for evidence of mass killings and other atrocities since the fall of the enclave in mid-July 1995.[20] Similarly, Secretary of State Warren Christopher's daily intelligence briefings did not present "any intelligence imagery that could confirm massacres" of "8,000 Muslim troops."

The number, though later modified as troops along with variously-aged civilian men and boys, was pulled out of the air by Bosnian government propagandists and fed to reporters who digested it and spun it into the repetitive cycle of unverified and unproven statistics that achieved the impregnable status of unquestioned fact.[21]

Less than a week after vicious Croat offensives in Krajina and Western Slavonia that stirred sudden resentments throughout the U.S. and Europe against the Croat government, then-U.N. Ambassador Madeleine Albright raised the pitch of her anti-Serb vitriol, waving eight satellite photos of mounds of dirt, which she said were mass graves

---

17. *Associated Press*, April 16, 1994.

18. Abner Katzman, *Associated Press*, April 24, 1995.

19. Vanessa Vasic Janekovic, "All the President's Questions," *Balkan War Report*, May 1995.

20. Paul Quinn-Judge, *The Boston Globe*, July 26, 1995.

21. Even though the previous seven years of exhumations by U.N. forensic teams from a variety of alleged mass grave sites in the Srebrenica area had yielded 3,200 supposedly identified remains through October 2002, reporters repeatedly made conflicting assumptions: "Forensics experts have exhumed more than 5,000 bodies, *1,620 of which have been identified* through DNA analysis and other techniques."—Almir Arnaut, *Associated Press*, July 11, 2003.

containing Muslims at Srebrenica.[22]

Remarkably, the "sensational" photos of the supposed mass graves were not widely published in the hoped-for sensation by the mainstream Western press.

Moreover, American readers had little access to—and Albright ignored—what was reported by the *Daily Telegraph of London* from Tuzla:

> "The Bosnian government deliberately increased the suffering of the Muslim refugees fleeing Srebrenica to put pressure on the international community, according to documents made available to the *Daily Telegraph*. The papers include instructions to the United Nations from the government of Alija Izetbegovic in Sarajevo that the refugees must be taken *in their thousands* to a single location rather than being spread around numerous available centers. The resulting television pictures and media reports of chaos among aid workers overwhelmed when the refugees arrived at the UN base at Tuzla were intended to bring about a decisive international response. *It is not the first time the Bosnians have manipulated events...*"[23] (Italics added)

The dearth of reporting a single retrieved or verified Muslim body from Srebrenica at the time caused *The Independent* to follow up with another startling account a week later from Tuzla which remained unseen beyond London readers:

> "After five days of interviews the United Nations chief investigator into alleged human rights abuses during the fall of Srebrenica has not found *any* first-hand witnesses of atrocities."[24] (Italics added)

The seeming mirage of mass atrocities and murders at Srebrenica was doubted further when Muslim refugees arrived from Zepa—just twenty miles south of Srebrenica—a few days later:

> "They brought tales of two weeks of living in caves in the wooded hills during the heavy bombardment of the U.N.-designated 'safe haven,' but did not recount atrocities like those people brought out of Srebrenica after the Serbs overran that 'safe area' on July 11... 'We were treated well by the Serbian soldiers', said Ms. (Ramiza) Kolovac, a law student in Sarajevo who was visiting her parents in Zepa..."[25]

The surprising reports from refugees and aid agencies about "no evidence of systematic abuses of the Zepa civilians" were desperately disputed by Bosnian government officials in Sarajevo who decided to bar journalists from camps holding the Zepa refugees. U.N. officials rebutted that it was part of Sarajevo's "propaganda line."[26]

But within a month came the devised remedy for the unraveling campaign of disinformation. The August 28 mortar incident and shrill media reactions successfully

---

22. Louis Meixler, *Associated Press*, August 10, 1995.
23. *The Daily Telegraph*, July 15, 1995.
24. *The Independent*, July 24, 1995.
25. Raymond Bonner, *The New York Times*, July 27, 1995.
26. Bonner, *ibid*.

blurred—again—the emerging exposure of diplomatic and journalistic collusion from previous months and years. The media shrieked for air strikes.

Syndicated American columnist David Hackworth called the artifice a failure:

> "...In Bosnia, despite what we're shown on the tube by Pentagon hucksters with their precision bombing commercials—NATO air power flunked the course big time...The CIA isn't convinced that the Serbs fired the mortar shells that killed 38 Muslims in the Sarajevo market. This tragic but convenient event triggered the bombing campaign, causing the United States to take sides in the three-way civil war and NATO to become the Bosnian government's air force. A CIA analyst suggests the Muslims were up to their old trick of shelling themselves and blaming the Serbs."[27]

Hackworth turned up the volume a week later:

> "America is at war. ...President Bill 'John Wayne' Clinton, who ordered the military solution, played golf in Wyoming when the bombs started to rain down. He was conveniently out of the way of a probing press, whose top guns were also on their August holidays."[28]

The media schemes around Srebrenica also covered up one of the most startling discoveries in the Yugoslav wars.

Journalistic fervor and aggressive reporting about the recent Iran-Contra scandal had apparently deflated when it was revealed there were government-sanctioned connections, explicitly approved if not instigated by the White House and Pentagon, with the Croatian army which carried out its ferocious blitz against Serb populations in Krajina and eastern Slavonia.

In another example of schizophrenic war reporting, *The New York Times* casually scrutinized what was shockingly uncovered in Zagreb:

> "At the Defense Ministry here, 15 Americans, retired military men, are training Croatian officers in what is termed 'democracy transition.' ...At a time when Croatian forces...are scoring battle-field successes that threaten the region's military balance, such emblems of American influence go far beyond a familiar relationship between superpower and client. ...Last year, the United States and Croatia signed a military cooperation agreement that provides for increased contacts between the American and Croatian armed forces, including Croatian access to a Defense Department training program. ...The arrival of 15 American military instructors raised eyebrows in Zagreb, *drawing comparisons between the U.S. mission and the way American advisers first appeared in Vietnam or Central America.* In December, the State Department licensed Military Professional Resources Inc.—

---

27. Hackworth, *King Features Syndicate, Inc.*, September 5, 1995.
28. Hackworth, *King Features Syndicate, Inc.*, September 15, 1995.

made up of high-ranking retired military officers and based in
Alexandria, Va.—to act as instructors to the Croatian army in a
course supposed to woo its officers away from old, communist
habits and instill the values of a democratic army."[29] (Italics
added)

The "company"—Military Professional Resources Inc.—was allowed to merely
deny it had tutored the born-again Croat army in "tactical training" or in cleansing
350,000 Serbs from Krajina.

Un-Packing The Journalists

The few journalists who began to free themselves from pack journalism and
self-censorship were led out of the propaganda morass by disillusioned
military experts and dissident diplomats, like retired Air Force General
Charles G. Boyd and George Kenney, the former Yugoslav Desk Officer at the State
Department.

Boyd, the Deputy Commander in Chief, U.S. European Command from November
1992 to July 1995, published a resounding expose on U.S. foreign policy in
Foreign Affairs, including statements that shredded illusions held by official
Washington and the media:

> "...The conventional wisdom in Washington...is stunted by a limited
> understanding of current events as well as a tragic ignorance
> or disregard of history... The linchpin of the U.S. approach has
> been the underinformed notion that this is a war of good versus
> evil, of aggressor against aggrieved... It has supported the legiti-
> macy of a leadership that has become increasingly ethnocentric
> in its makeup, single-party in its rule, and manipulative in its
> diplomacy. ...In short, the Serbs are not trying to conquer new
> territory, but merely to hold on to what was already theirs."[30]

Boyd singled out one of the leading promoters for the media's demonizing of Serbs:

> "Serbian people have suffered when hostile forces have
> advanced, with little interest or condemnation by Washington
> or *CNN* correspondent Christiane Amanpour."[31]

Kenney, who once subscribed to U.S. military intervention in Bosnia, quit his job
in disgust at the State Department only to later change his views as "multi-cultural,
sophisticated Sarajevo ...was turned over to coarse Muslim refugees who cared little
for pluralistic values."[32]

Kenney's disillusionment with the media bedlam over "genocide" gradually
succumbed to doubts about "the hollowness of the vague, unsubstantiated accounts
of mass murder":

---

29. Alan Cowell, *The New York Times News Service*, July 31, 1995.
30. Charles G. Boyd, "Making Peace with the Guilty: The Truth about Bosnia,"
Foreign Affairs, September/October 1995.
31. Boyd, *ibid*.
32. Kenney, "Bloody Bosnia," *Washington Monthly*. March 1995.

> "As one of the original interventionists, I must confess here, I'm guilty myself of having used the term genocide (rarely, with qualifications) in reference to Bosnia, yet I've never felt comfortable with insisting it was taking place. ...Where, one might ask, are the bodies? ...How many people died? ...250,000 is a number the press has used for some time. ...Friends in the U.S. intelligence community tell me their best guess for confirmed dead runs to tens of thousands. ...The number 250,000 probably evolved out of sloppy reporting of Bosnian government claims, a demonstration of the herd instinct at work among journalists."[33]

For his candor, Kenney was black-listed and no longer sought for frequent commentary by the *British Broadcasting Corporation,* and major U.S. media. He was dropped by the Carnegie Endowment. Also, he was harangued by *Newsday's* Roy Gutman, co-winner of the 1993 Pulitzer Prize for International Reporting. Kenney called a scathing critique by *The New Republic's* Charles Lane "a completely unethical, unprincipled, below-the-belt attack."[34]

But Kenney's was not the only example of harassment by the media's own mercenaries.

The Tragic Trail Of War Reporting

During 1993 and 1994, the author interviewed dozens of international correspondents and wire service editors who were based in Belgrade, Zagreb and at other news bureaus in Europe and the U.S. With few exceptions, journalists said censorship and prejudice, in varying degrees, was heavily applied to their reports to reflect a dominant anti-Serb bias.

The tragic trail of unethical and negligent war reporting is voluminous:

> • To date, there is no evidence that 50,000 rapes were committed by Serb soldiers against Bosnian Muslim women, as claimed by Bosnian officials who, along with Croatian propagandists, predicted waves of rape-induced births in November 1992. Nor is there evidence to support claims by *The New York Times'* John F. Burns, the other 1993 Pulitzer co-winner, that as of August 7, 1993, there were 200,000 Muslim war fatalities—an average of 450 per day! [35]

> • There was simply no documented proof to even preposterously suggest that there are "tens of thousands" of war criminals at large in the former Yugoslavia, as claimed by *Newsday's* Gutman on April 16, 1994.

> • There has never been acknowledgment for erroneous reports by *The Los Angeles Times* on April 28, 1994, that there were 3,000 Muslim civilians dead or injured from supposedly

33. Kenney, *ibid.*

34. Kenney interview with author, September 13, 1995.

35. Burns, *The New York Times*, August 7, 1993.

indiscriminate Serb shelling at Gorazde. The original sources were Bosnian Muslim ham radio operators, replaying their earlier on-air theater during the fighting at Cerska. Seventy-five percent of the 272 evacuees retrieved eventually by U.N. helicopters from Gorazde turned out to be men and soldiers with injuries that were mostly sustained during attacks against Bosnian Serb military positions and uprooting Serb civilians—in direct violation of U.N. rules for designating Gorazde a "safe haven."

•Media outrage at the killing of *ABC* producer David Kaplan by a sniper in Sarajevo suspiciously fell silent when U.N. officials said the shot could not have come from Bosnian Serb positions.

•German television producers apologized later for wrongly identifying a grieving father and his dead son as Croats in late 1991 near Laslovo in Eastern Croatia. Both were Serbs.

•European television showed dozens of Bosnian Serb bodies after a massacre in western Bosnia in late 1992. They were originally reported as Muslim fatalities.

•The February 21, 1994, issues of *Time* and *Newsweek* magazines showed photographs of the grave of a victim from the February 5 Markale market bombing. The captions implied the victim was Muslim, but the victim's name was visible in Cyrillic lettering on the Serbian Orthodox cross over the grave.

•In July 1993, the *MacNeil-Lehrer News Hour* showed scenes of Albanian children who allegedly were victims of chemical poisoning in the Kosovo town of Podjujevo. But the children were not receiving medical attention and were being prompted to rub their arms for cameras. U.S. Embassy officials in Belgrade later said the incident was a hoax.

•On March 7, 1994, the *Toronto Globe and Mail* published a photo of the remains of the ancient Ottoman bridge at Mostar, carrying the caption that the famous cultural landmark was destroyed by Serb shelling even though Croat officials in Zagreb had admitted blame and promised to rebuild the structure.

Why the Western and American media lost its conscience and objectivity in the Yugoslav civil wars is secondary to why it persisted with biased reporting.

Probably, the best answer was published in 1994 by Gregory Copley, editor of *Defense and Foreign Affairs Strategic Policy*:

"At present, more than ever, facts are interfering with 'truths' as perceived and espoused by leaders and writers. Accepting 'truths' enable editors and politicians to have a continuity of policy and, perhaps more important for their careers, continuity of perceived opinion and attitude. For an editor or a politician to say 'I was wrong' or 'I have changed my opinion based on later and better information' is a recipe for job loss."[36]

The reality became clear with President Clinton's decision to send thousands of U.S. troops to enforce intervention, not peace in Bosnia. The media only casually asked the Pentagon how many body bags were being sent with U.S. troops into the already roaring Bosnian winter:

> "Sooner or later—maybe it'll take a decade—they'll start filling them up and sending them home..."[37]

> "The Army refuses to disclose how many body bags it plans to bring to Bosnia. When pressed by lawmakers last week, Gen. John Shalikashvili, the chairman of the Joint Chiefs of Staff, said the U.N. experience in Bosnia offered an imperfect comparison. Since 1991, 212 blue-helmeted peacekeepers in Bosnia have been killed, including 66 in traffic accidents, and 1,673 were injured."[38]

Larger questions remained unanswered by the media themselves, such as how would journalists justify the New World Order collision with a New Cold War? Predictably, they simply declined to comment.

But discerning the media's role that led to the U.S. and NATO invasion of Bosnia, and later Kosovo, was possible. And the clues to the truth were abundant—as are the consequences for ignoring them.

---

36. Gregory Copley, "When to Lie, When to Lead," *Defense and Foreign Affairs Strategic Policy*, February-March 1994.
37. Anonymous Pentagon official.
38. Eric Schmitt, *The New York Times News Service*, December 5, 1995.

Chapter 3

'Zoos Can Tell You Something About A Country'

"There are no whole truths; all truths are half-truths.
It is trying to treat them as whole truths that plays the devil."[1]
—**Alfred North Whitehead**

"When the legend becomes fact, print the legend."[2]
—**Maxwell Scott**

There was a devil loose in Yugoslavia. Maybe dozens or hundreds of them by July 1991 when the war in Slovenia and Croatia was just a month old. The actual fighting was bad enough in Croatia. The uncertain ceasefire in Slovenia wasn't much better. The media war was becoming catastrophic. The first wave of reporters and correspondents arrived and was digging in. Credibility was starting to take heavy casualties.

Seven thousand miles from the front, the reporting and the action was only fingertips away from anyone who had access to the wire services.

This war was not like the others. Not even the previous war in the Persian Gulf. There was access to information from all sides, all the time. The communications technology had exploded unimaginably since the last war was fought in the Balkans a half-century earlier when it took days and sometimes weeks of waiting for news about individual battles and incidents that were now barely hours or minutes old when reports arrived on the wire.

I was not of any Yugoslav background, nor related or connected to any of the people or cultures of the six republics and two autonomous provinces that were called Yugoslavia. After twenty years, I had friends and acquaintances in and from each of them, but I was not one of "them." In between letters and visits, I tried to keep an eye on Yugoslavia by scrolling down the lists of wire stories each day.

---

1. *Dialogues of Alfred North Whitehead* (1953)
2. Lines spoken by Carleton Young (as Scott, editor of the *Shinbone Star*),
The Man Who Shot Liberty Valance, Willis Goldbeck, 1962.

Before the late 1980s, there wasn't much to read. To Americans, overall, it was vaguely believed to be a relatively unimportant region in the thaw of the Cold War.

Occasionally, a reporter on tour would wander through and attempt to describe the variety and complexity of the hybrid federation in brief paragraphs that appeared to have been lifted out of travel brochures.

After Josip Broz Tito died in 1980, there were tensions and periodic spasms, but there was a more sensible reluctance by journalists to risk the perils of getting lost along side streets or down the back alleys of inflammable Yugoslav politics and resurrecting nationalisms.

The Yugoslavs impulsively tried to educate foreign journalists who did ask the ridiculous questions. Depending on the location or the time of year, it likely provoked a vexing but passionate explanation about dusty European mosaics and the demised royal houses, after-shocks from two world wars, Communism, Tito and post-Tito. Serbs, it seemed, had a different story to tell, but after a few minutes' recitation that began with the Battle of Kosovo a half-millennium earlier, listeners' expressions went blank while their native tutors soon tired and withdrew politely behind their Balkan masks with some impatience at the listeners' absence of historical stamina. After all, how could centuries be compressed into such simple, black-and-white answers?

Kosovo for the Serbs was what Valley Forge or Gettysburg was to Americans. No, more accurately it was like the Alamo and Pearl Harbor. Kosovo was not just a resounding defeat of the Serbs by the ancient Ottoman Turks. It was the commencement of a brutal occupation by the Turks for 500 years! This was unable to register with American minds and history. But for the Serbs, it is the cosmic event in their history, culture, politics and basis for all life.

Tito, half-Croat and half-Slovene, had packed Kosovo with ethnic Albanian Muslims to neutralize the nationalist soul of Serbia, denuding its heartland, sowing controversy and conflict for years to come. The issue of Kosovo was eagerly manipulated by the Slovene and Croat secessionists.

In 1986, I was at a party in Zagreb where there were numerous sophisticated, young professionals. They were the privileged class of progressive, urban Croats, doing what privileged and well-educated young people do everywhere on Saturday nights. They talked, smoked, laughed and drank too much. They treated the lone American guest with warmth and, as they became less inhibited and proudly tried out their heavily-accented English. The highlight of the evening was Sanja's showing of her slides taken during a recent holiday in Holland. The lights were turned off and everyone was seated on the floor in front of the large screen. I stood off to the side and had a clear view as well of the audience as they dragged on their cigarets and fell silent with awe, almost reverence as they watched. Soon, I realized that every detail of background—affluent Dutch streets, dazzling Dutch beaches, chic Dutch clothes, substantial Dutch buildings, Dutch traffic, Dutch wealth, Dutch life—was being devoured by starving souls. The thirty or so viewers whispered occasionally, but mostly they remained breathlessly quiet, stunned, stupefied. They coveted Western life!

The slides were artfully arranged and included happy poignant scenes of my host and her Amsterdam boyfriend, framed by a romantic seaside sunset at the end. The audience cheered, lit up and topped off their glasses. It was, after all, the dream of every person in that room—the beckoning, seductive West with its promise of the "good" life.

The tall American seemed out-of-place, detached, catching a few glances from the curious.

The evening's entertainment wasn't over. Somebody picked up a guitar and started to strum first a few happy songs which everyone knew and accompanied lustily. Then he began to plunk with deliberately clumsiness, moaning and stammering strange lyrics that sounded Oriental. His listeners were overcome with laughter at his mournful, sad-faced expressions that only caused new rounds of whoops and back slaps.

My host sat nearby, joining in.

"What is he singing? What are the words?" I asked, wanting to understand the hilarity.

"He's singing Serbian nationalist songs like an Albanian," she answered between guffaws, as her eyes nervously questioned my lukewarm smile.

As late as 1989, it was best to give assurances instead of answers to English-speaking outsiders, even if running the risk that articles would later be written from scant lines in journals and notebooks on the basis of Western optimism, irony and allegory:

> "However you look at it—geographically, historically, ethnically—Yugoslavia is a patchwork of fragments: all beautiful, all different, like brilliant shards of stained glass. ...Even without the political labels, the diversity of the country makes a traveler gasp. ...This diversity is both blessing and curse."[3]

This by one writer from Minnesota after journeying through Yugoslavia and recording a postcard narrative about ancient Dubrovnik and the Dalmatian coastline. In Belgrade, she focused on the vulnerable imagery "of spray-painted graffiti in English" on a bridge.

And, a trip to the zoo was used to symbolize her sentiments about the Serb capital:

> "In the past two millennia, my guide announced brightly, 'Belgrade has been destroyed and rebuilt thirty-six times.' ...I'd gone up to the park to see Yugoslavs at rest, and to rest myself. But then I stopped in at the zoo, and it wasn't restful. Because they're not normally on the tourist trail, zoos can tell you something about a country. About values. About kindness. About priorities. At the Belgrade Zoo, a crazed black panther raced back and forth ceaselessly in a cage too low for climbing. Boys teased a pair of young alligators over and over. An old tiger missing some teeth and part of his tail, kept fumbling with his metal water dish, peering into it, nudging it with his nose; the dish was dust-dry."[4]

Apparently, the reporter never got to the park or spoke with any of the thoughtful Belgraders sitting restlessly on benches nor stood elbow-to-elbow on cold mornings in neighborhood bakeries, eating *burek* and sipping yogurt. But, she praised Montenegro, the picturesque Bay of Kotor, the lush scenery along the Adriatic and the idyllic cliche about Sarajevo.

For some reason, her article never mentioned Zagreb or Ljubljana where secessionist atmospheres and sedition were smoldering. The Slovenian, Croatian and Bosnian capitals also had stereotype zoological caricature.

---

3. Catherine Watson, *Minneapolis Star Tribune*, April 1990.

4. Watson, *ibid.*

Civilized Words And Discoveries Of Burial Pits

B y early 1990, Western journalists were being lured through the media conduit to Kosovo where nearly two million ethnic Albanian Muslims and a vastly outnumbered Serb minority at 200,000 were in a standoff over the same ground. Also being contested was media favoritism.

The mentors of the Kosovo Albanians were discreet officials of Western embassies in Belgrade and throughout Western Europe, who passed on names and leads and "contacts," anonymously:

> "In spite of Serbian claims of provocation and 'political violence'
> by the Albanians, diplomats who have investigated side with
> the Albanians."[5]

Actually, embassy tipsters investigated very selectively or very little, but they were appreciative a few days later for corroborating feedback from returned journalists who had become instant experts and were swayed to believing the original rumors and suspicions from desk diplomats in Belgrade. The right people awaited the journalists in Pristina:

> "'We are resisting only peacefully, with civilized words and
> without conflict, just like Gandhi,' Jashar Kabashi, an English-
> language professor at Pristina University, explained to a Western
> journalist beneath the brown awnings of the seedy Grand Hotel's
> outdoor cafe."[6]

At Pristina in 1985, it was no secret that "passive resistance" decoded for gullible journalists meant the "blood revenge" exchanged between Albanian Muslims and Serbs. But, Western journalists talked to understandably few Serbs in Kosovo because the ill-equipped visitors spoke no Serbo-Croatian, which was the shared language of the region. But, the language barrier wasn't the only difficulty for the first non-native journalists hurried into Yugoslavia to find out what was going on. They knew they were expected:

> "Young students dressed casually in Washington Redskin
> sweat shirts mix with older men nattily dressed in white suits
> and white shoes. They all drink tea from glasses as they read
> the local *Rilindja* ('Resistance') newspaper and patiently wait
> for Western reporters and TV crews to show up. ...The Albanian
> opposition has compiled volumes of eyewitness reports of
> unprovoked raids by Serbian police and rapes, arrests and
> beatings of Albanian students. In the coffee shop of the Grand
> Hotel, Albanian 'spin control' experts circulate to reporters
> English-language translations of the eyewitness reports and
> arrange interviews with Albanian students and leaders, oblivious
> both to the Serbs watching them and the beggars seeking
> money for food.'[7]

---

5 Watson, *ibid.*

6. Lance Gay, *Scripps Howard News Service*, July 27, 1990.

7. Gay, *ibid.*

And, to observe journalism's first rule of checking out the "facts" independently was to invite a beating or robbery at least or, if you wanted to confront local officialdom with the "facts," you were destined for a roadside ditch. Western reporters in Pristina seldom wandered very far from hotels or the university, except to leave town from the railroad station or the airport at Kosovo Polje.

Curiously, details were rare about "spin control experts" when stories were filed by reporters who mainly wrote about what was told to them, even though smacking of hearsay:

> "Serbia's communist politicians have whipped Serbs into a frenzy over the issue (of Kosovo), contending the Albanians are trying to steal their historic homeland with its cultural monuments to Serbian history. ... 'How many people have left their monuments on the fields in Europe? Should they all have the lands back where they left monuments? Kosovo is for the people who live here now,' said Kabashi."[8]

A million caravanning Serbs joined brother Kosovo Serbs at a historic gathering on June 28, 1989, around the nearby monument on the Plain of Blackbirds to commemorate the 600th anniversary of the battle and their unreconciled defeat at Kosovo. Officials feared violence from Kosovo's Albanian majority who were still enraged by the deaths of two dozen demonstrators during incidents three months earlier in Pristina. Their expectations were justified. Two departing trainloads of Serbs were stoned by Albanians that night on the way out of Pristina, causing injuries to passengers.[9]

A year later, Serbs and Albanian Muslims were still offering condescending apologies and reassurances to visitors:

> "The people of Yugoslavia and the citizens will find ways of solving this situation, said Gani Jachari, president of the local Communist League."[10]

By August 1990, the apologetics disappeared. The "news" that wasn't new—got worse:

> "Discovery of a burial pit filled with thousands of human bones has stirred old ethnic hatreds and political feuds in this troubled nation. ...Video tapes of the scene show human remains, more than ten yards deep in places, covering the floor of the cavernous grave, the last resting place of an army of 40,000 Croats who collaborated with the Nazis."[11]

Certainly, the ghoulish videotapes in the Zagreb and Belgrade press stirred up emotions, but the story itself was disturbing when it emerged on the *Associated Press* in August. The overline, written for news editors thousands of miles away, said that the discovery about thirty-five miles west of Zagreb at Jazovka was "new." But the eighth paragraph said something else:

---

8. Gay, *ibid.*
9. *Associated Press*, June 30, 1989.
10. *Associated Press, ibid.*
11. Slobodan Lekic, "Newly Discovered Mass Grave Revives Old Feuds," *Associated Press*, August 2, 1990.

"The grave, *found in June* after a former partisan involved in
the killings told journalists about it, has inspired debate about
the one million believed killed in fratricidal clashes from 1941
to 1945." (Italics added)

Why was there a two-month delay in getting the story? Or, why was there delay
in getting it on the wire to the outside world?

Reports were beginning to regularly appear about tensions and unrest in Slovenia
and Croatia, confrontations and local disturbances. It was all normal enough fare for
flexing nationalisms. But that was the superficial reporting. There were deeper, more
insidious intrigues along with hidden hands at work. The stakes were enormous,
and the real provocateurs were only occasionally glimpsed.

Germany Introduces The 'Ultimate' Competition

Nobel Prize nominee Branko Horvat, a respected Croat economist in Zagreb,
was alluding to the potential for emerging Central and Eastern European
nations now stirring themselves from the doldrums of post-Communism
to form their own economic coalitions. The European common market initially
showed disdain toward welcoming these states into the West European community
with full and equal standing. Germany controlled the membership roster, and total
subservience to Bonn was the only requirement and strict condition for admittance.

Horvat and others speculated about whether a hungrier common market next
door might succeed as a competitor, "stretching from the Baltic to the Balkans."[12]

Even in late 1991 after the commencement of the Slovenian and Croatian wars,
Horvat was still being asked about his ideas by the dissident Belgrade journal *Vreme*.
He was asked whether "Western Europe would allow this, given the enormous
natural and intellectual potential that exists here." Horvat's answer was peculiar,
almost cryptic:

"Nowadays you can only stop competition by introducing
some other form of competition. So if Western Europe feels
that such a counter market of around 150 million people would
be dangerous, it will then become easier for us and for Eastern
Europe countries to enter the European Community."[13]

But there was a more permanent option for ultimate "competition" Germany's
leaders intended to incite among the Yugoslav republics to prevent any competitive
threat against its European economic and political hegemony. Membership in the
European Community was secondary. The destruction of Yugoslavia, cloaked by
internal, manipulated incitements, was similarly introduced by Germany fifty years
earlier—fratricide!

The prerequisite by 1990 for vassalage and German favoritism depended on the
enlightened initiative of "democratic" Yugoslav politicians to extricate themselves from
the stubborn Balkan federation. German weapons and armaments had been flowing
into Slovenia and Croatia for years and were stockpiled for the inevitable.[14]

---

12. Horvat interview with Ivan Protic and Mitar Rocenovic in *Vreme* (Belgrade),
November 1991.

13. *Vreme, ibid.*

14. German arms exports to Yugoslavia in the period 1982-90 were worth 2.2 billion
deutschmarks. (Milos Vasic, "The German Connection," *YUGOFAX*, February 3, 1992.)

German diplomats quietly strategized beyond view of the media, which was senti-mentally captivated by the romantic idea of Balkan aspirations for democracies in southeastern Europe.

By the end of the year, the door was already closed on that legendary Yugoslav talent for improvising last-minute solutions and relief from the volcanic pressures about to erupt. Peaceful pretense was abandoned and the rhetoric was ignited. Slovenian President Milan Kucan's tone could hardly be interpreted as anything but belligerent when he was quoted in a lengthy, contradiction-laced interview in the widely-read German news magazine *Der Spiegel*:

> "If the irrational atmosphere continues in which our republics are trying to transform themselves into sovereign national states, then a civil war cannot be ruled out. ...Our goal is to be integrated into the European system as quickly as possible. ...For now, there seems to be little prospect for compromise. And that is why our bags are packed and waiting at the door."[15]

It was the eve of nationalist referenda in Slovenia and Croatia, and it was all a facade to legitimize the illegal secession of the Yugoslav republics and, later, the illegal—if not outright criminal—international recognition of these republics. Integration "into the European system as soon as possible," the codified rationale for armed rebellion, was not specified or explained on the ballots. The electorate was bombarded by old communist regimists and their new democratic rhetoric and affiliations with "progressive" parties cleansed of grimy socialist nuances. There was some hypocritical skepticism by *Der Spiegel* about the justifications for "new" opportunism at the expense of constitutional responsibility:

> "**Q**. Mr. Kucan, can the elections in the Yugoslav republics put an end to the country's political anarchy?
>
> "**A**. They will at least legitimize new representatives who will have been elected democratically and who will thus be entitled to negotiate in the name of their people and their republics.
>
> "**Q**. What could you do if Europe said it would integrate only a united Yugoslavia?
>
> "**A**. I don't believe there is anyone in the West who would take the responsibility for chaining us into a Yugoslavian federation if that endangered our existence. That contradicts the demo-cratic principles of the West. But naturally we understand the warning that, in pursuing our goals, we must show a sense of responsibility to the other Yugoslavian peoples and to the international community.
>
> **Q**. You're turning your back on a bankrupt Yugoslavia for a prosperous Europe?
>
> "**A**. Only by ensuring our sovereignty can we further the democratic process in Slovenia and have some influence on

---

15. *The New York Times News Service*, November, 29, 1990.

intensifying the process elsewhere in Yugoslavia. This will be much easier after the elections.

"**Q**. You yourself were a member of the communist leadership under Tito. At that time you insisted that fraternal relations and unity prevailed in Yugoslavia. Was that a lie?"

Kucan did not answer. *Der Spiegel*, not surprisingly, did not push it. Obviously, it was doubtful that more than a few major media outlets in the U.S. published the important and revealing interview, or whether any news editors recognized the lethal hypocrisy.

It all sounded good to Westerners. It sounded good to me, and I had some time in the country and at least knew the names of some of the players.

Western democracies. Free-market reforms. Democratic elections. Sovereignty. It all sounded good.

In June 1991—just seven months later—somebody opened the cages at all the zoos. It was feeding time. The media was slapping labels on people, personalities, governments, villains, and marauding military units faster than they could devour each other.

In the West, they wrote and read about the "rebellious republic of Slovenia" and "...renegade republic of Slovenia" and "...Slovenian territorial defense forces..."

In less than a month, the cauldron spilled over into Croatia with the "Serb rebels" and "...Serb guerillas" and "...secessionist Croats" and "... rebellious Serbs" and "...ethnic Serbs" and "...Croatian fighters" and "...Orthodox Serb rebels" and "... Croatian militiamen" and "...Croatian security forces" and "...ethnic Serb gunmen" and "...the independence-minded Croatian government" and the "...rival Yugoslav republic of Serbia..."

Struga: The 'Making' Of Memories

An entire lexicon was in the making as the Croatian war spread to the village of Struga, about seventy-five miles southeast of Zagreb on the Croatian border with Bosnia-Herzegovina. More significantly, Struga was located on the Una River about fifteen miles south of Kostajnica and about thirty-five miles southwest of the confluence of the Una with the Sava River at Jasenovac.

It is wasted geography upon Western media consumers, but the rivers were the grisly repositories for the remains of at least 700,000 concentration-camp inmates and victims of bestial massacres by Croats at Jasenovac a half-century earlier.

Also, the history was apparently lost on foreign reporters and correspondents who were streaming back and forth between Zagreb and Belgrade in early 1991. However, Struga became a landmark on the media map in the opening days of the Croatian war when the journalists were captives of the government information ministries intent upon molding the perceptions of the current war and any media memories of its predecessor.

During World War II, Jasenovac was the Auschwitz of the Balkans. Estimates vary, but claims are not unreasonable that 600,000 or more Serbs, 30,000 Jews and 29,000 Gypsies were gruesomely exterminated at Croat death camps of Jasenovac run by Croatian extremists—the Ustashe. The memories, including that 250,000 Serbs were expelled from Croatia and another 200,000 were forcibly converted to Catholicism, are vivid in the minds of Serbs who lived nearby and needed little prompting to organize local militia to bolster units of the Yugoslav army in hostilities against the Croat army and militia. This densely-populated swath of land was historically inhabited by Serbs who hastily created the autonomous region of Krajina, expecting the worst:

> "The Eastern Orthodox Serbs in Croatia, who have a living memory of war time atrocities by Roman Catholic Croats, say they are endangered in Croatia."[16]

Except for a few reconnaissance excursions that invariably required "official" government interpreters and escorts, most Western media newcomers did not stray very far from the security of hotels and international press centers in Zagreb and Belgrade. Especially in Zagreb, these became the major staging and indoctrination areas for "covering" the war. Most arriving correspondents spoke no Serbo-Croatian, and interpreters were often native journalists or "stringers" with practical understandings about correctness and what was preferred by post-communist, now nationalistic censorship in Zagreb to promote the "new democracy."

Media newcomers to Belgrade—where the Yugoslav federal information ministry included a mere half-dozen publicists—were previously accustomed to patronage, cooperation, access and answers in the West. But officials in Belgrade arrogantly tolerated the press with its anti-Yugoslav, anti-Serb bias. In the early days of the war, the international media's harangues in Belgrade were simply, though unwisely, ignored. So, as some correspondents admitted later, they wrote what they wanted, often in adversarial tones "and we never worried about our visas getting revoked." And, when Belgrade brass read the results, it only confirmed their original suspicions and short-sighted, passive policies toward media appeasement. Antagonisms became entrenched all around. If Belgrade had a legitimate story to tell, it went untold due to the combined negligence by official Belgrade and the media. Meanwhile, government publicists in Zagreb used persistence, intensity, intimidation and volume to win the sympathies of the West.

Before the summer of 1991, there was only a handful of Western correspondents based in Yugoslavia and Belgrade. But communications with the West by mid-1992 was transplanted in Zagreb. Establishing Zagreb as the media hub was all the more astonishing because of Croatia's well-known repression against domestic journalists and the resurrection of communist-era laws that threatened five years imprisonment for anyone in the media—domestic or foreign—who criticized the government.[17] Also, the Brussels-based International Federation of Journalists continuously refused membership to Croatian media. Dissident Croat journalists were sacked from newspapers and television stations where boards, as well as executive staffs, were quickly packed with government loyalists. But novice Western reporters were not dissuaded from writing dispatches based on or direct quotes from the government-controlled Zagreb media.

The foreign press produced few meaningful stories with Zagreb datelines which unfavorably illuminated government figures and the darker sides of the Croatian "democracy."

They winked at the replacement of the Yugoslav *dinar* by the new Croatian *kuna* resurrected from the fascist days of World War II. They did not seem to notice that libraries were being purged of all books and periodicals but those sympathetic to official policies. Western journalists looked the other way as the government

---

16. Chuck Sudetic, *The New York Times News Service*, July 31, 1991.
17. Mary Hueniken, "History Reveals Source of Serb's Anger," *London Free Press*, August 24, 1993.

reclassified requirements for Croatian citizenship. Nobody reported that citizens born outside Croatia were required to re-apply—at a price!—for citizenship by April 15, 1992, including refugees living temporarily abroad. Missing the deadline meant a monetary penalty equal to an average three months salary for late applications. Failure to comply meant exile (or worse) and the seizure of property by the state. But the Western media would not discover "ethnic cleansing" until the war spread to Bosnia.

New policies for religious instruction in Croatia's public schools were designed to encourage registration as, if not conversions to Roman Catholicism. Boulevards, other main thoroughfares and public squares were "cleansed" of Yugoslav identities and renamed for World War II Ustashe figures.

Likewise, Western media remained silent about the demise of democracy in Slovenia. One disappointing prognosis appeared just five months after the ten-day Slovenian war ended:

> "Slovene society has been militarized. Police repression is clearly visible. Attitudes to immigrants are marked by intolerance and racism. The democratic spirit of civil society is rapidly disappearing. This is the irony of post-communist Slovenia. After free elections, and the fall of communist rule, the possibilities for free and open discussions have receded."[18]

A Ljubljana sociologist advocated urgency:

> "Facism is already a creeping force within Slovenia, and measures need to be taken now to deal with it effectively."[19]

In the early days of the war in Croatia, the public relations front was obscured to the outside world except in rare published pieces by a few journalists, who stepped back for a clearer look at the images being manipulated in front of rookie war correspondents that obediently packed the nonstop press conferences in the Zagreb Parliament building:

> "One thing is certain: nobody can complain that the Croatian publicity machine is overcautious about unsubstantiated allegations. If it is colorful tales that you are looking for, then Croatia can always oblige. Day after day in the Croatian capitol, Zagreb, press conferences take place at which journalists seek facts and figures about the growing conflict in Yugoslavia. ...It sometimes seems the ministers who turn up to the press conferences live in a rhetoric-rich, fact-free fairyland."[20]

But one story about what happened in the Struga region in the first month of the Croatian war echoed eerily throughout subsequent years of war reporting in the Balkans. It would require a discipline to read, as the saying goes, between the lines.

The half-dozen or so wire reports that appeared on June 31, 1991, had described the frenzied attempts in Brussels and Belgrade to gain cease fire agreements and stop the shooting in Croatia. But one story from Zagreb jumped out:

---

18. Ali Zerdin, "After Free Elections, No Democracy," *YUGOFAX*, November 16, 1991.

19. Goga Flakera, "A Loss of Orientation," *YUGOFAX*, February 3, 1991.

20. Steve Crawshaw, *The Independent*, July 11, 1991.

"Tales of massacres and mutilation are emerging in Croatia's bloody ethnic conflict, feeding growing fury between Serbs and Croats and diminishing the chances for peace. Stories of gruesome bloodletting have become central ingredients to an unrelenting propaganda war. Details are often difficult to substantiate but their existence has stirred deep emotions."[21]

The story began by describing Croatian newspaper reports the previous week from the "village of Sisak" where a "human shield" of elderly Croat men, women and children were "forced to march ahead of ethnic Serb militiamen confronting Croatian forces..." The *AP's* Austrian-based reporter never questioned that Sisak was listed as a "village" (accurate maps were easily available in Zagreb) when in reality it was the seat of the district of Sisak-Moslavina and a manufacturing-industrial town of 50,000 or more people.

But "village" conjured up images of rural innocence, backwardness and vulnerability.

The Sisak account was "confirmed by interviews conducted by some Western journalists."

Then was unveiled the ghastly horror at Struga, a village with a Serb minority:

"The Croatian government on Tuesday played a tape of crying women from Struga and other villages south of the capital, Zagreb. 'The (Serbian) terrorists destroyed everything and killed at random,' said one Croatian woman, her voice choked by tears. 'They were shooting and burning houses, killing people and cattle,' another woman said on the tape, played at a news conference. People interviewed by a Croat reporter also spoke of rapes and killings with knives and bayonets by Serbs. They claimed the Serbs mutilated dead bodies and carved out eyes. The tape, first carried by Croatian radio, did not give the names of those interviewed."[22]

Another "old woman," again anonymous, was recorded and said she was seeing her third war this century, as the story continued:

"Struga, a flashpoint of recent violence, has also been mentioned in the government-controlled media in connection with the abduction of thirty to forty people. The Croatian government so far has failed to say what exactly happened to those purportedly kidnapped. It has also not given full details and the results of an autopsy of nine policemen, said to have been butchered by Serbian attackers in the Struga area Friday. A Serb source in Zagreb told *The Associated Press* he had been told by friends in the area that what happened in Struga was not a massacre but a grenade attack. The source spoke on conditions of anonymity."[23]

---

21. Roland Prinz, "Tales of Atrocities and Massacres Harden Croatian Conflict," *Associated Press*, July 31, 1991.

22. Prinz, *ibid.*

23. Prinz, *ibid.*

Anonymous sources, anonymous victims, hearsay, third—and fourth-hand hearsay, unnamed "Western journalists" who "confirmed" knifings, bayonetings, human shields, mutilations, carved-out eyes, slain animals, butchery, mass kidnapping, random killings, and rape?!

Not a single named source or identified attribution in the entire story. Only Croat reporters inspected the scene. No mention of whether any corroboration was demanded from Croat government officials who made and exhibited the recordings and broadcast them over Croatian radio. No description how the information was presented. In Serbo-Croatian with translation? With English transcripts? Did the Austrian correspondent speak Serbo-Croatian? The autopsy reports of the nine policemen "said to have been butchered" four days earlier were never mentioned again.

Such a story was a mutation of modern Western journalism. It was somehow judged credible by the insertion of a couple of disclaimers. The reporter should never have moved the story without specific information. The editors at the *Associated Press* "control" bureau in Vienna should never have moved the story. Editors at the *AP* bureau in New York should never have moved the story. News editors of newspapers and electronic media should never have used the story. But they did. It was not an "example" of the use of "unrelenting propaganda" in the Croatian war. It was THE propaganda itself! It was also a classic sample of the first evidence of the breakdown and collapse of news judgment and the abandonment of objectivity and fairness in reporting about the Yugoslav debacle.

Surely, there was another side to the story of Struga in Belgrade or at Knin where the Krajina Serbs had their headquarters. Somebody could have made a phone call from Zagreb, from Vienna, from New York or from anywhere. Nobody did.

Three years later, the *AP's* supervising editor in Vienna reflected about how the government publicists had been running wild, about how "other" sides to stories were rarely sought or were entirely neglected, how media top management steered war coverage to play up victims, and about how hindsight showed plenty of media gullibility and favoritism.[24] She gave one specific example of something worse —cover-up. Once the propaganda role of hired American public relations companies became blatant, a reporter filed a story about it. The story was moved to New York where editors snuffed it out.

Later, the *AP's* top news executive in New York flatly refused any specific response about the killed story or any general comment about the organization's bias in reporting the Yugoslav wars.[25]

By late October 1991, *Philadelphia Daily News* columnist Jack McKinney summed up the obvious:

> "Western reporters have been giving Croatians much more sympathetic coverage than the Serbs."

It was troubling others also:

> "Clarity was an early victim of the war in Yugoslavia and reality has become progressively enveloped in a blanket of fog. ...As the desperate attempts to win the hearts and minds of

---

24. Author's interview with Alison Smale, *Associated Press* bureau chief in Vienna, January 10, 1994.

25. Author's interview with Bill Ahearn, *Associated Press* senior vice president, June 17, 1994.

Europe grow, the claims become wilder, the proof skimpier. But the (government-controlled) Croatian media are convinced that officials in London and Washington can be outraged into submission, so the assault continues unabated."[26]

At the same time, Belgrade-based journalists and correspondents were confronting the arrival of 60,000 mostly Serb refugees from Croatia. They brought with them horrifying accounts, equaling the Struga episode, about atrocities and the destruction of scores of Serb villages. Almost 100 of the remaining 156 Serbian Orthodox churches had been razed in Croatia where more than 800 Serbian churches stood in Croatia prior to World War II. Media skepticism—though the refugee reports coincided with earlier claims by official Serbian and federal Yugoslav government information bureaus—prevented any serious reporting about "concentration camps" holding Serbs in Croatia, such as at Suhopolje in the Grubisno Polje commune where eighteen Serb villages were destroyed. Another was at Stara Lipa, among the remains of twenty-four Serb villages in the Slavonska Pozega commune where Serb populations were evicted.

The Struga style of war reporting was not valid when confronted with Serb victims. True enough, Serbs were accused as the primary aggressors in the Croatian war. True enough, travel to Croatian war zones was difficult and dangerous to verify allegations of atrocities. But there were plenty of refugees and humanitarian organizations to talk to in Belgrade. There were plenty of credible "Western journalists" around to confirm the possibility of such incidents. And somebody—whether in Belgrade, Vienna or New York—could have made some phone calls to Croatian information ministers in Zagreb who were always accessible for questions.

'Myths, Utopias, Illusions'

When the Yugoslav civil war passed its first anniversary, one convincing diagnosis emerged about the cause of "media noise" from Western (including American) journalists who were covering the exasperating conflict in Croatia:

"The greatest difficulty for West European politicians and commentators in dealing with Yugoslavia is that most knew next to nothing about the country when they first delved into its crisis. Now that everything has come loose, they are disgusted by the chaos and their powerlessness to change anything overnight. Worse still, in their disgust some have come up with so-called radical solutions. ...Yugoslavia is a chaos of nations, religions, languages, cultures, traditions, ambitions, frustrations, myths, utopias, illusions."[27]

The media became addicted to official government information and generally could not leave Zagreb; they reviled official government information but generally would not leave Belgrade. Indeed, "radical solutions" were needed for the "chaos" of war reporting in the media itself.

So, they resorted to one of the few reliable guides, they thought, to lead them through the twisted madness of Yugoslav fratricide.

---

26. Anne McElvoy (in Zagreb), *The Times of London*, November 10, 1991.
27. Slavko Curuvija, *The European*, May 14-17, 1992.

United Nations officials (primarily because they spoke English) became corroborating sources, spokesmen and patient instructors for journalists who lacked Balkan orientation but who needed to file stories immediately after "hitting the ground." Helpful U.N. officials often were uncertain themselves with details and veracity about incidents, but within minutes their background speculations were being reported as fact through Western media outlets.

The Western media was simply unprepared, if not unqualified, to do their jobs, according to Petar Lukovic, deputy editor-in-chief of *Vreme*, the major opposition newspaper in Belgrade:

> "I have met lots of Americans... and they came around here, around Belgrade and around Yugoslavia without the basic information. For someone sitting in an office in Chicago or Washington, thinking this was a fight between good guys and bad guys... they simplified it to the point so that any four-year-old kid could understand."[28]

And David Binder, a longtime Balkan expert and experienced *New York Times* correspondent, sized up the inexperience and consequences of American reporters and editors with the Yugoslav breakup thrust before them:

> "With very few exceptions, the performance of the press, in my opinion, has been miserable. It's been very biased and slanted... and it hasn't even done the ordinary thing that reporters should do, that is to go to all sides and talk to people from all sides... White hats and black hats. We cannot deal with a world in which there are multiple culprits, multiple perpetrators... We have to have one side that is good and one side that is bad..."[29]

The arriving media, U.N. staffers noted with growing bitterness, also were responsible for casting the U.N. as anti-Serb and then again, abruptly, as pro-Serb. The relationship between the media and U.N. officials in Yugoslavia would become one of the love-hate variety.

"I've worked with the press for a long time, and I've never seen so much lack of professionalism and ethics in the press," remarked Aracelly Santana, a U.N. official in Belgrade.[30]

Media disillusionment, distortion and manipulation began almost before the bells in the Zagreb cathedral stopped ringing on June 25, 1991, celebrating Croat secession from Yugoslavia.

Even Balkan experts would become careless with the "little" facts about the Yugoslav inferno, such as when they said that the Slovenians were the ones who apparently started everything.[31]

---

28. Lukovic interviewed in documentary, "Dr. Dove: International Involvement in the Balkan Conflict," 1997.

29. Binder, "Dr. Dove...," *ibid.*

30. Santana interview with author in Belgrade, February 10, 1993.

31. Susan Woodward, Brookings Institute fellow, during a panel discussion, entitled "Making Sense Out of Chaos," American University (Washington, D.C.), October 5, 1993.

"Two hours after Croatia's 6 p.m. secession declaration, neighboring Slovenia... followed suit."[32]

People uncorked champagne bottles in front of the Parliament building in Zagreb:

> "Inside, legislators roared their approval as Croatian President Franjo Tudjman, a fiery nationalist, defiantly announced secession. ... Tudjman said Bulgaria had recognized his republic, in a telegram he waved at a news conference. But a journalist from Bulgaria's state news agency said Sofia's ambassador in Belgrade had denied the assertion."[33]

Somebody made a phone call or two.

---

32. Dusan Stojanovic, *Associated Press*, June 25, 1991.
33. Stojanovic, *ibid*.

Chapter 4

Paul Revere 'Rides Again'

"Facts are stubborn things; and whatever may be our wishes,
our inclinations, or the dictates of our passions,
they cannot alter the state of facts and evidence."
– John Adams[1]

The scene showed some of Tom Prescott's men had smiles on their faces as they fired into the unarmed crowd on Boston's King Street. Five people died and six were wounded. It is one of the famous scenes in American history textbooks. Everyone has seen it. It is Paul Revere's famous engraving of the Boston Massacre in 1770, one of the events that sparked the American Revolutionary War.

It is also a distortion of the real facts and an example of deliberate and effective propaganda. Also, it is classical revisionism.

Revere's engraving, owned by the American Antiquarian Society, shows eight British soldiers, including Captain Thomas Prescott, sword raised, shouting commands. Muskets are firing into the faces of unarmed civilians. There are leering expressions on the faces of some of Prescott's men.

Revere wrote a poem condemning the event, which accompanied the printed copies of the engraving that he peddled. Silversmith Revere was not a journalist, and nothing is known of his abilities on horseback with the exception of an historic two-hour ride aboard a borrowed mount to Lexington, Massachusetts, on April 18, 1775, to deliver the alarm that British troops were on the march. Revere was captured when attempting to return to Boston where, after being released, he became an artillery officer.

In fact, "Boston Massacre" is a misnomer for the attack by about sixty enraged colonists against a single British sentry. Prescott arrived with several soldiers who were likewise attacked by the mob. The soldiers defended themselves, fatally shooting three people who died on the street. Two others expired later from wounds. But it was not the event shown in Revere's engraving or described by his poem.

Prescott, eloquently defended in court by John Adams, was acquitted of wrong-doing. Adams, who experienced insults and personal criticism while pressing his client's case for justice, was not popular among hawkish Boston colonists, who had little appreciation for anyone pointing out the true facts about the supposed

---

1 Adams, "Argument in Defense of the (British) Soldiers in the Boston Massacre Trials (December 1770)," *Boston Gazette*, 1774; *Bartlett's Familiar Quotations*, Boston: Little Brown and Company, Inc., 1992, p. 337.)

massacre. But Revere's engraving and poem took a permanent hold on popular history. Differing versions could be suspected of revisionism.

It was 219 years later and hot outside, and I was grateful to be in the cool, stately hallways of the elegant old Cosmos Club on Washington, D.C.'s Embassy Row. The Cosmos, said a brochure at the desk on that muggy June 7, 1994, is "the closest thing to a social headquarters for Washington's intellectual elite."

The 116-year-old club was a comfortable refuge for past members like Presidents Taft, Wilson and Hoover. Later rosters also enjoyed posh sitting areas, billiard table, dining rooms and the French-Italian baroque motif of the Warne Lounge and Cosmos' regal ballroom.

The Hall of Honors displayed photographs of numerous Cosmos members who were Nobel and Pulitzer Prize winners. I studied the portraits hurriedly, waiting for my ride to the Carnegie Endowment for International Peace on nearby N Street. It was an impressive display: Sinclair Lewis, Glenn T. Seaborg, Henry Kissinger, William Allen White, James Truslow Adams, Herman Wouk, Archibald MacLeish, Bruce Catton, Allen Drury, Walter Lippman, Daniel J. Boorstin, and Henry B. Adams.

So, Henry Brooks Adams was a member of the Cosmos! American history was full of Adamses. I never could remember how many, or if they were all related.

"No one means all he says, and yet very few say all they mean, for words are slippery," wrote Adams in 1907.[2] That statement stuck with me through the years.

Adams was right. That was the same problem in the media with the Serbs in Yugoslavia. There were Serbs in Serbia. There were Bosnian Serbs in Bosnia and Krajina Serbs in Bosnia and Croatia, Darko's and Zarko's, Pavle's, Franjo's, Slobo's, Vuk's and Alija's. It was slippery going. Journalists and headline writers lumped them all together at first. For instance, you read and heard stories about "Croatian Serbs." To Westerners, it supposedly made sense in the trend of hyphenated ethnicity. But nobody used, say, the ridiculous term "Mexican Texans." The media stopped it after awhile but picked it up again in early 1995. Bizarre multi-ethnic terms like the politically correct "Kosovar" and "Bosniak," contrived to sanitize and destigmatize "Albanian Muslim" and "Bosnian Muslim" respectively, suddenly sprouted on the linguistic landscape.

Henry Brooks Adams was right.

As far as Yugoslavia was concerned, all that was said wasn't all the media could have said or meant.

The words were strange, and who knew what to think and report about? Or how?

Invitation To An Ambush

That's why I was summoned to Washington. After I spoke out about the negligence and the omissions—and the bias. I was "invited" to explain my observations to some of my outraged fellow journalists on a panel, entitled "The War in the Former Yugoslavia: Are the Western Media Combatants?" I wasn't exactly asked to appear; my invitation was more like a summons from *Foreign Policy* Editor Bill Maynes. He was taking plenty of heat in Washington and showed me samples of angry, demanding letters that went to his boss, Carnegie board president Morton Abramowitz. It was no secret among Carnegie insiders that Abramowitz, who took his own public position on the Yugoslav issue, wanted to fire Maynes for publishing my article about biased war reporting.[3]

---

2. Education of Henry Adams, Chapter 31.

3. "Dateline Yugoslavia: The Partisan Press," *Foreign Policy*, Number 93, Winter 1993-94. pp. 151-172

Abramowitz, a former U.S. ambassador to Turkey during the Bush Administration, was aligned in his Balkan sentiments since 1992 with billionaire and currency speculator George Soros. Abramowitz, who was also a former ambassador to Thailand, was one of the main organizers behind the Action Council for Peace in the Balkans that was bankrolled by Soros in 1993. Soros' mysterious agenda in the Yugoslav wars was supposedly inspired by philanthropic motives involving scores of millions of dollars in humanitarian aid programs, such as construction of a water-purification and pumping facility in Sarajevo. However, once in operation, the plant became a public relations tool and was shut down whenever the whims of the Sarajevo government wanted to draw world attention to the city's bouts with thirst caused by supposed Serb bombardments. Often the water lines were turned off without any shelling.

Soros, immune from any serious or timely scrutiny by the Western media throughout the Yugoslav upheavals, wanted to enlist a Washington cadre of influence brokers to quietly exert pressure on the White House and hesitant members of Congress.

"Abramowitz played a considerable role in making contacts and shaping strategy."[4] But the strategy of discreet lobbying was later jettisoned as public outbursts spewed from so-called "peace" advocates for air strikes in Bosnia and even against Belgrade.[5]

My positions were already in print, regarding the question posed by the title of the panel gathering. Carnegie's "Face-to-Face" was "a forum facilitating dialogue among governmental and non-governmental participants on major international issues." Even as a career journalist, I never considered myself an authority about major international issues. But then, there wasn't much dialog provoked by my own or any other public critique of the media in the Yugoslav wars. Few cared. Most waited to be told what to believe.

The "forum," despite its high-brow format, could be an interesting discussion about media coverage in Yugoslavia. Instead, I smelled an ambush.

My main adversary was Charles Lane, an angry, petulant journalist and self-appointed champion of U.S. intervention in Yugoslavia who was at *Newsweek* and later at *The New Republic*. Lane was the bloodhound for *Newsday's* Roy Gutman and led the charge in early December 1993 to undermine my critique in *Foreign Policy*. But a few weeks before the Carnegie forum, I learned that Lane was investigating my personal background, beginning with my college days in the 1970s on up to my recent visits to Yugoslavia when he was trying to find "proof" that I was boarded and fed in hotels on the tab of the Belgrade regime.

There wasn't any proof because it never happened, and Lane couldn't find anybody in Belgrade to make such a claim. I wondered what kind of management at Lane's magazine would shoulder the expense of time and international travel to smear the reputation of another journalist. And, what was he "researching" about me in Berlin?!

---

4. Dick Kirschten, "Sarajevo's Saviors," *National Journal*, March 3, 1994.

5. An advertisement advocating the use of "force" was placed in *The New York Times* in January on the Sunday before President Clinton's inauguration in 1993. "Open letters" to Clinton, urging a lifting of the arms embargo and air strikes against Bosnian Serb targets, appeared in *The Washington Post* the following April and May. Curiously, the ads regaled Bosnian Serb forces that had generally ceased military operations except for sporadic reactions to provocation and continuing atrocities by Croats and Muslims. The latter two were currently locked in fierce battles with each other in areas such as Mostar. But such relevant factors were not mentioned in the ad or the open letters.

Another critic was Tom Gjelten, of *National Public Radio*. But, Gjelton was barred by his bosses from participating at the Carnegie forum. His book was about to be published and contained profuse flattery of *Oslobodjenje,* the government-supported Sarajevo newspaper that published throughout the Bosnian war under the approving eye of the ruling Muslim nationalists.[6]

What was National Public Radio afraid of?

The newspaper, although celebrated as an "independent" and non-government controlled publication, was staffed throughout the fighting by editors and reporters who observed the most conscientious self-censorship, according to former editor Kemal Kerspahic.[7]

There was no doubt about what Lane wanted to do at Carnegie. He and others were not interested in any substantive discussion about the media conduct in the Yugoslav wars. Lane was only interested in making personal attacks.

I kept my opening statement to the assigned ten minutes. Snarling and sneering, Lane took up twenty minutes, reading his prepared indictment. I watched moderator Maynes out of the corner of my eye. He wisely let Lane go out as far on the limb as he wanted. Lane began in solemn tones:

> "...By and large, I believe the media have done a good job in Bosnia. The present fact is that it is one of the few international institutions that has worked the way that it's supposed to. We've been no more combatant or partisan than anyone else. We have told an important story honestly. We have prodded the conscience of the world (despite) attempts to deny or explain away or obfuscate the existence of some of the most horrible crimes against humanity since the age of Hitler and Stalin..."

Lane read his standard indictment against any who would criticize the Balkan war coverage.

Maybe there were others in the room that asked themselves the same question I puzzled over as Lane ranted and fumed through his list of itemized complaints: What was behind such a tirade? An abhorrence for the facts and evidence?

He sounded like a courtroom prosecutor, demanding that the jury convict in the absence of facts.[8]

A Deeper Media 'Pathology'

The media and the reporting and conduct of some of the journalists and correspondents IS the bad news from the outset of the Yugoslav civil wars. And somebody started asking questions, and there were answers, facts and evidence. There was a paper trail. The frenzied media free-for-all—with its lopsided

---

6. *Sarajevo Daily:* A City and Its Newspaper Under Siege,
New York: Harper Collins, 1995.

7. Kerspahic interview with author, June 26, 1997, Washington, D.C.

8. Lane went on a leave of absence in 1996 to begin studies at the Yale University School of Law, returning a short while later as editor of *TNR* after publisher Martin Peretz, who wanted more lenient coverage of his friend Bill Clinton's campaign finance and sex scandals, fired editor Mike Kelly. Later, under Lane, *TNR* suffered a major setback with an infamously fact-free expose about a teenage computer hacker. Lane resigned soon after and went on to cover the U.S. Supreme Court for *The Washington Post.*

reporting about atrocities of torture, mass murder, rape and the made-for-media cliche "ethnic cleansing"—so far was rallied to a height of hysteria thought impossible for the public to ignore any longer.

The conflict was conveyed to media consumers with the most vivid reports of cruelty, tragedy and barbarism since World War II, excluding the utter capitulation of the Western press in reporting the Cambodian genocide. It was an unprecedented and unrelenting onslaught, combining effects of modern media technique, technology and tidal waves of advocacy journalism.

Eventually, all sides were condemned for systematic brutality. Bosnian Serbs were accused for carrying out most of the war's gruesome horrors against Muslim civilians, while equally grisly crimes committed against Serbs by Croats and Muslims—and later by Croats and Muslims against each other—were minimized and ignored in the press.

The media was obsessed with inflicting "a Massada psychology" in its siege against the Serbs.[9] The phenomenon did not escape notice by a few academics and a handful of informed journalists who detected flaws in the reporting, especially with such blatant examples as wrong identification of Serb victims as Muslims or Croats in newspaper photographs, magazine spreads and television footage:

> "The myopia and bias of the press is manifest. *The Washington Post,* France's *L'Observateur* and other leading newspapers have published pictures of paramilitary troops and forces with captions describing them as Serb, though their insignia clearly identify them as (Croatian) Ustashe."[10]

Although there was a patronizing trend to massage the consciences of readers, listeners and viewers, a total paralysis obstructed self-criticism from the professional media societies, national and international press associations about the Yugoslav war coverage. And there were suggestions about a deeper pathology:

> "Not all agendas about the Balkans have been revealed or debated; only the tragedy of innocent people dominates the news. ...What happens in the Balkans is not only a violation of human dignity, it is also an exploitation of human suffering, with the help of paid image makers and late converts to democracy who seek to smooth their way into the international arena. ...Mass media and policy-makers alike, perhaps unwittingly, have set the stage for repetition of the Yugoslav scenario in the Balkans at large. They have trivialized the core issues, stereotyped a nation (the Serbs). ...Selective victimology is a growing media business."[11]

The same writer described his own early study of media tendencies and slanted reporting:

---

9. Professor Carl Jacobsen, paper entitled, "War Crimes in the Balkans: Media Manipulation, Historical Amnesia and Subjective Morality," Carleton University (Ottawa), April 22, 1993.)

10. Jacobsen, *ibid.*

11. Nikolaos A. Stavrou, "The Balkan Quagmire and the West's Response," *Mediterranean Quarterly*, Vol. 4, Winter 1993.

"A qualitative and quantitative analysis I conducted over a three-month period, of stories appearing in a major newspaper in the eastern United States and fourteen randomly selected stories prior to the onset of the Yugoslav civil war in an equally well-established American newspaper, shows a disturbing pattern in news coverage. Of ninety stories reviewed in the eastern U.S. paper, excluding editorials, almost eighty-five percent include what could be called hearsay evidence. The authors seem to have made little or no effort to cross-check claims or seek the 'other side's' reaction. For the same period, the origin of almost ninety percent of the stories was Sarajevo, and only five percent originated in Belgrade from Serbian sources. An analysis of the fourteen randomly selected stories that appeared in the Western newspaper showed a similar tendency toward ethnic stereotyping. The Serbs were referred to as 'remnants of the Ottoman Empire,' and by implication primitive; the Yugoslav army officers were described as 'orthodox Communist generals' and the adjectives 'Eastern,' 'orthodox' and 'orthodox Communists' were repeatedly used in a pejorative context. Even the leader of the Democratic party in Belgrade, an implacable foe of Milosevic, was repeatedly described as 'Rasputin.' The only similarity between Rasputin and Vuk Draskovic is a beard. The Croats, on the other hand, were described as 'Western,' 'nationalist,' 'wealthiest and most advanced,' 'most developed,' 'Westernized,' and their system as a 'Western-style democracy.' Even photographs published in the eastern U.S. newspaper showed a gaping omission: no Serbs were shown suffering or being killed, their churches destroyed or villages burned. Almost eighty-five percent of these pictures depicted suffering Bosnians and problems caused by refugees housed in train depots in Croatia. One photograph showed a 'humane' Bosnian sniper: he was compelled by events to do a little sniping from his perch above a busy street. There was no mention of refugees in Serbia and certainly no pictures of them. Yet, as of December 1992, according to the International Red Cross, there were approximately six hundred thousand such displaced persons in Serbia, a great number of them Bosnian Muslims who sought refuge in their 'enemy's' territory."[12]

Media audiences were inundated with reports that:

•Only Serbs committed atrocities, violated truces, maintained concentration camps, and destroyed shrines and historic sites.

•Serbs "occupy" land belonging to Croats or Muslims, while Croats or Muslims "secure" disputed areas.

•Serbs have superior weapons while the Bosnian Muslims are virtually "unarmed" and peace-loving "victims."

---

12. Stavrou, *ibid.*

•Croats, Slovenes, and Bosnians abandoned the Yugoslav federation to avoid "Serb domination."

•The world, led by the U.S., should open the arms bazaar so that the Muslims can arm and defend themselves."[13]

Such one-sided vilification of Serbs by the Western media was without historical precedent. More precisely, it was without precedent because the modern insatiable media technology was able to "get" all sides of the story. Wire service correspondents in Belgrade may not have been able to talk by telephone to officials or members of their own organizations in Zagreb or Sarajevo. But their bureaus in nearby European cities could talk to both of them. Both sides could have been, should have been heard.

Numbers Tell A Different Story

The Yugoslav conflict was the unspectacular successor to the multi-media carnival during the previous Persian Gulf war. It was confusing to Western outsiders. It required patient and lengthy explanations. In the era of demands by news management for short articles, ostensibly to compensate for the diminished attention spans of readers and viewers, competent and ethical coverage of the Yugoslav wars collided with media business policies. "Selective victimology" was the answer. And, business-wise, it made good sense.

The tragic consequence was that slanted coverage of the Yugoslav civil wars overall was fed via monopoly to at least seventy million subscribers of more than 1,600 daily newspapers in the U.S. (and many millions more worldwide) by the *Associated Press* and *New York Times* wire services.

In October-November 1992, the author analyzed a tabulation of 1,526 articles collected from about 3,500 separate wire-service reports. Two identical five-month periods (May-September, 1991 and 1992) were examined in three categories:

•**1,087 breaking news stories,**
•**347 human-interest or feature stories,**
•**92 opinions, analyses, editorials, interpretive articles.**

These articles appeared under the bylines of 135 writers, correspondents or reporters, including only nine Serbs, two Croats, two Bosnian Muslims—and 122 non-Yugoslavs! During the early months of the wars, dependency upon newly arriving foreign reporters who primarily could not understand the language and did not know the histories in the region produced huge imbalances in the reporting—and some of the most flagrant errors!

Apart from the 135 identified writers, there were numerous articles without bylines, which were written or compiled by unidentified correspondents or editors in European and U.S. bureaus.

Chronological trends, datelines and analyses showed a dramatic predominance of Croat and Muslim perspectives, sympathies and suffering. Bias and slant were overwhelmingly obvious in the hundreds of stories with Sarajevo and other Bosnian datelines. Also identified were unfavorable or negligible treatment of Serbs or Serbian-oriented issues in the human-interest features and opinion pieces, analyses and editorials.

---

13. Stavrou, *ibid.*

A later tabulation of more than 4,000 wire service reports and articles, features and opinion pieces showed a minimum forty-to-one bias in the war reporting comparing datelines, sources quoted, editorial viewpoints, etc.—chiefly against the Serbian position. The ratio became excessively more lopsided in the reporting and commentaries by Western television journalists.

Media slam-dunking in the Yugoslav bedlam also spread to the pages of the slicks, running the gamut from the high-brow musings in *The New Yorker*:

> "'We are rewriting European geography,' a wise and experienced American expert says. 'We are doing this ad hoc and piece by piece. It is very dangerous'."[14]

...To T.D. Allman in *Vanity Fair* and his crass recollection of table talk with the police chief of Banja Luka (also present was *Newsday's* Gutman):

> "I sup with the Devil, and it occurs to me that I have neglected to bring a long spoon... I take another sip (of slivovitz) and ask, 'Do you want your children to be killers or computer salesmen?'"[15]

The same account describes cynical preconceptions before meeting with President Goran Hadzic of the Serbian Republic of Krajina at the piano bar of the Hotel Inter-Continental in Belgrade:

> "I'm here to meet the president with the eyes and beard of Rasputin."[16]

The repeated use of "Rasputin" when referring to dark-featured Serbs by the media throughout the early years of the Yugoslav wars a prevailing racism by commentators and correspondents. P.J. O'Rourke's hip sarcasm in *Rolling Stone Magazine* also contained undertones of racism toward Yugoslavs, i.e. the Serbs:

> "The unspellables were shooting the unpronounceables. ...It's hard to come back from the Balkans and not sound like a Pete Seeger song. Even those of us who are savagely opposed to pacifism are tempted to grab the Yugoslavs by their fashionably padded shoulders and give them what for: 'Even if you win, you assholes, all you've got is Yugoslavia! It's not like you're invading France or something'."[17]

Media variations also spanned the "meat-market" evacuations of wounded children from Sarajevo in the August 30, 1993, edition of *People* magazine to the typical assumption about the Serb-inflicted mass devastation at Dubrovnik:

> "Bad as the shelling was, the wonder is how well the city survived."[18]

---

14. John Newhouse, "The Diplomatic Round: Dodging the Problem," *The New Yorker*, August 24, 1992.

15. T.D. Allman, "Letter from Greater Serbia: Serbia's Blood War," *Vanity Fair*, March 1993.

16. Allman, *ibid.*

17. P.J. O'Rourke, "Gang Bang Bang," *Rolling Stone Magazine*, January 7, 1993.

18. Martin Fletcher (*NBC News*), "Dateline Dubrovnik," *Travel & Leisure*

The story of Dubrovnik was vexing. The city, supposedly, was continually under fire and was continually being rebuilt. In between came comments in the routine run of reports that it was remarkably unscathed with only slight damage in the old city. A joke began to make the rounds by early 1995: "They just keep rebuilding Dubrovnik more beautiful and more older than ever." One editor of a supermarket tabloid explained in mid-1994 why there was an unusual absence of macabre stories about the horrors of the Yugoslav civil wars leering from the racks beside grocery checkout lines:

> "The fact is that the mainline media and all the straight media are doing our jobs better than we could."[19]

There Were No Handshakes

I looked around the small meeting room at Carnegie. It was packed with repre-sentatives from most of the major news organizations and other groups who peered at me with frowning, pale faces and avoided eye contact. Congressional staff members, journalists from the *Associated Press, National Public Radio, Canadian Broadcasting Corporation, Voice of America, The Financial Times, St. Louis Dispatch, News Network International,* the Senate Foreign Relations Committee, the U.S. Department of Defense, the Atlantic Council, American University, University of Maryland, University of Chicago, George Washington University, Johns Hopkins University, the RAND Corporation, and others. *U.S. News & World Report, ABC,* and *The Washington Post's* Michael Abramowitz (the latter being the son of the Carnegie president and former U.S. ambassador) were all invited but didn't show up.

Mother Jones Magazine's Eric Alterman gave a chilling response during the testy question-and-answer session when he denounced what David Binder, of *The New York Times*, called "the first commandment of objective reporting" to get all sides of the story. Binder, heavily censored by the *Times* but who produced landmark stories during the Yugoslav wars, was a co-panelist.

"That's a fallacy of objective journalism!" blurted Alterman.

What was astonishing was the absence of any rebuttal by news professionals or educators to the issue of compromised objectivity in the war reporting raised by Binder. Lane's co-panelist, Ed Vulliamy, of *The London Observer*, gave a surprisingly frank and passionate oration about his own abandonment of objectivity the previous year in *The British Journalism Review*:

> "I am one of those reporters who cannot see this as just another story from which I must remain detached and in which I must be neutral. ...During the war in Croatia, I did try to be impartial. It was hard, but just about possible. Even after Omarska and Trnopolje I tried to be fair. But with Omarska and Trnopolje objective coverage of the war became a rather silly notion. If anything, I am embarrassed now by how objective I tried to be then. ...It is not only that I have to declare a partiality that I am on the side of the Bosnian Muslim people against an historical and military program to obliterate them."

Magazine, September 1993.

19. *The National Enquirer* editor requested anonymity in an interview with the author in mid-1994.

John Sawyer, of the *Post Dispatch*, telephoned several days later, sounding sympathetic to the argument about media bias and said he planned to "write something" about the Carnegie event. But nothing resulted. And, aside from a few who squirmed in their seats, Alterman's incitement failed to arouse any hoped-for "lynching."

NPR's Daniel Schorr, the media emeritus, sauntered to the front with a half-bottle of beer, offered a meandering soliloquy about the Yugoslav conflict being a "strangely ambiguous war" and said he was disappointed that he felt like he had "wandered into a bar room brawl." Schorr, who was asked later about how he could condone *NPR's* biased news policies toward the Yugoslav wars, apologized that he was "but a news analyst. I am not in the chain of command and have no responsibility for what others do on *NPR*."[20]

A few of the Carnegie directors glared around angrily when it was over. There were no handshakes. I was alarmed by the silence until I realized that the audience was there to assess damage control and whether any names would be mentioned for specific reporting misdeeds.

I let Lane and anyone else get their gripes out, but I leveled a final admonition, telling the audience that their crisis was authentic, that the media's co-combatant record was embarrassingly visible to all and demanded remedy.

But their response of silence meant only one thing: Cover-up.

Moments after the room emptied, I stood outside on the sidewalk next to Massachusetts Avenue. The evening air was soothingly cool. The Carnegie president and two-time U.S. ambassador came out the front door and quickly walked down the front steps, squinting at me contemptuously before turning up a side street. He had undoubtedly wondered whether his chances had paled at winning another diplomatic post from the White House and was embarrassed that his own institution's journal had published my damning article.

So, there was a paper trail to it all. There were names. There were facts and evidence. And there was a "cover-up"—a word that brought saliva to the media's mouth when it applied to the targets of their journalistic blood-hunts. Now, it was twisting in their guts since it was applied to them.

But, was there something else? Conspiracy? Another hated word. When did "pack journalism" become conspiracy?

Abramowitz hurried off. I wanted to go after him to ask what he thought of the Boston "massacre."

---

20. Schorr in a letter to British author Nora Beloff, May 25, 1995.

Chapter 5

'Only Muslim Victims...
Only Serb Perpetrators'

"Rape is usually a very casual by-product of many wars."[1]
– Judy Bachrach

"Mirrors should reflect a little before throwing back images."[2]
– Jean Cocteau

Nothing in the bestial Balkan carnival of wide-angle horror and atrocity fed media hysteria more than the barrage of stories and claims in late 1992 and early 1993 about mass rape in Bosnia.

Television and newspapers were inundated with waves of shrill reports about the "systematic" attacks against Muslim women, primarily. Correspondents and commentators insisted it was a policy and a tool of Serbs only to achieve ethnic cleansing. Systematic mass rape became a seductive media cliche.

Few spreads matched the cover-story treatment in the January 4, 1993, issue of *Newsweek* derived from Bosnian government claims, often quoted in the rhetoric of Bosnian Prime Minister Haris Silajdzic, that up to 60,000 rapes were committed by Serb soldiers during the previous nine months—a staggering average of 220 assaults per day!

Newsweek's "A Pattern of Rape—War Crimes in Bosnia" was eight pages of emotion-packed narrative with ten photographs. The two largest photos of sobbing, though posed, victims including the cover, were shot by German photographer Andree Kaiser whose work appeared frequently with *Newsday's* Roy Gutman and his Bosnia reports.

The large-type teaser on the top of the table-of-contents page showed no restraint and set the tone for hard-hitting sensationalism:

> "Now, on top of documented cases of systematic torture and murder in Bosnia, come charges of a new Serb atrocity—the rape of as many as 50,000 women, mostly Muslim. Wrenching testimonies from refugees tell of repeated rapes of girls as young as six, schools and hotels turned into bordellos, gang rapes so brutal their victims die and *deliberate programs to impregnate Muslim women with unwanted Serb babies."* (Italics added)

---

1. Bachrach, "The Unquiet Americans,"
The Philadelphia Inquirer Magazine, January 30, 1994.
2. *Des Beaux-Arts.*

Transparent disclaimers, including one in a rhetorical question, were remotely scattered into the text of the main article.

> "...No one knows how many victims there are, though estimates range from 30,000 to 50,000 women, most of them Muslim. ...Many reports are unconfirmed, and some may never be independently corroborated. But as anecdotal evidence piles up, Western media and women's groups are pressuring their governments to take some kind of action. ...How many women are victims of rape? The Bosnian government commission on war crimes in Sarajevo claims that there are 30,000; the (Bosnian government) Ministry for Interior Affairs goes as high as 50,000 women. When pressed, Bosnian officials concede that their estimates are extrapolations based on a relatively small number of testimonies. *There's no procedure for reporting such crimes.* ...Proving mass rape is difficult. ...The attempt to pin down numbers enrages some advocacy groups." (Italics added)

Missing from the story was any information about how the Bosnian government's War Crimes Commission in Sarajevo obtained its data and testimonies to support its allegations. There was "no procedure for reporting" because Sarajevo up until then was physically cut off from the rest of the country for months to come.

The principal writer of the *Newsweek* piece was Tom Post, who admitted later he had never been to Yugoslavia.[3] Contributing correspondents included researcher Alexandra Stiglmayer (who had said less than a week earlier in a *National Public Radio* interview that the numbers of rapes were unconfirmed), Charles Lane and Joel Brand. Lane conceded reluctantly a year later that the media routinely digested such whoppers from the Bosnian government and its PR handlers:

> "Too many reporters quoted the Bosnian government's *patently unconfirmable* claim that 50,000 Muslim women were raped by the Serbs."[4] (Italics added)

Pinned down five months later about his role in the original *Newsweek* story, and asked whether the record required more than his nineteen-word redress, Lane again brushed it aside, claiming he had "very little" part in writing the article.[5] Post said later that Brand's "second-hand" contribution to *Newsweek* came from Sarajevo where Brand, *The Times'* (London) correspondent, "is making his second home."

The *Newsweek* story marked the low-point in journalistic ethic and stands alone as a prime example of manipulated media and public opinion about alleged mass rape in the Bosnian war. But it staked a permanent claim in the minds of journalists and their audience. The contradictory findings that led to the European Parliament's final conclusions two months later were blanketed by media silence. After that, the clamor in newspapers and television toned down due to U.N. officials and other international authorities that drew attention to pointed disclaimers included in their official reports only to have them ignored or minimized by reporters and editors.

---

3. Interview with author on June 17, 1994.
4. "Washington Diarist," *The New Republic*, January 3, 1994.
5. Carnegie Institute panel, "The War in the Former Yugoslavia: Are the Western Media Combatants?," June 7, 1994.

But another audience, which had likely not kept pace with the daily production line of daily media incitements about mass rape, was more vulnerable.

Only Muslim Victims, Only Serb Perpetrators

Most audiences of popular "slick" magazines are assumed to be female readers who spend minimal time with major newspapers or watching Sunday's news panel shows or documentaries on television.

Editors of the slicks are not interested in the stiff official pronouncements from the United Nations or the European Parliament. Magazine journalism does not traditionally insist on getting other sides to stories.

Mass rape had maximum exploitable appeal to such publications as the *Ladies' Home Journal* where Ann Leslie anchored her story in the August 1993 issue on statements from a twenty-two-year-old Muslim woman, who claimed she was assaulted while in a detention camp.

Entitled "A Weapon Called Rape," the *Journal* article resurrected the shamble of estimates from the Bosnian government even though abandoned by the U.N. War Crimes Commission and the Warburton Commission five months earlier. Leslie described the woman as "one of an estimated 20,000 Bosnian women who have been subjected to systematic mass rape by Serb soldiers and paramilitaries. ...The Bosnian government puts the figure as high as 50,000." The meaningless disclaimer followed: "These figures, like all such atrocity statistics in this most brutal of wars, are virtually impossible to prove."

Stranger still was a casual afterthought toward the end that "...Serbs, too allege that their women have been raped by Bosnians and Croats." Period.

The *Journal* added an unsigned editorial summary, unaccompanied by any documentation, stating: "Serbia is using rape as an intentional, strategic weapon in its efforts to seize the republic of Bosnia."

Catherine MacKinnon, a professor at the University of Michigan Law School, wrote "Turning Rape Into Pornography: Postmodern Genocide" for the September 1993 issue of *Ms.* magazine. MacKinnon's steamy ramble recounted how "the campaign of expansion through ethnic extermination has included rape, forcible impregnation, torture, and murder of Muslim and Croatian women 'for Serbia'." MacKinnon used provocatively racist tones to assert that deviant behavior was part of contemporary Serbian character: "The national politics are fused with sex."[6]

MacKinnon prefaced her story with an admission that double hearsay was used from "original research and translated" by two women, whose identities, backgrounds and credentials were omitted.

Two months later, *Mademoiselle* magazine continued the emotion-packed marathon with Vivienne Walt's incredulous "Bosnia: What Are They Fighting For?" which used "mostly rough estimates compiled by United Nations agencies, the U.S. Committee for Refugees and the missions of Serbia, Croatia and Bosnia." However, Walt made a statistical leap that topped her predecessors:

> "20,000 to 100,000 Bosnian Muslim women had been raped as
> of the end of 1992, almost all of them by Serb fighters and
> officials who gang-raped them repeatedly in detention centers."

---

6. Catherine MacKinnon, "Turning Rape Into Pornography: Postmodern Genocide," *Ms.* magazine, September 1993.

The latter preposterously infers an average of between 100 and 500 rapes were committed daily during the first seven months of the war in Bosnia!

Seventeen magazine's June 1994 story, "Reality Bites" by unemployed actress Natia Dajani, started out with airy petulance but ended with a twist, surprising even from a media novice. She said she'd seen "a news report about Muslim orphans in the former Yugoslavia ...*hospitals were overflowing* with babies born to mothers who've been the victims of Serbian gang rapes." (Italics added)

Volunteering for three weeks as "a social worker" in a Croatian camp for Muslim refugees at Gasinci. Instead, she discovered Croatian brutality *against* Muslims: "I felt as if I'd been time-warped back to Nazi Germany."

No matter the unsubstantiated claims of 50,000 or more rapes of Bosnian Muslim women, the media never found it significant that the promised epidemic of rape-induced births—predicted by Bosnian and Croatian information ministries in October 1992—never materialized!

National Public Radio's Sylvia Poggioli, writing in the Fall 1993 issue of Harvard University's Nieman Reports, said such statistical disinformation "has stuck and the prevailing perception is that only Muslim women have been the victims and Serbian fighters the only perpetrators."[7]

Thrust into a hurried six-day investigation (December 18-24, 1993), the European Parliament delegation headed by Dame Anne Warburton reported that it had visited primarily Zagreb but obtained no direct access to alleged Muslim victims or refugee centers where victims were supposedly located. Croat propagandists would later mass-produce so-called "victims" for Western media and politicians. But Warburton's investigators did discover reports about rapes of Croat and Serb women and emphatically noted "the contrast between the extensive media coverage of the alleged rapes (against Bosnian Muslim women) and the lack of supporting documentary evidence."

Eventually, although it declined to specifically identify the source of "the most reasoned estimate suggested to the Delegation," Warburton's group gave in to media pressures and hesitantly estimated "a figure in the region of 20,000 victims."

At about the same time, there was a superseding inquiry by the U.N. Commission on Human Rights, with investigators emerging from Bosnia-Herzegovina, Croatia and Serbia to report on February 10, 1994, their findings that only 119 documented cases of multiple rape had occurred among Muslin, Croat and Serb victims with Muslim victims comprising the largest number. This followed another European Community delegation to Zagreb and Bosnia-Herzegovina on a five-day probe in early January where it held "a small number of in-depth interviews with individual (Muslim and Croat) victims."

But the delegation omitted any follow-up reporting about rapes by Muslim and Croat soldiers.

The European Parliament's Committee on Women's Rights held hearings a few days later in Brussels on February 17-18, 1993, to infuse credibility into the Warburton Delegation's tentative claim of 20,000 Muslim rape victims that was almost immediately rejected because of the lack of supporting evidence and testimony. The chairman of the U.N. War Crimes Commission, international legal expert Frits Kalshoven, said the evidence that had been gathered was insufficient, while Amnesty International and the International Committee of the Red Cross concurrently declared that atrocities and rapes were being committed on all sides. In a gesture interpreted as disapproval and disillusionment because of the mishandling of the investigation by the media and officials, Dame Warburton was notably absent from the hearings in Brussels. Next, a European Parliament resolution on March 10 cited rapes committed

---

7. Sylvia Poggioli, "Scouts Without Compasses: War in the Balkans Is Forcing Correspondents To Rewrite Their Guidelines," *Nieman Reports*, Fall 1993.

by all three warring groups, cautioning that evidence thus far "does not single out the Serbian soldiers as the sole perpetrators of rapes, nor Muslim women as the sole victims of the same crime."

Officials at the Brussels hearings were not interested in hearing testimony from a Belgrade gynecologist, Dr. Ljubica Toholj, who possessed grim and accusing affidavits from Serb victims about a variety of abuses. She had arrived in Brussels for the hearings but was refused a visa by Belgian immigration officials.

The gamut of public and official perceptions was sensitized by the huge *Newsweek* spread on January 4, 1993. It topped the list of "evidence" on February 25, 1993, about "many thousands of Muslim women (who) have been raped by Serbian soldiers," wrote Professor Shirley Williams, a faculty member at Harvard's John F. Kennedy School of Government.[8]

As Poggioli said, the media scam of 50,000 mass rapes stood as statistical coinage.

But the media cadence about "systematic mass rape" orchestrated by Bosnian and Croat government information ministries in late 1992 was also a distraction and a decoy. It is not too cynical to surmise that the media-wide mobilization in August 1992—when imitations of Roy Gutman's death camp stories in *Newsday* were taking over prime-time television, newspaper headlines and magazine covers—obscured an already lengthy list of shocking revelations of mass rapes against Serb victims. Serbs had protested for months and were becoming increasingly insistent about the existence and locations of several dozen "rape camps" controlled by Bosnian Muslims and Croats where Serb women were being subjected to unimaginable forms of rape, sodomy, torture and murder.

A few Western journalists said later they were aware of the allegations by the Serbs, but they nonetheless minimized the Serb claims.

Thom Shanker, a Berlin-based correspondent for *The Chicago Tribune*, wrote a revealing report[9] on August 6, 1992—just four days after Gutman's sensational reports in *Newsday* about Serb-run "concentration camps" and the hyped comparisons with the notorious Nazi-era camps. Later, Shanker called his "the first published report proving the Serb campaign of systematic mass rape."[10] But it did not prove systematic mass rape by Serbs. Instead, it proved that Shanker and others also knew about, but minimally reported mass rape against Serbs:

> "For every horror story advanced by Croatians, the Serbs have
> an *equally* grisly tale of violence, massacre or death of their people
> at the hands of Croatians or, perhaps, Bosnians. ...Unfortunately,
> though, the stories are proving almost impossible to verify
> independently."[11] (Italics added)

In the feverish aftermath of the electrifying *Newsday* reports that sent 350 Western reporters stampeding into Bosnia to duplicate Gutman's "discovery" of the resurrected practices from Auschwitz, journalists were distracted from any compelling suspicions to check out the earlier Serb claims of rape.

---

8. Letter from Williams to Radomir Putnikovic, February 25, 1993.
9. Shanker, "Sex slavery joins list of Balkan 'atrocities'," *The Chicago Tribune*, August 6, 1992.
10. Letter from Shanker to Bill Maynes, editor of *Foreign Policy*, December 29, 1994.)
11. Maynes' letter of response to Shanker on January 16, 1995, stated "...Ironically, your story did not get the attention of the stories in late November and early December 1992 precisely because it was so professional. It stuck to provable facts."

Bosnia's Camps And Press Decoys

If the *Newsday* stories had been calculated to divert attention away from emerging revelations about Serbian victims of rape, such a ploy could not have worked better. The result was the same.

Had reporters and correspondents taken a ten-minute walk from the International Press Centre in Belgrade to the unpretentious second floor office of the Serbian Council Information Center at Safarikova 7, a non-governmental organization headed by respected researcher Vojin Dabic, they could have discovered an abundance of affidavits, depositions and testimonies from raped, sodomized and tortured Serbs who were available at nearby refugee centers. Though many times tempted, Dabic and his staff of volunteers were able to sustain the organization's credibility and their investigations apart from any government affiliation or propagandistic taint.

But the herds of Western reporters in search of only Muslim victims and stories about mass rape were lured instead to Bosnia, ignoring documents submitted by Serbian agencies in Belgrade and by Bosnian Serbs to the European Parliament and to the U.N. that included such allegations as:

> •Late March 1992–Serbian females imprisoned at Breza were raped and then murdered by Moslems; their bodies were later incinerated.

> •May 27, 1992—Female prisoners from Bradina were taken to the camp in Celebici where they were repeatedly raped.

> •Mid-July 1992—Young Serb females and girls were confined at Sarajevo's Hotel Zagreb and Hotel Europa. Both hotels were converted into brothels for Muslim soldiers and were located a stone's throw from Western journalists who, as a rule, stayed at Sarajevo's infamous Holiday Inn.

> •July 26, 1992—An escapee from Gorazde reported Muslims forced Serb fathers to rape their own daughters before both were murdered.

> •August 2, 1992—The fifth floor of the Sarajevo main prison was used to hold an unknown number of juvenile and older Serbian females who were repeatedly raped. Also, Serb women prisoners at the Viktor Bubanj barracks in Sarajevo were subjected to repeated abuse and mistreatment.

> •August 27, 1992—An affidavit by Dr. Olga Drasko, a former inmate of a Croat-run camp at Dretelj, described rapes and mutilations of women, including herself, during her four-month confinement.

> •August 1992—UNPROFOR was requested to assist in obtaining release of Serb women who were being held and repeatedly raped in the Sarajevo train station by Muslim "green berets."

•November 1992—A group of Serbian women released from Tuzla were requesting late-term abortions after having been repeatedly raped by Muslims during lengthy captivities.

•December 7, 1992—Emilio Castro, Secretary General of the World Council of Churches in Geneva, sent letters to leaders of religious communities in former Yugoslavia, deploring rapes committed against women by ALL warring sides.

•December 10, 1992—In Belgrade, Serbian Orthodox Patriarch Pavle told officials of the Swiss Federal Parliament and representatives from European ecumenical movements that 800 Serb women were documented as repeated rape victims in twenty camps operated by Muslims and Croats.

The patriarch also cited parts of the report from the Yugoslav State Commission for War Crimes on August 2, 1992—the same day *Newsday's* "death camp" stories went on American newsstands!—that identified locations at Sarajevo, Tuzla, Bugojno, Bihac and Slavonski Brod where Serb women were confined and raped by Croat and Muslim soldiers.

Inexplicably overlooked by the media was the submission of a lengthy report (S/24991) by the U.N. Security Council on December 18, 1992 to the General Assembly. The report, including affidavits and depositions from Serb rape victims, also cited a catalog of sodomy, gruesome torture and murder.

There was never a specific response from U.N. officials about why the December 18 report was not circulated until January 5, 1993—the day following *Newsweek's* shocking spread!—even though it was unique as the only report produced by an international agency with documented testimonies and affidavits from *any* rape victims up until that time. It identified fifteen brothels being run by Bosnian Muslim and Croat forces where 560 Serb women were held captive and were individually attacked in multiple rapes. The report also referred to the data concerning the rape of "800 women of Serbian nationality" which had been submitted to U.N. and European parliament authorities. But a U.N. Security Council press release the same day instead condemned the "rape of women, in particular Muslim women, in Bosnia and Herzegovina"[12] without any supporting documentation, mentioning nothing about the report (S/24991) pertaining to the rape of Serb women and sexual abuse and torture of Serb men and women who were held by Croats and Muslims!

The report was quietly circulated only to a few at the U.N. while public attention was being distracted by the media clamor over undocumented claims by Bosnian government officials that as many as 60,000 rapes of Muslim women were committed by Serb soldiers.

Births Three Months After Rapes?

The Bosnian government's claims were allowed to stand unchallenged. No matter that from the commencement of the war in Bosnia in April until November 1992 there were thousands of refugees who fled into Croatia and other countries where extensive monitoring by humanitarian agencies and the media failed to disclose allegations or solid evidence of "systematic rape."

But by late November and early December, there was a sudden deluge of reports about mass rapes against Muslim women—only. The accounts originated from the

---

12. U.N. Security Council press release No. SC/5521, December 18, 1992.

information ministries of the governments of Croatia and Bosnia-Herzegovina and their imaginative public relations specialists.

They claimed hospitals had been bulging for the previous three months with babies born from Muslim rape victims. But the war had started in Bosnia only six months earlier, suggesting huge numbers of babies from rape victims were prematurely "born"—not miscarried—as early as August or September after just three months of pregnancy!

Although the routine rule of journalistic follow-up on the rape issue was abandoned, the media could have eventually discovered the resulting handful of rape-induced pregnancies and the clear contradiction against the Bosnian government's allegations about the offspring being born in droves and that were "overflowing" at Bosnian and Croat hospitals.

The omission was contrasted by the lone account from French journalist Jerome Bony, who described in a February 4, 1993, broadcast his trek to Tuzla, which gained notoriety as the most prominent Bosnian town for finding Muslim rape victims:

> "When I was fifty kilometers from Tuzla I was told to 'go to the Tuzla gymnasium (high school) (where) there are 4,000 raped women.' At twenty kilometers this figure dropped to 400. At ten kilometers only forty were left. Once at the site, I found *only four women* willing to testify."[13] (Italics added)

The privately-funded, eighteen-month project to create a "database of atrocities and aggression" at DePaul University School of Law in Chicago attempted to prop up the earlier claims of widespread rape against Bosnian Muslim women.[14] The DePaul team of lawyers, researchers and volunteers, produced a "summary" of the project for the U.N. which was instantly leaked to *Reuters* and *The New York Times* just before its official publication date on June 1, 1994, and before the U.N. could officially review the data and report its own conclusions to the U.N. war crimes tribunal at The Hague. Mark Bennett, a DePaul spokesman, said in mid-May that the findings covered just 5,000 or comparatively fewer than expected instances from a wide range of alleged atrocities—murder, torture, kidnapping, extortion, damage of private property, destruction of cultural structures—AND rape![15]

Bennett added that none of the results from the DePaul project, which he said was financed with $900,000 from billionaire George Soros, could stand alone as legal evidence in war crimes prosecutions and was only intended as a "road map" for further investigations. But, not surprisingly, the DePaul project, undertaken at a Catholic university without any official monitoring and using vast amounts of information from the Croatian propaganda ministry, was intended first and foremost as a propaganda tool. It was rushed to publication two months ahead of actual schedule and minus completion of its detailed annexes that insinuated overall that Serbs committed mass and systematic rape. However, the "summary" was succeeded by the U.N.'s "Final Report of the Commission of Experts," issued December 28, 1994—seven months later—with the finished and detailed annexes, and which demonstrated varying rape allegations from Muslim, Croat AND Serb girls and women for war crimes prosecutors at The Hague to sort out.

But, the earlier June 1, 1994, "summary"—which weakly suggested that the Warburton Commission's estimate could eventually be proven along with predominate Serb

---

13. Bony's report was broadcast on *France 2* television,
14. *Associated Press*, April 24, 1994.
15. Bennett interview with author.

blame for rape and other atrocities—obsessed the media which was uninterested in facts that disrupted the prevailing storyline by December 28:

> "...The earlier projection of 20,000 rapes made by other sources are (sic) not unreasonable."[16]

This lamely refuted former War Crimes Commission Chairman Frits Kalshoven, who had said in a February 1993 report to the European Parliament that evidence supporting the Warburton Commission projection of 20,000 rapes could not stand up in court. In December 1994, Kalshoven said he still stood by his 1993 conclusions doubting the Warburton Commission's estimate of 20,000 alleged rapes.[17] As late as January 1995, Tribunal chief prosecutor Richard Goldstone hinted that the vital annexes to the DePaul/Soros project remained incomplete, at least by his estimate, eight months later![18] Goldstone was also gauging the substandard quality of the completed DePaul/Soros project from an evidentiary viewpoint. He didn't elaborate.

Kalshoven's successor, DePaul Professor Mahmud Cherif Bassiouni, was the enthusiastic overseer of the database project. It was widely reported that Bassiouni, a Muslim and native of Egypt was miffed at not getting Goldstone's job at The Hague.

For all the media outcry produced from the allegations of systematic mass rape, the eighty-four page U.N. "summary" on the DePaul/Soros data-base contained slightly over five pages that described its "Rape and sexual assaults study"![19] Findings were sparse and conjectural, focusing on the information contained in the DePaul database and excerpted from limited information in a series of interviews by the Commission of Experts "in Croatia and Slovenia in March 1994." The 223 interviews identified just thirty-one female rape victims from Bosnia-Herzegovina and eleven female rape victims from Croatia.

The description in the "summary" of reported cases of rape and sexual assault in the database raised more questions than it answered:

> "The reported cases of rape and sexual assault contained in the data-base occurred between the fall of 1991 and the end of 1993. The majority of the rapes occurred from April to November 1992; fewer occurred in the following five months. In the same time period the number of media reports increased from a few in March 1992 to a high of 535 news stories in January 1993 and 529 in February 1993. This correlation could indicate that the media attention caused the decline. In that case, it would indicate that commanders could control the alleged perpetrators if they wanted to. This could lead to the conclusion that there was an overriding policy advocating the use of rape as a method of 'ethnic cleansing', rather than a policy of commission, tolerating the widespread commission of rape."[20]

---

16. Letter from U.N. Secretary General Boutros Boutros-Ghali to the President of the Security Council, S/1994/674, p. 84, May 27, 1994.
17. Kalshoven interview with the author at Geneva, December 16, 1994.
18. Goldstone speech to the World Affairs Council of Northern California, San Francisco, January 18, 1995.
19. S/1994/674, pp. 55-60.
20. S/1994/674, pp. 55-60.

The barrage of "news stories" and "media attention" on the reported cases of rape and sexual assault more than likely induced the exaggerated claims and accusations in the first place during January and February of 1993. Never doubted by the media was that the eight-month period (April-November 1992)—when the Bosnian government said the majority of alleged assaults supposedly took place—inferred an average of 10,000 sexual assaults per month, or an average of 556 per day that were supposedly inflicted upon Muslim women!

Not only did the huge numbers of press reports not even risk to make such a numerical claim, but the U.N.'s Final Report noted only a single instance of an alleged rape-induced pregnancy!

Too Many Unanswered Questions

Rape victims, rapists and responsible commanders were unidentified in the database, said DePaul researchers in their June 1, 1994, "summary," suspiciously mentioning only that "the reports contained in the Commission's (DePaul) database identify close to 800 victims by name or number."

The only known collective documentation about 800 rape victims submitted to the U.N. and the European Parliament was the U.N. Report S/24991 (December 18, 1992) that described 800 rape victims—who were all Serbs!

The Commission "summary" vaguely claimed "an additional 1,673 victims are referred to, but not named in reports of victims who indicate that they witnessed or know of other similar victims" and "some 500 reported cases which refer to an unspecified number of victims."

Who were the identified 800 victims in the DePaul database, and who were the rapists and their commanders?

Was there a coincidence in the statement about the alleged 800 non-Serb identified rape victims? Or, were they the 800 identified Serb rape victims previously reported to the U.N. and European parliament?

Why did the Commission limit its March 1994 investigation and interviews only to Croatia and Slovenia? Did the thirty-one female rape victims from "Bosnia-Herzegovina" include Bosnian Serbs? Did the eleven female rape victims from Croatia include Serbian women?

Why did the Commission not travel to Serbia to interview reported rape victims? A ludicrous answer was attempted:

> "It was not possible to conduct an investigation in the territory of the Federal Republic of Yugoslavia, as the Commission had requested from the Government."[21]

Even so, there was no need for the Commission to travel to Serbia and Montenegro in search of Serb rape victims. It already had enough information about 800 rapes against Serbian women from the December 18, 1992, U.N. report.

One of the more exceptional examples of media hype during the rape hysteria did not occur until January 30, 1994—a full year after the initial reports.

The Philadelphia Inquirer Magazine published the article by Judy Bachrach without any attribution, deploring how "the rape of more than 50,000 Bosnian women could be conducted without fear of reprisal."[22]

---

21. S/1994/674, p. 82.
22. Bachrach, "The Unquiet Americans," *The Philadelphia Inquirer Magazine*, January 30, 1994.

The timing of Bachrach's article was blatantly contradictory. A day earlier, a new U.N. General Assembly Report (A/48/858) was released, corroborating the negative findings by the U.N. and the European Parliament. Despite Boutros-Ghali's report a few months later on the DePaul database, the latest January 29, 1994, report debunked the litany from the Bosnian and Croatian governments about mass rape.

It detailed the Commission of Experts' pilot study from April to July 1993 that had collected and evaluated evidence and documentation about alleged rapes from the War Crimes Commission of Bosnia and Herzegovina. The experts had conclusively retrieved *"all* their information identified as relating to this issue." (Italics added)

It fell astonishingly short of the previous year's worth of media drum-beating, citing all of the Bosnian government's own records which had been the basis for complaints from humanitarian organizations and the press:

- **126 victims.**
- **113 incidents.**
- **252 alleged perpetrators.**
- **73 witnesses.**
- **100 documents.**

Again, the January 29, 1994, report from the U.N. was suspiciously ignored by the media.

Four months later, Bachrach said she had not seen the U.N.'s January report and would have doubted it anyway.[23]

She said she had obtained her "statistics" from various "agencies" and "experts," whom she would not identify. Bachrach also would not elaborate about her claim of 250,000 Bosnian fatalities. Although her article used vivid descriptions of scenes inside alleged Serb-run detention camps, Bachrach said she had "covered several wars"—but had never gone to Yugoslavia's war zones although her writing posed as firsthand reporting!

"Just read my article," she said irritably and hung up the phone.

Another of German photographer Andree Kaiser's photographs (used in *Newsweek's* January 4, 1993 spread) from his 1992 trip to Tuzla with Gutman reappeared in a montage to illustrate Jan Goodwin's 1995 article in *Cosmopolitan* about the global scale of abused women.[24]

Oddly, no mention of rape or anything about the Yugoslav wars was mentioned in Goodwin's text.

Only a confusing caption appeared next to Kaiser's photo: "Scores of Bosnian women have been raped at a Serb refugee camp." "Bosnian women," of course, implied Bosnian Muslim women. Tuzla was a Muslim stronghold where there was at least one Bosnian government-run refugee or detention camp which held scores of Serb women who were repeatedly raped, the U.N. finally reported in March 1996.[25]

Kaiser's photo at the Tuzla high school showed fifteen young women, identified as Muslims, who claimed they were rape victims from neighboring Borovo Polje.

The village of Borovo Polje had a detention facility that supposedly housed, according to the U.N. Final Report on December 28, 1994, "approximately 1,000 people," including about 150 young women who were allegedly raped by up to thirty men each.

But Kaiser's photo of fifteen young Muslim women at the Tuzla high school is the more curious when compared to other data published by Bassiouni:

---

23. Bachrach interview with the author in May 1994.
24. Goodwin, "The State of Women in the World," *Cosmopolitan*, March 1995.
25. U.N. Report No. E/CN.4/1996/36, March 1996.

"...Tuzla appears to be the site of several facilities where women were apparently held for the purpose of rape between approximately June and November 1992. The alleged perpetrators are identified as members of Bosnian Muslim, Bosnian Croat, and Bosnian Serb forces. ...The alleged victims were *primarily Bosnian Serb women*, though many of the reports do not provide the ethnic, national or religious background of the victims. ...One report alleges the existence of a camp for Bosnian Muslim women. The reports identify several locations where rape was allegedly committed by Bosnian Muslim and Bosnian Croat forces in Tuzla. One report cites a secondary school where about 100 Serbian women were reportedly held for the purposes of rape. Another report cites a house on the road towards Srebrenik (near Previla), where about 15 Serbian women were held. Four reports state that four different Serbian woman were held in one camp and raped up to five times a day for at least five months. Each woman was released in an advanced stage of pregnancy. Statements of the alleged captors and the pattern of release, indicate that women were uniformly not released until their pregnancy reached a certain stage. The reports do not provide detailed testimony from the victims, only a general description of how they were allegedly raped and the conditions in which they were held. Another report describes how unspecified perpetrators surrounded the village of Brezje, divided women and girls into groups, removed 36 youngsters, pillaged the village, and then transported the women to Tuzla. The reporter spent five months in a camp with 10 other women and was raped. ...She was, however, kept until her pregnancy was well-advanced.... Another report cites a sports stadium at Zivinice and former police offices in Tuzla as places where victims were held for rape. One report asserts that 200 girls, aged 15 and under, were held and raped in a camp in Lomnica. Another report states that there were rapes in Tuzla and Zivinice without providing further detail as to whether they occurred in detention facilities. Finally, one report states that women were raped prior to a prisoner exchange, but does not allege the exact location of this event. The dates of the incidents were fairly evenly distributed from July through November. ...Most incidents involving detention facilities allegedly occurred in mid-1992 (i.e. June or July). Three reports specify that they occurred from mid-1992 to November 1992."[26] (Italics added)

The above refers solely to Serb women who were raped, although Muslim and Croat rape accounts added to the whole sordid scenario of rape during the Yugoslav civil wars.

The point is: rapes of Serb women were generally ignored or omitted by the Western media.

Equally intriguing is the result—planned or not—from the eight-month delay in producing the DePaul/Soros project "annexes" and heard in Goldstone's remark in January 1995 that the U.N. Final Report was "incomplete."

---

26. U.N. Report No. S/1994/674/Add.2 (Vol.5), December 28, 1994.

With that perception, for as long as Goldstone and his successors wanted to assess the U.N. Final Report as incomplete or insufficient on an evidentiary basis, the large numbers of rape cases *against* Muslims and Croats would languish indefinitely if not altogether disappear.

Besides, the media had reached its verdict by early 1994. Asked about follow-up from the December 28, 1994, U.N. Final Report, one editor later scowled: "More rapes in Yugoslavia? Old news."

Seven years later, prosecutors at The Hague obtained the first convictions against three Bosnian Serbs accused of rape and forcible prostitution in the Bosnian Muslim town of Foca during a Serb takeover in 1992. But the sentencings, ranging from 28 to 12 years, were hollow sequels to expectations for numerous rape trials in the war's aftermath. It was clear that the claimed thousands of alleged rapes—even with the anticipated trickle of victims breaking silence in subsequent years—would not achieve validation by the Tribunal as a weapon of war.

After the sentencings, a more somber than usual Christiane Amanpour reported on *CNN Insight* for February 22, 2001:

> "The presiding judge today said that there was not sufficient evidence to say categorically that rape had been used as a weapon of war as ordered by the masterminds, as she said, of the Bosnian Serb political and military scene. In other words, there wasn't sufficient evidence to suggest that either Radovan Karadzic or Ratko Mladic had directly handed down the order for their people to rape women as a weapon of war... However, she said that there was plenty of evidence to suggest that rape was used as a systematic instrument of terror... And she suggested that these were not isolated incidents, that they had occurred in other parts, and certainly we reporters who were in Bosnia at the time heard many, many of these accusations and claims of mass rape when we were there."

Amanpour grudgingly noted the Foca rape trial lasted nearly a year and "was very painstaking. These allegations cover hundreds of victims. They were only able to bring 16 women, victims, to the court to testify." Amanpour could not resist parroting that there were "hundreds of victims" but gave no official source. Altogether, the dwindling debate about legally defining—or not—whether rape was specifically "a weapon of war" fell silent as did the original and unproven claims of 20,000 rapes from a decade earlier.

The U.N. Commission of Experts on War Crimes' 1994 report settled on 2,000 alleged rapes on all sides—and not the 50,000 claimed by the Bosnian government or the European Parliament's vaporous 20,000 estimate.

"The numbers game has been used throughout the wars in the former Yugoslavia to manipulate Western opinion," *The Cleveland Plain Dealer's* Elizabeth Sullivan concluded in 1999.

> "During the Bosnian war, European parliamentarians announced that they had confirmed, apparently through a handful of interviews with victims and a cursory review of other reports, that 20,000 women had been raped by Serbs in huge 'rape camps.' No 'commandant' for any of these camps has ever been identified or charged at The Hague. The number was simply incredible—yet it was repeated the world over."[27]

27. Sullivan, "Gullible Uncle Sam tours a land of lies,"*The Cleveland Plain*

"One of my biggest disappointments," said Sullivan, "is that no one has gone back and button-holed these people who were throwing all those big numbers around and forced them to explain why the real numbers turned out to be much, much lower."[28]

Dealer, November 15, 1999.
28. Sullivan to the author, February 12, 2004.

Chapter 6

'Where, One Might Ask, Are The Bodies?'

"By magic numbers and persuasive sound."[1]
– William Congreve

*"...(T)he press might do well never to publish
anything its reporters have not personally witnessed.*[2]
– Barbara Tuchman

The Corcoran Gallery of Art's two month exhibition of large, somber, black-and-white photographs had two weeks left to run. The eighty photos lived up to the exhibit's billing, as far as the Saturday morning crowd was concerned.

The images "elucidate with stark, wrenching realism the impact of the current war on the Bosnian civilian population."

It was April 16, 1994; cool spring weather for Washington, D.C. Some people were sniffling from colds as they milled about, studying the ghoulish scenes of agony and bodies wrapped in plastic. Some stared tearfully.

The title for a panel discussion that morning was "Understanding Bosnia: What Can We Do to Help?"

Newspapers and television reports in Washington and everywhere else were obsessed with the "siege of Gorazde," the latest "siege" in the Bosnian civil war. Those at the gallery would remember the photographs when they read, saw or heard the news about Gorazde that evening. Most of them could not properly pronounce the name of the eastern Bosnian town any better than the current occupant of the White House.

Philip Brookman, Corcoran curator of photography and media arts, described photographer Gilles Peress and his work in a brochure:

> "He presents his own impressions by *creating* a visual continuity from his perceptions, describing in almost cinematic terms the current experiences of Bosnian citizens. Numerous points of view are revealed in complex sequences. The psychological

1. The Mourning Bride, Act I, Scene I.
2. Tuchman, *Practicing History*, New York:
Alfred A. Knopf Inc., 1981, p. 66.

> impact of the massacres, sieges, and ethnic cleansing is considered, *creating* a physical and emotional journey through this devastated land."[3] (Italics added)

Creativity, after all, had a lot to do with the news photos and television images fed to millions in the West who swallowed variously manipulated images from the wars. Topping them all was the infamously rigged photo of Trnopolje "concentration camp" inmates behind a few sagging strands of rusted barbed wire—and flimsy chicken-wire!

There was tension, silent anger and stiff applause as the panel was introduced. *Newsday's* Roy Gutman sat with Aryeh Neier, who was president of billionaire George Soros' foundations and philanthropic funds; Warren Zimmerman, former U.S. ambassador to Yugoslavia; panel moderator Stephen Rosenfeld, *The Washington Post's* deputy editorial page editor, and Peress.

Gutman patronizingly complimented himself and other panel members, noting their unanimous interventionist views toward the Balkan civil wars.

"This is a very hawkish panel," he began, "but I think also a panel that has in our own individual ways a lot of knowledge of the facts and the history and of the most calamitously bad Western response."

He rapidly described what he thought was happening at the U.N.-declared "safe haven" of Gorazde, bemoaning the inadequacies of U.S. foreign policy in the Bosnian wars and most lately at Gorazde.

"The press is not in Gorazde," said Gutman in a worried tone. "One of the most revealing things that the Serbs have done in this particular case is to expel the American press, to expel *CNN*. In fact, they're even expelling people from Belgrade, from Serbia. And if there's anything that gives me fear of what is really planned in Gorazde, it is expulsion of the press. Because we won't be there to see what's happening. And you won't really have any vivid view."

Indeed, the Bosnian Serb government had started to revoke press credentials of certain journalists and news organizations. The media theater at Sarajevo, Srebrenica and Mostar had taught them there was nothing to lose by barring cameras and certain reporters they thought were unfair in their reporting.

Especially tedious was *CNN*, which in its previous February 5, 1994, coverage of the Sarajevo market bombing repeatedly rolled gruesome footage of the blasted market-place and victims to fill its hour-long news packages. No responses were aired from the Bosnian Serbs, who seemed to be convincingly blamed for the blast by the time the hour was concluded.

But unannounced, and following a series of commercials, *CNN* suddenly showed Bosnian Serb President Radovan Karadzic who was allowed to make a brief denial of Serb responsibility. It was the same media tokenism in television and wire service reports with long, repetitive accounts and quotes from Bosnian Muslim officials, reserving a few lines near the end—and well after standard editing cutoffs—for short paraphrased rebuttals by Karadzic and others.

One British reporter from the *The Independent* lamented that he was one of those being evicted by the Bosnian Serbs. Professor John Peter Maher, who earlier visited the Yugoslav war zones, said the same journalist told him in 1994 he used self-censorship and that his reporting was deliberately one-sided to meet the expectations of his editors.

CNN apparently had gotten the message after three of its correspondents were

---

3. Brookman, quoted in "Farewell to Bosnia: New Photographs by Giles Peress," March 5 to May 2, 1994.

booted on April 16, 1994.[4] Four days later Karadzic was given the unprecedented fifteen-minute segment to explain his side of the fighting at Gorazde to *CNN's* Judy Woodruff, who seemed mechanically indifferent about Karadzic's revelations. Karadzic's account was later substantiated by U.N. officials and others who stated publicly that the Gorazde hospital was used as an artillery platform by Bosnian government troops. Gorazde and other safe havens doubled as military staging areas for the Bosnian army in violation of U.N. edicts. Woodruff avoided the appropriate and obvious follow-up questions about Karadzic's descriptions that Muslim guns next to other buildings occupied by the U.N. and humanitarian agencies were shelling Serb civilians across the Drina River.

But it turned out that Gutman's worries were unnecessary about the press being excluded from Gorazde: Whatever the Western press and *CNN* were not there to see did not and would not happen. But, they had missed what happened two years earlier when Bosnian government troops cleansed nearly 13,000 Serbs from Gorazde. No clearer account of ethnic cleansing of Serbs from their homes in Gorazde was expressed than by General Sir Michael Rose, then commanding UNPROFOR troops.[5] Rose told reporter John Simpson that U.S. satellite photos of hundreds of stark shells of homes in Gorazde, argued by American intelligence officials as houses "destroyed" or "damaged" by the Bosnian Serbs, were in reality former Serb homes deserted during "ethnic cleansing" two years before. Rose pointed out that the houses were virtually undamaged from shelling, noting instead they were visibly stripped of all roofing material, doors, and window frames, as opposed to other Bosnian Muslim dwellings hit by artillery fire.

The hoax at Gorazde would be replayed at Bihac in late 1994 and early 1995 before reporters and photographers arrived and discovered that Bosnian Prime Minister Haris Silajdzic's claim of 70,000 government and civilian casualties to media in Sarajevo did not occur as Silajdic claimed. Red Cross personnel at Bihac reported that the accurate number was fewer than 1,000 mostly Bosnian army casualties and was later corroborated by U.N. officials.

Hysterical reports were arriving from Gorazde that 3,000 Muslim civilian fatalities supposedly resulted from indiscriminate Bosnian Serb artillery barrages. But *The Times* of London quoted the director of the hospital in Gorazde as saying the report of 2,000 injured and 700 killed "was an exaggeration."

Bosnian Muslim ham radio operators, as they had done during previous fighting around Cerska, claimed they were transmitting from Gorazde to the Western press corps in Sarajevo and even staged an incredulous plea from a man who identified himself as a "surgeon" and who called on his colleagues throughout the world to go on a twenty-four hour strike to protest refusals by Western governments to intervene militarily in Bosnia![6] News stories about Gorazde omitted the vicious "ethnic cleansing" by Bosnian government troops in a replay of negligent reporting from Srebrenica in 1993 when Bosnian Muslim forces were eventually contained after two months of murderous rampage and destruction of scores of nearby Serb villages.

Only the final artillery exchanges—provoked from inside Srebrenica by tank-fire from Bosnian government troops—positioned next to the town's hospital!—were substantially reported.[7]

---

4. *Associated Press*, April 16, 1994.

5. John Simpson, "Rose's War," *PANORAMA* television (London), December 1994.

6. *Associated Press*, April 21, 1994

7. Tim Judah, *The Times* (London), April 15, 1993; and author's interview with retired Swedish and UNPROFOR Lt. General Lars Wahlgren, at Goteborg, Sweden, on December 3, 1994.

Reporters and photographers in Sarajevo waited excitedly for the return of U.N. helicopters that were used to retrieve supposedly thousands of wounded men, women and children from Gorazde on April 26. But seventy-five percent of the total 272 victims evacuated from Gorazde were men and not large numbers of women and children, as Bosnian government officials and ham radio operators had claimed. Also, a third of the evacuees had war injuries that preceded the stepped-up coun-terattacks on Gorazde in April by the Bosnian Serbs. The Serbs had complained to the U.N. for the previous six weeks about local provocations and offensives by the Bosnian government's army that used the U.N.-declared "safe haven" at Gorazde as a staging center for raids against Serbs. Peter Kessler, spokesman for the U.N. High Commissioner on Refugees, said on April 26 that U.N. representatives in Gorazde had been sending information about the huge numbers of casualties "on the basis of unchecked Muslim reports."

The U.N.'s last two helicopters from Gorazde landed on April 26 in Sarajevo —empty! And General Rose, obviously incensed and voluntarily tape-recorded by reporters, said that some of the young men evacuated from Gorazde hopped off their stretchers once in Sarajevo and went into town on their own.

On April 29, *The Washington Post's* John Pomfret reported that Muslim casualties in Gorazde were "only a fraction" of the 1,970 wounded and 715 dead claimed by the Bosnian government.[8] In reality, far fewer fatalities had occurred.

Cooking The Numbers

The pace for the hyped reporting of casualties at Gorazde and Bihac was set by *New York Times* correspondent John F. Burns, co-winner with Gutman of the 1993 Pulitzer Prize for International Reporting. Burns was abruptly reassigned to India in January 1994. He had been in Sarajevo since May 1992 and was considered an "insider" at the Bosnian government presidency.

Among Western journalists and the Yugoslav press, it was common knowledge that in 1993 ambitions to "win the Pulitzer" drove the war reporting. And, to one journalist who had worked closely with Burns, "he was on a mission."[9]

It was Burns who first wrote that 200,000 Bosnian Muslim deaths had occurred in the fighting as of July 1993. The statistic stuck and was used routinely by most other journalists. *The Los Angeles Times'* Carol Williams and others attempted during 1994 to boost the tally to 250,000[10] which was the number eventually quoted by President Clinton before sending U.S. troops to Bosnia in December 1995.

Bosnian government sources, again, were Burns' only attribution for his August 7, 1993, claim that up to 200,000 Muslims had been killed—an average of 450 per day which rivaled even peak casualty counts three decades earlier of Viet Cong and North Vietnamese troops! Burns had reported two months before that between 150,000 and 200,000 "mostly Muslims" had died or disappeared overall, while the previous April 4 he wrote that 140,000 were dead or missing. That four-month death toll translated to an average of 15,000 per month, or 500 per day—the average daily Bosnian Muslim death count Burns pegged for twenty months of fighting!

Burns, who other reporters said ventured less and less outside Sarajevo, consistently reported the government's inflated casualty counts during the war.

Correspondingly, as of late 1993, the U.N.'s estimates of 130,000 fatalities had

---

8. *The Washington Post*, April 29, 1994.
9. Author's interview in February 1993 with Belgrade journalist Duska Anastasijevic, Burns' translator during 1992.
10. *The Los Angeles Times,* February 3, 1994.

not changed, using Serb claims of 45,000 dead and Croat claims of 32,000 (including 10,000 who died in the 1991 war with Serbia). The net balance of about 53,000 Muslim fatalities was not immediately verifiable.

The New York Times celebrated Burns for his Pulitzer win, noting in a congratulatory advertisement that in "a 275-day stretch, he sent 163 articles from the former Yugoslavia, 103 with Sarajevo datelines..."[11] The newspaper said the correspondent "was assigned by the *Times* to cover the conflict in early 1992 after a diagnosis of lymphoma and months of treatment."[12] But Burns' coverage appeared more to coincide with the steady stream of government-supplied "facts" spinning out from the Bosnian presidency.

Repeated attempts were unsuccessful to interview Burns about his one-sided reporting and sources for his statistics when he was briefly in Toronto in June 1993 and when he was in New York, Cleveland and other U.S. cities the following December and January. In Cleveland and elsewhere, Burns made private presentations to certain groups, including the Council on Foreign Relations, which were not open to the public and where there was a ban on tape-recording any of his remarks. He then left for his new assignment in India after allowing only a brief interview on January 10, 1994. This one occasion for overdue confrontation was sidestepped by interviewer Charlene Hunter Galt on *The MacNeil/Lehrer News Hour*.[13] Though she possessed several examples of Burns' biased reporting, Hunter Galt never challenged Burns' blanket denials of bias and let him drone on without interruption. She sat passively even as Burns dramatically announced that a "new" U.N. investigation "within the last few weeks" had examined the site of the May 27, 1992, "breadline massacre" and had turned up gouges in the pavement by exploded mortars and not from the planted, remote-controlled explosives that munitions experts originally concluded were used. Incredulously, Burns claimed it could now be blamed on the Serbs—nineteen months later!

But the supposedly "new" U.N. investigation cited by Burns was apparently not reported elsewhere nor was any such report distributed to U.N. Security Council members. More significantly, there were no reports in *The New York Times* by Burns or anyone else describing any "new" U.N. investigation.

Burns was either mesmerized with his own rhetoric, or else he just plain wasn't listening to Hunter Galt's questions that began with the statement that his breadline-massacre report in 1993 "resulted in your getting the Pulitzer Prize with the bread-line massacre"! Amazingly, Burns nodded in agreement. However, the celebrated centerpiece of Burn's Pulitzer Prize-winning entry was not the debunked breadline reporting but his rambling account of supposed murders and multiple rapes from a confession beaten out of a deranged Serb militia member, Borislav Herak!

Without missing a beat, Burns then outdid himself with exaggerated claims that there were two million Bosnian Muslims at the start of the war and that as many as 300,000 had been killed, up to 900,000 wounded and that they are "dying by hundreds-a-day now"!

Hunter Galt herself refused to be interviewed about her session with Burns.

Curiously, one of Burns' first stories after his arrival back in Sarajevo from a short furlough in July 1993 contained a reference to the "breadline massacre," which was contrived the previous year to pressure the U.N. on the eve of its vote for sanctions against Serbia. A year after widespread concessions that Muslims—not Serbs—set

---

11. *American Journalism Review*, May 1993.
12. *The New York Times*, April 13, 1993.
13. *The MacNeil/Lehrer News Hour*, January 10, 1994.

off explosives outside the Sarajevo bakery that killed twenty-two civilians,[14] Burns and *The New York Times* still clung to the falsehood that a Serb mortar was the cause. But Burns' July 4th story itself had suddenly described Bosnian paramilitaries in Sarajevo who were firing mortars on nearby Bosnian army units! It was a surprising revelation from Burns whose news reports from Yugoslavia were characterized by habitual anti-Serb bias and tenaciously pro-Muslim.

The following illustrate Burns' trademark slant throughout his war reporting:[15]

•June 26, 1992—Burns assigned sole blame to Bosnian Serb gunners for obstructing U.N. relief flights to the Sarajevo airport and did not disclose until the eighth paragraph that Bosnian government commandos had first commenced firing on Serb positions.

•January 5, 1993—Burns did not identify ten victims who froze to death as including Serbs, nor did he report that others among the 108 residents of the nursing home were also Serbs. He also neglected to describe how their location in Nedarici, a Serb-controlled area, was subjected to almost daily sniper fire and shelling from Bosnian Muslim lines nearby. More than 100 of the 300 previous occupants had died already, including twenty who were picked off by snipers and during other Bosnian Muslim attacks. Burns also omitted that Serb victims were buried in an Orthodox cemetery. The implication, characteristic of most reporting by Burns during his seventeen months in Sarajevo, was that the only victims in the war were Bosnian Muslims!

•October 16, 1993—In reporting the breach in one of the more publicized Sarajevo cease fires, Burns assigned sole blame to Bosnian Serb forces while in the seventh paragraph giving only passing mention to a Serb denial. Burns then continued a lengthy recitation that the incident followed a so-called "pattern" of Bosnian Serb artillery attacks during the previous eighteen months. Burns apparently missed or ignored a statement by an UNPROFOR spokesman at a press conference the same day that said the latest attack was directly provoked by Bosnian government commandos who opened fire first on Serb positions. Because the UNPROFOR statement was prominently included in other news reports, Burns hastily stuffed it into the ninth paragraph of a story the next day that tediously resumed

---

14. "*Newsweek* columnist (and retired colonel) David Hackworth, on February 14, 1994, made a trip in 1992 to Sarajevo to solve the breadline blast and other questions. "Such tricks are the oldest ruses of war," said Hackworth concluding that the breadline murders were caused by a planted Claymore mine. Hackworth added he was told by a U.N. soldier, who was an eyewitness, that "Muslim gunners" also fired a mortar salvo toward Bosnian President Alija Izetbegovic and British Foreign Secretary Douglas Hurd on July 17, 1992. Izetbegovic didn't mind his role as target in another public relations event when he and Marrick Goulding, U.N. Undersecretary for Special Political Affairs, came under fire in Sarajevo on May 6, 1992, when the Bosnian war was barely a month old.

15. All references are from *The New York Times News Service* with Burns byline.

the argument that the Serbs were at fault after all. But it was too late to influence New York Times columnist Anthony Lewis who turned out his latest savage attack against Bosnian Serb President Radovan Karadzic before Burns' follow-up report arrived. Lewis spewed his anti-Serb vitriol and added a factual error about the supposed Serbian origins of the phrase "ethnic cleansing"[16] Lewis never corrected his error.

Use Of Chemical Weapons

Burns and other wire service correspondents ignored the astonishing public announcement by Bosnian government leaders over Radio Sarajevo on June 9, 1993, that government troops were preparing to use "chlorine-filled" artillery projectiles and other chemical weapons.[17] Bosnian President Alija Izetbegovic had even said the use of chemical weapons had been planned.[18] U.N. officials subsequently reported that analyzed soil samples confirmed the use of chemical grenades had occurred near Boskovici in August and at other sites in October.[19]

In the late summer and fall of 1993, the *Times* virtually ignored the critically important schism in Bihac and, to a lesser degree, in Tuzla where Muslim separatists openly broke with Sarajevo and the Bosnian government, choosing to seek their own peace agreement with Bosnian Serbs. The episode exposed the myth of a unanimous constituency throughout Bosnia for the extremist Izetbegovic government except among the horde of Muslim refugees that had packed into Sarajevo from rural towns and villages, replacing the many longtime Sarajevans who had fled the country earlier. The "newcomers" and shredded remnants of the original civilian population were pitilessly exploited as media fodder and were endlessly victimized for propaganda purposes. But the suffering by nearly 90,000 harassed Serbs who still resided in Sarajevo—down from about 139,000 original Serb inhabitants—was invisible in the media throughout three and a half years of the city's siege until noted in December 1995 as potentially disruptive to the Dayton-Paris "peace" agreement!

Rather than report about the threatened and imminent use of chemical weapons, Burns belatedly focused on the personalities in the Bihac dissident leadership, resurrecting "numerous allegations" about their past connections with the "Agrokomerc scandal" of the former communist regime from five years earlier.

On October 7, 1993, while being interviewed on *National Public Radio* on the eve of his departure for India, Burns at last divulged that marauding gangsters in Sarajevo had "tentacles running right into the Bosnian government." With his lengthy and intimate knowledge about the Sarajevo regime—after all, several at *The New York Times* recalled a boast that were it not for Burns the Izetbegovic government would

---

16. The origins of the phrase "ethnic cleansing" were debated by journalists at intervals in the Yugoslav civil wars. Konstantin Fotich (see *The War We Lost,* New York: The Viking Press, 1948, pp. 118-119) gives perhaps the most relevant 20th Century origins of the phrase, quoting Croat Ustashe figures who used it as incitement against Serbs during World War II.

17. See Youssef Bodansky, "Terrorism Update: Iranian and Bosnian Leaders Embark on a New, Major Escalation of Terrorism Against the West," *Defense & Foreign Affairs Strategic Policy,* August 31, 1992.

18. Bodansky, *ibid.*

19. *Defense & Foreign Affairs Strategic Policy*, September 1993; see also UNPROFOR Situation Report, October 18, 1993.

have collapsed long before—Burns finally wrote his stories just before his final Sarajevo exit that described the criminal profiteering that had openly infested and depleted Sarajevo for months. *The Daily Telegraph* correspondents Patrick Bishop and Robert Fox wrote extensive articles about the Sarajevo mafia six months earlier![20]

Officials at *The New York Times* refused to respond to specific questions about Burns' reporting involving these and other examples.

Likewise, Burns (along with Roy Gutman, *ABC's* Peter Jennings, Charles Lane and others) had ignored the disappearance by mid-1993 of almost 50,000 Serbs from the pre-war population of Mostar. However, Burns' editors received an odd message from Sarajevo about the migration of news coverage when it was shifting to the Muslim-Croat fighting in Mostar. It stated cynically that "the brethren" in the Sarajevo press corps had decided that the next location under the media spotlight would be Mostar. The use of "brethren" evoked similarities to the same term used to describe the U.S. Supreme Court. Sarajevo correspondents, including Burns, not surprisingly had ordained themselves as supreme judges and, as rabid advocates for military intervention, accomplice executioners and not just reporters in the Bosnian wars.

After January 1993, Burns' new assignment in India "with his Muslims," as one *New York Times* correspondent noted later, placed him beyond the reach of any face-to-face questions about his Sarajevo record that was attracting growing criticisms.

Breaking Up The Pack

The media, and sometimes members of a single newspaper staff, were often beset with disputes due to statistical manipulation. One such dispute—concealed from public view—became evident in the news columns.

On January 23, 1993, *New York Times* reporter Michael Gordon wrote that anonymous U.S. intelligence sources claimed there were as many as 70,000 inmates currently in all detention camps operated by Serbs, Croats and Muslims. Buried in Gordon's story was that Red Cross officials affirmed that no more than 10,800 people were ever held and that only 2,750 were still confined! Gordon was furious a few days later when a story by the *Times'* David Binder from Geneva quoted peace negotiator (and *Times* board member) Cyrus Vance who shot down Gordon's reporting of the 70,000 figure as "rubbish." Even Yugoslav Prime Minister Dobrica Cosic lodged a rare official complaint against Gordon's article which, it turned out later, was ascribed to a statement by a U.S. State Department official who blamed a typographical error!

But Gordon, in a late-night telephone call to Geneva, roused Binder from sleep with "screaming and yelling and cursing." Unmentioned by Gordon was that fellow *Times* reporter Chuck Sudetic, whose anti-Serb sentiments had caused complaints to the *Times'* management, reported two days earlier on January 21 that the latest statistics from the International Committee for the Red Cross (ICRC) showed a total of 2,924 inmates were in all detention camps in Bosnia.[21] The Bosnian government "and its Croat allies" held 1,564 prisoners while Serbs held 1,360 inmates. Binder was facing increased obstructions in his attempts to rectify the unbalanced reporting at his newspaper:

> "No one agrees on the number of casualties in the Balkan strife. Leaders of the Bosnian government, for example, say that 200,000 people have lost their lives in the fighting that began with the Serbian attacks last year, but negotiators here

---

20. Bishop (writing from Kiseljak), *The Daily Telegraph*, March 1, 1993, and Fox (writing from Zagreb), *The Daily Telegraph*, March 2, 1993.
21. *The New York Times*, January 21, 1993.

(Geneva) say that Bosnian officials are acknowledging privately that something more like 20,000 have been killed."[22]

Journalists had generally persisted in looking the other way about the issue of detention camps by early 1994 when the U.N. released its report, which quoted from the ICRC. The report provided more reliable insight into responsiveness by individual governments and their willingness to close down the camps:

> "As of 31 December 1993 there were 5,500 (detention camp inmates in Bosnia-Herzegovina) still on the 'active' register. According to reliable estimates, around forty percent of the detainees are held by Bosnian Croat authorities, twenty-five percent by the (Bosnian) government, thirteen percent by the Bosnian Serbs and the remainder by the forces of the so-called 'autonomous (Muslim) province of western Bosnia'."[23]

The manipulation of inflated war fatalities went to the heart of widespread allegations of genocide in and by the media.

Genocide And 'Sloppy Reporting'

The most succinct insight into the media obsession about the complaint of "genocide" came from George Kenney, a former U.S. State Department dissident and one-time advocate for the multi-ethnic facade of the Bosnian government leadership before its takeover by hardcore Muslim nationalists. Kenney, who earlier subscribed to U.S. military intervention in Bosnia, quit his job in disgust at the State Department only to later change his views when "multi-cultural, sophisticated Sarajevo ...was turned over to coarse Muslim refugees who cared little for pluralistic values."[24]

Kenney's disillusionment with the media bedlam over "genocide" eventually succumbed to doubts about "the hollowness of the vague, unsubstantiated accounts of mass murder...":

> "Full-throated advocates of intervention in Bosnia often dwell on the question of genocide in the hope that the high moral imperative of 'never again' may influence policy. As one of the original interventionists, I must confess here, I'm guilty myself of having used the term genocide (rarely, with qualifications) in reference to Bosnia, yet I've never felt comfortable with insisting it was taking place. ...Where, one might ask, are the bodies? Genocide, of course can't be merely a question of numbers, but one may use numbers as a rough—a very rough way—to figure out a threshold for declaring that genocide happened. Looking back after three years of war in Bosnia, a review of what we know about the numbers is sobering. How many people died? ...250,000 is a number the press has used for some time. The United Nations High Commission for Refugees has no numbers for dead Bosnians, nor does the U.N.'s peacekeeping office in

---

22. *The New York Times*, January 9, 1993.
23. U.N. report No. S/1994/265.
24. George Kenney, "Bloody Bosnia," *Washington Monthly*, March 1995.

New York. Sources at the International Committee of the Red Cross in Washington and Geneva tell me their estimates range from 20,000 to 30,000 dead. ...Friends in the U.S. intelligence community tell me their best guess for confirmed dead runs to tens of thousands. (It's worth noting that Secretary of State Warren Christopher's office has sometimes demanded the numbers, only to discover they don't exist.) Intelligence sources add that official Bosnian statistics simply 'come out of the air.' The Bosnian Ministry of Health, for example, reports 200,000 dead or missing. Although we'll never know for certain, the number 250,000 probably evolved out of sloppy reporting of Bosnian government claims, a demonstration of the herd instinct at work among journalists. The question is not whether 250,000 dead is a wildly inflated number, but by how much it is wildly inflated."[25]

Ex-Yugoslavia desk officer Kenney's defection stunned the interventionist press and diplomatic ranks. Kenney also took issue with David Rieff's claims in *Slaughterhouse,* as an example of the media's willful gullibility.[26] Rieff "paints no great and terrible picture of genocide. To the contrary, he awkwardly daydreams through a jumbled series of anecdotes, throwing in occasional half-baked theories about policy formation. ...It isn't based on facts."

Kenney's reversal was predictably ill-received, and he dug in to survive attacks from colleagues. Among the first to revile him was *Newsday's* Roy Gutman, co-winner of the 1993 Pulitzer Prize for International Reporting, who chastised Kenney for using unidentified and confidential sources, and that his conclusions about greatly reduced fatalities were invalid.

But Gutman's own war reporting habitually used unnamed sources.

Kenney, who was black-listed and no longer sought as previously for frequent commentary by the *BBC* and major U.S. media, described his upbraiding by Gutman, who had become an enforcer against defectors from pack journalism, as harassment. "Gutman called me up for one of his harangues and insisted, no, demanded that I reveal my sources!" said Kenney. "And I said, 'Here you are a journalist, and you want me to give up my sources?!'"

The conscientious ex-State Department officer was also condemned in a scathing rebuke by *The New Republic's* Charles Lane, which Kenney called "a completely unethical, unprincipled, below-the-belt attack."[27]

Kenney hung on doggedly, challenging the inflated death counts through NATO's Kosovo campaign.

Later reviewing Noam Chomsky's 1999 book, *The New Military Humanism: Lessons From Kosovo* for *The Nation*, Kenney examined the Kosovo "genocide" chronology:

"...Chomsky contends that almost everything you have read or heard or seen on television about Kosovo has been a partial truth or outright falsehood.

"On March 18, the day the Rambouillet talks broke down, David Scheffer, the State Department's ambassador at large for war crimes

---

25. Kenny, *ibid.*
26. Rieff, *Slaughterhouse*, New York: Simon & Schuster, 1995.
27. Kenney's interview with author, September 13, 1995.

issues, proclaimed that 'we have upwards to about 100,000 men that we cannot account for' in Kosovo. Depending upon the sophistication of the press organ involved, this statement was variously construed as a warning or, as the *New York Daily News* put it in a headline the next day, '100,000 Kosovar Men Feared Dead.' The specter of mass murder critically supported public acceptance of NATO airstrikes, which began less than a week later, on March 24. After two months of bombing, the Yugoslav regime was still, to the Administration's deepening chagrin, in the fight. By this time there were increasing murmurs of discontent in the press regarding the effect of NATO airstrikes on unmistakably civilian targets. Ambassador Scheffer stepped to the plate again in mid-May, calling for 'speedy investigations' of war crimes (by Serbs) while now noting that 'as many as 225,000 ethnic Albanian men aged between 14 and 59 remain unaccounted for.' Several wire services quoted him on different days as saying that 'with the exception of Rwanda in 1994 and Cambodia in 1975, you would be hard-pressed to find a crime scene anywhere in the world since World War II where a defenseless civilian population has been assaulted with such ferocity and criminal intent, and suffered so many multiple violations of humanitarian law in such a short period of time as in Kosovo since mid-March 1999.' It was a profoundly ignorant remark, of course, but what's important is that the Administration's laser-like focus on allegations and innuendoes of genocidal acts securely established the legitimacy of continued bombing for an at-that-time unknown, perhaps lengthy period."[28]

The ploy was unraveling.

"...Sensing that Washington—Scheffer and a battalion of like-minded flacks—had gone too far out on a limb, in June and July the British started publicizing their reduced estimate that 10,000 Albanian Kosovars had been killed. For whatever reason that number stuck in establishment circles. In fact, however, it appears to be still too many. The actual number is probably somewhere in the low thousands.

"In mid-July sources from the NATO-led peacekeeping force in Kosovo, known as KFOR, were telling the press that of 2,150 bodies found by peacekeepers only 850 were victims of massacres. Nevertheless, still eager to bolster the Serb = devil argument, National Security Adviser Sandy Berger, in an address to the Council on Foreign Relations on July 26, poignantly mentioned 'the village of Ljubenic, the largest mass-grave site discovered so far from this conflict, with as many as 350 bodies.' Berger may not have been aware that the Italian in charge of the site, Brig. Gen. Mauro Del Vecchio, had told the press several days earlier that the exhumation had been completed at the site

---

28. George Kenney, "Kosovo: On Ends and Means," *The Nation,* December 27, 1999.

and that seven bodies had been found. All press mention of Ljubenic ceases after that point."[29]

Finally, Kenny cited an *El Pais* (Madrid) article two months later, which dealt the heaviest blow yet to claims of genocide in Kosovo, reporting that:

> "...Spanish forensic investigators sent to Kosovo had found no proof of genocide. The team, which had experience in Rwanda, had been told to expect to perform more than 2,000 autopsies in one of the areas worst hit by fighting, but it found only 187 bodies to examine. No mass graves and, for the most part, no signs of torture."[30]

By November, Kenney traced the sinking spiral of Kosovo deaths in such outlets as *The Nation, Los Angeles Times, De Volkskrant* (Amsterdam), and *The Sunday Times* of London, which "...added an interview with the head of the Spanish team, Emilio Perez Pujol, who was 'disillusioned' by the 'war propaganda machine.' Pujol says the death toll may never exceed 2,500."

Kenney noted that even Carla Del Ponte, the chief prosecutor for the war crimes tribunal at The Hague, told the U.N. Security Council on November 10 "that its investigators had found 2,108 bodies at 195 sites, out of 529 reported locales."

The State Department clung to its unsupportable claim that the death count of the Kosovars was 8,000 or higher.

While the media adhered to its incoherent claims of up to 300,000 killed in the Bosnian war alone, Kenney's researched estimates settled on 100,000 or less, which was buttressed when the Stockholm International Peace Research Institute later published nearly-identical figures in its yearbook.

The Cleveland Plain Dealer's Elizabeth Sullivan, one of the few noted for her objective reporting in the Yugoslav wars, was clearly as skeptical by November 1999 about the hyped body counts in Kosovo and Bosnia as she was doubtful about officialdom's abilities to substantiate the exaggerations:

> "Likewise for the death count in Bosnia's three-year war, usually put at 250,000. After the war ended in 1995, a Canadian working for the Organization for Security and Cooperation in Europe contacted municipalities all over Bosnia to try to get lists of their dead, to be used in correcting the election rolls. Few had any lists or even names to give him. The overall numbers never have been confirmed. Military analysts are dubious that a war in which only tens of thousands were injured could have produced that many dead."[31]

In the end, the interventionist polemic was always: I can claim that thousands more bodies exist if you can find thousands less!

---

29. Kenney, "Kosovo:..", *ibid.*
30. Kenney, "Kosovo...", *ibid.*
31. Sullivan, *ibid.*

Chapter 7
'A Partial Story' And Half A Pulitzer

"Rumor is a pipe
Blown by surmises, jealousies, conjectures,
And of so easy and so plain a stop
That the blunt monster with uncounted heads,
The still-discordant wavering multitude,
Can play upon it."[1]
– William Shakespeare

"I had heard reliable rumors."[2]
– Roy Gutman

In 1981, *Washington Post* reporter Janet Cooke won a Pulitzer Prize for fiction-writing. But the piece was submitted as factual in the News Feature category, and was therefore judged a lie. The reporter was stripped of the prize and left the newspaper.

In 1993, Roy Gutman and John F. Burns won Pulitzer Prizes for "persistence" and "thoroughness," respectively. But there are questions about consistency, bias, methods, about how and what kind of information was obtained, when and where and from whom they got it. There are larger doubts about objectivity and omissions.

Cooke had to return her Pulitzer Prize.

Gutman and Burns kept theirs.

Appointment At Villprot

A manure spreader was nosed out onto the narrow street, blocking the way to Roy Gutman's house, which was also the European bureau of *Newsday*, the Long Island-based newspaper with, at the time, a national distribution in the U.S.

It was a crisp winter day in 1994 with a sudden clear sky and brilliant sunshine. I set aside the day for a face-to-face meeting with him at his home in rural Villprot, a small village outside of Bonn. Gutman won part of a Pulitzer Prize in 1993 for his sensational dispatches from Yugoslavia and especially his electrifying stories about

---

1. *King Henry the Fourth*, Part II, Induction 1. 15.
2. Gutman interview with Sandra Gair, WBEZ Chicago, September 16, 1993.

"concentration camps" in the late summer of 1992. He gave appearances of not trying to duck the persistent questions and challenges about being selective in his reporting and about the prominence and amounts of hearsay information that made it into print. He simply sidestepped them. He was more upset about my article in *Foreign Policy* and was stammering with anger when he called me a month earlier from Zagreb. No, he hadn't actually read the article yet, but he didn't like what he heard!

Before "Dateline Yugoslavia: The Partisan Press" was published, we had agreed to meet. I suspected he would back out, but he wasn't irked enough, apparently, to scrub our appointment at Villprot. I showed up a week early—just in case. I entered *Zukunftwegstrasse* and swerved around the manure spreader parked near Gutman's quaint rural house beside an empty field. So, this was *Newsday's* European Bureau? *Zukunftweg*, I consulted my sparse inventory of German, translated to "the future way." With regard to method and ethics in media—I hoped not.

I stayed the previous night in the river town of Linz. The small Wald Hotel was a welcome refuge from the darkness and rain that made driving dangerous, coming into the lighted warmth after a long weary January day that began the journey by train from Vienna and ending on the twisting country roads of northwestern Germany. The owner of the hotel apologized that the one-room restaurant on the ground floor was still closed after the earlier floods from the Rhine River that lapped a few yards from the front door. There were water stains on the walls above my head. I wasn't that interested in eating.

It seemed I was barely asleep when I heard children's voices outside. It was morning and they were off to school before sunrise.

The rolling, white-capped swath of the Rhine was still angry as the ferry churned across to the western bank later with its load of early morning commuters.

It was then a short drive to Villprot. The sun wedged through the clouds, shimmering across the hills and valleys. It was going to be a beautiful day, and I looked forward to confronting Gutman.

Frankly, I didn't know much about him or his activities in and around the Yugoslav wars before I first spoke with him on the phone when all he wanted was to complain. Occasionally, I heard his name mentioned, especially in Belgrade during February 1993 after the uproar caused by his "concentration camp" stories the previous August. But even the dissident journalists and correspondents there voiced resentment toward Gutman. Jealousy, I supposed. I didn't know exactly why and wasn't too interested to find out at the time.

When the Pulitzer Prizes were awarded on April 13, 1993, I became suspicious.

Pulitzer day in newspaper journalism is supposed to be festive. Champagne is stocked in newsrooms in case of a celebration for local journalists. The finalists have their Oscar speeches ready. Everyone reflects upon their own work from the previous year, making private comparisons with what begins to appear on the wire services as the award winners trickle out in short takes from New York.

The Pulitzer judges gave the award for Spot News reporting to *The Los Angeles Times* for "balanced, comprehensive, penetrating coverage" of the 1992 Los Angeles riots.[3]

The Wall Street Journal won for reporting about the management upheavals at General Motors. "We just poured everything we knew into what we wrote," said Joseph B. White, one of two *Journal* reporters.[4]

Oddly, two prizes were given for International Reporting, beginning with *The*

---

3. *Associated Press*, April 13, 1993.
4. *Associated Press, ibid.*

New York Times' John F. Burns, recuperating from cancer and praised by Pulitzer judges for his "courageous and thorough coverage of the destruction of Sarajevo and barbarous killings in the war in Bosnia-Hercegovina."[5]

The judges cited Gutman for "'courageous and persistent' reporting that disclosed atrocities and human rights violations in Croatia and Bosnia-Hercegovina."

"Gutman, speaking from *Newsday's* offices on New York's Long Island, said: 'The story that matters is what happens to people... The story goes on, the atrocities go on, the killing goes on. I don't think one can celebrate anything. This is not over.'"[6]

There was a sanctimonious edge to such gloomy remarks. Likely he was miffed because Burns was given a share of the Pulitzer's International Reporting prize "even though his (Burns') work was not among the three entries nominated by the international reporting committee," said Pulitzer publicist Fred Knubel. "The seventeen-member board may award the prize to any entry, regardless of whether it was one of the finalists nominated by the committee."[7]

Gutman and Burns did not have to share the Pulitzer cash prizes even though they had to share the prestige. Figuratively, they each got $3,000—in blood money!

Formula For A Pulitzer

Burns and Gutman rarely covered the same story but baited the pack-reporting with their focus on two episodes during the end of July and beginning of August 1992. The "news" coming out of the Bosnian war during those days made no sense—except to a few skeptics who were beginning to eye the media more closely.

During the week of July 27, the U.N. repeated a claim by the Bosnian government that 11,000 Bosnian Muslim prisoners were being held at a Serb-run detention camp in the former mining complex at Omarska—*after* Burns and Gutman wrote stories about Omarska the previous week.[8] The U.N.'s information was speculative and was derived from Bosnian government sources, like the "anonymous" sources that had instigated Gutman's story six days earlier about sealed freight cars full of deportees "like Auschwitz."[9]

On the bloody Sunday of August 2, Burns was in Sarajevo and wrote his story about the ambush of a bus evacuating infants and toddlers. Two were killed. Burns blamed it on the Serbs, even though two days later mourners at the Orthodox cemetery were shelled with mortars during the burial of one of the victims.[10] Nobody found it odd or refuted that Bosnian Serbs had attacked an Orthodox funeral service! Also, Burns never explained why burial services would be held for a "Muslim" in a Serb cemetery. Burns then wrongly identified the dead two-year-old Serb girl as a Croat and never corrected his first report in his second follow-up story when the information became known to other reporters. Also, he neglected any explanation about why Serbs would first shoot up a bus full of toddlers, including Serbs, and then take nine of them (identified as Serbs) off the bus before it continued its journey the next day.

The same day—August 2—*Newsday* published Gutman's horrifying accounts about Omarska in Bosnia, but which were reported from Zagreb primarily from the

---

5. *The New York Times*, April 13, 1993.
6. *Associated Press, ibid.*
7. *Associated Press, ibid.*
8. *The Chicago Tribune*, August 3, 1993.
9. Reprinted by Gutman in *A Witness to Genocide*, New York: Macmillian Publishing Company; 1993, p. 36.
10. *The New York Times*, August 5, 1992.

accounts of two alleged camp survivors. One man was identified by Gutman only as "Meho," a sixty-three-year-old building contractor who supposedly had been an inmate at Omarska "for one week in June (3rd through the 10th) before being released."[11] Gutman's Meho estimated 8,000 prisoners were at Omarska when he was there, but he did not say how he calculated his estimate. Gutman said the previous week's report of 11,000 prisoners at Omarska came from the U.N. High Commissioner for Refugees that was obtained from the "official Bosnian State Commission on War Crimes,"[12] a propaganda mill, adding that Omarksa was the "largest of the ninety-four camps known to the commission."

Gutman said he first heard about Omarska in Zagreb and included a disclaimer that the International Committee of the Red Cross and other international agencies were not able to visit Omarska. In other words, nobody knew anything firsthand for sure—including Gutman. Also, Gutman had not personally gone to Omarska and did not describe how the Bosnian State Commission on War Crimes, which was cut off and isolated in Sarajevo, could make such claims. Gutman was in Zagreb—200 kilometers from Omarska and 400 kilometers from Sarajevo.

Burns wrote a story from Sarajevo on June 20 saying that "according to Bosnian government claims, more than 10,000 Muslim Slavs...are in Serbian camps."[13] Burns was clearly referring to *all* Serb camps. Burns had gone to none of the camps.

Left unexplained by Burns, Gutman, the U.N. or any credible international agency was the obvious statistical disparity of how a number exceeding all of the estimated inmates in ninety-four alleged Serb-run camps six weeks earlier had been counted at Omarska by July 27. To account for the inmate population at Omarska, the other ninety-three alleged "camps" would have to have been emptied and inmates hauled to Omarska—an unlikely logistical undertaking to transport thousands of prisoners over hundreds of miles through war zones in less than six weeks!

After all, the one unquestioned statistic that appeared in Michael Gordon's later report on January 23, 1993 in *The New York Times* was that the International Committee of the Red Cross had determined six months earlier—at the end of July and on the eve of Gutman's stories about Omarska the first week of August 1992—that there were never more than 10,800 inmates in detention camps run by *all three sides* in Bosnia!

Gutman continued to orchestrate inflated claims more than two years later, attempting to buttress the sagging credibility of his original stories that juxtaposed phrases about "death camps," "concentration camps," and "prisoner-of-war camps," depending on the audiences.

Reporting later he'd talked only with unidentified "U.S. officials," Gutman said "20,000 to 25,000 people were killed in camps. The worst slaughters occurred in June and July 1992."[14] (Gutman obviously considered that his anonymous sources were more credible than George Kenney's.[15])

Cricket, Fair Play And A Nuremburg Neurosis

Roy Gutman telephoned from Zagreb on December 8, 1993. He was upset about what his editors read to him over the phone from the article that questioned Gutman's 1992 death camp reports. He was upset that he wasn't

---

11. *Newsday*, "Survivors Tell of Captivity, Mass Slaughters in Bosnia." August 2, 1992.
12. *Newsday, ibid.*
13. *The New York Times*, June 20, 1992
14. *The San Francisco Chronicle*, May 11, 1994.
15. See Chapter 5, 'Where, One Might Ask, Are The Bodies?

contacted him before the article came out. "It isn't cricket," he spluttered. "It isn't fair play."

Actually, Gutman had only been mentioned regarding "questions" raised by British journalist Joan Phillips in a May 1993 article, entitled "Who's making the news in Bosnia?" that appeared in the British journal, *Living Marxism*.

Gutman was not interested in discussing anything about biased reporting in the Yugoslav wars. But he confirmed that he'd had conversations with Phillips. He referred to her as: "This Joan Phillips cat is—wow! She has to be described a little bit more carefully." Gutman avoided direct denials against anything written about him by Phillips and instead said she had "really tracked me down." More importantly, he didn't deny the substance of what Phillips wrote.

His scoffing tone about *Living Marxism*, which published her report, was plainly intended as leftover Cold War nuance meant to discredit Phillips personally and, more importantly, her reporting about Gutman. He sloughed off the growing concerns about objectivity and facts in the war reporting raised only by "alternative" journals, such as *Living Marxism* and others. Phillips' reports displayed impressive quality and depth.[16] She was well-traveled in the Balkans with a reporting style that was modulated, cool-headed, focused and insightful. Her reporting was reputable among other British and U.S. journals, including *The Nation*,[17] *Covert Action Quarterly*,[18] and other periodicals.

Gutman then alluded to his "lawsuit" in Belgrade, protesting censorship of his responses to allegations in a *TANJUG* report (Jovan Babic, "Blatant Lies for 500 Pounds," January 28, 1993.) that he was an "American agent code-named 2-IC." TANJUG is the official Yugoslav news agency.

Gutman hung up the phone before he could be asked again about his relationship with a British mercenary Robert Allen Loftus, or an alleged reporter contact of Loftus', code-named "2-IC."

There were growing questions concerning his reporting about the alleged "concentration camp" run by Serbs at Omarska. Alleged mass murders at Omarksa and other camps were at the heart of Gutman's package of stories submitted to the Pulitzer Prize judges. Even when his 1992 Omarska reports appeared a year later in his book, the questions remained. But, confronted at Villprot in early 1994, Gutman was suspicious, cagey and defensive. He refused to discuss it further. The only recourse was to scrutinize what he wrote and what he said.

Beginning with his July 19, 1992, report from Banja Luka, he cited an unidentified "witness" who told him "six to ten people die daily" at Omarska. That count disputed Gutman's own "Meho" (quoted in his August 2, 1992, *Newsday* story) who spent eight days at Omarska and claimed 8,000 had been slaughtered—tenfold more than were cited two weeks earlier! Obviously, Meho was not a credible witness and was passing on hearsay. An attempt was made to cover the defects in his stories by hedging that "*nothing definitive is known* about Omarska" which "*may be* a genuine prisoner-of-war camp." (Italics added)

Who, then, were the sources or "source" other than Meho?

Also, Gutman vaguely mentioned an unnamed "local Red Cross official who said

---

16. "The dangers of secession," September 1991; "Frontier War: Europe's new East-West divide," January 1992; "Whose war is it anyway?", February 1992; "How to invent a nation," March 1992; "Who's to blame?", August 1992. All were published in *Living Marxism*.

17. Joan Phillips, "The Case Against the War Crimes Tribunal," *The Nation*, February 1995.

18. Joan Phillips, "Dangerous Interventions," *Covert Action Quarterly*, 1995.

he knew of 'no civilians' in Omarska.''[19] But in Gutman's thinking, places like Omarska were the destinations for trains with sealed freight cars and cattle cars carrying thousands of unarmed civilians when he wrote his second story, also datelined Banja Luka, on July 21, 1992. "It was like Jews being deported to Auschwitz," he wrote. A Nuremberg neurosis had set in.

A man in the article, identified only as sixty-six-year-old "Began Fazlic," described the unsanitary conditions on one train. Fazlic was obviously recruited for the Gutman interview, along with several other supposed former Omarska inmates in Zagreb, by a supposed Muslim humanitarian agency. Such "humanitarian" groups were also involved, it was well known, in weapons smuggling and propaganda. Fazlic later posed for a staged photo inside a boxcar.[20] The effect of the photo was to establish Faslic as a "real" person and boxcars as the means to transport camp inmates and deport other Muslims. Aside from Fazlic, the article listed statements from four unidentified sources, along with Banja Luka Police Chief Stojan Zupljanin, Mayor Predrag Radic (both Serbs) and Bosnian Serb army spokesman Major Milovan Milutinovic.

Gutman's third story about Omarska again carried a dateline from Zagreb on August 2, 1992, and boldly labeled Omarska as a "concentration camp." Gutman's source was the supposed former inmate named "Meho" and another alleged witness who was unidentified and who claimed "thousands of men were also being held in an open outdoor pit." But Gutman also obtained a statement from an identified geological engineer "who helped design the mining facility" and who said that Meho *could not* have seen the pit from his own confinement in a large cage inside an ore loader. So where, Gutman never was compelled to answer, did Meho obtain his information, and how reliable was it? Or, whose words were put into Meho's mouth?

In Gutman's fourth story about Omarska, datelined Zagreb on August 5, 1992, he used information from a second alleged inmate identified only as a fifty-three-year-old survivor named "Hujca." Another "indirect account" came from a thirty-one-year-old member of the Bosnian Muslim defense force, who said a fifteen-year-old boy, identified only as "Gredelje," told him he'd once been confined in the Omarska pit. This time, Gutman reported "hundreds of prisoners" were held in the pit—not thousands. Gutman also cited two other "indirect accounts"—totaling three double-hearsay sources!

"*Kristallnacht* for the Bosnian Muslims came not in one or two nights, as it did for Germany's Jews in November 1938," Gutman wrote on September 2, 1992, from Tuzla. It was one of his numerous articles that were colored with nuances and direct comparisons with the Holocaust. Living in Germany, Gutman later declared he'd long carried fixations about the Holocaust that clearly set the precedent and overlaid his disposition and reporting about the Yugoslav wars:

> "Well, I'm Jewish and, yes, the Holocaust is something I believe must never happen again. Somewhere, back in my first thoughts about going into journalism, I considered that maybe if reporters had been out there to issue warnings at the time, they could have stopped it. And, maybe that's the way to stop

19. *Newsday,* "There Is No Food, There Is No Air," July 19, 1992.
20. Fazlic appears in a photo on the third page of an eight-page photo display in Gutman's book. Interestingly, there is a photo on the first page taken by Gutman himself, showing a "deportation train" and refugees from Kozluk in eastern Bosnia. But pictured is not a cattle car but a "first class" passenger car.

the killing in Bosnia now. But I never expected I would be the warning system for some other ethnic group."[21]

Gutman's next reference to Omarska in was on October 4, 1992, in a report from Karlovac. It began:

> "After four traumatic months in captivity, the first large group of survivors of Serb-run concentration camps in Bosnia has reached freedom with eyewitness accounts that confirm charges of mass murders of civilians during the Serb conquest."[22]

But with such a large collection of ex-Omarska inmates, Gutman waited until the eighteenth paragraph to include a single, short quotation from a supposed twenty-one-year-old former inmate, identified only as Admir Krajisnik who supposedly saw "four or five bodies laid out on the grass" each morning. The man was not described as being a civilian or part of any military unit or militia. Also, Gutman did not give the length of Krajisnik's incarceration at Omarska.

The sixth article about Omarska was the October 18, 1992, *Newsday* report that used an Omarska dateline but failed to establish that Gutman had achieved his only firsthand trip to Omarska. Also, it occurred long after Omarska was closed.

Gutman attempted to sort out the jumble of hazy statistics he'd reported earlier. *Newsday's* headline was "Death Camp Horrors: The Killing Went on Almost Everywhere." It takes up twelve pages, again resorting to interviews from a handful of supposed refugees in London and Karlovac and from unidentified members of the U.S. Embassy in Zagreb who were passing on hearsay:

> "*Newsday's* estimate of the death toll of more than 1,000 is based on eyewitness accounts of daily killings by three former detainees who spoke in separate interviews. ...Extensive *Newsday* interviews with prisoners indicate that at least 2,500 to 3,000 detainees were held in Omarska at any one point. International Red Cross officials have a working estimate that up to 5,000 prisoners were taken to Omarska and that well over 2,000 are accounted for. Despite the imprecision of the statistics, the story of Omarska and other concentration camps in Bosnia constitutes one of the most savage chapters of modern European history. ...But even the United States Embassy interviewers have been unable to determine the number of people held at Omarska, the number killed or the number missing..."[23]

Gutman's original claims of 8,000 or 11,000 inmates at Omarska had seriously eroded. Gutman eventually posed rhetorical questions about Omarska, inferring that the reduced official counts of the camp's population were the result of rapid inmate transfers, insinuations of large-scale executions or disappearances of thousands of inmates:

---

21. Gutman interview with Sherry Ricchiardi, "Exposing Genocide...For What?" *American Journalism Review*, June 1993, pp. 32-36. A biographical note described Ricchiardi, a journalism instructor at Indiana University, as having "covered the war in the Balkans for several American newspapers and (who) directs International Media Fund Project in Croatia."
22. *Newsday,* "Back From the Dead," October 4, 1992.
23. *Newsday,* October 18, 1992.

"...But the biggest mystery is what happened to the people transferred from Omarska at the time of its closing. ...Were other Omarska prisoners killed in other ways? Were they dispersed to other camps? *No one has an answer...*"[24] (Italics added)

And that included Gutman. Nobody had hard proof to back up his excited speculations about mass, Nazi-styled concentration camp killings and volumes. Also, there was no proof to support Gutman's claims about how many people were ever originally detained at Omarska.

Gutman's own uncertainties were evident in yet a seventh report about Omarska that appeared with an Omarska dateline on November 8, 1992.

Again, interviews with a few unidentified former inmates were used to shore up Gutman's renewed arguments of about "10,000 or more former Omarska detainees."[25]

Later in his book, Gutman selectively updated the debunked January 1993 claim by the U.S. State Department "that there were as many as 70,000 detainees" in Serb-run camps alone. He added a terse contradiction that "Red Cross sources said they could not verify this figure."[26]

Gutman ignored any mention of the much lower number of 10,800 total inmates, according to the International Red Cross, in camps run by all sides throughout the Bosnian war that had not changed and was easily available during final revisions of Gutman's book in mid-June 1993.

Twenty Testimonies 'Do Not A Death Camp Make'

Joan Phillips' evaluation of Gutman's "concentration camp" stories was generally unavailable to American and most other audiences. But her conclusions should have alerted the 1993 Pulitzer Prize selection committee:

"As Gutman himself points out, more than 350 journalists headed into Bosnia to find the 'death camps' in the weeks after his first reports. They didn't find them, nor did they find any evidence that they had existed. Even the testimony of twenty former prisoners, whom Gutman spoke to later, do not a 'death camp' make."[27]

Phillips' few critics—mostly American journalists, like Gutman and *The New Republic's* Charles Lane—stooped to "Red-baiting" when attempting to attack Phillips personally. But complaints about her reporting[28] paled quickly after the profoundly revealing television program "Free for All" aired August 24, 1993, during prime time on Britain's *Channel 4*. Phillips, using focus and sensitivity, obtained surprisingly candid answers from several journalists who covered the "concentration camps" episode. No similar public or media dialogue had occurred with American journalists.

Her opening interview was with *The Guardian's* Maggie O'Kane, who broke the "camp story" in the British press on July 29, 1992, and who led the 350 or more

---

24. *Newsday, ibid.*

25. *Newsday,* "*In Town After Town, Bosnia's Elite 'Disappeared.'*" November 8, 1992.

26. *A Witness ..., p. 141.*

27. Phillips, "Gutman: still guilty," *Living Marxism*, August 1993.

28. Phillips, regarded among her peers as highly competent and professional, joined the staff of *The Economist* of London in April 1995.

journalists that flooded into northern Bosnia in the wake of hers and Gutman's very first articles. Phillips' calm questions and O'Kane's demolished responses were riveting:

> O'KANE: "As far as I was concerned, there were large concentrations of people—men, women and children—being held in appalling conditions, who weren't being fed. And there were executions taking place, particularly in Omarska. So, when we can sort of, as I see it, I think that was a fair description. I wouldn't call them death camps because *there wasn't a consistent and systematic policy of exterminating people*, as such. There certainly (were witnesses)..., and you can talk to them in London, how people were taken out regularly and executed and high torture went on as well. So, I mean, I think you should call a spade a spade, and as far as I'm concerned, that's a concentration camp." (Italics added)

> PHILLIPS: "But when you call it a 'concentration camp,' anybody reading that in Britain will immediately think of Nazi-style camps, and that's what 'concentration camps' mean to most people. So, do you think that was a legitimate thing to do, to give that impression?"

> O'KANE: "(pausing, shaking her head) I'm not sure. No."

> PHILLIPS: "Because I think that's the danger, you see, that once you say 'concentration camp' people immediately think of the Holocaust, Second World War, the Nazi's, and so on."

> O'KANE: "(nodding) Yes, I think that's a valid point. I think that it is. Yes, it's a valid point."

Phillips next talked with Phil Davison of *The Independent*:

> DAVISON: "Things had gone slightly quiet. Suddenly, we had 'death camps.' We had 'concentration camps.' We had direct comparisons with the Second World War. I felt, at that stage, there was an exaggeration. There were certainly prisoner-of-war camps, and they were bad, as we later found out. Again, without trying to justify too much, you also have to remember that these prisoner-of-war camps existed on both sides but were certainly worse on the Serbian side. There was a blockade on Serbia. There was very little food around. Everybody was hungry. That may sound bad, but it is the case that people on that side were eating little as well. It's an explanation for why the prisoners of war were badly treated on that side and less badly treated on the other."

Alex Mitchell, London editor for the *Sydney Sun-Herald*, added his views about the camps:

MITCHELL: "They looked to me, looking at them on television, better than Long Kesh was, that the British had in Northern Ireland only ten years ago. And they are certainly better than the camps that the British constructed in Kenya for the Mau Mau. They were certainly illegal. They were certainly appalling. And rightly, the U.N. and other people stepped in to close them down, and what have you. But to give them the kind of horrendous status that the press and television did in this country—it was nauseous because of its hypocrisy!"

PHILLIPS: "The Serbian camp story was a media sensation, but other voices went unheard. The International Red Cross stated that Croat and Muslim forces were also running camps, but few journalists gained access to them. The Red Cross concluded that Serbs, Croats and Muslims all run detention camps and must share equal blame."

MITCHELL: "No one will really remember the fact—it's not established in the public's mind anywhere—*that in fact all sides were doing this, or both sides were doing this.*" (Italics added)

PHILLIPS: "On the first of October last year (1992), all sides agreed to release their prisoners. While the Serbs released most of their detainees, the Croats and Muslims did not. By July this year, Red Cross figures revealed that the Croats and Muslims together had more prisoners of war than the Serbs. But this information hasn't made the news. By depicting Serbs as murderous aggressors, the 'death camp' story helped conceal the causes of the conflict."

Who Was '2-Ic?'

The use of presumption based on hearsay without facts in reporting against the Serbs stands out in the checkered journalistic saga of the Yugoslav wars. Little was ever disclosed about Roy Gutman's connections to a series of mysterious personalities that anchored his reporting, including the British mercenary Robert Allen Loftus. For several years, a full accounting escaped a succession of opportunities for questions during appearances in radio and television interviews, magazine interviews, testimony before Congress, and during a variety of speeches and panel discussions. Gutman's own articles omit anything about Loftus. Likewise, Gutman would not offer or volunteer any of the documents used in his Belgrade lawsuit that might discuss or describe his relationship with Loftus.[29] Clearly, most of Gutman's interviewers, talk-show hosts, Congressional committee members, audiences, co-panelists and Pulitzer Prize judges had never heard of Loftus, who was a British fugitive when he arrived in Bosnia in September 1992:

"(Loftus went) to fight with the Muslims, because he believed media reports blaming the Serbs for all that was happening there.

---

29. In 1994, an appeals court in Belgrade rejected Gutman's complaints about being censored as "groundless."

Ironically, the tables were turned once Loftus arrived in Bosnia. He became a source of stories about Serbian atrocities for any journalist who would listen."[30]

Joan Phillips was one of only two Western journalists known to have examined Loftus' diary shortly after it was found in the wake of a Muslim retreat from Mount Majevica in January 1992. The official Yugoslav news agency, *TANJUG*, claimed that Loftus had actually been captured, but Phillips discounted this because Loftus returned to Nottingham in April. "He had been wounded in the head."[31]

The mercenary's supposed Serb captors never produced Loftus, who possibly was later released through intervention by British or Belgrade officials. Phillips reported that British Foreign Office officials said little about Loftus and preposterously suggested he was a "humanitarian relief worker." Neither Phillips nor anyone else has reported further about Loftus. However, Phillips quoted from his diary:

> "(Loftus) had some unfinished business in Nottingham. 'I ran from the mistake I made because of shame. But having come close to death several times has made me think that life is too precious to run away from and come what may I will answer to my peers for my stupidity.' (November 6, 1992) Loftus was running away from the police. Having returned to Nottingham in April, he then disappeared again."[32]

According to the diary, Loftus also had provided accounts of atrocities in exchange for money to make his life easier in Bosnia:

> "He was always broke; a mercenary's pay didn't go far. His days off were spent on the phone to Barclay's Bank in Nottingham trying to transfer money to the bank of Tuzla."[33]

Who deposited money for Loftus at Barclay's is not known.

Gutman wrote three stories with Tuzla datelines between August 23 and September 2, 1992, which were reprinted in his book.[34] He made no mention of meeting Loftus.

Phillips said the first mention in the diary about Gutman was on October 13, 1992, more than two months after Gutman's first sensational stories about the camp at Omarska. Only five days after that entry, Gutman wrote his grisly, more detailed sequel about Omarska in *Newsday* on October 18.

Gutman's name is next mentioned in Loftus' diary, according to Phillips, on October 15:

"Remember to find Mr. Tanovic's phone number/Zagreb Roy Gutman-re-Marlboro + whiskey."

Phillips said Gutman's name was written on the diary's back page next to "figures (presumably deutschmarks) totaling 950." She said no other evidence was produced to connect Loftus with Gutman. Phillips said Gutman admitted speaking to Loftus "several times" on the telephone, adding Gutman told her "that the guy called me out of the blue." Gutman told Phillips he was "thrilled" to hear from Loftus and he had encouraged Loftus to feed him information while saying he could not publish

30. Phillips, "Who's making the news in Bosnia?" *Living Marxism*, May 1993.
31. Phillips, *ibid.*
32. Phillips, *ibid.*
33. Phillips, *ibid.*
34. *A Witness* ..., pp. 68-83.

anything from Loftus without official corroboration. "There is no evidence that Gutman used any information from Loftus for his stories. The *Newsday* reporter also denies that he paid Loftus money."

Phillips added that Gutman gratuitously invited her to "check my bank statements if you want."[35]

Phillips indicated no further references to Gutman from the diary. But French journalist Jacques Merlino reported that when he examined the diary, it showed that Gutman was present on one occasion with Loftus and his unit near one of the combat fronts in Bosnia. Loftus, according to Merlino,[36] said he was amused that supposedly Gutman became agitated after he was shot at by a sniper.

This contradicts an article written by Liljana Smajlovic in *Vreme*, a dissident journal published in Belgrade. Smajlovic wrote that Gutman answered her specific questions about Loftus by admitting he spoke with Loftus on the telephone. But Gutman denied he paid Loftus for information and said that he "had personally never met him (Loftus)."[37]

Phillips also criticized Gutman for his three-month delay to report about a massacre of seventeen Serb civilians by Muslims and Croats at Serdari, a small village near Banja Luka. Gutman was in Serdari after the murders in September 1992, but his story did not run in *Newsday* until December 13, 1992:

> "Why did he wait almost three months to report a massacre of Serbian civilians in a place which he had visited? After all, he wasted no time before writing stories about Serbian atrocities in places he had not visited on the basis of secondhand statements."[38]

Gutman wrote a lengthy rebuttal and claimed he was delayed in getting to Serdari and to the local coroner, and that "it was baffling that the corpses had been removed."[39] Also, he claimed his editors were reluctant about the story until he later verified the massacre when he was introduced to an unidentified Muslim in Zenica who, Gutman said, helped commit the crime!

Gutman made only casual mention of Loftus without providing more details about their relationship. The main urgency in conversations with Phillips was to shore up any emerging cracks she had found in his death camp stories:

> "The death camp stories are very thinly sourced. They are based on very few accounts from alleged survivors. They rely on hearsay and double hearsay. They are given the stamp of authority by speculation and surmise from officials."[40]

Besides several "outlandish" allegations about Loftus and Gutman in the Belgrade press during early 1993, the Loftus controversy was touched on briefly in the December 12, 1993, issue of *Globus*, a Zagreb news magazine. The article focused on some of the reporting contained in Gutman's book, which was published in Croatian.

---

35. Phillips, *ibid.*

36. *Les Verites Yugoslaves Ne Sont Pas Toutes Bonnes A Dire* (All Truths About The Yugoslav War Are Not Being Reported Honestly), Paris: Albin Michel, 1993.

37. Smajlovic, *Vreme*, March 1, 1993.

38. "Who's making the news in Bosnia?" *Living Marxism*, May 1993.

39. Gutman's response, *Living Marxism,* July 1993.

40. Phillips, *Living Marxism*, May 1993.

The Loftus references in *Globus*, along with Gutman's book, caught the eye of Professor John Peter Maher, a Chicago linguist and Slavic languages expert who had long been critical of media trends in the war coverage from Yugoslavia.

"Roy Gutman's *A Witness to Genocide* is a false witness," wrote Maher in 1995:

> "Although the Pulitzer Prize winning writer of *Witness to Genocide* speaks American English, one must infer from the text of 'his' book that someone other than Roy Gutman wrote at least parts of 'his' book. ...No American, but a Yugoslav hand wrote at least several passages of *Witness*. That hand unwittingly left his/her signature all over the document."[41]

Maher listed twenty separate passages in Gutman's book, detailing grammatical and stylistic defects common to non-English speakers and particularly telltale of Yugoslav or Serbo-Croatian-speaking translators.

Maher's observations gouged out chunks of credibility: (Author's Note: *italics* denote the grammatical irregularities.)

> • "By December, Milosevic had no more use for Panic and easily ousted him in *tampered* elections." (p. xxxv)

> • "Some 1,800 passengers, including 70 mothers carrying infants were expelled from the east Bosnian village of Kozluk after two armored tanks *crashed* into the main square..." *Newsday*, July 2, 1992.

> • "There are hundreds of armed police and military guards for the estimated, 3,000 prisoners, and the *watchmen* use German shepherd dogs..." *Newsday,* July 19, 1992.

> • "Mirsad Sinanbegovic, 35, recounted the night of July 22 when he said Serb guards fired *gas bombs* into a large room in a factory building..." *Newsday*, October 4, 1992.

> • "In the hospital for six weeks with his leg suspended from a bar, Elkaz never recovered because Serb *ill-wishers* came by and poked the wound with a stick..." *Newsday,* October 18, 1992.

> • "Here in two *hangars* where grain was once stored, hundreds of Bosnian Muslim and Croat detainees..." *Newsday*, January 24, 1993.

"I have saved one of the choicest nuggets of 'Gutman's' book for last. Pen your own one-liners for this one," scoffed Maher:

> "Mrki was taken to the White House because he was standing in a prominent location when a guard came into the room looking for *scapegoats*." *Newsday*, October 19, *ibid*.

---

41. Maher, "The Annotated Gutman," *Chronicles* magazine, May 1995.

The same phenomenon occurred several times in *Forging War: The Media in Serbia, Croatia and Bosnia Hercegovina*, by British author/editor Mark Thompson and published by *Article XIX*, the London-based International Centre Against Censorship. *Article XIX* was partly subsidized by the Soros Foundation.[42]

Gutman sent a congratulatory note to *Article XIX* executives about *Forging War* on June 12, 1994. But, Gutman's note raised another disturbing question:

> "My book just appeared in Croatian, and last week I went to a
> book presentation, organized by the publisher, Nenad Popovic
> of Durieaux/Zagreb *and the U.S. embassy.*" (Italics added)

Joint sponsorship by the U.S. Embassy of Gutman's private publishing venture in Zagreb was inappropriate unless there was some official U.S. government connection to producing the book, or unless the government had a deeper hand in supplying some of the information for the book.

There were more questions. Such as, judging from his concerns about skepticism surrounding his connections to the British mercenary, did Gutman ask the Bosnian Serb government to let him examine the Loftus diary himself?

Gutman's 'Methods'—And 'An Exception'

There were cracks in Gutman's facade of exaggeration, loquaciousness and the more intriguing silences, when gullible interviewers—whether in the media or in Congress—took giant leaps in speculation and assumption about what Gutman reported *and* what he hadn't reported, what he ignored, what he had witnessed—*and* what he had not witnessed.

After all, he was a celebrity and a public figure. And, he knew there were doubts about his "methods." That's why he said he went to a local library just before he was interviewed by the Sherry Ricchiardi for the *American Journalism Review* a few weeks after he was awarded the Pulitzer. Gutman had anticipated Ricchiardi's question about why and how he had "to step away from the basic tenet of objectivity." Gutman used paraphrase to quote the late Edward R. Morrow and former *CBS News* president Fred Friendly:

> "I just went to the library today to get the quote. ...And here's
> how Friendly put it: 'Though objectivity is part of responsible
> reporting, all arguments, as Murrow had said, are not equal.'
> ...Some issues simply are not equally balanced and we can't
> give the impression that for every argument on one side, there
> is an equal one on the other side."[43]

Gutman noted to Ricchiardi that Friendly was actually talking about Murrow's reporting on migrant workers in the U.S.—while twisting Friendly's words in an attempt to apply them to alleged Balkan genocide or holocaust!

"Simon Wiesenthal himself calls it genocide," blurted Gutman, referring to the World War II concentration camp survivor and famous Nazi hunter.[44]

---

42. Mark Thompson, *Forging War: The Media in Serbia, Croatia and Bosnia Hercegovina*, Avon: The Bath Press, May 1994.
43. Ricchiardi, *ibid.*
44. Ricchiardi, *ibid.*

But four months later, Wiesenthal's views about the Yugoslav wars were voiced during a nationwide television talk show with host Larry King:[45]

WIESENTHAL: "What we have in Yugoslavia is a civil war with
bestialities that cannot be compared with the Nazi times."
KING: "Bosnia is not a holocaust?"
WIESENTHAL: "No, it is not a holocaust."
KING: "It is a civil war with bestiality on all sides?"
WIESENTHAL: "Yes."
KING: "...I guess your answer to all of this is you have always
desired to be fair?"
WIESENTHAL: "Yes."
KING: "And if you don't have the evidence, you don't lay the charge."
WIESENTHAL: "I never accuse without evidence."

Gutman's book was being released simultaneously and included an acknowledgment to Wiesenthal:

> "The idea for this book arose from a conversation with Simon
> Wiesenthal, the famed Nazi hunter, who has devoted his life to
> documenting genocide and bringing justice to the victims. He
> gave me an eloquent reason: 'All of us need an alibi so that we
> can say we were not silent, that we informed people, that we
> did *everything to bring knowledge about this to the public.*'"[46]
> (Italics added)

Gutman's reporting showed a different perception about doing "everything" aside from Wiesenthal's context of comprehensive fairness in refusing accusations without evidence.

In his book, Gutman wrote that he originally intended to search out Bosnian Muslim and Croat camps holding Serb inmates and that "I made a mental note to search for evidence of Serb camps of the same description."[47] But he showed no results of any such search and, holding to his high standard of reporting methodology, he nevertheless admitted taking a deliberately different course about the Omarska reporting and "immediately made an exception and wrote about the Omarska camp... **which I had not visited, based on the secondhand witness account...**"[48] (Italics added)

Obviously, Gutman's "methods" about evidence differed from Wiesenthal's.

Sondra Gair, a radio talk-show host with the *National Public Radio* affiliate in Chicago, aired an insightful interview with Gutman on September 16, 1993. Gair continuously referred to Gutman himself as an actual "witness" to Bosnian war incidents and that he had "personally been an eyewitness to these horrors." She queried Gutman about "what *you saw*...in the Serb-run death camps." Gutman was only a witness to his ambiguous method of reporting:

> "I have to tell you this. Those of us who went to those camps
> *did not, could not report truthfully and fully what we were
> seeing* when we were seeing it because whatever we reported

---

45. "Larry King Live," October 6, 1993.
46. "Larry King Live," *ibid.*
47. *A Witness...*, p. x.
48. *A Witness...*, p. xii.

was only a partial story. The only way to have reported this... was to talk to people who had gotten out of the camps. So, *it was really some months* before I was able to construct or reconstruct the story of what happened at one of the camps, at Omarska. ...It was a very tough thing to report in *a full and truthful way.*"[49] (Italics added)

Gair did not detect the subtle shifts or turns to avoid full and honest answers to her questions. Without mentioning which camps were or were not visited—or when the camps were visited—Gutman served up one of his typically outrageous anecdotes from, of course, a lone unidentified witness:

> "In one case near the town of, or, I think, in the town of Kozarac, and they took the head of the Muslim party there and in front of witnesses, *and I talked to one witness.* They took an electric drill and they drilled holes in his body, in his heart and killed him. They took, I think, the children and decapitated them all and put their heads on pikes—all in full view."[50] (Italics added)

Single-source reporting and all, Gutman always claimed he was ethical in his reporting, despite his disproportionate volume of accounts from Muslim victims that contradicted his intentions for getting all sides to a story. Ricchiardi asked him about his differences with "so many journalists (who) seemed to take the middle ground in reporting this war." The question itself displayed more of Ricchiardi's illusions that the war reporting overall was somehow neutral and not stacked in favor of the Bosnian Muslims. His response was mind-boggling:

> "Unlike many of my colleagues, I did spend more time with the Serbs, reporting them and watching them, rather than spending time with the victims in Sarajevo who were being shot at from a long distance. I wanted to get inside the machine, and I made a lot of effort to do that. If you weren't in the thick of it where they were actually doing the cleansing and running the camps, you could hardly discern the truth. ...You have to collect everything you can, put the entire story together, then go to the other side for comment."[51]

But was the "thick of it" in Zagreb where Gutman talked primarily with Muslims and Croats and where much if not most of Gutman's reporting originated? And inside which "machine" did Gutman spend his time reporting and watching? Judging from his reporting, little resulted from his time "inside the Serb "machine." And, far sooner than the lapse of "some months" he said were required "to construct or reconstruct the story of what happened at one of the camps, at Omarska," enough "data" was practically immediately provided to Gutman in Zagreb for the basis of his infamous "concentration camp" stories in August 1992.

---

49. Interview with Roy Gutman by Sandra Gair, WBEZ Chicago, September 16, 1993.

50. Gair, *ibid.* In Gutman's book, he told the same general story and attributed the source to Began Fazlic, an alleged Omarska survivor *Newsday*, July 21, 1992.

51. Ricchiardi, *ibid.*

Gutman reported that "within a few days" he was provided with a "team of experts" organized by a Bosnian Red Crescent "volunteer... sociologist" who led him to former Omarska and Brcko Luka camp imates. Gutman's editors ran the story with *the dramatic cover treatment that only a tabloid can."*[52] (Italics added)

The "data" and the witnesses were recruited for Gutman who was steeped in his premise about the resurrection of the Holocaust and Nazi-era "concentration camps." Describing how his stories began to unfold, Gutman again discloses that while "transiting Zagreb" he got the "tip that Serbs had begun full-scale 'cleansing' in Banja Luka."[53]

Gutman never identified his Zagreb tipster. But he instantly assembled a "tight but unique team" that included an interpreter and German photographer Andree Kaiser. They arrived in Banja Luka a few days later, looking for the "reversion to Third Reich practices" and instead discovered that "'Ethnic cleansing' had not really begun here." Instead, Gutman's brief "three-day visit" turned up more "tips" that pointed to supposed "concentration camps" and systematic rape.[54]

Whether it was "a week" in Zagreb or "few days" in Banja Luka, Gutman's references to that period, recited in later interviews and speeches, vaguely describe as many as "about ten days (where) I and several Muslim charitable foundations searched to find survivors of the camps."[55]

The vagueness of so recent a memory of such an important break in his story was curious.

Even months after the International Red Cross and others showed serious doubts toward the first estimates about detainee populations or atrocities at the camps, Gutman had his context fixed on the historical past:

> "This was the worst genocide in Europe since the Holocaust, so I didn't feel I could treat it lightly."[56]

Congress ...Out To Lunch

"Were your stories attacked for not being substantiated?" Terry Gross asked Gutman two days before his interview with Gair. Gross hosted *Fresh Air* on WHYY, the *NPR* affiliate in Philadelphia. Gutman's response was intriguing about his sensational stories on Omarska and Brcko Luka which were published by *Newsday* on August 2, 1992:

> "Oddly enough, they weren't. Because for one thing just the fact of having the pictures made it clear that these were real people. *Secondly, the story contained comments from every responsible international organization, including the Red Cross."*[57] (Italics added)

But the August 2, 1992, report quoted only the anonymous Omarska inmate, named "Meho"; and Pierre Andre Conod, a Red Cross official in Zagreb; then

---

52. *A Witness...*, p. xiii
53. *A Witness...*, p.viii.
54. *A Witness...*, p. ix.
55. Gair interview, *ibid*.
56. Ricchiardi interview, *ibid*.
57. Interview by Terry Gross, *Fresh Air*, WHYY, Philadelphia, September 14, 1993.

Yugoslavian Prime Minister Milan Panic, unnamed "international relief agencies," the Bosnian Muslim charity Merhamet, anonymous secondhand hearsay reference from a UNHCR report, and an unidentified daughter of the Prijedor mayor. The second story was based solely on statements from an alleged former inmate at Brcko Luka named Alija Lujinovic.

How credible were Gutman's sources? Specifically, the "charity" Merhamet was a propaganda conduit and a suspected channel for weapons smuggling during the Bosnian wars, and it was clear that Merhamet recruited the pair of former camp inmates and "witnesses" for Gutman's reports on August 2, 1992. But Gutman, when confronted twice in 1994 by the author, refused to answer questions about anything, including his connections to Merhamet.

During September 1993, when Gutman was interviewed by Gross and Gair, he also appeared as one of a "panel of experts" before a hearing of the House Committee on Foreign Affairs in Washington, D.C.[58]

He was noticeably cautious and self-restrained from repeating phrases about "concentration camps" or "death camps" or "holocaust" that he'd liberally used in his *Newsday* reports. In his prepared statement for the committee, which was submitted in writing for the record of the hearing, he consistently referred to "detention camps" only.[59] In fact, Gutman conceded to the committee that "of course, *everybody is involved* in the atrocities to some degree, but especially the Serbs and Croats."[60]

Even in response to baited questions by Congressman Frank McCloskey, a "Bosnia hawk" from Indiana, Gutman was unusually cautious. He was no doubt mindful that statements to congressional committees were considered as being *de facto* under oath:

> McCLOSKEY: "Mr. Gutman, in your book *Witness to Genocide,* based on your trail blazing news dispatches, you describe the conditions in the concentration camps, the acts of the Serb captors and so forth. Can you tell us what happened to those camps and those prisoners after you got the word out? Specifically, do the camps still exist and had there been Western access to them? Are the Serbs out of the genocide business in that particular area?"

> GUTMAN: "Congressman, the news reports, followed by a great deal of public attention and statements by governments, focused the world on the Serbs and focused the Serbs on themselves. ...Almost overnight one of the major camps, Omarska, where there were at least 2,000 or 3,000 men, was closed down and the prisoners were dispersed. ...There was a significant reduction in the genocide. ...There were so many delegations coming through, so many questions being asked, so much interest, that it was not possible to carry on with this process.

58. The hearing was entitled "The Crisis in the Former Yugoslavia and the U.S. Role," and was held on September 29, 1993, resulting in a transcript published by the U.S. Government Printing Office. Other panelists included author Misha Glenny, American Enterprise Institute senior fellow and former U.N. ambassador Jeanne Kirkpatrick, and Professor John Lampe, director of East European Studies at the Woodrow Wilson Center.

59. Congressional hearing, *ibid*, pp. 37-43.

60. Congressional hearing, *ibid*, p. 16.

The interest regrettably diminished at the end of the last year. There was not a great deal of follow up or follow-through by Western governments."

Officials he quoted as claimed Serb guards killed as many as 5,000 men at Omarska of the 13,000 or so who were processed there."[61]

Also, nobody at the hearing was interested to hear from co-panelist Professor John Lampe, "about what has been happening on other sides in this unfortunate matter of ethnic cleansing."[62] Lampe was referring to new and shocking reports about the "grim medical consequences" due to embargoed shipments of food and medicine to Serbia[63] that had created a "catastrophe" for innocent Serb children and other helpless victims, including Muslims in Kosovo and Muslim refugees from Bosnia.[64] Lampe favored removal of the red tape, i.e. U.S.-imposed sanctions, that "delayed or denied" permits to ship food and medical supplies, describing it as a "mockery."

Lampe also submitted an article from *The Washington Post* for the hearing record that described:

> "While the Western media have concentrated their attention on Muslim suffering in Sarajevo and more recently in Mostar, the Bosnian army has systematically pushed the Croat population out of many ethnically mixed towns such as Fojnica all across the industrial heartland of Bosnia. Thousands of Croat civilians have fled because their homes were destroyed in the fighting, they feared Muslim retribution and rule, or they were ordered to leave by their own retreating protectors. ...A five-month Croat blockade of all roads into central Bosnia has only served to worsen conditions for the remaining Croat population. The blockade has prevented delivery of humanitarian food supplies..."[65]

The committee promptly recessed without any discussion about the Serb health catastrophe or the imperiled victims of Muslim attacks. It was noon and time for lunch.

Propagandist With Five Aliases

There are questions about Roy Gutman's association with a remarkable Croat woman named Jadranka Cigelj—or Jadranka C., Jadranka Cigev, Jadranka Cigay or a Mrs. Jadranka—and whether she was the "tipster" that launched his search for detention camps in Bosnia during his short Zagreb stopover.

Cigelj is described discreetly in Gutman's book only as a forty-five-year-old attorney and political activist from Prijedor in northern Bosnia. She was also, Gutman

61. *A Witness..*, *ibid*, p. xiv.
62. Congressional hearing, *ibid*, p. 35.
63, Lampe, Congressional hearing, *ibid*, p. 54.
64. Congressional hearing, ibid. Lampe included in the hearing record "Serbia's Health Catastrophe: U.N. Sanctions on 'Pariah' Block Medicines," *International Herald Tribune*, August 23, 1993.
65. Congressional hearing, *ibid*, p. 56. "Bosnian Muslims Gains May Have High Cost," *The Washington Post*, September 12, 1993.

claimed, a victim of multiple rapes in the Omarska detention camp where she was an inmate for seven weeks, from June 14 to August 3, 1992.[66] Gutman wrote that she was first raped on July 18 at 1:15 a.m. by a Bosnian Serb "reserve officer named Nedeljko Grabovac."[67] Gutman wrote that she was also raped by at least three other men, including Zeljko Mehajica who was the commander in charge of guards at Omarska, and Mladen Radic and Kos Miloica who also raped her "on four nights. Every night, a different one."

German journalist Thomas Deichmann later reported that Cigelj was erroneously identified in a June 3, 1993, photo in the *Minneapolis Star-Tribune*, where she was called a "Bosnian Muslim victim."[68]

Deichmann had surfaced as a tenacious skeptic about Gutman's writings and an overall critic of the war reporting in Yugoslavia. He zeroed in especially on Cigelj's relationship with Gutman because of her whirlwind international campaign in front of the German Parliament, U.S. Congress, European and American television, a host of political and human rights organizations and universities as a high-profile "victim" against the rapes committed in the Bosnian war.

Deichmann put Cigelj under the microscope at about the time she went to Minneapolis to receive an honor from the Minnesota Advocates for Human Rights "for outstanding contributions to international women's rights." She was also soliciting donations, said Deichmann who had discovered Cigelj's four aliases as well as an array of astounding details about Cigelj's background that Gutman didn't detail for his readers—and became irate about when publicly asked for more specifics about her.

"I personally take offense at your question," Gutman said in a huff when questioned about Cigelj at the University of Goteborg in Sweden on December 2, 1994. He called the question "frivolous" about whether he knew Cigelj was a paid propagandist at the time he interviewed her at the Croatian Information Centre (CIC) in Zagreb. Gutman's *Newsday* interview with Cigelj was datelined February 21, 1993, from Zagreb.

Deichmann said Gutman told him he first met Cigelj "by chance." Deichmann said Cigelj had been working for the CIC and was also the "vice chair of the Croatian section of the International Society for Human Rights (ISHR), whose headquarters are situated in Frankfurt am Main, Germany."[69] Deichmann added:

> "The ISHR predecessor organization has well-documented historic links with the Nazi authorities in World War II and later with the CIA and the German secret service BND. ...The ISHR Zagreb office and personnel double as the CIC."

Deichmann's November 4, 1994, article in *Die Woche* was backed by a longer report two months earlier about the ISHR which he described as "the second largest organization for human rights in Europe."[70] Deichmann's article was reprinted by the Belgian daily *De Morgen* on November 8, 1994, and by the Swedish daily *Helsingborgs Dagblad* on November 26, 1994.

---

66. *Newsday,* February 21, 1993.

67. *Newsday, ibid.*

68. Deichmann, *Die Woche* news weekly, Berlin, November 3, 1994.

69. Deichmann, *ibid.*

70. Deichmann, "IGFM - Human Rights in Focus," *Novo*, No. 12, September/ October 1994. *IGFM* is the acronym for *ISHR* in German (Internationale Genossenschaft fur Menschrenrechte).

Deichmann said he found some of Cigelj's Croatian aliases "in numerous publications of the ISHR":

> "She is sometimes described as a forty-four year-old Croatian from Prijedor, sometimes as a Croatian in her early forties from Vukovar."[71]

Deichmann wrote about his telephone interview with Gutman in August 1994, adding that Gutman "affirmed that he still regards his rape witness, Jadranka Cigelj, as a reliable source." He continued that Gutman and Cigelj remained in "close contact":

> "The fact that Gutman met Jadranka Cigelj when he launched the Croatian edition of *A Witness to Genocide* in the Zagreb Culture and Information Centre in June 1994 also suggests that the author and his witness have not lost contact. The CIC has also stated that Cigelj had helped Gutman with his research trips in Bosnia and that it had always passed all 'valuable information' to him. ...When I asked Roy Gutman on the phone on what occasion he had last seen Jadranka Cigelj, he failed to mention the presentation of his book together with Cigelj in Zagreb which had taken place only a few weeks before our conversation. He began stuttering and pretended having forgotten this event that made him the most important and celebrated Western journalist in Croatia. He also stated that, apart from a very brief and insignificant contact this summer, he had never heard of the International Society for Human Rights (*ISHR*) and that he did not know that Jadranka Cigelj has been the vice-chair of its Croatian section in Zagreb since December 1993."[72]

Deichmann wrote that by the time Gutman met Cigelj she had already testified before the German Parliament about "systematic rape in Bosnia-Hercegovina" in December 1992. The following March, a month after Gutman's story about Cigelj and rapes at Omarska, "she appeared at the annual conference of the *ISHR* in Koenigstein near Frankfurt...as Jadranka Cigev."[73] Cigelj also made numerous television appearances in Germany, the U.S., France and Great Britain.

There is no mention about Cigelj or the *CIC* in the Acknowledgments or Author's Note in *A Witness to Genocide*. In fact, the *CIC* is mentioned with lower-case vagueness as only "the Croatian information center" where Gutman interviewed Cigelj.[74] He could hardly have missed the nature of materials at the location or the nature of the organization's purpose. What bothered Deichmann were contradictions by and about Cigelj in Gutman's book and *ISHR* publications. According to Deichmann, Gutman answered that it was a mere omission when asked why he referred to Cigelj as "Siget"—yet a fifth alias—when he wrote to Bosnian Serb officials to get responses from Mejahic, who denied he had raped Cigelj. In the *ISHR* brochure *God's Forgotten Children,* Cigelj claims she was raped *only by one person,* Omarska guard Grabovac, and

---

71. Deichmann, *Die Woche*, November 3, 1994.
72. Deichmann, *ibid.*
73. Deichmann, *ibid.* In a footnote, Deichmann cited *ISHR* publications as his source.
74. *Newsday,* February 21, 1993*, ibid*

not Mejahic. However, Gutman wrote she was raped by Mejahic, Grabovac, Radic and Miloica.

Also, Deichmann noted that in *ISHR* documents Cigelj said she was transferred from Omarska on August 3, 1992 to the "concentration camp Trnopolje" where she remained for four days.

Gutman said she was "released" on August 3. Deichmann said he asked Gutman about the inconsistencies in the rape allegations and her confinement dates:

> "Roy Gutman says the explanation for this may be that Cigelj only overcame her trauma in stages, until she was finally able to articulate all the details of her horrific experience. This seems unlikely since the *ISHR* brochure was published in the same month as Gutman's article, in February 1993. Two months later there was even published another long interview with Cigelj in the German *Frankfurter Allgemeine Zeitung* (April 5, 1993). Like in the *ISHR* brochure, she claims that the camp commander did not rape her. In this interview it becomes very clear that she is a propagandist."[75]

In the April 5, 1993, interview, Cigelj also claimed that 11,800 inmates had been killed at Omarska before she arrived on June 14, 1992. On October 18, 1992, Gutman reported that Omarska was opened on May 25, 1992.[76] Official documents of the International Criminal Tribunal for the Former Yugoslavia at The Hague state that Omarska was opened on May 26, 1992.[77] No credible evidence from the U.N. or anyone else has verified that an average of 4,000 deaths occurred during each of the three weeks prior to Cigelj's arrival.

Deichmann also cited a television interview in which Cigelj was asked directly if Mejahic had raped her. "The way she answered was not 'yes' or 'no'," said Deichmann.[78]

Cigelj Dumped As Hague Witness?

The indictment on February 13, 1995, by prosecutors at The Hague did not specifically charge Mejahic with rape although he was held responsible for alleged rapes by those under his command at Omarska.[79]

Jadranka Cigelj is very probably the victim referred to in a "sample" case file included in the "data-base" of alleged war crimes prepared at DePaul University and sent to The Hague tribunal in 1994.[80] But disparities are immediately obvious about other statements and records, which include an "audiotape recording of an interview with a witness, supplemented by a written statement." A "summary description" of the rape incident shows the exact details about Cigelj's first alleged rape at Omarska, which Gutman reported had occurred on July 18, 1992 at 1:15 a.m. But the DePaul file shows the date of occurrence to be at 1:15 a.m. on June 30, 1992. The source of

---

75. Deichmann, *Die Woche*, November 3, 1994.

76. *Newsday,* October 18, 1992. *ibid*

77. Judgements against defendants, No. CC/PIS/63-E, July 24, 1995.

78. Deichmann interview with author, April 17, 1995.

79. Document No. CC/PIO/004-E, International War Crimes Tribunal at The Hague, February 13, 1995.

80. Terry Sullivan, "Managing the Information of Ethnic Cleansing," *DePaul University Magazine*, Spring 1994.

the DePaul documentation is identified as the "Croatian Information Centre."[81]

The *CIC* produced volumes of information, including audiotapes, testimony and affidavits from supposed Croat and Muslim victims of war crimes to the DePaul project which, it is remembered, was almost totally financed with $900,000 from billionaire philanthropist George Soros.

Deichmann's doubts about Gutman, Cigelj and the *CIC* are compelling:

> "When he wrote his article about Jadranka Cigelj in February 1993, Gutman was aware of her connections with the governing Croatian party and the *CIC*. It is perplexing that Gutman has never expressed any doubt about the credibility of this institution and its personnel."[82]

For several reasons, Gutman could not afford to undermine his support of Cigelj or the *CIC* when pestered by questions at the University of Goteborg in December 1994:

> "She was the first person to testify out of the women held at Omarska that she had been raped. And the other women have come forward in the meantime. ...There is no question about what happened to her unless there's some question in your mind. ...The Croatian Information Centre (produces) a number of books and articles about what happened during the Croatian war and during the Bosnian war. *And I think that those that I've seen have been more or less scholarly. I can't testify for everything that they've written.*"[83] (Italics added)

Gutman indeed knew a good deal about the *CIC*, contradicting what he told Deichmann about his first interview with Cigelj.

Five months later, prosecutors at The Hague suddenly announced that an unidentified female witness in the Dusan Tadic case would not be testifying in the upcoming trial.[84] There was little doubt that they were talking about someone who identically fit the profile of Cigelj, whose testimony and veracity as a professional lawyer herself would be ripped apart under oath. The prosecution could not afford that kind of embarrassment in the first war crimes trial at The Hague and risk a devastating defeat. Not only would there be a catastrophic loss of credibility before the public, but the United Nations would be further dissuaded from financing the costly $100 million per year experiment with international justice in the New World Order.

Ejecting Cigelj, if indeed she was the witness, was not only necessary in order to salvage Gutman's reporting about Prijedor—and the waning esteem for his Pulitzer Prize—but because Prijedor was one of the main areas focused on by U.N. investigators, according to Boutros Ghali's report in May 1994 to the U.N. That report was based primarily upon the "data-base" project from DePaul University that included a large

---

81. Sullivan, *ibid.*

82. Deichmann, *ibid.*

83. Gutman, University of Goteborg, December 2, 1994.

84. *Associated Press*, May 11, 1995. The Tadic trial was the lone instance of war crimes prosecution against the only defendant who was then in custody at The Hague. Tadic was accused of a variety of atrocities and human rights abuses connected to the Omarska camp.

volume of information received from the Croatian Information Centre—including the flawed report about Cigelj's alleged rape at Omarska. There was the very possible danger that Cigelj could be tied to other information produced by the *CIC* for DePaul and Tribunal investigations.

Cigelj's demolished credibility, which could have affected an unknown number of war crimes cases against Serbs and would be attacked by any reasonably skilled defense attorney with a nose to follow the scent of perjury, cracked the cornerstone of the Prijedor case at The Hague.

Undaunted, Cigelj's career as the war's most celebrated rape victim was subsequently launched in the hour-long 1996 film "Calling the Ghosts: A Story About Rape, War and Women" preceding a promotional tour through twenty-five U.S. cities. She lectured from coast to coast, including American University, Boston University, Princeton and Yale Universities, UC-Berkeley and others. She also found time on her packed media itinerary to address the exclusive Council on Foreign Relations and made calls on Capitol Hill's most vocal Bosnia "hawks" like Representatives Tom Lantos and John Porter and Senators Diane Feinstein and Frank Lautenberg.

Along with her "co-star" and fellow Prijedor lawyer Nusreta Sivac, also a rape victim at Omarska, she was named *Ms.* magazine's "Woman of the Year" while the film was featured on *CBS 60 Minutes*, received promotional boosting from *Time* Magazine, and was shown nationally via *HBO-Cinemax*.

The movie, funded in part by Soros, scooped up a sparkling list of a dozen cinematic prizes and film festival showings, landing a pair of Emmy Awards where a sympathetic U.S. envoy Richard Holbrooke hurriedly walked out of the televised ceremony before "Calling the Ghosts" co-director Karmen Jelincic took her trophy and blasted the plodding war crimes tribunal at The Hague.

The production established openly that Cigelj was as a member of the *CIC* in Zagreb—a point lost on American audiences—where she was working at collecting and compiling alleged rape testimonies for prosecutors at The Hague.

Easily, the most memorable feature was Cigelj's "starring role"! Her dramatic flair almost destroyed the documentary aspect of the film. From tears to chain-smoking to tight shots of her face shadowed by subdued lighting, to her numerous solo scenes showing her varied theatrical abilities with candles, ice cream cones and more tears.

Her low, husky voice-overs with doleful strains from a lonely cello in the background added effect to her role as an Omarska rape victim turned crusading film narrator/star:

> "In the beginning I was in a state of shock ...I felt the need for revenge ...and the only way to get revenge was by collecting testimonies. I thought that by making them public, I would be able to get revenge..."[85]

Strolling as a pensive solitary beside a field of maize, back turned to the camera, her hair blowing gently, she questions her past ambivalence when seeing and forgetting reports of abused women in other lands: "Maybe this is God's punishment!" At the end of "Calling the Ghosts," she stands and ponders small Dutch children riding past her on a merry-go-round: "This is like a dream ...really!"

Jadranka Cigelj's "dream" for revenge and incidental justice collided with the U.N. Commission of Experts' pilot study from April to July 1993 that was taken from

---

85. "Calling the Ghosts: A Story About Rape, War and Women,"
Bowery Productions, 1996.

the War Crimes Commission of Bosnia and Herzegovina. That study resulted in 126 victims, 113 incidents and 252 alleged perpetrators—drastically lower numbers than were claimed later by Cigelj and others. The following year, the summary report on "rape and sexual assaults" in the DePaul/Soros data-base reported the Commission of Experts had completed 223 interviews that identified just thirty-one female rape victims from Bosnia-Herzegovina and eleven female rape victims from Croatia. The alleged offenses occurred between the fall of 1991 and the end of 1993.[86]

But investigators and various organizations could be counted on to comb through the emotional wreckage in the region for years to come, searching for the elusive 20,000 cases they believed to be "out there."

The Race For The Pulitzer

There are questions about Roy Gutman's connections with the overly dramatic Muharem Krsic, a former Muslim political party leader in Banja Luka. Gutman recalled it was July 9, 1992, when he got a telephone call from Krsic that Gutman described as a summons back to the Nazi era.[87]

It had been almost two months since John F. Burns, *The New York Times* correspondent in Belgrade, had left for Sarajevo. Burns had been writing block-buster stories, including the dramatic piece only three weeks before with the Bosnian government's claim that there were 10,000 Muslims in Serb detention camps. Most Western reporters involved in the war coverage, along with local journalists in Belgrade and Sarajevo, knew Burns and Gutman were locked in the race for the Pulitzer Prize.

Two days earlier, Burns had reported that Bosnian President Alija Izetbegovic would meet with President Bush in Helsinki, where Izetbegovic said he planned to renew his plea for arms from the West in order to stave off "slaughter" by the Serbs.[88] What was nerve-wracking to other Western reporters was that Burns had an exclusive hour-long interview with Izetbegovic. UNPROFOR General Lewis MacKenzie said it was as though Burns "practically lived" at the Bosnian presidency.[89]

Burns was in the right place, and Bosnian government propagandists knew the crowded refugee and detention camps would yield a bonanza of anti-Serb media if they could only lure the right journalists at the right time, using the right words. The Serbs had left themselves vulnerable during large-scale rail transport of non-Serb residents from areas in northwestern Bosnia. They used chartered trains with passenger cars, but because of the large numbers of evacuees, they were also imprudently using some box cars and cattle cars. On July 3, 1992, Gutman wrote his story about *"deportation trains"* chartered to carry "expellees" not to nearby "concentration camps" but to the Hungarian border from Bosnia.[90] But the nuanced comparisons with Jews deported to Auschwitz and other Nazi concentration camps during World War II were intentionally obvious. Numerous photos in 1992 showed occupants of the trains leaving at will to gather water and food during the arduous journeys by rail. It was nothing like the gruesome deportations to the infamous World War II Holocaust camps—except in Gutman's mind and reporting.

In Sweden almost three years later, Gutman read aloud Krsic's words from July 9, 1992, from Banja Luka:

---

86. S/1994/674, p. 56.
87. *A Witness* ..., p. vii.
88. *The New York Times*, July 7, 1992.
89. *MacKenzie interview with the author, October 1993.*
90. Gutman at Goteborg, *ibid.*

"Please try to come here. There is a lot of killing. They are shipping Muslim people through Banja Luka in cattle cars. ...They were so frightened. You could see their hands through the openings. We were not allowed to come close. Can you imagine that? *It's like Jews being sent to Auschwitz.* In the name of humanity, please come."[91] (Italics added)

In Sweden almost three years later, Gutman sat with co-panelist Krsic. Not by coincidence, the panel presentation was entitled, "In the Name of Humanity, Please Come!"

Gutman indicated that the reason he did not identify Krsic in his *Newsday* stories or his book as the man who'd called him from Banja Luka was supposedly because Krsic had been briefly jailed in Banja Luka. At the time, Gutman didn't know how much of Krsic's problems were tied to him. Krsic, who spoke passable English, had gotten his family out of Bosnia early in the war. He said his mission in Banja Luka had been to gather information to submit to U.N. and other officials with the aim of convincing the Western world that genocide was being committed by Serbs. The goal of disseminating such information was to instigate decisive Western military intervention against the Serbs. In other words, Krsic was at least a propagandist!

"I was in my hotel room in Belgrade, having heard a tip about ethnic cleansing having started in Banja Luka," Gutman recalled dramatically in Goteborg. "And the idea that there might be so-called ethnic cleansing, that is to say the mass removal of a population, was a staggering idea."

Gutman said that he "had to check it out and see if I could go there." He also said he'd been given Krsic's phone number by "somebody at the American embassy" who'd known Krsic "for many years, but I'd never met him before myself. And I got on the phone, and I asked him: 'What is going on today in Banja Luka? Is it true that there is massive removal of people?'"

At the time, former Ambassador Warren Zimmerman was in charge of the U.S. Embassy in Belgrade. Zimmerman later was exposed as having recommended to President Izetbegovic on March 25, 1992, that if he was dissatisfied with the Lisbon Agreement to avert a Balkan war, which the latter had signed a month earlier, then he simply didn't need to live up to it.[92] The Lisbon agreement was reluctantly signed the previous month by Bosnian Serbs, Croats and Muslims, who agreed to confederate Bosnia-Hercegovina into three ethnic regions in lieu of all-out war.

Gutman said Krsic gave him "very specific information, first of all, about the trains. I felt that this itself was one of the most dramatic things I'd ever heard—people being shipped in cattle cars in the heat of summer without water through the town."[93]

Gutman marveled at the exactness of Krsic's information:

"Based on this experience, that his information was so accurate and so precise, I listened with great care to everything else he had to say. And he told me that they had, he and his colleagues, *had just gotten* information, that they'd been collecting information *for some time* about camps being set up—detention camps, concentration camps—where people were being taken and held until they died or were tortured to death."[94] (Italics added)

---

91. Gutman, *ibid.*
92. David Binder, *The New York Times*, August 29, 1993.
93. Gutman at Goteborg, *ibid.*
94. Gutman, *ibid.*

It is worth remembering that Omarska and other camps opened on or about June 26, 1992, and Krsic's phone call came to Gutman in Belgrade on July 9, 1992.

Gutman said he was given a "very precise list of the locations." Ten days after arriving in Banja Luka, Gutman wrote about the Manjaca detention camp, which he'd just visited, and about the "worst sounding" Omarska "concentration camp," which he'd only heard about. Gutman didn't hold back. His *Newsday* stories based on Krsic's information during those few days in late July used phrases like "concentration camps," "Nazi Third Reich" and even the fictional post-World War II movie "Stalag 17."[95] Two days later he repeated the hearsay about Omarska being a "death camp" and that the drama was "like Jews being deported to Auschwitz."

In his Goteborg remarks in December 1994, Gutman repeated how he decided "to spend a few weeks, searching for survivors from Omarska." But when he was interviewed in Chicago by Sondra Gair in 1993, he had said precisely it took only ten days for Muslim "charity" groups in Zagreb to bring just two alleged survivors to him. At Goteborg, with Krsic sitting alongside, Gutman claimed that "maybe as many as 5,000 were killed in the course of just a couple of months (at Omarska)." Not surprisingly, Gutman avoided quoting Jadranka Cigelj, whom Deichmann had exposed, and her statement on April 5, 1993, that 11,800 inmates had allegedly died at Omarska. "A minimum of a thousand people were killed there," Gutman then conceded in a huff after being surprised with a challenge from the audience by Nikola Janic, a businessman of Serbian background from Varmdo, Sweden.

How Valid A Witness?

At Goteborg, as in many of Gutman's post-Pulitzer appearances, he shored up the credibility of the sources he used in his reporting and writing of his war time articles. He especially lauded Krsic as a prime source of information for numerous other correspondents. Painting Krsic as credible to other journalists only caused suspicions about Krsic's real role as a government propagandist.

Krsic "is such a valid witness on the events. ...His information was accurate, in terms of what he told me. My colleagues in the press went to him again and again. He basically was a source for all of us."

Gutman, who never named his "colleagues," turned to Krsic on the Goteborg panel, announcing loudly that he had a question for the former Muslim political leader from Banja Luka, the local contact for the U.S. Embassy in Belgrade and Gutman's primary source for articles about revived Third Reich practices. The inquiry was theatrical:

> "And my question is: How, in the midst of this terror that he was living in, did he manage to collect accurate information, and to collate it and to produce it so that we and the rest of the world could find out about the camps and the terrible practices going on in this area?"

As though choreographed, Krsic took his cue and began describing the packed trains that had rolled through Banja Luka with deportees from Kosarac and Prijedor, recalling it was "something we couldn't have imagined in our imaginations at all." He continued, without stating the exact date, that he had once left the railway station and returned home where his emotions overtook him, and he said he tearfully contacted the local Catholic bishop and Muslim mufti who provided no help.

---

95. *A Witness* ..., p. 30.

Gutman and the audience received a muddled, clumsily over-dramatic answer to his question. Gutman then diverted the frowns from Krsic's presentation and, almost mystically, described the supposed element of spontaneity in the routine of journalism:

> "There's a great degree of accident in what we do as reporters, when we do original reporting. There's not a lot of planning. There's a lot of spontaneous thinking and traveling. And if you come upon the story, you come upon it. And often you don't."

He briefly told about how it was one of the goals of the Serb forces to cut through northern Bosnia, linking Serbia in the east with Bosnian Serb regions around Banja Luka and the Serb Krajina in northwestern Bosnia with a narrow but defensible life-line. Gutman said that this "corridor" had been opened "by coincidence, just that same weekend that I heard this tip and the same weekend that I made this phone call." Moments later, Krsic offered his rehearsed corroboration:

> "But luckily, in destiny and coincidence, Roy Gutman gave me a ring on the same day. And, so, started this story."

Krsic said he had only a twenty-four-hour notice when he was invited to participate in the weekend program about the Bosnian and Yugoslav conflicts at the University of Goteborg. Speaking some of the time through an interpreter, Krsic then made an astonishing statement:

> "In spite of everything, this challenge has been so big to me that I'm going to risk everything. I'm going to risk something *false* here, because that's better than not to come." (Italics added)

Krsic seemingly meant he wasn't going to worry about accuracy. Carefully omitting any details about his past vocation or profession, the extroverted Bosnian recalled how he was elected at the end of 1991 as the leader of the Democratic Action Party in Banja Luka, a city which before the war had a predominant population of over 100,000 Serbs and a remaining 100,000 Muslims and other non-Serbs. He said Banja Luka, the second largest city in Bosnia Hercegovina, was frequently visited by Western diplomatic officials, journalists and American congressmen. Krsic said conditions for non-Serbs worsened, causing him to "start to collect information secretly, to select it and to distribute it. We had direct information from concentration camps. Even Serbs used to deliver information to us, some of them in military uniforms."

Describing one alleged incident when over 250 people were murdered during a single twenty-four-hour period. Krsic said 188 corpses were later discovered, and he reported the massacre to local Red Cross officials who said they could only transfer the information to the International Red Cross in Geneva. He said he reported another planned murder of forty men to U.S. Embassy officials in Zagreb, including First Secretary Henry Kelly and Ambassador Peter Galbraith. Krsic boasted his information even reached Bill Clinton, who was campaigning for the U.S. presidency at the time. Krsic said the executions were subsequently prevented.

Krsic said he was also involved with "appeals to international Jewish organiza-tions" to prevent growing Israeli sympathies with Serbia. He said appeals were also sent to the Vatican (!) "but we didn't dare to send the same appeal to the Islamic side because it would be counter-productive." Krsic also told how Serbs in Banja Luka allegedly planned to massacre 5,000 civilians who were rounded up and held in a park named for a famous Jewish citizen. Their scheme, said Krsic, was for a local Serbian commander, whom Krsic did not identify, to murder some of his own soldiers and for blame to be placed on the Muslim mob. But through "coincidence," said Krsic, another Serb commander arrived with his unit "who did not know this scenario and prevented" the slaughter. Gutman gave no indication he'd ever written a story about the sensational scheme described by Krsic, who added that Muslims in Banja Luka had been ready to bring their weapons out of hiding. "It would have been the same thing (as) Warsaw and the Jewish ghetto."

Krsic then tried to return to Gutman's question about how he collected information in Banja Luka about Serb atrocities committed against Muslims:

> "I personally used to go out in the night in dark clothes, looking for information. The more difficult thing was how to send this information out of Banja Luka. I can tell you we used all different methods except (carrier) pigeons. ...In Banja Luka, altogether 350 Bosnians and Muslims were killed, mostly by knives."

Krsic then shouted at the audience in anger:

> "And nobody is responsible for that! Can you imagine that if somebody killed five persons here in Goteborg, and nobody was responsible? Even five dogs?!"

Krsic said the "job for the mass media has not yet been completed."

What had become Krsic's fate as the former Muslim political leader from a remote Bosnian community, the former media hotwire between the U.S. Embassy in Belgrade and hideous "concentration" camps, the former sleuth in black garb who skulked along dark Banja Luka streets to compile death counts for selection and distribution to Western journalists, the U.S. Embassy in Belgrade and the international community? His achievements over a two-year period did not go unrewarded. Without any previous experience in foreign service, he had arrived at Goteborg with his new title as Bosnian Consul in the capital city of Oslo, Norway!

This Trip Was Necessary

In January 1994, Roy Gutman was in his office/home in Villprot on *Zukunftwegstrasse*. He was on the phone, and I sat across the room, looking at his stacks of books and periodicals. I arrived a week early, wondering whether he would answer the many questions about his mysterious associations and his "methods" as a journalist. A large transparent plastic calendar hung on the wall in front of me. In the center was written in large letters: "Is this trip necessary?"

He would recall three months later for another audience what he told Sherry Ricchiardi, Sondra Gair, Terry Gross and others about how he spared no risk of life and limb while searching out the clues, reasons, facts and observations behind the baffling war between Bosnian Croats and Bosnian Muslims in 1993. "It was the war that none of us could write about. It was so damn confusing," he said.[96] So he risked mine fields, arrests and hired an armored vehicle at $1,000 per day to get to the bottom

---

96. Gutman speech at the Freedom Forum, Washington, D.C., April 10, 1994.

of the fighting in Mostar, to get both sides of the story.

"I began by going to the Croat side of the conflict," he said, adding how his World War II fixations were further bolstered. "At times I thought of the correspondents in war time Berlin, talking to *Der Fuhrer,* or to Goebbels or Himmler."

Gutman said he knew the importance of getting both sides—if not all sides—to a story. The task was described as logical and simple.

"So, having seen the Bosnian Croat side, I decided it was time to go over to the Bosnian Muslim side," he said.[97] Even though he risked such a trip to what he described as "hell on earth...(and) the most dangerous place I had ever seen," Gutman's twenty-four-hour stay in Mostar failed to result in any account about the disappearance of more than 25,000 Serbs who had populated Mostar before the war.

"I'm but a reporter who works—I'd like to say, one should get one's fingernails dirty—by digging out information at the scene, by finding people who will tell the story and by telling you the readers what I've found," he said, adding peculiarly that he'd gone to northern Bosnia "somewhat by accident" in 1992.[98] In his numerous public appearances, Gutman routinely read passages from his book, frequently the passages about rapes. "The story about systematic rape, unfortunately, is a true story. It's happened."[99] He spoke about the town of Foca in southeast Bosnia:

> "There was a sports hall where women were kept for two months or so, a group of sixty or seventy women. And rape was routine, every night. This location was incredible though. It was right next to the police station, but the police were unable to do anything about it. How is this possible? Well, you know politics in Los Angeles or any town we live in. Because the people who were doing the crime were protected by top politicians. And in this case the top politicians turned out to be some of Radovan Karadzic's closest associates. One man who was a minister in his government was the man in charge of Foca. A man named Velibor Ostojic. And I was able to get *everybody* to identify him as the man running Foca."[100] (Italics added)

"Everybody," in Gutman's retelling of two stories he wrote about Foca, turned out to be five identified Bosnian government officials, one identified member of a Muslim "benevolent association" and several unidentified sources—all in Sarajevo, almost 100 kilometers from Foca. He also twisted part of a response from Karadzic and tersely added the substance of Karadzic's denial in four sentences at the bottom of the same account Gutman wrote for *Newsday*, datelined Sarajevo. Only initials and fictitious first names of rape victims were used in an accompanying *Newsday* story, datelined Turkey on April 19, 1993.[101]

Same Questions, No Answers—And A Joke!

Roy Gutman was thought by some as usually capable of doing thorough and balanced reporting, which was ascribed to his first book, *Banana Diplomacy: The Making of American Policy in Nicaragua 1981-1987*, about the American

---

97. Gutman, *ibid.*
98. Gutman speech to the Los Angeles World Affairs Council, October 19, 1994.
99. Gutman, *ibid.*
100. Gutman, *ibid.*
101. *Newsday,* "April 19, 1995.

government's chicanery in Central America.[102]

"A reporter's career is an eventful career, as eventful as one wants it to be, in a sense," Gutman told his audience at the Los Angeles World Affairs Council exactly one year later. "It's one of the great professions ...especially if one has the privilege of working for first-class news media, as I have."

There is no doubt that Gutman's disclosures in the summer of 1992 about the Serb-run camps saved lives—maybe other than Muslim lives.

But Gutman had languished over the Serdari massacre for three months. He continually doubted, minimized and scoffed at what Serbs told him. It is not known if he even asked questions about the missing 25,000 Serbs from Mostar. By contrast, when it came to non-Serbs, he took phone calls in his hotel rooms in Belgrade, Zagreb and Sarajevo, and wrote stories only a short time later based on hearsay and double hearsay from supposed "witnesses" provided to him through Bosnian government channels.

Why?

Thinking over all the questions while sitting in his office in Villprot, one couldn't help but notice the photo of about a half-dozen men on the wall. They were posed defiantly, like on a rock band album cover, against a backdrop of what looked like rubble in a war zone, probably in Bosnia. Probably in Sarajevo. I was looking closer at the photo to see if he and John F. Burns were in the group when he hung up the telephone, walked briskly around his desk. He didn't wait for any questions and was already in the midst of complaint. Why, he whined, hadn't I called him before publishing Joan Phillips' criticisms? I started to say that I'd seen his responses to Phillips and that they didn't invalidate her reporting about him. He was agitated and babbled, raising the pitch of his whining.

"People don't always respond to me, but I usually get them eventually," he said. "But that's the thing, you know. If you don't do the basic thing of getting someone to comment, to explain something where there may very well be a legitimate explanation, and not only a legitimate but a serious explanation, it doesn't work."

That's why I was there, I told him, repeating that I wanted to ask him if that applied to any Serbs he'd interviewed or might have interviewed before the appearance of his own stories about alleged "concentration camps" and mass rape.

"...It's not reasonable. It's not factual. And, so, you may write anything you want to, but I suggest you watch out," he went on, without taking a breath. "Because if you claim things that you haven't done, if you haven't done the thorough search that you're supposed to do as a part of any article, as I do as a part of daily journalism, then you can't expect anybody to talk to you."

What was his impression about the overall assertion of media bias and negligence in the Yugoslav wars?

"The substance of your article? Whew!" he continued, shaking his head. "I dig my facts out. And I dig my facts out not just for one story. If you don't check the other side..."

He didn't finish and, no, he wasn't going to answer any of my questions. Why? What was he afraid of?

I got up from the chair. Gutman stood in front of me the entire time. He introduced me to his wife and then said he couldn't talk further and that he was rushed with "ten different things" he had to get done.

Ten months later, I went to Goteborg to question him again—this time in public.

---

102. *Banana Diplomacy: The Making of American Policy in Nicaragua 1981-1987,* New York: Simon and Schuster, 1989.

There were new questions. No, he said. His editor wouldn't allow him to speak privately with me.

Gutman liked to end with a flare at his public appearances. He capped his speech at the Freedom Forum in April 1994 with "a joke" about an "emaciated" concentration camp inmate that was told to him by the Muslim mayor of Mostar. The man, being asked by the camp commandant named Joko if there was anything he needed, only wanted to know the outcome of an episode in an American television soap opera he'd missed. The humor was in poor taste, judging from the few uncertain twitters from the audience. Nobody laughed or applauded. Next, he offered an ironic invitation that suitably applied to his own reporting:

"If you're looking at the American press, please judge us not by what we're doing but what we should be doing."

The Los Angeles Times got its Pulitzer Prize in 1993 for "balanced, comprehensive, penetrating" reporting. *The Wall Street Journal* won its Pulitzer that year for pouring "everything" into its reporting. Gutman and Burns each got half a Pulitzer Prize for one-sided reporting in 1993—both halves on the same side.

Gutman was right when making his somber pronouncement on getting his Pulitzer. There was nothing to celebrate.

Chapter 8

'Can Anybody Hire Ruder-Finn?'

"I'm a journalist. I got my Master's from Northwestern University. I know a little bit about this business."[1]
– **James Harff, of Ruder-Finn Global Public Affairs**

"The danger is that the propaganda has fueled those atrocities by heightening hatreds and inventing untruths. The propaganda has resulted in the inevitable backlash from the other, aggrieved side as they commit an act of revenge."[2]
– **Tom O'Sullivan,** *The Independent.*

Brookings Institute fellow and Balkan expert Susan Woodward eyed her fellow panel members at American University in Washington, D.C., and momentarily chilled the 1993 discussion, stating with piercing conviction that the media is "indisputably a weapon of war, and everybody knows it!"[3]

The crucial propaganda wars in Yugoslavia were won in 1991 and 1992, Woodward said, by Slovenian, Croatian, and Bosnian government information ministries—and their hired public-relations guns. She was then asked but hesitated to name those who had paid for Balkan propaganda, what they bought or to explain how a series of horrifying news reports had manipulated diplomacy and exploited public opinion through a succession of mysterious catastrophes.

The answers were sitting in office buildings just across town on K Street, as everyone knew.

Probably, the most decisive PR success occurred with the spectacular weekend bombing at the market in Sarajevo on February 5, 1994, which caused sixty-eight deaths and about 200 wounded. The mortar blast was later documented by United Nations investigators as originating from nearby Bosnian government troops and not from a single, pinpoint-accurate 120mm mortar fired from distant Serb positions.

---

1. Harff interview, June 1993.
2. "Truth is the first casualty in PR offensive," *The Independent,* August 21, 1992.
3. Woodward, in a panel discussion, "Making Sense Out of Chaos: Reporting the War in Bosnia," American University, October 5, 1993.

The Bosnian government knew they were murdering civilians, including Muslim citizens. They planned it that way. It happened on a Saturday—market day for all Sarajevans. It was a terrorist disaster planned for the media—specifically, for *ABC's* Peter Jennings who "happened" to be nearby, touring Sarajevo's newly rebuilt water system.

"Under no circumstances were we pre-positioned," Jennings insisted, adding he and his camera crew were "three, four, five minutes away by car when the market was attacked. And we took off immediately, and being that close got to the market virtually immediately. I remember 'virtually immediately' because I remember thinking at the time how astonishingly brave my camera team was. ... Having seen one mortar come in *I was convinced we might get another one*. I remember myself hanging back for just a second and the camera team plunged ahead into the market. I thought, 'man, that's gutsy.' So, we were there very, very quickly."[4] (Author's emphasis)

But, Jennings and his camera crew had "seen" nothing "come in" and reacted only to hearing the explosion.

Jennings' arrival at the scene of the explosion "three, four, five minutes" later—and his hesitation to approach the explosion site closer because "I was convinced we might get another one"—was a response from someone who was aware that an initial explosive device was typically followed by a similar delayed detonation of a second planted bomb designed to kill rescuers or, in this case, the top TV news celebrity at *ABC*. Had that happened, the network most responsible for sensationalizing the martyrdom of Sarajevo could have been counted on to push longer and louder for decisive American military intervention in Bosnia.

Succeeding mortar fire on the market would have certainly resumed within "three, four, five minutes" but could never have hit the exact same site. Also, Jennings' camera crew was suspiciously certain enough the attack would only involve a single mortar and that a second explosion would not occur when they rushed into the market-place. But a "star" may have had misgivings about any assurances his crew could have had.

UNPROFOR Commanding General Lewis MacKenzie recalled that Jennings had telephoned him in Sarajevo in early 1993, telling him he was planning to come to the Bosnian capital and asking "about what could be expected. And, I warned him in no uncertain terms that within days after his arrival there would be an enormous event, some kind of massive event."[5]

Jennings was preparing an hour-long *ABC* special program, "Land of Demons," which aired in March 1993.

The program attempted to explain the chaos in Bosnia during the first year of the war, using a mosaic of new and older video. Several remarkable segments featured footage of camera crews actually present with snipers in Sarajevo shootings of civilians! The camera work was provocative as snipers actually shot at victims for the benefit of photographers:

> •Two segments involve stopped Sarajevo trams. First, there is a just-immobilized tram with a body of a man next to it. The camera zooms back into a window and the face of the concealed shooter—a Bosnian government soldier wearing a beret with the Bosnian blue insignia clearly visible and holding a smoking rifle. In another scene, the second tram is stopped as a rocket-propelled grenade (RPG) hits the track about fifty

---

4. Jennings interview, January 8, 2004.
5. MacKenzie interview with author, February 2, 2004.

meters in front of or behind it. No killed or wounded victims are visible.

•Next is a scene of a small blue truck with a dark tarp over the back that is taking fire. One man jumps out the rear of the truck and runs to the front of the truck. The same scene resumes at the end of the program when a second man jumps out the rear as the truck is hit by a low-trajectory RPG. He is wounded in the right leg and falls a few yards away. While on the ground and screaming for help, he is hit by rifle-fire, his right shoulder jolting backward, from an unknown shooter in front of him. The downed man is facing slightly to the right side of the nearby cameraman's position. The shooter is close to the cameraman.

•In another segment, a cameraman is filming a pair of snipers who are firing from inside a building. The photographer pans over the shoulder of the second sniper who drops an unarmed man carrying parcels in front of a building entrance, hitting him in the foot. No uniform or insignia is visible on the uniformed shooters except that they are both firing AK-47s with scopes used predominantly among Bosnian government soldiers.

•The program also uses footage that pans across the body of a dead man, a supposed Bosnian Muslim in Sarajevo who is wearing a striking red coat. The same frame was used as a still in *Newsweek* (Jan. 4, 1993) and again identified as a Bosnian Muslim fatality. In fact, the man was a Serb killed in Vukovar in late 1992.

•The program also features a cameo of Bosnian army rogue commander and later indicted war criminal Naser Oric who, unacknowledged by Jennings, between 1992 and 1995 had marauded through the area around Srebrenica, burning and destroying scores of Serb villages and hamlets, forcing thousands of Serb civilians to flee and murdering nearly 3,300 others. For Jennings and others, Oric posed as a freedom-loving patriot defending Srebrenica despite inciting the 1995 encirclement of the enclave by Bosnian Serb soldiers whom Oric constantly provoked with artillery attacks, using Muslim civilians as shields. He was belatedly arrested in late March 2003 and extradited to The Hague for war crimes prosecution.

The above segments offended Jennings' critics because there are not enough *ABC* disclaimers, and viewers were left with no choice but to accept Jennings' words that introduced the program's closing mosaic of "twelve months worth of images, recorded by our reporters and camera teams here who've watched it happen." In other words, without explanation of whether the footage was obtained from other sources, *ABC's* "reporters and camera teams" could be assumed to have been pre-positioned with the snipers!

And, while Jennings may insist that he and others on his reporting and camera teams were not knowingly pre-positioned in 1993 and 1994, the Bosnian government knew of their precise location and was able to time when the fatal events were triggered.

MacKenzie emphasized that regarding the February 5, 1994, marketplace explosion, there was "no possible way" that Serbs could have targeted a single 120mm mortar to hit the Sarajevo market with such accuracy. "And, certainly not following with a second mortar."

Jennings never wavered in his later accounts about the market bombing:

> "'Good timing makes for good news,' *ABC's* (Peter) Jennings said in a recent interview in which he explained how he and his crew *happened* to be in Sarajevo—just two blocks from the central marketplace—when the fateful shell exploded on February 5 (1994)."[6] (Italics added)

A year later in Sarajevo, Jennings opened another special program, "The Peace-keepers: How the U.N. Failed in Bosnia"—with his dogged reaffirmation about the February 1994 market bombing:

> "We're going to begin this program here in Sarajevo's central market because it was here, just a little more than a year ago, that we came upon the worst single example of terror that this city has ever seen. *A single mortar shell launched into a marketplace* so shocked the world that the major powers finally decided something had to be done to stop the Serbs from shedding civilian blood day after day after day."[7] (Italics added)

Jennings' drive-by Balkan specials were breathtakingly emotional, one-sided and filled with leftover media "objectivity" from the Cold War era. Jennings said he felt "morally obligated" to identify with Sarajevo and the Bosnian war "because it has so many echoes of an earlier war. I did not want to look back some years hence and say either to myself or my kids that I didn't go and bear some witness to what was happening."[8]

But Jennings never answered how he and others in the media drove the pace in the Yugoslav wars or about the part he and *ABC* had in overt efforts to coerce political and battlefield reactions, which included very real casualties on the ground. Clearly, the artillery provocations by combatants in and around Sarajevo adhered to media and diplomatic deadlines.

Jennings and other interventionists were never satisfied during the subsequent sporadic NATO air attacks against Bosnian Serbs (which began a month after the February 5, 1994, market blast) until the full-scale bombings of major Serbian cities occurred in 1999.

Coincidentally, the February 1994 market bombing occurred between the previous weekend's Super Bowl frenzy and the following weekend's start of the 1994 Winter Olympics and the media-hyped showdown between American skaters Tanya Harding

---

6. Dick Kirschten, "Sarajevo's Saviors;" also, "So far, K Street's doing OK," *National Journal*, March 19, 1994.

7. Jennings, "The Peacekeepers—How the U.N. Failed in Bosnia," April 24, 1995

8. Kirschten, *ibid.*

and Nancy Kerrigan. Also, commencement of debate over the controversial national health care issue in the Congress and the Whitewater scandal was poised to preoccupy television news and front pages for weeks and possibly months to come.

In other words, the timing, public relations-wise, was right.

But was it really contrived for the Western media? Was such a question too cynical despite a history of "tragedies" in the Bosnian wars being loosed on the eve of critical diplomatic events? What about the suspicious "timing" of these episodes if staged to blanket media audiences and manipulate responses and policies of governments in reaction to public opinion?

"Throughout twenty-one months of war in Sarajevo, however, no physical evidence has ever been found that suggests Muslims purposely shoot themselves, and at this stage the notion is as preposterous as it is insulting to Bosnian honor," said a testy Tom Gjelten, of *National Public Radio*.[9] Despite plenty of evidence, Gjelten was attempting to divert suspicion that Bosnian Serbs were not responsible after all for the notorious breadline massacre in Sarajevo on May 27, 1992. That explosion outside the bakery on Vasha Miskin Street killed twenty-two and injured about 100 people, including several Serbs—a fact which should have roused media suspicions. More importantly, the controversial incident stampeded the United Nations vote to impose a broad range of lethal economic sanctions against Serbia and Montenegro a few days later. But in the same breath Gjelten conceded that the "accusation that one side in a conflict kills its own people in order to get its enemy blamed for the atrocity is not new in the annals of war propaganda."[10]

All of the questions about the February 1994 market massacre in Sarajevo were answered with subdued media notice on June 6, 1996, when Yasushi Akashi, the U.N. Under-Secretary-General for Humanitarian Affairs and the former head of the U.N. Mission in Bosnia, verified "the existence of a secret U.N. report that blames the Bosnian Muslims..."[11] Self-inflicted terrorism wasn't new in the Bosnian wars, according to Newsweek's military writer and columnist Colonel David Hackworth who made a trip in 1992 to Sarajevo to solve the breadline blast and other questions.

"Such tricks are the oldest ruses of war," said Hackworth, adding that the breadline murders were caused by a remotely detonated Claymore mine![12] Hackworth also reported he was told by a U.N. soldier and other eyewitnesses that "Muslim gunners" also fired a mortar salvo toward Bosnian President Alija Izetbegovic and British Foreign Secretary Douglas Hurd on July 17, 1992—a Friday. (Izetbegovic didn't mind his role as a target in another public relations stunt when he and Marrick Goulding, U.N. Undersecretary for Special Political Affairs, came under fire at the Bosnian Presidency in Sarajevo on Wednesday, May 6, 1992, with the Bosnian war barely a month-old and as Goulding was attempting to negotiate a crucial cease-fire.)

MacKenzie, who was UNPROFOR commander in Sarajevo at the time of Hurd's visit, recalled:

> "On Sir Douglas's arrival, there were ten to fifteen members
> of the TDF (Bosnian Territorial Defense Forces) on either side
> of the building's entrance as a sort of honour guard. Once he

9. Gjelten, "Blaming the Victim," *The New Republic*, December 20, 1993.

10. *Ibid.* Gjelton again insisted Bosnian Serbs were to blame for the 1992 breadline killings in his book, *Sarajevo Daily,* which was published in early 1995. However, his tone had become more modulated in his brief reference to the 1994 Merkale murders—when three times as many people had died!

11. Hackworth, *Newsweek*, February 14, 1994.

12. Hackworth, *ibid.*

had entered the main door, the group of TDF on the right of the entrance joined their colleagues on the left, and the entire group walked round to the west side of the building and took cover. Thirty seconds later, ten mortar rounds landed immediately across the street from the Presidency, and seven innocent citizens were killed or seriously maimed. A pre-positioned pair of ambulances and the local television cameramen on the east side of the building rushed to the scene of the tragedy, collected and filmed the dead and wounded, and moved off in the direction of the Kosevo hospital. There was only circumstantial evidence, but everyone who witnessed the event had an uneasy feeling that it had been orchestrated by the Presidency to place the Serbs in a bad light in front of Sir Douglas and the international media."[13]

The Timing Of Tragedy

As if timed, the flashpoints among Yugoslav and especially Bosnian war dispatches—which produced the loudest outcries from politicians, columnists, editorial writers and members of television news panels—happened at mid-week, just before weekends or near holidays. This was ideal timing, especially for the American press, that was laying out big spreads in the large Sunday newspapers and for scheduling topics for Sunday morning news panel shows on television. But also ideal because weekends and holidays prevented any serious attempts for timely rebuttals from official Serb sources or other authorities.

For example:

- Roy Gutman's infamous *Newsday* stories about alleged Bosnian Serb "concentration camps" at Omarska and Brcko broke on a Sunday, August 2, 1992, the same day that other front-page spreads and television news programs led with the story about the ambush and killing of infant orphans aboard an evacuation bus in Sarajevo.

- John F. Burns' exhaustive interview with "confessed" mass rapist and murderer Borislav Herak in Sarajevo was published and distributed by *The New York Times Wire Service* on Thanksgiving weekend in 1992.

- On a Sunday in 1992, the *BBC* broadcast to 300 million listeners worldwide the false, fantastic story about how Serb snipers were paid a bounty of $600 for every Muslim child they shot.

- The shooting down in 1992 of an Italian cargo plane carrying relief supplies to Sarajevo—at first blamed on the Bosnian Serbs and later challenged by Hackworth and others—happened on a Thursday.

---

13. MacKenzie, *Peacekeeper: The Road to Sarajevo,* Vancouver/Toronto: Douglas & McIntyre, 1993, p. 301.

•The 1992 murder of *ABC* television producer David Kaplan in Sarajevo, also falsely blamed on Serbs, occurred on a Thursday.

• *Time* and *Newsweek* simultaneously produced huge spreads about alleged mass rapes against Muslims by Bosnian Serbs on the long 1993 New Year weekend. (Roy Gutman's and Judy Bachrach's articles about rape were both published in Sunday editions of *Newsday* and *The Philadelphia Inquirer*, respectively.)

•London's *Sunday People* on January 17, 1993, unfurled the headline that read "Crazed Serb bombers may blitz Britain" above a story, quoting an anonymous Foreign Office source who said Serb fanatics might bomb Britain to retaliate if forceful measures were used against them in Bosnia.

•On Wednesday, March 3, 1993, *The New York Times'* Paul Lewis and Chuck Sudetic joined *The Financial Times* of London, the *Associated Press, National Public Radio*, and American television networks in a frenzy of stories about how at least 500 Muslims had been killed by Serbs in the enclave of Cerska. The *AP* took at face value the claim by the Bosnian government that 1,400 people were dead. Some supposedly had their throats slit and *AP*, quoting a source from forty miles away in Tuzla, said Cerska had been flattened after Serb tanks drove around, blasting the town to ruins. A few days later, UNPROFOR Gen. Philippe Morillon reached the area, found it relatively peaceful with no evidence or signs that mass murders or atrocities or total devastation had taken place. Morillon's report was essentially ignored by the media.

•Burns' heart-tugging story in *The New York Times* about Irma Hadzimuratovic broke on Sunday, August 8, 1993, launching a media exploitation of the five-year-old girl who became a world-wide sensation in what U.N. doctors in Sarajevo called a "meat market" fanfare over air evacuations of a handful of injured children. Western governments and humanitarian organizations were swimming in media hype, clawing their way over each other in the PR orgy about air-lifts for wounded tots while left behind were adults and elderly who were in worse condition. Not surprisingly, only Burns blamed the Serbs in another of these curiously timed tragedies that involved a single mortar shell that killed Irma's mother and critically wounded the child who later died in 1995 without similar fanfare in a London hospital.

•Paul Lewis' botched story, "Rape Was Weapon of Serbs, U.N. Says," on October 20, 1993, appeared in *The New York Times* on a Wednesday and misrepresented a U.N. report which actually had identified 800 Serbian women as rape victims. Lewis wrote that the U.N. had identified the "800 victims by name" and omitted that they were Serbs. An unprecedented front-page retraction, acknowledging error in the reporting, appeared later.

•A well-prepared press audience was on hand for the first NATO air strike with American F-16s against Bosnian Serbs at Gorazde on Sunday, April 10, 1994. Another air sortie received lavish coverage when four NATO jets obliterated an obsolete anti-aircraft gun retrieved from a U.N. compound near Sarajevo by Bosnian Serbs, grabbing headlines on Friday, August 5, 1994.

'Honesty...It's Just Not Our Job'

James Harff and Ruder-Finn Global Public Affairs distributed the gruesome story to the American media about Serb snipers who were supposedly paid bounties to shoot Muslim children.

"And the story is almost certainly not true," wrote Karl Waldron shortly after the notorious *BBC* broadcast in 1992.[14] Waldron detailed how it originated from a "volunteer aid worker," who was told the story by Croats and Muslims while he was in a truck convoy to Sarajevo. The story was repeated and written by a Muslim journalist in a Croatian newspaper. It later was aired by *Radio Croatia International* and was monitored by the *BBC*, said Waldron, who pinpointed the tale as having its origins from a faxed message "from the fax machine in the offices of *Ruder-Finn* in Washington."[15]

Waldron followed the trail of the story, obtaining a response from a Ruder-Finn spokeswoman about how the story was spread throughout the media after a company spokeswoman, Rhoda Paget, said it came from "a minister in the Croatian government" and that they checked the truthfulness of it before distributing it. Truthfulness wasn't the PR firm's job and it was up to reporters to check the facts. Waldron was told.[16]

Waldron noted that Ruder-Finn claimed it was being paid a meager retainer of $18,000 per month by the government of Croatia. But, David Finn tried feebly to persuade the monthly magazine, *Midstream*, that his company had even charitably donated its PR services to the Croatian government since August 1991, when the war was barely two-months-old.[17]

Waldron and others noted the "bounty on children" story had the ring of a predecessor during the first Persian Gulf War and the fictitious testimony by the Kuwaiti ambassador's daughter before the Congressional Human Rights Caucus which listened—wide-eyed and open-mouthed—to tales of hospitalized infants brutally murdered by Iraqi soldiers. The Washington PR firm of Hill & Knowlton Inc. was a principal instigator in that incident.

After being exposed as propagandists in the bungling of the Kuwaiti hospital story, Hill & Knowlton had become sensitive about its latest war-time propaganda roles and rushed to challenge *Konkret* magazine's Boris Groendahl in Hamburg in March 1994, threatening legal action. The firm wanted an immediate retraction for *Konkret's* reprint of the *Foreign Policy* article which said Hill & Knowlton was one of several American public relations agencies operating in Yugoslavia during the

---

14. Waldron, "Spin doctors of war," *New Statesman & Society,* July 1992.

15. Waldron, *ibid.*

16, Waldron, *ibid.*

17. Finn, in a letter of response to *Midstream* published in the journal's August/September 1994.

federation's disintegration in the late 1980s.[18]

Groendahl produced U.S. Justice Department documents, showing Hill & Knowlton had in fact been a registered agent for Yugoslav interests—ostensibly for tourism work—under the Foreign Agents Registration Act in the late 1980s.

The bluff added light to the firm's murky activities that were scrutinized in 1993 by San Francisco journalist Johan Carlisle who traced Hill & Knowlton's links directly to the White House, the Central Intelligence Agency and the American media.[19]

Carlisle was managing editor of the periodical, *Propaganda Review*. Hill & Knowlton was also mentioned in a 1992 report by *The Independent* that described how "in Britain, Croatian representatives were negotiating with lobbying firms, including Hill & Knowlton, offering 500,000 British pounds (about a million dollars U.S.) for a campaign to win official recognition and raise the profile of Croatia."

Carlisle's eye-popping expose reported that "in 1991, the top fifty U.S.-based PR firms billed over $1,700,000,000 in fees"(!), according to the 1992 edition of *O'Dwyer's Directory of Public Relations Firms*.

In late 1993, when President Clinton was receiving his strongest criticisms from the media for the administration's inaction on U.S. military intervention to quell the Bosnian wars, former Hill & Knowlton executive Howard Paster left his post as White House advisor/strategist and returned to Hill & Knowlton to take over as chief executive officer. Paster's influence on the Clinton Administration's early policies toward the Balkans is not specifically known, but the favoritism toward Croatia and Bosnian Muslims from the White House and its antagonism toward Serbia coincided with Paster's influential tenure in the Clinton Administration:

> "Public relations and lobbying firms are part of the revolving door between government and business that President Clinton has vowed to close. It is not clear how he will accomplish this goal when so many of his top appointees, including Ron Brown and Howard Paster, are 'business as usual' Washington insiders. ...Paster, former head of Hill and Knowlton's Washington office, directed the confirmation process during the transition period and is now Director of Intergovernmental Affairs."[20]

Carlisle's conclusions were shared by others who were alarmed about the high percentage of press releases spawned by PR agencies that reached the news columns of prestigious newspapers:

> "One of the most important ways public relations firms influence what we think is through the massive distribution of press releases to newspapers and TV newsrooms. One study found that forty percent of the news content in a typical U.S. newspaper originated with public relations press releases, story memos, or suggestions. *The Columbia Journalism Review*, which scrutinized a typical issue of the Wall Street Journal, found that more than half the Journal's news stories 'were based solely on press releases.' Although the releases were reprinted 'almost verbatim or in

---

18. Groendahl interview with the author, March 1994.

19. Carlisle, "Public Relationships: Hill & Knowlton, Robert Gray and the CIA," *CovertAction*, Spring 1993.

20. Carlisle, *ibid*.

paraphrase,' with little additional reporting, many articles
were attributed to 'a *Wall Street Journal* staff reporter.'"[21]

Other disturbing observations from Carlisle included:

> "While the use of the U.S. media by the CIA has a long and
> well-documented history, the covert involvement of PR firms
> may be news to many. ...Reporters were paid by the CIA, some-
> times without their media employers' knowledge, to get the
> material in print or on the air. But other news organizations
> ordered their employees to cooperate with the CIA ...and the
> CIA had 'tamed' reporters and editors in scores of newspaper
> and broadcast outlets across the country. To avoid direct
> relationships with the media, the CIA recruited individuals
> in public relations firms like H&K (Hill & Knowlton) to act as
> middlemen for what the CIA wanted to distribute."[22]

Justice Department rules and enforcement of foreign agent registrations are soft
if not inherently negligent:

> "Nor does the updated Foreign Agents Registration Act have real
> teeth. The act—legislated in 1938 when U.S. PR firms were
> discovered working as propagandists and lobbyists for Nazi
> Germany—is rarely enforced."[23]

Identified by Carlisle as one of "H&K's highly paid agents of influence" was
"Democratic power broker Frank Mankiewicz." Mankiewicz simultaneously responded
in 1993 when *Newsday's* Roy Gutman falsely denied that Hill & Knowlton had not
represented Yugoslav clients—contrary to Justice Department records that Gutman,
apparently, never bothered to check![24]

Three-Way PR In A Five-Sided War

Ruder-Finn Inc. was unique among PR operatives in Yugoslavia's five civil
wars and until June 1993 handled propaganda for Croatia and its Bosnian
Croat ally which was locked in fierce combat with another Ruder-Finn
client—the government of Bosnia-Herzegovina. Ruder-Finn's third client at the time
was the faction of dissident Muslim Albanian secessionists in Kosovo.

---

21. Study by Scott M. Culip, ex-dean of the School of Journalism and Mass
Communications at the University of Georgia, cited in Martin A. Lee and Norman
Soloman, *Unreliable Sources: A Guide to Detecting Bias in News Media*, New York:
Lyle Stuart, 1990.
22. Carlisle in *Covert Action,* quoting from Susan B. Trento's *The Power House:
Robert Keith Gray and the Selling of Access and Influence in Washington,*
New York: St. Martin's Press, 1992
23. Carlisle, *ibid.*
24. See Gutman, "Letters to the Editor," *Foreign Policy,* No. 94, Spring 1994, p. 158.
Hill & Knowlton Inc. was on file at the U.S. Justice Department as a
Yugoslav agent on its Pending Foreign Principals list: Registration No. 03301,
May 10, 1987 and February 22, 1988.

According to David Finn, Phyllis Kaminsky, of Phyllis Kaminsky & Associates of Potomac, Maryland, was Ruder-Finn's "senior international adviser" during February 1992.[25] Kaminsky handled public relations for the secessionist Republic of Slovenia through 1992.[26]

"Slovenia is the one that broke up Yugoslavia and caused all the wars!" exclaimed Susan Woodward.[27]

Harff was far from secretive about Ruder-Finn's Balkan clients:

> "Our role is to identify the aggressor and the victim which has been obscured by either a lack of information or Serbian propaganda. ...The overriding objective was to develop a Croatian profile when competing against other foreign policy initiatives in Washington. Our main targets were the media, Capitol Hill and the Bush administration. There was a dearth of information among policy-makers on the Foreign Affairs Committee."[28]

The Independent's Tom O'Sullivan said that "the Ruder-Finn strategy has been to build a congressional and Senate coalition in the U.S. in support of Croatia."

Canadian journalist Mike Trickey wrote that Ruder-Finn had "decades of experience in representing foreign governments in Washington" noting that the firm:

> "...(S)cored another coup in the final days of the Bush administration when the White House warned Belgrade it would not tolerate aggression against Kosovo. That was quite a change from the previous year when the emphasis was on the integrity of the borders. 'Getting (former secretary of state Lawrence) Eagleburger to name names and talk of war crime trials was obviously a breakthrough,' says Mr. Harff, who had worked for three congressmen over an eight-year period. It is those kinds of successes, some of which could drag a third country into war, that encourage voiceless nations and factions to hire the lobbying pros."[29] (Italics added)

The "getting" of Eagleburger was left tantalizingly unexplained by Harff and Trickey.

But by mid-1993, as Bosnian Croats along with regular Croatian troops began to slaughter and be slaughtered by Bosnian Muslims, Ruder-Finn faced a bizarre conflict of interests. It was decided to hand the Croatian PR account to Waterman Associates —but not before Ruder-Finn received its 1993 "Silver Anvil Award from the Public Relations Society for its Bosnia work." Its mercenary role focused exclusively on promoting the oft-tainted causes of its Bosnian Muslim and Albanian Muslim clients.

Waterman was not new to promoting interests of former communist states of the U.S.S.R. It had represented the Chechen Republic since January 1993 and demonstrated a wide variety of access to official policy-makers, organizing briefings with the U.S. Department of State, Department of Defense, the "intelligence community as

25. Finn letter to the editor, *Midstream*, August/September 1994.
26. O'Sullivan, *The Independent*, August 21, 1992.
27. Woodward, American University panel discussion on "Making Sense Out of Chaos: Reporting the War In Bosnia," October 5, 1993.
28. O'Sullivan, *ibid.*
29. Trickey, "War propagandists for hire: Croatia, Bosnia use Western public relations firms to win support," *Hamilton (Ontario) Spectator*, February 12, 1993.

well as private sector individuals who are interested in Checcinya (sic)."[30]

Waterman also organized four specific meetings and/or presentations on Croatia's behalf with Israeli and American Jewish community representatives. Waterman set up sessions for visiting Croatian President Franjo Tudjman with Senators Robert Dole, Joseph Biden, Richard Lugar, and U. S. House Members Tom Lantos, Charles Wilson, Dana Rohrabacher and Susan Molinari—all with exploitable biases for Croatia and demonstrated animosities against the Serbs. Waterman reported to the Justice Department that it had pocketed $150,000 from Croatia from March to June 1993, including that Waterman consultant David M. Barrett had donated a conspicuously modest $500 campaign contribution to Lantos. Waterman, which had signed a $300,000 contract with the Croatian government,[31] was also representing a vaguely identified client, presumably with Islamic orientations, called the "Lebanese Forces," headquartered in Juniyah, Lebanon, according to its August 1993 report filed with the Justice Department.

Outwitting The Jews

Small doubt that copies of Yohanan Ramati's essay in *Midstream*, published for a small circulation in New York City, spread like wildfire throughout Jewish communities in North America and Europe in April 1994. Ramati was the respected and outspoken director of the Jerusalem Institute for Western Defense.

Ramati wrote about how the Croatian and Bosnian Muslim publicity campaign had specifically and successfully targeted and "outwitted" the Jewish community in North America. The article also referred to Harff, who was usually glib but later refused any comment about Ramati or Ruder-Finn's representation of Croat and Bosnian/Kosovo Muslim clients.[32]

Especially stinging in Ramati's outburst against the biased media coverage in the Yugoslav wars were condemnations aimed directly at complicity among the Jewish community:

> "The American Jewish organizations and leaders outwitted by Ruder & Finn can now pat themselves on the back. They have played a major role in gaining the world's sympathy for anti-Semitic regimes in Yugoslavia. They are 'politically correct.'... It may take more than the embargo, Ruder & Finn and the equivocations of democratic politicians and journalists—among them some Jews—to break the spirit of a proud people."[33]

Ramati said the "organized anti-Serb and pro-Muslim propaganda" omitted accounts about "the killing and maiming of Serb women and children by Muslim fire in Bosnia or by Croat fire in Croatia." He said it was reminiscent of another sensitive era for Jews:

> "It recalls Hitler's propaganda against the Allies in World War II. Facts are twisted and, when inconvenient, disregarded. The selectivity in reporting and comment is far too blatant to

---

30. U.S. Justice Department, six-month report for foreign agent registration No. 4738, August 2, 1993.
31. *O'Dwyer's Washington Report,* Vol. III, No. 12, June 7, 1993.
32. Harff interview with the author, April 1995.
33. Ramati, "Stopping the War in Yugoslavia," *Midstream,* April 1994.

be accidental. The Western governments do not control their
media sufficiently to be responsible for it. So who is? Who is
bankrolling and masterminding this vast effort to destroy a
people the United States, England and France have no reason
to hate in order to establish a second Muslim state in a Balkan
province where the Muslims are a minority?"[34]

Ramati was suspicious about who was paying the costly expenses for Ruder-
Finn's work with Croatia, the Bosnian Muslim government and the Kosovo
Muslims:

> "It seems unlikely that the governments of Bosnia-Herzegovina
> and Croatia could raise the money required. Are we dealing
> here with Arab money? With the money of U.S. oil companies
> operating in the Arab states? With the money of international
> banks? Can anybody hire Ruder & Finn?"

Three months later came David Finn's carefully worded reply for *Midstream* in
a letter to the editor. The response in chronological form raised more questions than
it answered. Finn claimed Ramati's report included the account of a short interview
by French television journalist Jacques Merlino with Harff in 1993 that, Ruder-Finn
claimed, was a "fabricated conversation." Finn continued:

> "There is, in fact, no mystery about who paid Ruder-Finn...
> We *were* paid by the governments themselves... We worked
> for these governments without a profit for our firm because
> of our great sympathy for the sufferings of their people. In fact,
> we contributed more than $100,000 in *pro bono* advice and
> counsel." (Finn's italics)

He attempted to erase concerns with the World War II comparisons penned by
Ramati, saying that Ruder-Finn had internally resolved the issue:

> "Knowing about Croatian anti-Semitism during the Hitler
> years, our ethics committee thoroughly discussed the issue
> before accepting Croatia as a client. It was only after we received
> a statement in support of the present government from the
> Jewish community of Croatia, that we felt we could proceed."

Finn referred to a "statement" from the "Council of the Jewish Community in Zagreb"
on October 7, 1991, "condemning indiscriminate attacks on the Croatian civilian
populations and historical monuments, including Jewish sites." The Council's statement was unsigned. The Yugoslav federal army, which was "controlled by Serbs,"
was blamed. But the incidents, including the desecration of the Jewish cemetery and
synagogue in Zagreb, occurred during a period when the surrounded federal army
was either captive inside its garrisons or was withdrawing eastward toward Serbia.
In Zagreb, such "attacks" that whipped up anti-JNA fervor were widely regarded
as faked. Also, the alleged attacks on "Jewish sites" occurred simultaneously
and incredulously with the Croat dismantling of the memorial at Jasenovac where

---

34. Ramati, *ibid.*

at least 60,000 Jews and Gypsies along with 600,000 or more Serbs were brutally murdered during World War II. Finn's spin was that "efforts to depict Croatia as anti-Semitic and neo-Fascist" were false, attempting to blur the contradiction with the stark statement by the Zagreb Council. Finn claimed anecdotally that Tudjman had even given refuge to the son of a "leading Jewish physician (who had) fled Croatia" during World War II.

But it is well-known historically that persecuted Jews in Croatia and elsewhere in the region fled *to* Serbia during World War II to escape the Nazi's and their Croat Ustashe collaborators.

What Finn did not say was that swastikas again proliferated in Zagreb and throughout the rest of Croatia along with other Nazi and Ustashe regalia since the late 1980s. Also, the "new" Croatian unit of currency was the *kuna*, which was used by the Ustashe puppet government during the Second World War. The resurrection of the *kuna* not only sent a strong warning to Serbs living in Croatia, but also to Jews. But more telling was the strong and detailed denunciation of President Tudjman's regime as "fascism" by the former president of the Jewish community in Zagreb, Slavko Goldstein:

> "A new wave of political terrorism that has been spreading across Croatia quietly and covertly until recently has come into the open. ...It is an open secret that telephones are tapped by the Croatian Ministry of the Interior...(and) the kind of terrorism which shows itself permanently as a system of government. In other words, it is fascism."[35]

Goldstein was the internationally respected head of the *Erasmus Guild* publishing house and "became an idol of the Croat public during the 1980s thanks to his publishing and other cultural activities independent of the communist regime.

He was a founder of the first non-communist political party in Croatia, the Social Liberal Party, which led the anti-Tudjman opposition."[36]

Goldstein's "declaration" also called outright for the removal of Gojko Susak, the Croatian defense minister and previous "pizzeria operator from Canada."

In his *Midstream* rebuttal, Finn quoted from a February 18, 1992, letter to Tudjman from Chief Rabbi of Jerusalem Noah Weinberg in which Tudjman was praised for his "important work of safeguarding religious freedom."

According to Finn, Weinberg "added, 'our involvement stands as a symbol of understanding—a testament to Croatia's investiture in religious freedom. We have been assured that the place of the Jewish people is now secure in your democracy.'"

No matter that Finn's praises of the new regime came at a time when Israel itself balked at extending diplomatic recognition to the Republic of Croatia.

Ruder-Finn's vigorous agenda on behalf of the Bosnian government after May 1992, said Finn, included representative activities such as "Organization of the Islamic Conference emergency session on Bosnia-Herzegovina held in June (1992); the Conference on Security and Cooperation in Europe in Helsinki in July (1992); the London Conference on Former Yugoslavia in August (1992); and the United Nations General Assembly in October (1992)."[37]

---

35. Stephen Schwartz, "Tudjman Regime Rebuked," *The Jewish Forward*, November 4, 1994.

36. Schwartz, *ibid*.

37. Finn letter to *Midstream*.

He also noted "private meetings" were arranged by Ruder-Finn for the propaganda-happy Bosnian Prime Minister Haris Silajdzic with former British Prime Minister Lady Margaret Thatcher, then presidential candidate and Senator (later Vice President) Albert Gore, Saudi Ambassador to the U.S. Prince Bandar, President Bush and Secretary of State James Baker in Helsinki.

Finn was generous in extolling his firm's connections.

He recited an impressive list of contacts with the media and Congress, along with connections made with the intelligence community and humanitarian agency activities that were carried out in the U.S., Europe and the Middle East, concluding with self-congratulation for a blatant conflict of interests:

> "We feel that our work for all three governments has been conducted in accordance with the highest standards of professional integrity. It has been difficult to work within the limited budgets provided by governments that are defending themselves militarily, but it has been a privilege to be of help to people who are enduring such great suffering."[38]

The Pogroms Of Sarajevo

Finn's letter to *Midstream* attempted at least one example of propaganda when he described the "Serbian naval and land artillery attacks on defenseless, and *Serb-less*, ancient Dubrovnik." (Italics added)
Initial inspections showed the old city appeared to be only slightly damaged:

> "The old city received forty-nine shells in its three-month bombardment, but only seven were primed to explode."[39]

The predictable "official" revisions later claimed damages and casualties were much higher:

> "...(T)he Yugoslav Army bombarded Dubrovnik by air, land and sea. Two thousand shells fell on the city. ...More than 200 people died during the siege, and 632 people were injured."[40]

But "Serb-*less*" Dubrovnik"? In fact, the few examples of serious damage in Dubrovnik were from explosions and fires set off in and around the 17th Century Serbian Orthodox Church, its adjoining library and manse.[41] Reports submitted to the United Nations also describe the "ethnic cleansing" of 4,000 Serbs from Dubrovnik.

The Dubrovnik saga also overshadowed if not intentionally obscured the fate of the Jewish community in Sarajevo that was appallingly concealed and ignored by correspondents who obliviously and tediously celebrated the city for its multi-ethnic, religiously tolerant character.

---

38. Finn, *ibid.*
39. Gillian Darley, *The Financial Times*, October 15, 1994.
40. Margot Patterson, "Dubrovnik after war: Recovery and remembrance," *National Catholic Reporter*, November 2, 2001.
41. From videotape (shown on *Chicago Public Television*) and report of on-site inspections in 1992 by Professor John Peter Maher three months after the supposedly devastating bombardments.

Eluding Finn—not to mention *Newsday's* Roy Gutman, *The New York Times'* John F. Burns, *CNN's* Christiane Amanpour and others—were incidents that instantly sounded storm warnings to Jewish leaders in Sarajevo and mobilized a prompt and quiet exodus.

The simplistic presumption about the abandonment of cosmopolitan Sarajevo by the Jews was that it was due to the havoc from Bosnian Serb artillery that raked the city. But the memories of persecution, murder and deportation at the hands of the Nazis and their Muslim collaborators in World War II were more compelling.[42]

National Public Radio's Tom Gjelton, with his attempt in 1995 to produce the definitive volume on Sarajevo's demise, gave only astonishingly superficial treatment to the latest exodus of Jewish evacuees, noted only that half the city's population had evacuated by early 1994, "including a majority of the Serbs *and Jews* and many Muslims and Croats who had financial resources or international connections."[43]

Western journalists could have probed the deeper causes of Jewish flight from Sarajevo had they visited the city's decimated synagogue and inquired for the whereabouts of its former members.

Gjelton and others could have probed the deeper causes of Jewish flight from Sarajevo had they visited the city's decimated synagogue and inquired for the whereabouts of its former members.

Gjelton could have consulted with columnist and essayist, Zlatko Dizdarevic, who was on the staff of *Oslobodjenje*, as to when—if not why—the Jewish exodus actually began. After all, the celebrated newspaper's valiant endurance as the only surviving news outlet in Sarajevo, although admittedly under various phases of government control, was Gjelton's backdrop for extolling Sarajevo's exaggerated pluralism which was more believed by the media than by the scores of thousands of its original citizens who fled.

Several pre-war newspapers and news journals had healthy circulations before the war but eventually folded while *Oslobodjenje* attracted international support from Western media and financial contributors with pro-Muslim sympathies. It actually served the propaganda purposes of the Sarajevo government as a centerpiece of supposed democracy in its local media.

Dizdarevic himself was deeply troubled by the crumbling multi-cultural fabric of Sarajevo in his August 18, 1992, essay that Sarajevo's "Jews will *return* one day, I'm sure of that" He questioned whether the essence of the city's character would continue "after the departure of its Jews, *who have already packed their bags. The last seven hundred are about to go...*"[44] (Italics added)

Dizdarevic took up the theme of the departing Jews again on February 2, 1994, bemoaning that the Jews, who had populated Sarajevo for a half-century and assigning blame not just to "the evil committed against us all but also by the world's indifference"—and by the Zagreb regime![45]

---

42. Sarajevo's Jewish population numbered 8,196 on the eve of World War II and was wiped out by November 1941 when Germans and local Muslims deported 14,000 Bosnian Jews from the area—including 4,000 men, 4,000 women and 6,000 children—to the Loborgrad, Jasenovac and Stara Gradiska death camps. Less than 1,000 survived the war. See Martin Gilbert, *The MacMillan Atlas of the Holocaust*, New York: DaCapo Press Inc., 1982; p. 75.

43. Gjelton, Sarajevo Daily: A City and Its Newspaper Under Siege, New York: Harper Collins, 1995, p. 16.

44. Dizdarevic, *Sarajevo: A War Journal*, New York: Henry Holt and Company, 1995, p. 136.

45. Dizdarevic, *ibid.* p. 186.

Dizdarevic, apparently, was not referring to a permanent residency in view of Jewish persecution and deportation to Holocaust camps during World War II. The chorus of journalistic protest about the Jews' leaving now was almost too much of an invitation to look for other ...reasons.

Two months after Finn's letter in *Midstream*, the *Jewish Chronicle* reported that leaders of the Jewish community in Sarajevo had recently disclosed "an apparent campaign to discredit the community and its leaders." The article cited a series of arrests and interrogations of "a number of Sarajevo Jews, some of whom hold dual Bosnian-Israeli citizenship" and the seizure of "passports and communal documents."[46] The report detailed an incident on July 14, 1994:

> "...(W)hen a car with four Jewish passengers was searched and its occupants detained for 'informative talks.' Later, the vice-president of the community, Danilo Nikolic, was reportedly held for five days, during which he was interrogated ten hours a day. Sonya Elazar, head of a Jewish women's organization in Sarajevo, and the niece of the late Lieutenant-General David 'Dado' Elazar, the Israeli chief of staff during the 1973 Yom Kippur War, has also been questioned. Ivan Ceresnjec, president of the Sarajevo (Jewish) community, said the police seemed intent upon establishing that Jews had been conniving with the enemy. ...Seeking the return of the passports and papers, Mr. Ceresnjec met the Bosnian Prime Minister Haris Silajdzic, and the Chief of State Security, Nenad Ugljen. ...Mr. Silajdzic assured communal leaders that the police action had been an 'unfortunate' episode and that the documents would be promptly returned. 'But I waited for two weeks, and nothing happened,' said Mr. Ceresnjec, (adding) ...allegations by Bosnian officials that Jews were acting against Bosnian national interest were totally unfounded."[47]

As of late 1998, there was no measurable or loudly public repatriation of any of Sarajevo's Jewish community despite forced resettlements of Muslim, Croat and Serb refugees under the Dayton agreements.

The War Rooms On 'K' Street

Finn said that his firm "worked closely" with the Bosnian government for eight months, beginning in May 1992 when Ruder-Finn "was approached by the then Bosnian Foreign Minister Haris Silajdiz (sic) to assist his government with news media relations in the U.S. and internationally." Ruder-Finn also continued to work for Croatian "tourism officials" through March 1994 despite the announcement that it was unloading the Croatian government as a client in mid-1993.[48] "Harff insists that they've not worked for them since December 1992," said Dick Kirschten, of *The National Journal*.[49] But Harff was highly visible when he appeared with Silajdzic in June 1993 at the International Human Rights Convention in Vienna.

---

46. Valerie Monchi, "Sarajevo Jews arrested," *Jewish Chronicle*, September 2, 1994.
47. Monchi, *ibid.*
48. Dick Kirschten, *ibid.*
49. Kirschten correspondence with the author, June 4, 1994.

After the two-week convention was opened, the rules were abruptly set aside to allow Silajdzic's drum-beating on the plight of Bosnia and his unfounded claim of 200,000 Bosnian Muslim deaths, offering no proof for the average of nearly 500 daily fatalities. Delegates from 160 countries and a thousand humanitarian organizations allowed the convention's agenda to be hijacked by Silajdzic's high-pressure salesmanship that eventually succeeded in mustering an 88-to-1 vote to officially condemn the U.N. for prolonging the war.[50]

The convention was also coerced into demanding that the arms embargo be lifted for Bosnia, and the grandstanding also included a specious $20,000 award to Sarajevo's regime-friendly newspaper *Oslobodjenje* from the Houston-based Rothko Chapel's Oscar Romero Foundation for "truth and editorial courage."[51]

Harff's activities in Vienna were observed by George Jahn, covering the event for the *Associated Press*' Vienna bureau and a longtime Balkan correspondent. Jahn featured Harff and Ruder-Finn in a story about the maneuvering at the Vienna convention. The story would have added significant insight about the phenomenon of media and political manipulation by Washington PR specialists. Jahn's boss, *Associated Press* bureau chief Alison Smale recalled how the story was put on the wire to *AP's* New York City bureau, but Smale said that the New York editors for the world's largest news-distribution organization held back the story from newspapers and television.[52]

"It was a great story," said Smale stiffly. "But they killed it in New York."

Several attempts were made to ask Vice President and Executive Editor Bill Ahearn questions about the *Associated Press*' policies and performance in coverage of the Yugoslav wars—and about Jahn's story on Harff. But, surprisingly for a career journalist, Ahearn refused any comment. "I'm not going to talk to a journalist who's convoluted and twisted the facts as you have," Ahearn snapped over the telephone from New York, refusing to explain his accusations. "That's as far as I'm going to go."[53]

Jahn didn't sound surprised when describing the story and why it was kept off the national wire in the U.S.

"I have to tell you I actually tried to do a story about him, and it never cleared my senior editors," Jahn said, chuckling. "...I thought it was a pretty credible story because I exposed all sides of it, and I basically said what this guy does. And he gets paid for it."[54]

The Western media could not have waged a more formidable campaign of bias in the Yugoslav wars had policies for news coverage been devised directly from the K Street war rooms of the high-dollar public relations firms in Washington, D.C. and elsewhere. This was where strategies were meticulously worked out for the media offensives by American PR strategists who were the hirelings of Slovenian, Croatian, Bosnian Muslim and Kosovo Muslim clients. And it was simply hypocritical to plead, as did Finn, that they were doing it out of sympathy—or for free.

'National Treasure Or Messianic Manipulator'

There could not have existed a more formidable "commander-in-chief" in the Balkan media wars than the Hungarian-born George Soros, a naturalized U.S. citizen but almost publicly invisible billionaire and eccentric Jewish philanthropist.

50. Alan Riding, *The New York Times*, June 16, 1993.
51. *Associated Press*, June 16, 1993.
52. Smale interview with the author in Vienna, January 10, 1994.
53. Ahearn interview with the author, June 17, 1994.
54. Jahn interview with author, April 1995.

An eight-page *Business Week* magazine cover story in 1993 pictured Soros standing defiantly beside the Kremlin.[55] The story headline read: "The Man Who Moves Markets."

The article branded him as "super-investor and benefactor George Soros (who) is the scourge of Europe's central banks" but only superficially explored Soros' manipulations with Yugoslav "charities" and his ambitious media investments in Central and Eastern Europe.

The best source for clues about the magnitude of Soros' character and his motives as a self-anointed monarch and supreme mover/shaker within the Balkan cauldron came from Soros himself. His calling and confession are glimpsed in an introspective passage from Soros' book, *The Alchemy of Finance*, written in 1987:

> "There is a point beyond which self-revelation can be damaging, and one of the flaws in my character, which I have not fully fathomed, is the urge to reveal myself."[56]

The New Yorker magazine dug further into the Soros mystique, describing him as "an unregulated billionaire with a messiah complex." The marathon twenty-four-page profile was aptly titled "The World According to Soros."[57] Soros and others occasionally pondered his imagined messiah-ship. *Newsday's* Roy Gutman secularly described Soros as "a sort of would-be secretary-of-state."[58] But *The New Yorker* put a sharper focus on Soros' freelance political portfolio:

> "He has opened a Washington office, which, as one Soros associate (said) will function as 'his State Department.'... 'People in government used to sort of dismiss George—this crazy guy interested in Hungary,' said Morton Abramowitz, the former United States Ambassador to Turkey, who is now the president of the Carnegie Endowment for International Peace, and has participated in a Soros-funded advocacy group on the Balkans. 'He's now become a player—but it's very recent, a new phenomenon.' Abramowitz went on, 'He's untrained, idiosyncratic—he gets in there and does it, and he has no patience with government. As I frequently say about George, he's the only man in the U.S. who has his own foreign policy—and can implement it.' ...Whether national treasure or messianic manipulator, this much is plain: Soros, the archetypal outsider all his life, has finally found a club to which he wants to belong. ... 'There is a certain thrill in dealing with affairs of state."[59]

Soros never hesitated to publicly push for outright U.S. recognition for the former Yugoslav republic of Macedonia, an act that many said would ignite a new front in the Balkan wars with Greece, Bulgaria, Albania, Turkey and Kosovo inevitably drawn into the mayhem.

Eyebrows in Congress were raised in confused surprise during mid-summer of 1993 when President Clinton, after quiet consultations with members of the still-

---

55. *Business Week*, August 23, 1993.
56. T*he Alchemy of Finance*, New York: John Wiley and Sons Inc., 1987; p. 363.
57. Connie Bruck, *The New Yorker*, January 23, 1995.
58. Gutman speech at Freedom Forum, October 4, 1994.
59. Bruck, *ibid.*

unrecognized Macedonian government, ordered Company C of the U.S. Army's Berlin Brigade to affix the United Nations' insignia to its newly repainted white armored personnel carriers while 300 U.S. soldiers put on blue helmets and departed on July 4th for Macedonia.[60] Soros, however, did not appear to be pacified with this consolation gesture of Macedonian occupation by American troops.

There was no audible protest from Congress about the Macedonian "invasion," which was practically kept secret from the American public that was then immersed in new anxieties after a sudden missile attack against Iraq. Also, the bizarre strategy for U.S. soldiers to dig in along the Macedonian frontier next to Kosovo was obscurely coat-tailed to a new commitment to use American air power under NATO in Bosnia:

> "The American announcement ... coincided with a commitment by NATO to use its warplanes to defend U.N. peacekeeping troops throughout Bosnia, if they come under attack and ask for NATO's help. France, Britain, Turkey, and the Netherlands joined the United States in offering air units for the mission. The rules of engagement for the air units remain to be defined by the United Nations. ...*The American idea* to send peacekeepers into Macedonia, the independence of which has not yet been recognized by the United States, *was dismissed as unnecessary by a number of European leaders...*"[61] (Italics added)

Clinton was removing his mask of skepticism about eventually inserting the U.S. directly into the Bosnian war's hot spots of so-called "safe havens" which he had once called "shooting galleries."[62]

Nevertheless, the Sarajevo government had finally succeeded in mobilizing NATO—the American military's European subsidiary—as its "Bosnian air force" as the war was escalating dramatically.

And Soros had his Macedonian ambitions safely quarantined for future diplomatic and/or commercial exploitation. Infuriating especially Greece, Macedonia's political opportunists had staged their own cosmetic election for secession in 1991.

Provocation and punishment had unmistakable roles in the U.S. deployment of troops to Macedonia, which was dramatically amputated from Yugoslavia, while Greece and Bulgaria were being punished for being soft on U.N. sanctions against Serbia and allowing a thriving black market of goods and merchandise to flow across their borders to their Orthodox Christian cousins in Serbia.

Insightful media treatment of the Macedonian adventure was virtually nonexistent, except in rare instances such as an editorial by *The Milwaukee Journal*, which questioned why a U.S. combat force was being sent to Macedonia that "for now, is peaceful."

Serbs had shown no signs of staging a clamp-down on Macedonian secessionists, while the American presence on the border with Kosovo incited only increased agitation by Albanian Muslim separatists in Kosovo:

> "The Clinton administration's decision to send 300 U.S. troops to join an international peacekeeping force in the Balkans is extraordinarily risky. ...In fact, some diplomats fear that, far from deterring the Serbs, deploying the American troops could actually provoke the regime in Belgrade...

---

60. *Associated Press*, July 2, 1993.
61. *The New York Times*, June 10, 1993.
62. *The New York Times, ibid.*

Other risks and questions center on the mission of the force..."[63]

Soros, who disapproved of Clinton's foot-dragging to recognize Macedonian independence "wrote a sharp letter to the President, raising parallels with 1938 and appeasement."[64] With the occupation of the Macedonian border by Americans, along with Clinton's eventual decision to deploy U.S. troops to Bosnia in November 1995, Soros was appeased—for the moment—if not satisfied.[65]

Referring to Soros' schemes in Macedonia and elsewhere in the Balkans, a "well-placed" Clinton administration official told *The New Yorker*:

> "Nor were all Soros' efforts so overt. The Soros-funded Action Council for Peace in the Balkans launched a major effort on Macedonia. ...The Action Council letterhead lists fifty people—including members of its steering committee and its executive director and its program director—but not Soros."[66]

The New Yorker also noted that Soros was "for many years a major contributor to Helsinki Watch (and) according to one person, he recently made a long-term commitment to the *Council on Foreign Relations*—under the condition, however, that he be an anonymous donor." The elite Council's inner workings are secret, even though it publishes the upscale *Foreign Affairs* journal which consistently produced biased essays about the Yugoslav tragedy, blaming almost solely Serbian leaders and detouring away from explanations about the deeper intrigues behind the Yugoslav federation's demise.

Several members of the *Council on Foreign Relations* were on the letterhead of the *Action Council for Peace in the Balkans*, Soros' "state department" in Washington.

Soros' *Action Council* was designed to operate discreetly—at first:

> "When Soros, the phenomenally successful Hungarian-born financial speculator, decided in December 1992 to direct $50 million in philanthropic assistance to Bosnia, he sought advice on how best to assure that the money would be put to good use. *Sawyer Miller Group* partner Mark Malloch Brown, who describes Soros as a former client, helped pull together an international advisory committee to oversee the Soros grant. ...(When) Soros shifted his focus from humanitarian relief to trying to influence U.S. policy, two major PR shops, the *Sawyer Miller Group* and the *Wexler Group*, offered advice. ...Abramowitz played a considerable role in making contacts and shaping strategy for the expanded effort. A new group, the *Action Council for Peace in the Balkans*, was formed with a steering committee of marquee-worthy names from across the political spectrum. Former Secretaries of State Edmund S. Muskie and George P. Shultz signed on, as did former White House national security

---

63. *The Milwaukee Journal*, June 14, 1993.
64. Bruck, *ibid.*
65. Soros said his earlier impatience with Clinton had caused him to consider giving support to a Clinton opponent in the 1996 election. However, with Clinton's later decision to occupy Bosnia, Soros said all was forgiven. From *Charlie Rose*, *Public Broadcasting System*, November 30, 1995
66. Bruck, *ibid.*

advisers Zbigniew Brzezinski and Frank C. Carlucci III. The list of two dozen names included a half-dozen Members of Congress and former officeholders. ...But the *Action Council's* influential steering committee got nowhere with its strategy of relying upon private contacts with Administration officials and occasional op-ed pieces. ...Just before the marketplace massacre, however, the *Action Council* shifted gears and went public. It held its first press conference on January 6 and soon thereafter opened offices in Washington and Amsterdam to conduct ongoing public advocacy activities. 'When they didn't see the light we realized they'd have to feel the heat,' *Wexler Group's* (Thomas F.) Gibson said. Gibson, Wexler vice president, was a former Reagan White House aide."[67]

In the same *National Journal* article about Soros, *ABC* news anchor Peter Jennings was excessive in shoring up the credibility of *The New York Times*' John F. Burns:

"If anyone has come close to *saving* Sarajevo, I think it is Johnny Burns," said Jennings."[68] (Italics added)

Burns, who did not limit himself as a Sarajevo correspondent and propagandist, was featured in a "documentary" entitled "Sarajevo Ground Zero" and produced with Soros' money. Soros also subsidized numerous other films and "cultural" productions that celebrated the martyrdom of Sarajevo. Soros also bankrolled Sarajevan Ademir Kenovic's film, "Confessions of a Monster,"[69] based on the doubtful "confession" of a captured Serb soldier who, in front of Burns and Bosnian Muslim captors, eagerly admitted to a score of grisly murders and rapes for which he was later convicted without evidence in a Sarajevo show trial.[70]

Such episodes fit Soros' vision for a comprehensive and controllable media policy and method to fill the gap left by traditional East-West news coverage in the dramatic demise of Communism in Europe. While news pundits strained over how—or if —the profession should evolve, Soros acted.

"The cold war provided us with a coherent global road map, in terms of what to cover and how to cover it," said John Walcutt, former correspondent for *Newsweek* and *The Wall Street Journal*.[71]

"Since the fall of the Berlin Wall and elimination of the cold-war news filter, the task of making sense of global events has become less manageable for the media," said Don Oberdorfer, a former diplomatic correspondent for *The Washington Post*.[72]

Foreign Policy Editor Bill Maynes said leadership "has abdicated the diplomatic

---

67. Kirschten, "Sarajevo's Saviors"; also, "So far, K Street's doing OK," March 19, 1994.

68. Kirschten, "Sarajevo's Saviors," *ibid.*

69. "Funding the Survival of Bosnia," *Open Society News*, Winter 1994, p. 7.

70. The credibility of the production was directly compromised when supposed murder victims of Herak's and his accomplice were discovered alive and well in Sarajevo (*Washington Times*, February 28, 1997), bearing out a later plea by Herak that he was tortured into making false confessions.

71. Leon Hadar, "Covering the New World Disorder: The Press Rushes in Where Clinton Fears to Tread," *Columbia Journalism Review*, July-August 1994.

72. Hadar, *ibid.*

news agenda-setting role of the presidency to the media."[73]

Soros and his supposedly philanthropic network had new road maps, news filters and millions to spend—and could not be written off as eccentric dabbling by the quixotic billionaire, public-policy manipulator and media magnate.

David Ignatius, a former correspondent for *The Washington Post*, concluded that "what George Soros does is as important as what the Fed's Alan Greenspan decides..."[74]

And, what George Soros decided to do was to harness the influence and propaganda peddlers of Washington, D.C., including news professionals themselves. His scheme was to hedge the future of "democratic media" in Central and Eastern Europe. He spent millions for newsprint, newspaper and electronic media payrolls for "literally dozens of publications" and dissident broadcast outlets staffed by angry, cynical anti-nationalist reporters and editors in former communist countries. Soros also spent bundles for cross-pollination of European and American journalists with his "internships" and "training" programs at *CNN* and the *Institute for War & Peace Reporting*, a Soros beneficiary in London[75] that regularly published essays from anti-regimists and dissident journalists from "ex-Yugoslavia." But Soros was not limited to using saturation news outlets like *CNN*. He also hired journalists to further the goals of Soros' media vision, such as Stuart Auerbach, "on leave from *The Washington Post*":

> "Since the end of communism, a variety of Western organizations have tried to instill the principles of a free press in the region. The most common tool is a workshop. ...With three regional media specialists, the Soros Foundations try a different method. Working with the local offices, we go directly to the journalists in their clubs and offices. Because we are based permanently in the region, we are able to return over and over to build a level of trust with the local journalists. These meetings have produced some revealing exchanges."[76]

The common thread that weaves through the media and public relations web in the Yugoslav wars was Soros, who recited to *The New Republic's* Michael Lewis on January 10, 1994, how he had "carried some rather potent messianic fantasies with me from childhood."

Certainly, troubling media waters—if not pretending to walk on them—Soros persisted with his eccentric meddling in the Balkan wars, pumping more than a million dollars into construction of a new water works in Sarajevo, which was used intermittently by the Sarajevo government whenever it wanted to prolong and manipulate the city's PR image of being under siege, arbitrarily switching it off in time for evening news deadlines in the West. Soros also bankrolled the opposition media in Belgrade, such as *NIN* and *Vreme* magazines and *Studio B TV*, along with Sarajevo's government-controlled *Oslobodjenje*. In 1993, the Soros Yugoslavia Foundation published a volume, entitled "Toward Democratic Broadcasting," a work of questionable importance other than to celebrate Soros' media philosophy—and, more importantly, a primer for those who wanted access to the Soros payroll.

---

73. Hadar, *ibid*

74. Hadar, *ibid*

75. Hadar, *ibid*

76. Hadar, *ibid*. Quoting Auerbach, "'The Role of Reporters: Journalists in Eastern Europe' ponder basic questions in trying to understand their new responsibilities in transitional societies," p. 7.

'People Don't Feel As Depressed As They Should Feel'

The bitter cold and wintry grayness in Belgrade lifted suddenly for a few days around Orthodox Christmas and New Years in 1994. Everybody was outdoors during the day and early evening, walking along the *Terazije* promenade or the newly renamed Avenue of Serbian Leaders (or "Princes," depending on who was asked) formerly *Bulevar Marsala Tita*. People warmed themselves in the sunlight under the blue sky. Several windows in the seventh floor offices of *Vreme* were opened. Denisa Kostavic, a husky-voiced journalist in her twenties, and Aleksander Ciric, nicknamed "Sasha," who spoke in a deep, resonating tone, were being questioned about Serbia's devastated reputation abroad and whether they knew how bad it was, and if they knew anything about the aggressive public relations campaign to smear Serbia. Or that Soros was involved. How much outside news did they get about themselves anyway?

It was strange that *Vreme*, backed by Soros money, had no wire machines for monitoring international news. They were cut off and isolated, even though Kostavic and Ciric insisted they got adequate information from a variety of sources. They were preoccupied with debate over what was or wasn't happening inside Bosnia, avoiding any inquisitiveness about Serbia's demolished international image or its infamy of being under United Nations sanctions. The same questions were previously asked to *Vreme* writers Stojan Cerovic and Duska Anastasijevic. Cerovic appeared to briefly glimpse the magnitude of defamation and shrugged without saying anything. Anastasijevic, John F. Burns' former translator, was irritated and self-consciously helpless. "That's your problem!" she blurted.

Ciric and Kostavic couldn't add anything more to the conversation, and the balmy outdoors were more inviting. I remarked to Kostavic about the "beautiful weather" as she walked me to the door. She stunned me with a response that was part of the uniformity of correct insolence and cynicism. It was routine for youthful dissidents.

"I usually love nice weather," she said almost dreamily. "But I hate it for one reason only: it helps the regime because the people don't feel as depressed as they should feel!"

I stepped out onto the sidewalk along *Narodnog fronta*, unbuttoning my jacket for the pleasant stroll back to my borrowed flat.

I remembered James Harff's condescending tones from the year before: "I feel sorry for the Serbian people."[77]

Harff defended his and Ruder-Finn's work. If I was perplexed or had any questions about propaganda or bias, he recommended I should talk to people like *The New York Times'* Burns, *Newsday's* Roy Gutman or *CNN's* Christiane Amanpour. "They're the ones who are telling this story," said Harff. "Granted, people like us help in the sense that we make sure people are aware of what they're writing."

On the previous weekend, as Harff and Silajdzic launched their public relations salvos at the June 1993 human rights convention in Vienna, Bosnian President Alija Izetbegovic met with Pope John Paul II in Rome to cement their diplomatic ties announced ten months earlier. The occasion included the diplomatic introduction of Archbishop Francesco Monterisi as the Vatican's first ambassador to Bosnia-Herzegovina. Monterisi was an experienced envoy at tough venues, having previously served in Madagascar and South Korea[78]– rugged diplomatic posts for Roman Catholic prelates who encountered rigorous antipathy toward the Vatican's legacy for political and religious proselytism.

---

77. Harff interview with the author, June 1993.
78. *Associated Press*, June 11, 1993.

Chapter 9

God's Lonely Rider

"Many millions of words have been written since the election of Karol Wojtyla in attempts to analyze and understand what kind of man he is...It is to be regretted that the severely moralizing speeches of His Holiness cannot, apparently, be heard backstage... With the election of Karol Wojtyla quiet discretion has become a rare commodity."[1]
—David A. Yallop

"Roma locuta est; causa finita est (Rome has spoken; the case is closed)."[2]
—Saint Augustine

It is the identification of religions with nationalities which makes the situation explosive," wrote church historian Stella Alexander almost a year before Yugoslavia disintegrated. "It is always a lethal mix."[3]

The passive reporting about the religious implications of the Yugoslav wars was second only to the story of the war time media bias itself. Habitually, the Western media protested that the Yugoslav wars were not civil wars and were not based on ancient religious enmity and schism. The press insisted the barbarism was loosed by political powers in Belgrade, Zagreb and Sarajevo.

But even the most casual Balkan specialist admits it is preposterous to sever religious influences and manipulations from the historic and contemporary calamities among South Slavs and, most definitely, Catholic Croats and Orthodox Serbs. Likewise, the more recent encroachment by Islam and the denigrated—by Croats and Serbs alike—hybrid of Slavic Muslims.

Thus, the dearth of authentic coverage about the Yugoslav wars, the religious connotations, strategies and provocations. Beyond self-censorship, the press opted for near silence. For American readers and reporters especially, religion and the Balkan war coverage were seldom mixed beyond shallow categorizing amidst battles, soldiers,

1. Yallop, *In God's Name: An Investigation into the Murder of John Paul I,*
New York: Bantam Books, 1984; pp. 301-3.
2. *Sermones*, 131.
3. Stella Alexander, "Religion in Yugoslavia Today," *Occasional Papers On Religion In Eastern Europe Today,* Volume X, Number 3; October 1990.

civilians and casualties.

It was curious to hear some Western journalists later speculate generally about journalism which overlooks the religious characteristics and consequences of political upheavals.

ABC's Peter Jennings, consistently pro-Muslim in his Yugoslav war coverage and commentaries, and others rarely went beyond the mere recording of the presence of and statements by religious personalities and institutions that occasionally stepped into public view during the wars. Off camera, Jennings apparently believed there was no contradiction with his professional philosophy and his own Balkan war reporting:

> "...I have reported on....(and) seen first hand what a *profoundly destructive force* religion has been in the former Yugoslavia... And I am completely convinced that there is such a dimension to many news stories, and that when we report on that added ingredient we *more accurately* capture the human experience and thus we are *more relevant* as reporters."[4] (Italics added)

If Jennings and other correspondents had adhered to digging out and defining that "dimension" with the frequency and importance it was due, which would have resulted in a better comprehending of "the human experience" in Yugoslavia, he and others could be commended for achieving journalistic relevancy.

In fact, plumbing too deeply the religious roots of the conflict carried the obligation to vigorously scrutinize recent 20th Century history in particular. And, for the media, this would have meant giving serious consideration to justifiable contentions by Serbs about their unresolved controversies over mass slaughters by Croats and Muslims during World War II:

> "Religious affiliation in Yugoslavia was closely linked with the politics of nationality; *centuries old animosities among the country's three main religions*—Eastern Orthodoxy, Roman Catholicism, and Islam—remained a divisive factor in 1990. Forced conversions of Orthodox Serbs to Roman Catholicism by ultra-nationalist Croatian priests during World War II had made a lasting impression... Religious tension existed even in the most prosperous regions..."[5] (Italics added)

Up until late 1995, the Western press ritually denied the presence and significance of thousands of Muslim mujahedin, or "holy warriors," fighting in Bosnia. Only when the United States publicly ordered the Sarajevo government to expel thousands of religious mercenaries in 1996 did the embarrassed press meekly cease to deny their existence.[6]

4. Jennings' speech, given November 15, 1995, at the Harvard Divinity School's Center for the Study of Human Values in Public Life, from *Nieman Reports*, Vol. XLIX, No. 4, Winter 1995

5. Chuck Sudetic, *Yugoslavia: A Country Study*, Washington, D.C.: Federal Research Division, Library of Congress, p. 106. Sudetic, a Croat-American, was a correspondent for *The New York Times* in Yugoslavia during 1991-1995.

6. Brendan O'Neill's "How we trained al-Qa'eda," *The Spectator*, December 6, 2003: "...The Bosnian war taught Islamic terrorists to operate abroad. For all the millions of words written about al-Qa'eda since the 9/11 attacks two years ago, one phenomenon is constantly overlooked—the role of the Bosnian war in transforming the

Renate Flottau, a veteran correspondent in Yugoslavia for *Der Spiegel* said she accidentally ran into Osama bin Laden while they both sat in the Bosnian government presidency while waiting to see Alija Izetbegovic in 1993. Flottau said she did not know who he was at the time but recognized him years later as bin Laden's terrorist reputation became known.

"We were just sitting and waiting together, and we had a kind of general conversation," said Flottau. "I remembered him later only because of his strange, uneasy behavior in the waiting room."[7]

To openly examine the record of religious instigation in Yugoslavia was quicksand for the media and a Pandora's box for Western diplomats, both of whom had anointed non-Serbs with favoritism from the outset. There were too many witnesses still alive from the generation which remembered the condoning, incitement and participation by some Croat priests in the barbaric slaughters of Serbs, Jews and Gypsies a half-century before.

Whenever compelled to mention the late Archbishop Alojzije Stepinac, the controversial prelate of Zagreb, the press did so in apologetic tones though there was abundant documentation that Stepinac—still venerated by Croats and loathed by Serbs—stood by as forced conversions and mass killings abounded early in the Second World War:

> "Although the role and position of the Roman Catholic archbishop in Zagreb at the time, Alojzije Stepinac, remain fiercely disputed —he did write to (Croatian Fascist leader Ante) Pavelic in 1943 to denounce Ustashe excesses—the archbishop greeted the installation of the Pavelic regime as 'God's hand at work' and never publicly denounced the onslaught on Serbian civilians."[8]

Fifty years later, the media accepted at face value denials by the Vatican that it fomented the current disintegration of Yugoslavia. And, certainly after the Croatian war started in 1991, the reporters—as they had done for many years before—ignored the bitter memories in Belgrade nurtured toward the late Stepinac. His infamous union with the Ustashe was denied with equal vehemence by Catholic Croatia and the Vatican for over four decades. Convicted and briefly imprisoned for war crimes during the regime of Marshal Tito, Stepinac died in 1960—six years before the Vatican became the last state to officially recognize socialist Yugoslavia. Eight years earlier, Stepinac had been named a cardinal by Pope Pius XII on November 29, 1952 —a cynical coincidence in that it he was given the position on Yugoslavia's National Day.

Had they bothered to look more closely for similar nuances and subtle provocations that flourished between Rome and Belgrade, contemporary journalists and readers would have been stunned to learn that when Tito made his triumphal re-entry to Zagreb after World War II, he boasted to a group of Catholic leaders that he was both "a Croat and Catholic."[9]

---

mujahedin of the 1980s into the roving Islamic terrorists of today... From 1992 to 1995, the Pentagon assisted with the movement of thousands of mujahedin and other Islamic elements from Central Asia into Europe, to fight alongside Bosnian Muslims against the Serbs."

7. Flottau correspondence with the author, February 22, 2004.
8. Roger Cohen, *The New York Times News Service*, September 5, 1994.
9. *Official Gazette of the Zagreb Archdiocese,* October 5, 1945.

Embracing 'The South-Slavic Problem'

Outspokenly intolerant of schismatic ruptures between Catholic Croats and Orthodox Serbs, Bishop Josip Strossmayer was the head of the diocese of Djakovo just east of Zagreb in the late 19th Century. He resolutely espoused Yugoslav unity until he died at ninety in 1904.

"Where," asked a young Serb and federal army physician, sipping his beer morosely near the main square in Zagreb a few days before fighting erupted in nearby Slovenia, "is the spiritual heir to Strossmayer?"

"As apostolic administrator of the Catholics in Serbia he lost no opportunity of fostering good relations between the Catholic and Orthodox Churches," noted Stella Alexander. "...(H)e abstained until the last moment from voting in favour of papal infallibility at the First Vatican Council, knowing the offence this would give to the Orthodox."[10]

Strossmayer founded the Yugoslav Academy and the University of Zagreb. Alexander pointed out that Strossmayer and the Serbian Metropolitan Mihajlo "met in Belgrade in 1868 and embraced as a token that religion must not separate sons of the same nation, a gesture which was enthusiastically welcomed by Serbian students."[11]

In few news reports since the breakup of Yugoslavia in 1991 was there remembrance of Strossmayer's conciliatory call despite the numerous monuments and landmarks in Zagreb today that commemorate this famous Catholic and Croat who was revered by Serbs as well. Strossmayer, who seized upon any potential bond between Croats and Serbs, was the promoter of humanitarian answers to centuries of "the South-Slavic problem," as the late Slovenian-American writer Louis Adamic [12] and others referred to the region's inherent lapses into fraternal carnage:

> "This Catholic bishop's liberal-nationalist policy found further expression in his friendly relations with the Orthodox clergy in Serbia, Greece and Russia. And following the example of a Croatian bishop, Grgur Ninski, who had lived nearly a millennium earlier, Strossmayer encouraged the Old-Slavic liturgy known as the Glagolitic Rite, which survived in part of Croatia, and secured for it the protection of Pope Leo XIII. He was a contemporary of the Slovenian writer and bishop of Maribor, Anton Martin Slomshek, who created the Apostolate of Saints Cyril and Methodius, the purpose of which was to promote contact between the Catholics and the Orthodox. Cyril and Methodius, mainly credited with the Christianization of the South-Slavs, are regarded as saints by both Churches."[13]

The month before the war began in Slovenia and would shortly spread to Croatia, a solitary accolade for Strossmayer was penned by Mark Frankland in *The London Observer*:

> "Scarcely anyone has a good word for the Yugoslav federation except for Western diplomats who know they will have to help clean up the mess if disintegration occurs... Some might say

---

10. Alexander, Church and State..., *ibid*, p. 58 fn.
11. Alexander, *ibid*, p. 58 fn.
12. Louis Adamic, *My Native Land*, New York: Harper & Brothers, 1943.
13. Adamic, *ibid*, pp. 275-276.

that Strossmayer ...was just the sort of political personality that Yugoslavia needs today: Rose Macaulay called him 'a child of light, exempt from darkness and terror.' Strossmayer was also a Catholic bishop who tolerated no prejudice against the Orthodox Serbs, an example forgotten by Croatia's present president, Franjo Tudjman, who, when he was in London last week, disparaged Serbia as a "different civilization' from Catholic Croatia."[14]

Buried deep in the narrative of sparse news reports the previous week had been the dramatic but futile attempt by present Croatian Catholic and Serbian Orthodox leaders 123 years later to emulate the embrace between Strossmayer and their predecessors in what was wrongly-termed "an unprecedented meeting at the traditional seat of the Serbian church at Sremski Karlovac, forty-two miles north of Belgrade...":

> "The head of the Serbian Orthodox Church, Patriarch Pavle, and the Roman Catholic Cardinal of Croatia, Franjo Kuharic, called on political leaders Tuesday not to allow the defeat of 'soul, and heart, reason and human dignity.'"[15]

Kuharic and Pavle met again three months later in Slavonski Brod and called for an end to the fighting in Croatia in a joint appeal, which was ignored by the Western media and the combatants.

Their third meeting on September 23, 1992, in Geneva, was not only substantially ignored by the mainstream press but was unattended by Sarajevo's invited Islamic leaders:

> "...The chief of the Islamic Community, Ra'is ul Ulama Jakub Selimoski and his delegation, who had stated that they would come to participate in the conversations, were unable to travel out of Sarajevo..."[16]

Pavle and Kuharic used strong words to condemn "the blasphemous and insane destruction of places of prayer and holy places" and branded war criminals and rapists as "monsters...no matter what name they give themselves."

But the dramatic denunciations from the Cardinal and the Patriarch could not be heard above the clamor of war that roared through Bosnia-Herzegovina for the previous six months and showed little signs of relenting.

Headlines and television were reserved for blood, gore, horror, concentration camps, ethnic cleansing, mass rape and incessant propaganda.

After all, amid religious urging for calm and tolerance during the first year of war in Yugoslavia, there was clearly heard instead the shrill notes of incitement and provocation from those with the callings and vows of "peacemaker."

---

14. Mark Frankland, *London Observer* Service, May 13, 1991.

15. Ivan Stefanovic, *Associated Press*, May 8, 1991.

16. "Joint statement from Patriarch Pavle and Cardinal Kuharic," *Occasional Papers On Religion In Eastern Europe*, Volume XII, Number 5, October 1992; pp. 50-51.

The German-Vatican Connection

Besides Croatian president Franjo Tudjman, the two figures with the most popularity among secessionist-minded Croatians in mid-1991 were Pope John Paul II and German Foreign Minister Hans Dietrich Genscher.

And, Genscher was never timid about Bonn's manipulations in the Balkans as the chief booster of Croat secession.

The diplomatic path between Bonn and the Vatican was a crowded thoroughfare.

German hegemony over Central Europe—and especially the Balkans—had its price as well as invaluable dividends, and two of the most important popes in the 20th Century recognized the practicality of lasting interdependence that was galvanized by treaty in 1933.

Cardinal Eugenio Pacelli was the Vatican's secretary-of-state when a treaty was signed with Nazi Germany on the eve of World War II. As the future Pope Pius XII with the calling to keep a spiritual eye on his flock, he readily signed the pact with its determined destroyer:

> "Hitler saw many potential benefits in the treaty, not least the fact that Pacelli, a man already displaying marked pro-Nazi attitudes, might prove a useful ally in the approaching world war. History was to prove that Hitler's assessment was accurate. Despite a great deal of world pressure, Pope Pius XII declined to excommunicate either Hitler or Mussolini. ...His was a papacy that declined to condemn the Nazi invasion of Poland because, he said, 'We cannot forget that there are forty million Catholics in the Reich. What would they be exposed to after such an act by the Holy See?'"[17]

But there was an important incentive for the Vatican in the concordat:

> "For the Vatican, one of the major advantages to emerge from the very lucrative deal with Hitler was confirmation of the *kirchensteuer* (church tax). This is a state tax that is still deducted at source from all wage earners in Germany... This tax represents between 8 and 10 percent on income tax collected by the German government. The money is handed over to the Protestant and Catholic churches. Substantial amounts derived from the *kirchensteuer* began to flow to the Vatican in the years immediately preceding the Second World War. The flow continued throughout that war ($100 million in 1943, for example)."[18]

As the post-war economy of West Germany steadily mushroomed (prior to reunification with the German Democratic Republic), so did the Vatican's share of the *kirchensteuer*, especially from industrial centers, prosperous Catholics in Bavaria and, especially, the Diocese of Munich.

It should be remembered that the German bishops strongly influenced the seating of John Paul II on the papal throne. Indeed, some suggest that the Pope "owes" his election to the Catholic hierarchy of Germany.[19] In exchange, the Catholic

---

17. Yallop, *ibid*.
18. Yallop, *ibid*.
19. Merlino, *ibid*.

Church in Germany enjoys autonomy and wealth (its annual budget during the late 1980s ranged from $4-to $5-Billion!)[20] almost unmatched, though not lightly envied, throughout the Catholic world.

While the election of a Polish cardinal surprised the world, there was widespread belief by the Italian press that he was more than routinely promoted among the German cardinals. Further, it was widely reported—and could not be emphasized enough—that Wojtyla had recently headed a Polish delegation to the German episcopacy and that he had said mass in the cathedral at Cologne, reciting the liturgy in flawless German.

Peace, Reconciliation And Incitement

The papal reigns of ambitious and all too mortal men spawn human drama at its most intense level. Although his predecessors applied necessary theatrics and dramatic expression to accomplish their ends, none more than John Paul II had more attracted the modern media with the recognition of its global potential for manipulating images and history. As a teenager, he was already adept on-stage with an air of irresistible melancholy that endeared him to theater-goers in his native Wadowice:

> "At the age of fourteen, Karol Wojtyla discovered the theater. It struck him like a thunderbolt. It was as if he had suddenly come face to face with his destiny."[21]

Like no other medium, drama exploits contradiction.

John Paul II's "impulse" to visit Poland and Hungary in mid-August 1991 could not have been more timely to boost nearby Croatian morale after two months of losing clashes against the Yugoslav National Army. But it was also seen as the worst time for him to make the first-ever papal visit to Hungary, where the center-right government in Budapest had just restored relations with the Vatican in 1990 after a forty-five year estrangement. Also, Hungarian Cardinal Laszlo Paskai and other bishops were being publicly accused by radical clerics as previous informants for the officially disbanded Hungarian communist secret police:

> "Another point of criticism has been the high cost of the papal visit—estimated at $6.6 million—for this debt-ridden nation struggling to revitalize its economy after Communist misman-agement."[22]

But the pope was eager to get to tiny Pecs, a quiet town in southwestern Hungary beside the Croatian border. But, Pecs had always been his main destination. His appearance at World Youth Day events in Czestochowa in Poland and his emotional prayers at the tomb of Cardinal Jozsef Mindszenty at Esztergom, Hungary, whetted dramatic expectations.

When finally standing before the sweltering crowd of 10,000 Hungarians and Croat pilgrims in Pecs on August 17, the pontiff had enthusiastically greeted Croatian Cardinal Kuharic and five Croatian bishops. His remarks unmistakably signaled

---

20. Merlino, *ibid.*

21. Carl Bernstein and Marco Politi, *His Holiness: John Paul II and the Hidden History of Our Time,* New York: Doubleday, 1996; p. 35.

22. Roland Prinz, *Associated Press*, August 16, 1991.

stepped-up confrontation and conflict with Serbs to the more than four million Croats within earshot and television viewing proximity just over the border. The stage was set for Pecs the previous day in Budapest, when he endorsed the newly rewritten Croatian constitution which suspended laws for protecting minorities—principally including Croatia's 600,000-plus Serbs!

Instead of evoking themes of peace and forgiveness, tolerance and the abandonment of violence, John Paul II posed before a troupe of diplomats, while really addressing radio and television audiences in Croatia, to state that "minorities must accept the constitution of the country in which they live."[23] His other admonitions about upholding rights of equality were negligible sidebar.

If there was ever a time for urging prayers for Serbo-Croat reconciliation at the tomb of Strossmayer, it was just before his departure from Budapest for the Croatian frontier.

But in the open-air gathering at Pecs and with Kuharic standing at his side, the pope aimed his clear support of Croatian nationalism, speaking in Croatian, past the upturned faces of adoring Hungarian Catholics:

> "Once again, I can assure you that I am close to your *legitimate* aspirations, renewing my appeals to the *international* community so that they help you in this difficult hour of history... I am hopeful to be able one day in the near future to visit you."[24] (Italics added)

Although "it stopped short of an explicit endorsement of Croatia's independence drive," he meant it as an explicit enough incitement and, as the world's premier internationalist, he clearly called for internationalizing the Yugoslav civil wars.

On Hungarian soil, the pope knew his recollections of that nation's brutal communist experience would resonate in Croat ears as endorsement for open hostility against Serbia and the Serbian Orthodox Church:

> "An ironclad organization imposed on the nation an atheistic pseudo-culture, and wanted to make it a way of life."[25]

These were not words of charity and constructive dialogue from the Vatican's preeminent diplomat. His remarks were identical to those of Rome's envoys who succeeded throughout the previous quarter century in undermining Soviet rule in Poland, Hungary, Czechoslovakia, Latvia, Lithuania, Estonia, East Germany, along with pacifying Portugese and Spanish dictatorships.

Within days of the papal provocations from Pec, sporadic violence in Vukovar in far eastern Slavonia—though minimally reported in the Western press—rapidly escalated to open terrorism and murders of Serb civilians by Croat paramilitaries and militia. The federal army responded with a sustained artillery barrage which eventually crushed Vukovar—once the small picturesque Danubian town shared by almost equal numbers of Serbs and Croats.

The belated response to attacks against Serb civilians in Vukovar would also rally forces against the federal army itself throughout Croatia. By the wintry end of the six-month Croatian war, the U.N. conservatively estimated that 10,000 people on

---

23. Victor L. Simpson, *Associated Press*, August 17, 1991.
24. Stephen Kinzer, *The New York Times*, August 17, 1991.
25. Kinzer, *ibid.*

both sides had lost their lives. Scores of thousands of Serb refugees arrived in Serbia, where estimates were compiled by war archivist Vojin Dabic and others that at least 10,000 Serbs alone had been killed in the Croatian war.

Meanwhile, the Croatian government, through their hired publicists, loudly proclaimed their sufferings as true victims of the 1991 war. International diplomats and correspondents never bothered to inspect the fate of the first cleansing of the Serb population from Croatia before the huge exodus from Krajina came four years later.

'Danke Deutschland, Danke Herr Genscher'

It was Christmas Eve in 1991 in Zagreb, and long lines of Croats were lined up at the city's banks. They were not there to withdraw cash for last-minute shopping.

They were there to exchange *dinar*, the old currency of the federal Yugoslavia, for the crisp new banknotes of the Republic of Croatia. People stood in lines a hundred yards long, craning their necks to glimpse the new brightly colored *kuna* being waved in the air by smiling recipients who hurried off with the new bills "emblazoned with evocative nationalist symbols."[26] The *kuna* was officially reinstated as the currency used by the fascist Ustashe government in World War II.

Meanwhile, the fighting went badly for the Croats, who lost about a third of their territory and watched the continuing decimation of their economy. A few people scurried off to shops to buy something to celebrate with and not just for the Christmas commemoration. Everything was transacted with paper currency; there were no new coins minted.

After all, it had been the worst kept secret of the last two weeks. The *kuna* had arrived from printing presses in Sweden, a country appearing to now have oddly diverted from its reputed neutrality. Other predominately Catholic countries—including Iceland and the tiny Baltic states—were the first to recognize the independence of Croatia and Slovenia a few days earlier. But it was Germany which waved away warnings the previous week from U.N. Secretary General Javier Perez de Cuellar at a "fractious" meeting of European Community leaders. Germany would recognize the two Balkan republics "even if it had to do so alone."[27] The European Community also approved a resolution setting January 15 as the first day for formal recognition by EC members.

The lines outside Zagreb banks were not the only noticeable gatherings as pedestrians clustered in front of television sets in storefront windows around the *Trg*—now renamed *Jelacic Square*—and listening to blaring radio broadcasts. In the last few hours, it had been reported that German Foreign Minister Hans Dietrich Genscher was on his way back to Bonn after secret talks at the Vatican. Genscher's ministry, oblivious to the frowns on German faces watching television news programs, announced that Bonn had given the ultimate Christmas gift of formal recognition to Croatia and Slovenia. In Zagreb, crowds of Croats cheered wildly.

"Whether Germany has...acted too quickly was described in Bonn as a matter of interpretation," wrote Stephen Kinzer, of *The New York Times*,[28] noting Chancellor Helmut Kohl had justified his government's action as "a great victory for German foreign policy" while denying charges that "Germany was building a sphere of influence that would form the basis of a 'Fourth Reich'."[29]

---

26. Nada Buric, *Associated Press*, December 23, 1991.
27. Stephen Kinzer, *The New York Times*, December 24, 1991.
28. Kinzer, *ibid*.
29. Kinzer, *ibid*.

An unidentified spokesman for Genscher said it was hoped recognition would actually "quell the violence in Yugoslavia... We are sticking to the arms embargo that was imposed by the EC."[30] (Actually, Germany had already sent weapons worth billions of *deutchmarks* to Croatia and Bosnia before the wars and before the U.N.'s openly violated arms embargo winked at by Western and Arab governments.)

Attempting a dubious candor, the large and influential Munich newspaper *Suddeutsche Zeitung* criticized the government's recognition of Slovenia and Croatia:

> "(It is) a foreign policy reaction to domestic political pressure.
> We have goaded and provoked the Serbs and we will disappoint
> the Croats. We are not going to send them a single soldier or
> *give* them the weapons they are hoping for."[31] (Italics added)

No, the Croats and their international sponsors paid cash for the continuous shipments of clandestine weapons. And, German soldiers instead would take logistical roles by the time NATO occupied Bosnia in 1996.

A pair of new songs, "Danke, Herr Genscher" and "Danke, Deutschland," made the rounds at Zagreb pubs, adding to the boisterous holiday merriment in Croatia. If most of the celebrating sounded half-hearted, it was because the Croat economy had reached losses of $16-to $20-Billion "and the fighting has destroyed the region's tourist industry (worth $2-Billion annually) and curtailed foreign investment."[32]

Hapsburg Memories Of Things To Come

In the spirit of the Vatican's disdainful delay to establish diplomatic relations until 1966 with Tito's Yugoslavia, it likewise demonstrated just enough contempt toward Serbia (and Serbian Orthodox Christianity) by rushing ahead of the European Union's approved date for formally recognizing Slovenian and Croat independence. The announcement of recognition came on January 13, 1992, which reversed an earlier vow "that the Catholic Church would delay its symbolically important recognition of the two separatist states until January 15."[33] Vatican officials felt no need for public explanation about why it had abandoned its earlier assurances not to preempt recognition by European Community governments.

But the Vatican's announcement went beyond diplomatic formality and contained wording that could not be interpreted as anything less than prodding expansion of the war:

> "(The Vatican) hoped that with their entrance into the community of
> sovereign and independent nations, Croatia and Slovenia would
> know how to contribute to the pacification of the Balkan region
> and to the construction of a *more broadly united world.*"[34]
> (Italics added)

Macedonia and Bosnia were vigorously maneuvering for independence.

Germany would stampede the rest of the European Community into formalizing recognition of independence for Croatia and Slovenia two days later. In case there

---

30. Buric, *ibid.*
31. Kinzer, *ibid.*
32. Slobodan Lekic, *Associated Press*, January 15, 1992.
33. Alan Cowell, *The New York Times*, January 13, 1992.
34. *Associated Press*, January 13, 1992.

was any residual skepticism about whether the Vatican and Germany were again converging to subjugate and capitalize upon Balkan vulnerability, direct admission occurred on the same day:

> "In an interview... Germany's ambassador to the Vatican, Hans-Joachim Hallier, said there was a 'substantial coincidence of views' between Germany and the Vatican on the conflict in Yugoslavia."[35]

Italy, always eager to exploit disunity among Adriatic Slavism and in step with the Vatican and its former World War II ally, dispatched President Francesco Cossige for a high-profile visit to Ljubljana, the Slovenian capital, on the very next weekend.

The pope sent a hypocritical note to Belgrade, "saying its recognition of the republics was not intended 'in the least bit a hostile gesture toward Yugoslavia.'" [36]

Persistently chastising nervous European Community members who were giving reluctant recognition to Croatia and Slovenia, Germany's Genscher boasted in a radio interview the same day:

> "'The German policy on Yugoslavia has proved correct.'...Genscher said it didn't matter if all 12 countries made their individual announcements today. 'What's important is that the signals toward recognition are clear. If one or other countries grant recognition one or two days later that's surely not so bad.'...A senior British official ...said Britain was what he called 'one of the lesser enthusiasts' for the idea."[37]

Genscher's cheerleading went far beyond exaggeration, even raising eyebrows from Zagreb to tiny Lipovac to Dubrovnik that Croatia "has achieved the highest imaginable standard of respect for minority rights." The cruel ethnic cleansing by Croats of several hundred thousand Krajina Serbs just four years later would attest to Genscher's mendacity, intuited at the time by few in the German press who were concerned with the quickening drift toward the reincarnation of Goebbels-style media:

> "'Germany is acting in a highly sensitive psychological environment,' said a commentary this week in Bonn's principal newspaper, the *General-Anzeiger*. 'The fear of German dominance and unilateralism has grown.'"[38]

Croats obviously had mixed practical feelings about the results of the Vatican-German "diplomacy" to date:

> "The mood on the streets of the capital was considerably less triumphal... The Central Office of Statistics in Croatia estimates that up to 40 percent of its factories have been damaged or destroyed, with costs of rebuilding put at $18.7 billion. More than half a million people are refugees."[39]

---

35. Cowell, *ibid.*
36. Tony Smith, *Associated Press*, January 15, 1992.
37. Raf Casert, *Associated Press*, January 15, 1992.
38. Stephen Kinzer, *The New York Times*, January 15, 1992.
39. Stephen Engelberg, *The New York Times*, January 15, 1992.

Aside from Genscher and the Vatican, Europeans winced at the irony of Germany's darkening of bleak Balkan days. Observed Serbian Foreign Minister Vladislav Jovanovic:

> "It is deplorable that a country that was divided for 50 years should try to destroy our country's unity by promoting inequality and unilateral secession."[40]

The fifteenth cease fire between Croat soldiers, Serb rebel forces and the *JNA* was holding, but assurances from German and Vatican leadership that the rush to recognize Croatia and Slovenia would end the bloody breakup of Yugoslav did not survive for even ninety days.

Meanwhile, the Vatican energetically began preparations for John Paul II's promised visit to "independent" Croatia.

The pontiff had never conceived of his future visit to anything but a seceded Croatia although wrought at excruciating human cost. Nobody understood this better at the time than the conspicuous leftover of Austro-Hungarian imperialism, Otto Hapsburg and his family who were part of John Paul II's current entourage at Pecs. The royal House of Hapsburg had ruled the Holy Roman Empire for 400 years with descendants sitting on European thrones from 1200 to the early 1900s.

The Hapsburg presence at Pecs was officially noted in Zagreb on the front page of the Catholic newspaper *Glas Koncila*: "The Pope's mass in Pecs was also attended by Otto Hapsburg and his family."[41] Undoubtedly, they understood what John Paul II was saying when he voiced his desire to go to Croatia "one day in the near future."

"The Torino daily *Stampa* interpreted this statement as 'the Pope's wish to go to Croatia, but to an independent Croatia,' that the Pope 'has never so far linked in such a direct way the problem of the independence of Croatia and the possibility of visiting that country.'"[42]

John Paul II was sincere about "legitimate aspirations" for Croatian independence even if the means were the carnage traditionally practiced in Europe. Rome was expert in legitimizing such barbaric means to obtain its ends, almost as though by historic script.

Karol Wojtyla's dramatic flair never lapsed.

Bosnia exploded in April 1992. Regrets in Rome and Bonn sounded hollow; the Yugoslav civil wars were now successfully internationalized.

Contemplations Amid Melancholy

As with all Serbs, he begins with a history lesson. Milan Bulajic joined the Yugoslav liberation army in 1941. He was thirteen-years-old and was wearing short pants, literally, when he became a partisan. Along with many other teenage boys who would become experts overnight in guerilla warfare, he did not have to lie about his age even if he was asked. He was Montenegrin and tall enough.

On November 30, 1994, the harsh winter wind was slashing through Belgrade and across the stoic granite face of the huge federal office building on Marx and Engels Square.

There were no lights visible beyond the first-floor entry except for the glow of a

---

40. *Le Monde*, January 15, 1992.

41. *Glas Concila*, No. 34, August 25, 1991.

42. Milan Bulajic, *The Role of the Vatican in the Break-up of the Yugoslav State*, Belgrade: Ministry of Information of the Republic of Serbia, 1993, p. 183.

small television set in the watchman's booth. The audio was off. I could barely make out the face of the man inside who said a couple words and motioned for me to find my own way upstairs. He then shoved a card over the hole in the glass to block the escaping heat from the cramped enclosure.

Bulajic answered the door to his second-floor office. At sixty-six, he looked younger. And although in good health and tall, he seemed fragile and weary. His office was lit only by a tall window. He offered some brandy to supplement the feeble warmth, nudging the small, oscillating floor heater toward me.

A member of the Yugoslav diplomatic corps from 1949 to 1987, Bulajic was now director of the Museum of Genocide Victims. The sparse furnishings in his office included a row of file cabinets along one wall opposite his small desk and chair.

When talking, Bulajic gazed straight ahead at his files as his voice became strained, imploring and, at times, despairing. The drawers contained a massive assortment of half-century-old documents, statements, reports, maps, ghastly photographs of slaughtered Serbs, individually and in mass graves and pits, leering Croat fascist soldiers, executioners—and Catholic priests (presiding at forced mass conversions and baptisms), nuns, bishops, archbishops, Vatican diplomats and emissaries!

This was the torment of the collective, irresolvable Serbian soul and never adequately grasped by the outside world, and which never ceased to haunt elderly peasants and scholars of history alike, who demanded, as Bulajic did, that the Vatican confront "the truth."

If Western journalists and politicians did not acknowledge and convey this—then the historic injustice continued and would perpetuate itself.

Walking through the gray morning chill to Bulajic's office, I recalled his opening words at the beginning of his book about the *The Role of the Vatican in the Break-up of the Yugoslav State:*

> "I am contemplating the purpose of writing about the Vatican's mission in the Independent State of Croatia, about the responsibility for what was created on the bloody ruins of the Yugoslav state, when a genocide was carried out and when hundreds of thousands of men, women and children were slaughtered, when around two hundred and fifty thousand Orthodox Serbs... were converted to Catholicism, when hundreds of thousands of people were forced to leave their homes—only because they belonged to a different nation behind which stood a different religion... I am contemplating in 1991, fifty years later, when we are witnessing the repetition of the same scenario for breaking up the Yugoslav state... I am contemplating whether there is any point in investing superhuman efforts to prove historical facts from the past, when the present events are proving them."[43]

Published in Serbian, English and Greek, the book—along with Bulajic—was casually written off as the work of a propagandist. The Belgrade government published it, and many doubtless used it that way. But it also received the ultimate censorship from the Vatican—silence!

While Bulajic and others detected some curiosity from Western correspondents and journalists, who picked up occasional copies at the International Press Centre when they first arrived in Belgrade and were desperate for background, it was never mentioned in detail or emphasis by the Western media or by shuttling diplomats.

---

43. Bulajic, *ibid*, pp. 9, 10.

Sitting in his Socialist-Gothic era office with its high ceilings, and looking almost comical as his large frame was straddled across the seeming miniature desk and chair, Bulajic seemed every bit his own despairing self-description in his book, as "God's lonely servant, a lonely rider—a historian."

Documenting and publishing a book about mass murder and atrocity against Serb victims in 1993 (from Belgrade!) and attempting to find an international audience was a doomed endeavor. Targeting the Vatican as an infamous and immediate provocateur was doubly futile.

Such books appear infrequently and are rarely more than brief sensations, veiled reverently from any timely mass enlightenment, discussion and influence among disbelieving policymakers or media, who only describe religious wars and never study their origins, their pathologies.

Remarkably, some works from major publishers—such as British author David A. Yallop's *In God's Name: An Investigation into the Murder of Pope John Paul I*, published by Bantam Books in 1984—achieved a significant readership. Yallop's book was an American and European bestseller.

Books printed by smaller presses, demonstrating less profuse but accurate enough documentation—although too often negated by rhetorical excesses—have gained occasional and enthusiastic audiences and even multiple printings.[44]

But Bulajic was a melancholy figure. His own 221-page book is a condensation of a much larger two-volume work—a grim, exhaustive recitation of desperately chronicled Vatican infamy before, during and after World War II in Yugoslavia:

> "The supplement of this book gives the names of 694... Catholic priests and bishops who bear direct responsibility for the Ustashi crimes of genocide against the Serbs, Jews and Gypsies. None of those who have been proved guilty have been called on by the Holy See to answer for this."[45]

In November 1994, Bulajic had just returned from the United States where he gave lectures on the Jasenovac "system" of World War II Croat extermination camps at the U.S. Holocaust Memorial and Museum in Washington, D.C. His main purpose, however, was to gain display of his elaborate "Jasenovac Exhibit":

> "With Jasenovac, the American public can see the genesis of the Yugoslav crisis. Without an understanding of this, there can be no understanding."[46]

He had obtained an invitation to bring the exhibit and returned to Belgrade to begin preparations for transporting it to Washington. But, a letter arrived, and the invitation was withdrawn. He read aloud: "...We regret to inform you that the Museum has decided it is unable to sponsor your exhibition."[47] The letter said exhibit space was inflexibly booked for several years.

---

44. See Avro Manhattan's, *The Vatican's Holocaust*, Ozark Books, Springfield, Mo., 1986. This volume exhaustively implicates the Croatian Catholic priesthood in the atrocities and genocide against Serbs, Jews and other non-Catholic minorities during World War II.

45. Bulajic, *ibid*, p. 184

46. Bulajic interview with author, November 30, 1994.

47. Letter from the curator of the U.S. Holocaust Memorial and Museum, November 10, 1994.

Bulajic looked at his closed file cabinets as though they were tombs, speaking in a dirge-like tone about the "necessity for truth."

"Instead of an 'easy absolution,'" wrote Bulajic, "in the Orthodox spirituality there exists the discipline of repentance, gradation in moral responsibility (who committed the crime, where, when and in what place) in both the good and the bad sense... The precondition for determining 'the whole truth' is the launching of a dialogue of truth."[48]

Bulajic was also an advocate for reconciliation. As occasional speculation arose about a papal visit to Yugoslavia, reconciliation was discussed, he noted, by three outspoken priests from the Croatian Catholic mission in Paris.[49]

But Catholic hierarchy in Yugoslavia was unyielding in denying its clerics had aided and abetted atrocities in any 20th Century war, especially at the Jasenovac camps, according to Archbishop Vinko Puljic in Sarajevo, who was quoted in a 1991 interview: "We do not feel responsible for what happened in Jasenovac."[50]

Puljic's new diplomatic colleague in Sarajevo, Archbishop Francesco Monterisi and the Vatican's first ambassador to Bosnia-Herzegovina, agreed.

I left Bulajic later, noticing that the entire second floor was empty. The whole building seemed deserted.

Only the small television set inside the watchman's booth offered any animation inside the huge, crypt-like office building. But even he had disappeared.

The wind tore at the facade of the old structure as I walked outside, thinking how the historian's calling was a lonely one.

The Yugoslav religious morass was precisely "the despair of tidy minds," as Stella Alexander rightly said.

Bending into the wind and heading for the Café Verdi, I remembered a story:

> "In Bihac there's a pile of stones. The story—and I believe it—is this: The Ustasi dynamited the Orthodox church in '41. They razed it to the ground. Then the Catholics in Bihac used the stones from the ruins of the Orthodox church to add an annex to the Catholic church across the street... Toward the war's end the British bombers destroyed Bihac, the Catholic church with its new annex included. The few surviving Serbians gathered the stones from the wreckage of the new annex to the Catholic church and piled them across the street where the Orthodox church used to be..."[51]

A Papal Kiss Or Embrace?

Two years after the Bosnian war began, John Paul II still had not visited independent Croatia. And, delays for such a visit were annoying. In April 1994, he fell in his bathroom at the Vatican, fracturing his right leg which required surgical bone replacement. It was his latest physical malady adding to rumors that he was suffering from blackouts, Parkinson's disease and bone marrow cancer. He recovered from a dislocated shoulder six months previously, along with successful surgery to remove a large stomach tumor and had recuperated from a gunshot wound after an assassination attempt in 1981.

---

48. Bulajic, *ibid.*
49. Le Monde, June 18, 1991.
50. *L'Actualite*, No. 91, August 15, 1991.
51. Louis Adamic, *The Eagle and the Roots*, New York: Doubleday & Co., 1952, p. 415.

But by August, he was taking vigorous walks during his annual vacation in the mountains of Northern Italy.

He wanted to go to Sarajevo, Zagreb and even Belgrade in September, as the Vatican had announced the previous January. Religious reconciliation was the theme of a dramatic first-ever papal visit to Belgrade.

Such a trip received exhaustive media billing but was obviously unrealistic after the pontiff's stinging condemnations that same month:

> "...The Serbs were angered when the Pope called for 'all forms of action aimed at disarming the aggressor' in Bosnia, an appeal many Serbs interpreted as a Vatican endorsement of military action against them."[52]

To Serbs, "all forms of actions" did not exclude bombardment of civilian populations,[53] alarmed officials in Pale and Belgrade noted. "The Pope has never done that (urged bombings of civilians)," snapped Roger Cohen of *The New York Times'* Paris bureau, oddly self-interpreting the pontiff's call as nixing some forms of action when the pope had said to use "all" means to disarm.[54]

Understandably, U.N. officials and Serb leaders voiced security concerns—the latter fearing likely attempts on the pontiff's life at Sarajevo and certainly in Belgrade would be blamed on Serbs.

"It seems that he desperately wants to go," said a U.N. spokesman.[55]

The dramatic fervor began to spread. Bosnian Prime Minister Haris Silajdzic sought some of the limelight as well: "It is a recognition to all those who did not answer the call of blood and fire, a recognition to those who still believe in what Bosnia symbolizes."[56]

Then came the predictable and last-minute choreography of Serbs being blamed first for shooting and shelling incidents in Sarajevo with sudden sensational front-page stories that the former Olympic skating rink and airport had come under fire. Accurate reports clarified the reports afterwards:

> "A U.N. military spokesman... said Bosnian government forces were responsible for a sniping incident, originally ascribed to the Serbs, at the skating rink where the pope planned a mass. U.N. officials also reported that government forces fired a mortar shell that hit the Sarajevo airport runway..."[57]

The Belgrade trip was obstructed by the Serbian Orthodox Church which recalled John Paul II's incitements in Pecs. Then the Sarajevo trip was canceled altogether to a chorus of lament and scorn by the media and emotional sidebar from the pope and his Bosnian archbishop:

---

52. John Tagliabue, *New York Times News Service*, September 6, 1994.

53. But in a strange comment inserted into his story eight months later, *The New York Times'* Roger Cohen interpreted that the pope had not meant "all forms of action" including bombardment.

54. Cohen, *The New York Times*, September 5, 1994.

55. Hrvoje Hranjski, *Associated Press*, August 24, 1994.

56. *Associated Press*, August 30, 1994.

57. Clare Nullis, *Associated Press,* September 5, 1994.

"The Italian news agency *ANSA* reported that Archbishop Vinko Puljic of Sarajevo had sent a message to the pope saying: 'We cannot guarantee 100 percent the security of the Holy Father, but we very much desire his visit. We live in conditions of Christian insecurity, and we want to share this insecurity with our Pope.'[58]

...'The Pope's visit to the city of murdered hopes was delayed,' said Puljic. 'The inability of the pope to come to Sarajevo is another... in our many wounds.'... Workers at the speed skating rink where John Paul II had planned an open air mass gazed forlornly at the painted iron cross they had erected... Graffiti on a poster hailing the pope's arrival poignantly summed up the feeling of abandonment. 'Hurry up, God,' it said."[59]

As expected, John Paul II took to his balcony above St. Peter's Square and said he had decided to cancel his Sarajevo visit with "deep pain."[60]

His dramatic announcement achieved international coverage. His soliloquy was broadcast over radio and television in Sarajevo and was immersed in religious metaphor, concluding with an agonizing appeal: "I, the first Slavic pope, go on my knees to cry out: From plague, from hunger, from war, liberate us!"[61]

President Clinton reacted angrily, declaring that the U.S. was ready to formally scuttle the U.N. arms embargo, even if it was required to act alone.

In fact, the White House was always willing to look the other way while weapons were pouring into Croatia and Bosnia via Muslim and European countries.

Bosnian President Izetbegovic lost no time in venting his wrath at U.N. special envoy Yasushi Akashi:

"In an unusually bitter public attack, made the day after the pope postponed his visit, President Alija Izetbegovic said that... Akashi had shown consistent hostility toward the interests of Bosnia and that the Bosnian government would like to see him replaced. The president singled out a letter sent by Akashi to the Holy See...in which, he asserted, the U.N. official recommended that the papal visit be canceled. 'This postponement was godfathered by the United Nations Protection Force... I believe the pope has been deceived.'"[62]

The pro-government *Oslobodjenje* obediently shouted: "Akashi should be tried as the worst criminal."[63]

Reporters were caught up in the emotional free-fall of the event, variously reporting, as did *The New York Times*, that the pope's sermon included his offer to Serbian Orthodox Church of a "kiss of peace."[64]

---

58. John Tagliabue, *The New York Times News Service*, September 6, 1994.
59. Clare Nullis, *Associated Press*, September 7, 1994.
60. *Associated Press*, September 6, 1994.
61. John Tagliabue, *The New York Times News Service*, September 8, 1994.
62. Roger Cohen, *The New York Times News Service*, September 7, 1994.
63. Clare Nullis, *Associated Press*, September 7, 1994.
64. Tagliabue, *ibid.*

Or, as the *Associated Press* heard it, the pope held out only "a spiritual embrace."[65]

With predictable anti-climax and despite provocations by Bosnian government forces (verified by the U.N.), the *Associated Press*' Jasmina Kuzmanovic, based in Zagreb, said the pope's cancellation was caused after all by concerns about "Serb gunners"![66]

The surmise was without any justifying evidence and, in fact, conflicted with reports of Bosnian Muslim plots.

Nostalgia, Martyrdom And King Lear

Reporters differed about Vatican history. It is a kind of secular public sport which is beneath any response from the Holy See but *The New York Times*' Roger Cohen stated flatly: "No pope ever visited Yugoslavia."[67] Jasmina Kuzmanovic, of the *Associated Press*, said otherwise:

> "It has been more than 800 years since a pope last reached Croatian territory. And even then, it was by mistake. A ship carrying Pope Alexander III to Venice was blown onto a Croatian island during a storm in 1177. Catholic Hungary ruled Croatia then and for the next eight centuries, and the Vatican deemed a visit to Croatia unnecessary."[68]

It appears that Jasmina Kuzmanovic lacks expertise in history. There was never a country of Croatia in history until it was internationally recognized in 1991. "Catholic Hungary" ruled over ethnic Croats who were vassals, enslaved by the Austrian Empire until the end of World War I. The Pope may have accidently visited Balkan territory in an alleged "storm in 1177," but his ship certainly was not in "Croatia."

John Paul II's arrival in Zagreb was arguably not a visit. Croatian President Franjo Tudjman saw it as a strategic presence, saying "the papal visit gave 'moral support' to his country's struggle to regain what it lost."[69]

That went far to inspire the brutal ethnic cleansing of hundreds of thousands of Serbs from the Krajina a year later to which world leaders raised feeble objection and threat while the Vatican said nothing.

Journalists repeatedly began to sense there was more than immediacy behind the pontiff's determination to make a Balkan appearance even though he had failed to go to Sarajevo:

> "The Croatian visit will be the 62nd foreign trip of John Paul's nearly 16 year-long papacy but only his first since he toured the Baltic republics a year ago... Despite worries about his health and the personal risks in such a trip, the pope had been determined to visit Sarajevo..."[70]

> "...'The pope was eager to go ahead, no matter what,' said (French Catholic writer Christine) de Montclose, who has close

65. Nullis, *ibid.*
66. Jasmina Kuzmanovic, *Associated Press*, September 7, 1994.
67. Cohen, *The New York Times*, September 5, 1994.
68. *Associated Press, ibid.*
69. *Associated Press, ibid.*
70. Victor L. Simpson, *Associated Press*, September 8, 1994.

ties to senior Vatican officials. 'The Bosnian Serbs' insistence that they could not guarantee his safety did not influence him. *I really think he was prepared for martyrdom.'* ...He was ready to risk it, but was dissuaded by warnings that his death could have unforeseeable, potentially catastrophic consequences, she said. 'He was reminded that the assassination of Austrian Archduke Franz Ferdinand in Sarajevo led to the First World War and that no one could say what might happen if he, too, were murdered there,' she said." [71] (Italics added)

John Paul II grimaced as he walked on his painful leg in Zagreb, deciding to take an elevator instead of using the twenty-seven stairs that others climbed to reach the platform at the open-air mass in the city's Hippodrome beside the Sava River.

State television said a million had turned out, while the *Associated Press* and *The New York Times* counted 800,000 and 400,000, respectively.

He preached peace and reconciliation. But he interestingly "said the war was 'without any justification'"[72] that contrasted startlingly with his views at Pecs two years earlier where he codified Croatia's "legitimate aspirations" for secession.

His homily to the crowd at the Hippodrome also contained an eerie ring, impressing some "that he came close to suggesting the rebuilding of Yugoslavia":[73]

> "(He spoke of the) 'unbreakable ties' of culture and language that link south Slavic peoples as a bridge to peace and reconciliation in the Balkans... (T)he pope pointed toward the river as the image of unity among the peoples of the former Yugoslavia... The Sava, he noted,' flows through Croatia, along the northern border of Bosnia-Herzegovina, and on to Serbia and Belgrade, where it meets the Danube. In this metaphor of the rivers, we can almost see the footsteps on the way God wants you to follow in this difficult moment of history.'...(T)he pope said he felt nostalgia for the time 'when all the believers of this region were united.'... The pope's expression of nostalgia for a time of greater unity in the region... and his repeated appeals to Croats to rediscover their links with other south Slavs amounted to an extraordinary declaration, given the Vatican's policies toward the former Yugoslavia. The Vatican was the last state to recognize Yugoslavia, in 1966, and one of the first to recognize predominantly Roman Catholic Croatia's secession... At times, the pope even appeared to stretch historical facts in an attempt to promote reconciliation. Religious tolerance, he asserted, was part of the heritage of the region, a tradition that had survived for almost a millennium."

But had John Paul II been sincere about sending the message of peace and reconciliation, he would have gone to the tomb of Strossmayer before departing Zagreb. Instead, he kneeled cynically at the tomb of Stepinac in the Zagreb cathedral.[74]

---

71. Bernard D. Kaplan, *The New York Times,* September 8, 1994.
72. Kevin Costelloe, *Associated Press*, September 12, 1994.
73. Roger Cohen, *The New York Times*, September 11, 1994.
74. Ceaselessly fanning Serb-Croat provocations in the jittery peace after fighting ended in the Yugoslav wars, John Paul II announced he would beatify

No such pilgrimmage was made, nor was there any indication that one was ever contemplated.

The real message to Serbs and Serbian Orthodox Christianity that hot Sunday in September was clear.

While the pope juggled religious platitudes, others seized the potential for exacerbating disunity and conflict:

> "The thrust of the pope's remarks contrasted with the themes underscored by the Croatian president Franjo Tudjman and the archbishop of Zagreb, Franjo Kuharic. Tudjman spoke on Saturday of Croatia's deliverance from the 'hell of communism.' And on Sunday, Kuharic said that the 'Croatian people have received their sovereign state as a gift of God, and thereby the right to a name and voice among nations.'"[75]

For the time being, martyrdom eluded Karol Wojtyla even though he promised to go to Sarajevo "as soon as circumstances allow" and despite the seeming abhorrence of his aides who feared his demise there would cause historic catastrophe.

The frustrated mission to Sarajevo was "one of the most galling reverses and hard-fought battles of his sixteen-year papacy..." and partly contributed to "a sense of foreboding":[76]

> "'In the Vatican there is already an end-of-regime atmosphere, an ambiguous climate that has nothing to do with real chronology,' wrote Marco Politi, Vatican correspondent of the Italian paper *La Republica.*' It has been a bitter year for the pope... It seemed it would close with a grandiose and romantic passage from a chapter of 'Quo Vadis.' Instead, from the ruins of Sarajevo emerged the profile of 'King Lear.' Perhaps John Paul II recognized this, too. 'There is always a moment when the disciples sleep and leave the master to his solitude,' he said, in apparent reference to the last moments on earth of the biblical Jesus."

The Anti-Passions Of April

On November 1, 1994—two months after the failed visit to Sarajevo—John Paul II named Vinko Puljic as cardinal. Puljic, then forty-nine, was the youngest of thirty new cardinals nominated by the pope and the youngest worldwide.

In contrast to the habit of reclusiveness practiced by his fellow cardinals, Puljic was one of the most visible cardinals to the media and political theater. The title of cardinal benefitted Puljic in his main task of exerting high pressure diplomacy on behalf of Vatican interests in the Balkans.

President Alija Izetbegovic, whose artillery and soldiers had two months before shot up the airport and skating rink in Sarajevo and caused the cancellation of the papal visit, sent a congratulatory note of empty reassurance to Puljic:

Stepinac—the initial step toward sainthood—on October 3, 1998, at a Croatian shrine in Marija Bistrica. (*Associated Press*, May 8, 1998)

75. *Associated Press, ibid.*

76. Costelloe, *ibid.*

"We will do everything to build a country where everybody will feel free, whatever their religion, ethnicity or political opinion."[77]

For Puljic and others capable of Balkan designs, the first days of the month of April carried special opportunity to commemorate—and aggravate—Serbian indignation and miseries.

Specifically, April 6 carried unique insult and affront to Serbs. True, it was the day of liberation for Sarajevo from Nazi occupation—an event which included thousands of Serb partisans among the liberators.

More importantly, it was the day in 1941 when Hitler's bombers rained an especially hellish bombing raid upon Belgrade. Also, it was the day officially recognized as the beginning of the Bosnian war, although at the suggestion of Ambassador Warren Zimmerman and other advisors Izetbegovic had figuratively torn up the Lisbon Agreement (signed less than a month before) and unleashed Bosnian secession.

It was the same day European countries and the United States contemptuously recognized Bosnian independence.

It was not surprising then to find Cardinal Puljic in the first week of April 1995 on a media circuit in major American cities, saying mass at seven Croatian Catholic churches and issuing appeals for U.S. intervention in the Bosnian war along with condemnations for inaction:

> "'If (Americans) do not help, they will be accomplices of the future... A godless army began this war,' he said, his left fist clenched. 'This war was planned in Belgrade. It's a political aggression to occupy the territory.' Puljic echoed the oft-repeated charge that the Eastern Orthodox church, Serbia's dominant religion, is working hand-in-hand with the military.'"[78]

Puljic obtained access to the White House where he pressed his demands for intervention with an eloquence dutifully recorded by his media entourage:

> "Forever insecurity. While we're talking now, grenades are probably falling in Sarajevo.'...He claimed that the 150 priests still living within the Sarajevo archdiocese have remained 'outside political movements.'"[79]

In early 1997, Puljic was again in Washington, pushing for increased U.S. enforcement of the Dayton accords.

In making a presentation at the Carnegie Endowment for International Peace, he gave assurance that the Catholic hierarchy in Sarajevo was doing what it could to promote reconciliation. Morton Abramowitz, the exiting chairman of Carnegie and pro-Muslim challenged Puljic about contradictory notions of religious reconciliation "to maintain the unity of Bosnia":[80]

> ABRAMOWITZ: "You have preached a gospel of reconciliation ...Do you believe most of *your* Catholic Croats share that aspiration?" (Italics added)

---

77. Alan Cowell, *The New York Times News Service*, September 12, 1994.
78. Jan Ferris, *Religion News Service*, April 7, 1995.
79. Ferris, *ibid.*
80. Carnegie Endowment for International Peace, Washington, D.C., February 21, 1997.

>PULJIC: "There are few who can hear our voice of reconcilia-
>tion. There are many more who hear the voices on television...
>There are different words coming from television and our
>pulpits... If you give me the television, you can see what kind
>of change there will be."

Puljic's evasiveness, along with his trademark smile when volleying tough questions in public, was as obvious as was his repetitive mention about the failings and advantages of controlling media and television.

In early April—the 13th—of 1997, Karol Wojtyla stood on the tarmac at the Sarajevo airport, blinking and squinting as a blustery wind billowed through his papal raiment. Cardinal Puljic was at his side.

The buildup to the pope's arrival had been as noisy as just before his canceled 1994 plans. But, overall, his actual presence was anti-climactic and his departure after twenty-five hours was eagerly anticipated by his hosts. Security was smothering.

The airport greetings were subdued. A small girl brought a small white box of local soil and held it up for a kiss from the seventy-six-year-old pontiff who was obviously too frail and unsteady to kneel to the ground. "Never again war. Never again hatred and intolerance," John Paul II admonished the dignitaries at the small reception.[81]

His white "popemobile" then took him to the Sacred Heart of Jesus Cathedral, speeding past small groups of Sarajevans who applauded respectfully. Just hours before the pope's arrival, Bosnian police said they'd located twenty-three explosive devices rigged to a remote detonator. The bundle was located under a bridge along the route to be used originally by the motorcade. If responsibility was determined by investigators, they declined to make any public finding.

John Paul II arrived at Kosevo Stadium on Sunday and preached about peace and reconciliation in the face of daunting squalls of sleet and rain. Aides struggled to hold a large umbrella over him as the long-ago Polish apprentice actor from Wadowice struggled through his message. It was not one of Karol Wojtyla's best performances.

Returning to the airport for departure, he passed near the spot where Otto von Hapsburg and his son Karl—members of the German and Austrian parliaments, respectively, and descendants of the former Hapsburg ruling families—had just dedicated a post with the inscription: "Let peace rule the earth." The location marked the site where their ancestor Archduke Franz Ferdinand was shot on June 28, 1914.

The Hapsburgs installed the post the week before—again, contemptuously, on April 6.

Certainly there was something more than irony and closer to theater (if not hypocrisy) about the almost simultaneous arrival of the Hapsburgs and John Paul II in Sarajevo as previously at Pecs, symbolizing the ancient bulwark of the Vatican and the Austro-Hungarian empire against the encroachments of Islam onto the European mainland.

For Germany and Rome, retrenching a strong Catholic Croatia was the mandatory first line of defense against the northward surge of an Islamic Bosnian state.

---

81. Tom Hundley, *Chicago Tribune*, April 13, 1997.

Chapter 10

A Beating, A Confession, A Pulitzer Prize

"Do not veil the truth with falsehood,
nor conceal the truth knowingly."[1]
—**The Koran**

"Errors are volitional and are the
portals of discovery"[2]
—**James Joyce**

Max Frankel, executive editor of *The New York Times* said, "I think, the entire world of journalism rejoices in the award that went to John F. Burns, who did a breathtaking job at pursuing the story in Sarajevo at great personal risk."[3]

Frankel was talking about half of the 1993 Pulitzer Prize for International Reporting that was just awarded to Burns. The other half went to *Newsday's* Roy Gutman for his reports about alleged "concentration camps" in northern Bosnia.

The centerpiece of Burns' Pulitzer entry was a gory seven-hour "interview" with a captured Bosnian Serb, Borislav Herak, portrayed as a twenty-one-year-old psychopath and crazed member of a local militia. It turned out to be a manipulated confession and interrogation in which Burns was the key participant.

The huge 3,500-word story was moved by *The New York Times News Service* on November 27, 1992, the day after Thanksgiving and just in time for the huge Thanksgiving weekend newspapers. In an advance promotional note to editors across the nation, Burns' story was billed as:

> "(T)he brutal tale of Borislav Herak, a young Serbian soldier accused of war crimes, with twenty-nine murders, including eight rape-murders. Based on seven hours of interviews, this

---

1. *Chapter 2,* verse 42.
2. *Ulysses*, 1922.
3. *Associated Press*, April 13, 1993.

163

chronicle of six months of wanton slaughter and rape in a ten-mile area north of Sarajevo offers insight into the way thousands of others have died in Bosnia."[4]

Burns' interview had taken place two weeks after Herak was captured along with another soldier, Sretan Damjanovic, and Damjanovic's wife. All were in custody of the Bosnian government that decided it had found a public relations bonanza in Herak, who could be shown off as a stereotype, demented Serb.

Buried deep in Burns' story about Herak was a short paragraph with a second-hand response about Damjanovic who reacted with disbelief to what Herak had confessed and who threatened to kill Herak if put in a cell with him. Burns wrote that Herak was "asked repeatedly if he had been put under pressure to talk" and that "in hours of talking he never changed a detail." Burns said he'd inspected Herak's "upper body" which "had not been bruised." But he appeared deeply frightened, and asked after one long session if Burns would seek the prison governor's assurance that the Muslim guards would not beat him once he had finished telling his story. The governor, Besim Muderizovic, gave assurances that Herak would not be harmed. But at Herak's and Damjanovic's show trial in March 1993, Damjanovic said a "confession" was beaten out of him.

"Almost immediately," said Burns about the pair's capture, "Herak began telling investigators of his gruesome experiences."

Burns included many details from the interview, including Herak's acting out some of the supposed murders "in a room with potted plants in the Viktor Bubanj military prison" in Sarajevo. Burns said Herak told his story "partly in the presence of prison officials and partly with nobody from the Bosnian government or army present." But he did not say a Sarajevo video production crew was present and that interrogations were conducted by investigators—and by Sarajevo film director Ademir Kenovic!

Burns described Herak's mood swings between nonchalance and remorse from his "fried" conscience, "looking pallid, with sunken eyes and with fingernails so deeply bitten that some have virtually disappeared."

Burns also went to Herak's hillside home in Sarajevo and talked with his father and traced Herak's family history.

Burns said Herak now speculated about being executed, or being traded in a prisoner exchange, or wanting to fight on the Bosnian side if released. He described Herak's supposed experiences and observations at a Serb-run bordello, a restaurant and motel called "Sonja's."

But, vital pieces of the Herak story of mass rape and multiple murders were conspicuously missing. First, there was no evidence, corpses or victims or eye-witnesses to implicate Herak—except for hearsay from Bosnian government "investigators." Second, Burns had deliberately omitted Herak's outrageous allegation, made during the same interrogation, that UNPROFOR's former commandant General Lewis MacKenzie had raped young Bosnian Muslim women at Sonja's. Oddly, only two stories by Burns were distributed by *The New York Times News Service* during Herak's three-week trial, on March 13 and March 27, 1993 (both were for Saturday editions). Burns did not mention evidence or eye-witnesses or the MacKenzie allegation. He reported that Herak had suggested that he be shot, following his conviction for "thirty-five killings and sixteen rapes."[5]

Burns later refused to respond to requests for interviews when attempts were made to contact him in New York, Toronto and Sarajevo during late 1993 before he

---

4. *New York Times News Service*, November 27, 1992.
5. *The New York Times*, March 27, 1993.

was reassigned to India in January 1994.

Oddly, the War Crimes Tribunal—although it was not organized until July 1993—never publicly showed any interest in extraditing Herak even though the Tribunal's rules gave it the option, if not the moral responsibility, to take jurisdiction in cases which appeared to be prosecuted negligently or were conducted as outright show trials. Herak's proceedings fit both criteria. But the Tribunal could not impose death sentences and could not risk intervening where a case of insanity or mental aberration would result with a virtual acquittal.

Newsday's Gutman later reported about Sonja's—he called it "Sonja's Kon-Tiki"—and about U.N. soldiers, who allegedly availed themselves of the "Muslim and Croat women forced into prostitution."[6] Gutman omitted the allegation about MacKenzie. Using unidentified Bosnian Muslim sources and a one-time commandant at Sonja's, a Bosnian Serb named Branislav Vlaco, who was the "commander of the camp from May to November 1992," Gutman reported that fifty U.N. peacekeepers—from Canada, New Zealand, France, Ukraine and an unidentified African country—were clientele of Sonja's. Gutman indecisively described Sonja's as a "detention camp," a "possible concentration camp" and a "concentration camp" outright. Gutman, refusing later interviews, reported Herak was convicted of "raping sixteen women and executing twelve of them."[7]

Burns incredulously argued that the Herak proceedings were not those of a "show trial," citing that the prosecutor and one of the five judges, along with Damjanovic's defense lawyer, were Serbs.[8] Also, Burns and his editors ignored doubts about Herak's mental competency and the fact that Herak's credibility as well as the validity of the charges and the trial itself were shredded by the bizarre accusation against General MacKenzie—which was concealed by Burns and his editors.

Even more bizarre was Sarajevo director Kenovic's prison interview with Herak that was featured in "Sarejevo Ground Zero" in 1993. The overly dramatic video attempted to fuse the plight of the suffering city with heightened artistic effect using actors and singers. Even Burns went on-camera with soliloquies and an examination of Herak's torso (apparently for reassurance that there was no abuse by prison guards) as Kenovic coaxed the fantastic confession from Herak who unconvincingly demonstrated how he'd slit throats of some of his supposed victims. During the filming, Kenovic sat with crossed legs, asking Herak questions about the fine points of his "crimes."

Astonishingly, at the outset of the film, Kenovic said he had received permission to film Herak just three days after his capture—and before he was officially interrogated!

Kenovic's video was bankrolled by George Soros.

Alison Smale, Vienna bureau chief for the *Associated Press*, said in 1994 that correspondent David Crary, who she said accompanied Burns to the initial interview with Herak, had filed "daily" reports during the Herak trial. However, the stories never got onto the wire distribution nor was any mention made about the outrageous MacKenzie allegations which were patently defamatory. Smale's expression went blank with surprise a year later when told the *Associated Press*' follow-up stories about the Herak episode affair were derailed by her editors in New York.

She observed that sentiments in Sarajevo had lately swayed toward sympathy for Herak. "They'll never find any evidence or the victims," she said.[9]

---

6. Roy Gutman, "Sex Accusations Against U.N. In Bosnia," *San Francisco Chronicle*, November 1, 1993.

7. Gutman, *ibid.*

8. Burns, *ibid.*

9. Alison Smale, interview with the author in Vienna, January 10, 1994.

MacKenzie later told the side of the Herak story that Burns left out. The former UNPROFOR commander's own account about the Herak incident showed how Burns had helped orchestrate the Herak interview and had encouraged a cover-up of Herak's accusations against MacKenzie (which were excluded as well from Kenovic's production). MacKenzie himself had observed how Burns was susceptible to biased reporting and took the role of a participant in the events he covered. Burns' frequent upbraiding of officials at press conferences were notorious among other Belgrade and Sarajevo reporters and correspondents.

Also, Burns "virtually lived" at President Izetbegovic's offices in Sarajevo:

> "He was able to talk himself into a spot in the Presidency and, therefore, he really did become a participant. And we discussed this at some length that the more he was there the more it was really impossible for him to be able to get over to the other side."[10]

MacKenzie said it was because Burns was an insider at the Bosnian Presidency that Burns was able to later explain to MacKenzie about the accusations by Herak which were publicized by the Bosnian government:

> "In fact, he was the one that gave me the background on the Herak accusations against me and was very generous in telling me what actually happened and was shocked when I contacted him in London, where he was visiting his boy at public school, and said this story has broken. He said: 'My God, *I told them not to because it will destroy the credibility of what I've written.*'"[11] (Italics added)

MacKenzie said for a short time Burns "was very good in attempting to sort of keep me up to date with the accusations and how they were being fabricated." MacKenzie, using paraphrase, repeated how Burns gave him details about the interview with Herak and how the accusations occurred:

> "What he (Burns) said was, 'Look, I was doing the interview with Herak, and I'm part way through it, and I've got a representative of the Bosnian government standing there. And Herak starts saying that 'MacKenzie came to this Sonja's place north of Sarajevo, and we were saving four girls. And he drove off with them in jeeps and there were a couple of other U.N. folks with him.' And Burns said, 'Hold it just a second. When did this happen? How did you know it was MacKenzie?' (Herak's paraphrased answer) 'Well, I didn't, but then I saw him on TV that night.' (Burns continued) 'Okay, when did it happen?' He said, 'Well it was around the middle of August.' *And Burns turned to the Bosnian official and said, 'Look, MacKenzie went home on the 31st of July or the first of August. This is really a non-story. You're crazy if you take any action on this. It'll destroy the credibility of what I'm writing.'*...Well, on the day that Izetbegovic arrived in Riyadh for the Islamic conference,

---

10. General Lewis MacKenzie interview with the author, October 1993.
11. MacKenzie, *ibid.*

the story broke from the judiciary in Bosnia that they were asking for my immunity to be lifted, and that I be tried as a war criminal ...and mentioning the accusations about raping Bosnian girls. And I caught John in England, and said 'Do you know anything about this?' And that's when he told me the story. He said, 'Know about it? I was there. I was the guy doing the interview, and *I am shocked because it will erode some of the credibility of what I've written.*'...And John, at that stage, was 'living' in the Presidency and very much became part of the team, it almost seemed."[12] (Italics added)

MacKenzie explained that Burns was not physically "living" at the presidency, but that it seemed so judging from the slant of his reports and his close access to Izetbegovic. Burns abruptly broke off communications with MacKenzie who tried several times to contact him later. "But it's been over ten years since I've heard from him," said MacKenzie.[13]

According to *The Washington Post*, Burns' story about Herak "knocked everyone (on the Pulitzer jury) over..."[14]

The New York Times itself used peculiar wording about Burns' Pulitzer-winning performance in a self-congratulatory advertisement that appeared in the *American Journalism Review:*

> "(Burns) has written of the destruction of a major European city and the dispossession of Sarajevo's people. *He virtually discovered these events* for the world outside as they happened. In a 275-day stretch, he sent 163 articles from the former Yugoslavia, 103 of them with Sarajevo datelines."[15] (Italics added)

The tactics used to get a share of the Pulitzer for Burns were almost as bizarre, causing *The Washington Post's* media sage Howard Kurtz to follow his nose:

> "...(S)ome members of the jury on foreign reporting are questioning how Burns came to win a Pulitzer ...after they failed to rank him as one of the three finalists. The Pulitzer board overruled the jury and cloned the award, giving one to *Newsday's* Roy Gutman, who was a finalist, and another prize to Burns.

> "'Over the years I've always heard that the *Times* has exerted influence on the process. ...I consider this confirming evidence,' said Edward Higgins, editorial page editor of the *St. Louis Post-Dispatch* and one of four members of the foreign reporting jury. 'It's a little upsetting.'

> "Asked if the *Times* had mounted a lobbying campaign, Max Frankel, the paper's executive editor, said that 'we were very unhappy' that Burns was not a finalist. 'We didn't hide our disappointment,'

---

12. MacKenzie, *ibid.*
13. MacKenzie interview, February 2, 2004
14. *The Washington Post*, April 15, 1993.
15. *American Journalism Review*, May 1993.

he said. 'We went around muttering about it.'"[16]

Kurtz, who noted that fellow *Post* reporters Blaine Harden and Mary Battiata were also-rans in the Pulitzer competition, described the panic at the the *Times* that pulled strings at the Columbia University School of Journalism and the Pulitzer board to snatch a share of the Prize for Burns:

> "The annual Pulitzer ritual, administered by Columbia University, matters ntensely to members of the journalistic community. The *Times* has won 66 awards in the 77-year history of the Pulitzers, far more than any other newspaper, and regularly touts the figure in its advertising. Had Burns not won, the *Times* would have been shut out for the first time since 1985—and lost the foreign award to *Newsday*, its crosstown rival, for the second straight year.

> "...Sydney Schanberg, a *Newsday* columnist and chairman of the foreign reporting jury, said: 'I think there was a lobbying campaign. That's bloody sad because this is the best award in journalism. If we care about our profession, we shouldn't diddle with it.'

> "Schanberg said his comments had nothing to do with the fact that he quit the *Times* in 1985 after the paper abolished his column."[17]

The 1993 Pulitzer shenanigans may have been at the back of John Hughes' mind when he wrote his "essay" four years later, as a Pulitzer judge on the international-reporting panel. But Hughes, editor of *The Deseret News* and a former Pulitzer winner, had "concern" about the low numbers of Pulitzer competitors in the foreign category:

> "Though the quality of the reporting was high this year, the quantity—or lack of it—should be of concern to all of us. The international category drew only some 40 or 50 entries, compared with several hundred other categories. This means that news organizations are paying less attention to events in the world at large—events of immense significance to Americans."[18]

Hughes correctly diagnosed that journalism's financial investment in foreign reporting was being reduced:

> "Budget-cutting is hampering foreign correspondence. TV networks in particular have closed some and decimated many of their foreign bureaus. Print journalism has also been set back.

---

16. Howard Kurtz, "*New York Times* used clout to win, juror says," *The Washington* Post, April 15, 1992.

17. Kurtz, *ibid.*

18. John Hughes, "From Journalism's Summit, a Note of Warning," *Associated Press*, March 12, 1997.

While several large newspapers that have traditionally attached importance to foreign coverage have by and large maintained their staffs, others have cut back, particularly in capitals where the upkeep of a resident correspondent is especially costly.

"...If the American people are to make intelligent judgments about (regional crises)—and on such issues as when and where the United States should intervene—our foreign press corps, like our military, needs to be expert, well-positioned, and well-supplied with resources."[19]

The "foreign press corps," as far as the Yugoslav war reporting went, was non-expert. It was ill-positioned on the side of bias, favoritism, negligence and co-belligerence, so that it was moot about whether it was "well-supplied with resources."

The Herak story was a *New York Times* and American journalism disgrace, as was clear enough when other reporters and correspondents in Sarajevo abandoned the theatrics as obvious propaganda behind the Herak eposode.

But *CNN* suddenly reported on January 27, 1996—three years after Burns got his Pulitzer—that Herak was publicly denying the entire incident, saying he had been repeatedly beaten to confess, and was trying to get his case heard at The Hague.

The New York Times and *Associated Press* foreign desks and editors reacted skeptically when notified about Herak's reversal. Both Ed Marx, on *The New York Times* foreign desk, and Judy Ingram, *Associated Press'* international desk editor, on January 27, 1996, said they were unaware of Herak's denial.[20] But, with a blush rising among *The Times'* editors about the sudden and serious threat to the veracity of Burns' Pulitzer-winning entry, they dispatched Kit Roane to visit Herak in Sarajevo and pick up the pieces about his sensational reversal, assessing any threats to Burns' prize. Roane's tentative report appeared four days later:

"Thin and pale, Borislav Herak does not fit the picture of the rapist and killer he confessed to being nearly three years ago. He is quiet and subdued, an ex-store clerk residing in a 6-by-12 foot prison cell."[21]

Yes, Roane reported, Herak had recanted his infamous confession to Burns, whose reaction was not known and, if even sought, was not reported in the story.

"The editors just looked the other way. It's the damnedest thing. Here the guy's Pulitzer entry has been destroyed, and no one had the guts to confront him. No one was even talking about it."[22]

At the time, Burns was scavenging through the dank, smoky tenements of Baridara in Bangladesh, producing 2,000-word novelettes about impoverished female garment workers. Next, he was jetting off to Kabul, Afghanistan, to chronicle more misery amidst endlessly dueling warlords. And before the month was out, Burns was in India, plying through corrupt Hindu politics that had snared Prime Minister P.V. Narasimha Rao. Then, a year later, Burns was transiting Kabul for Calcutta when

---

19. Hughes, *ibid.*
20. Author's interviews with both on January 27, 1995.
21. Roane, "Symbol of Inhumanity in Bosnia Now Says 'Not Me'" *The New York Times*, January 31, 1996.
22. Anonymous *Times* reporter to the author, February 3, 1996.

The Times' Chris Hedges dealt the final blow to the Herak frontispiece of Burns 1993 Pulitzer sensation:

> "Two Muslim brothers whose supposed murders were used as evidence in highly publicized war crimes trial to condemn two Bosnian Serbs to death are found living in Sarajevo suburb; revelation is major embarrassment for Bosnian Govt (sic); finding of brothers raises questions about how guilty verdict was reached; trial of two Serbs, Sretko Damjanovic and Borislav Herak, in March 1993 was first attempt by Sarajevo legal system to try Bosnian Serbs for genocide and other war crimes."[23]

Although Hedges' story affixed the embarrassment on the Bosnian government, the shame rested with Burns. *The Times'* was officially silent. But Burns' charmed favoritism with his editors persevered. And, the Pulitzer jurors never remonstrated for awarding the Prize for international reporting—based on fiction!

'The Agony Of Yugoslavia Keeps Replaying Itself'

Burns was not alone in deceptive reporting about the Yugoslav wars. Examples show the range of media negligence, fabrications, and blatant falsehoods:

> •Street scenes of ravaged Vukovar in 1991 were shown on Western television networks a year later and were represented as combat footage from minimally damaged Dubrovnik. The "siege" of Dubrovnik itself was enhanced by the Croatian army, which ignited huge piles of old tires that produced clouds of thick black smoke for the background of filming the "destruction" of the old city.

> •A German television channel had broadcast a dramatic account about casualties, showing the corpse of a mutilated "Croatian soldier" who was later identified as a young Serb killed in late 1991 at Laslovo in eastern Slavonia. The program's producers later apologized.

> •An August 17, 1992, a full-page photo in *Newsweek* showed a shirtless, skeletal man who was described as being a Muslim prisoner in a Serb detention camp. Instead, there were credible claims, including a later entry in the Congressional Record, that the man was a Serb who had been arrested and confined on charges of looting. The man, appearing more dramatically emaciated than others who wore shirts in the picture, had suffered from tuberculosis for ten years, according to a woman identified as his sister in Vienna.

> •The *BBC* filming in 1992 of an ailing, elderly "Bosnian Muslim prisoner-of-war in a Serb concentration camp" resulted in his later identification by relatives as retired Yugoslav Army officer

---

23. Hedges, "Jailed Serbs' 'Victims' Found Alive, Embarrassing Bosnia," from archival abstract, *The New York Times*, March 1, 1997.

Branko Velec, a Bosnian Serb, who was being held in a Muslim detention camp.

•In late 1992, European television showed scenes of dozens of Bosnian Serb victims and coffins after a massacre at Kupres in western Bosnia. But the bodies were described as Muslims.

•Citing only a Bosnian government source, a story by the *Associated Press* appeared on February 17, 1993, about alleged cannibalism being practiced by starving Muslims in eastern Bosnia. The story achieved instant headlines in the U.S. However, receiving little if any similar play the following day was a vigorous denial by U.N. officials in Bosnia who had quickly gone to inspect the supposedly starving villagers and discovered them to still possessing livestock and chickens.

•On January 4, 1993, *Newsweek* published a photograph of several bodies with an accompanying story that began: "Is there any way to stop Serbian atrocities in Bosnia?" The photo was actually of Serb victims, including one clearly recognizable man wearing a red coat. The photo, with the same unmistakable man in his red coat, is identical in a scene from television footage taken at Vukovar a year earlier.

•*CNN* aired a report in March 1993 from the scene of a massacre of fourteen Muslims who were killed by Serbs. The victims later turned out to be Serbs murdered by Muslims.

•In July 1993, the *MacNeil-Lehrer News Hour* showed old video-taped scenes from an alleged chemical poisoning of Albanian children in the Kosovo town of Podujevo. But the footage was only of children rubbing each others arms in front of the camera. There were no adults, no teachers or medical personnel seen. And yet the camera kept rolling while the children were obviously instructed to keep performing. Officials at the U.S. embassy in Belgrade said personnel were immediately sent to investigate and later concluded it was a hoax.

•In early August 1993, *The New York Times* described in a photo caption that a Croatian woman from Posusje was grieving for a son who died as the result of recent attacks by Serbs. In fact, the Croat village of Posusje is in Bosnia near the Dalmatian coast, and was the scene of bloody fighting between Muslims and Croatians that had caused thirty-four Bosnian Croat deaths, along with the one in the photo.

•On March 7, 1994, the *Toronto Globe and Mail* became the latest in the media to show the destroyed landmark of Adriatic tourism—the ancient Ottoman bridge at Mostar. The *Reuters* photograph included the caption that the historic span had collapsed the previous November after months of Serb shelling.

In fact, the bridge was indiscriminately shelled by Croat forces, and officials in Zagreb later admitted blame and promised to rebuild the structure at the end of the war.

•Omitted from any coverage by Western media was the trial in Zagreb, stemming from the rape and murder of a twelve year old Serb girl and other members of the Zec family. Accused and later acquitted were the bodyguard of the Croatian Minister of Defense and other members of the Croatian Ministry of Internal Affairs.

• *The Associated Press* reported on April 25, 1995, that "Bosnian Serbs have nearly achieved their goal of driving other ethnic groups out of northern Bosnia... There are 67,000 Muslims and Croats in the Serb stronghold of Banja Luka, down from a pre-war population of 530,000." The city of Banja Luka never had a population above 200,000, of which less than 100,000 were non-Serbs. *The Associated Press*' Carolyn Henson was contacted in the Geneva bureau two days later. She had misquoted from the U.N. report which had applied the statistics to the wider area of the "environs" around Banja Luka and had not made any such specific mention about the drastically de-populated city which appeared in the story.

A typically-slanted article about the Yugoslav wars was the *Time* cover story in early 1993, which began:

> "The agony of Yugoslavia keeps replaying itself with new bombardments, massacres, rapes and 'ethnic cleansings.' At each horrifying recurrence, world opinion is outraged and opinion leaders call for an end to the barbarism."[24]

Deeper in the narrative of the same article appeared a statement from Sadako Ogata, U.N. High Commissioner for Refugees, who had told members of the U.N. Security Council:

> "Civilians, women, children and old people are being killed, usually by having their throats cut."

Ogata then said her uncorroborated statement was derived from uncorroborated broadcasts by unidentified ham radio operators in eastern Bosnia. Such transmissions had become an increasing source of "on-the-scene" propaganda and were frequently disproved after U.N. troops arrived. But, Ogata added that "if only ten percent of the information is true, we are witnessing a massacre," causing *Time* to confess that, contrary to the article's lead statement, "in fact Ogata, like other U.N. officials and foreign journalists, had no firsthand knowledge of what was happening."

---

24. *Time*, March 15, 1993.

Breaking The First Commandment Of Media Objectivity

What was the truth about supposed "world opinion" and the "opinion leaders"? Television reporting of the Yugoslav wars conjured up its "truth" and molded it into the illusion described in torrents of bias that poured from the mouths of its opinion-makers. There was almost no specific commentary about the advocacy role of American television coverage in the Yugoslav civil wars. What did emerge as critique was only tentative mention from the print media.

The Center for Media and Public Affairs, a nonprofit research organization in Washington, showed that prime-time news programs on major networks in 1993 had aired 233 stories on Bosnia and only 137 stories on first-year President Clinton's economic plans:

> "The trend intensified after April 1, the Center said, and culminated in the graphic broadcasts three weeks ago of refugees fleeing in the face of a horrific Serb attack on the Muslim enclave of Srebrenica. Media analysts said...it was no accident that Srebrenica was the turning point for Clinton Administration policy in Bosnia. ...It is the latest example of the extraordinary role played by television in setting the national agenda— especially in foreign affairs."[25]

A week earlier, another report by *Knight-Ridder's* Marc Gunther questioned the "depressing regularity" used by *ABC's World News Tonight* which saturated broadcasts with "images of homeless families, ravaged villages and armed civilians, even on nights when *CBS* News and *NBC* News turn their attention elsewhere. ...Is *ABC* doing too much with the story, or are its rivals not doing enough? And what accounts for the different approaches?"[26]

The *Knight-Ridder* story was based on *The Tyndall Report,* which monitored evening newscasts and found that *ABC's* Yugoslav war coverage had "provided 301 minutes of coverage, compared with 179 for *NBC's Nightly News* and 177 minutes for the *CBS Evening News* during the eleven months that ended in March 1993," continuing:

> "In 1992, excluding the election, the most covered story on *ABC* was the Balkans. *CBS'* top story was the Los Angeles riots, while *NBC* devoted the most minutes to Somalia. *ABC's Nightline,* meanwhile has devoted more than a dozen programs to the Balkans since last year, many consisting entirely of reporting from the scene of the fighting."

The Tyndall Report suggested that *ABC's* commitment to the Bosnian war was driven by Roone Arledge:

> "(Arledge) has a personal connection to the war because, as president of *ABC* Sports, he produced coverage of the 1984 Winter Olympics in Sarajevo. Last year, David Kaplan, a producer for *ABC's PrimeTime Live*, was killed by a sniper's bullet while preparing a report on the war."

---

25. Matthew C. Vita, *Cox News Service*, May 6, 1993.
26. Marc Gunther, *Knight-Ridder Newspapers*, April 29, 1993.

The *Knight-Ridder* article also underlined Peter Jennings's "personal convictions" and Jennings' admonitions that the world community failed to ease the suffering in Bosnia. Further noted was that Ted Koppel of *ABC's Nightline* was fixated on the story because he is the son of World War II holocaust survivors.

A network official, speaking anonymously, said the article's conclusions about *ABC's* fixations were "right on the money."[27]

By mid-1993, several major news organizations appeared determined to fan public outcry and to rouse political pressure for U.S. military intervention. They resorted to a campaign of skewed public opinion surveys.

But no matter how pollsters sculpted their questions, there was staunch opposition to all forms of armed intervention, especially if U.S. troops were involved.[28] More representative of overall public sentiments toward the U.S. media during the Yugoslav wars was a poll by *The Los Angeles Times* in March 1993 which showed only seventeen percent of the sampling believed the media was doing a "very good" job overall, a decline from thirty percent in 1985.

In fact, almost seventy percent of those polled agreed that:

> "The news media give more coverage to stories that support their own point of view than to those that don't."[29]

A month later, the issue was put more squarely:

> "Poll after poll shows the media sinking in public esteem and credibility."[30]

Finally, an *ABC News-Washington Post* poll emerged on August 11, 1993, saying six out of ten Americans "supported NATO air strikes to free Sarajevo of Bosnian Serb domination." The poll said Americans did not want the U.S. acting alone and that they overwhelmingly rejected "unilateral air strikes by the United States."

But the poll results were dubious because no questions sought responses to reports that Bosnian government forces fired on their own positions and populations in Sarajevo and manipulated artillery attacks elsewhere in Bosnia for public relations purposes in compelling U.S. intervention.

A *Washington Post* spokeswoman said such opinions were not asked because pollsters were "not sure the public would understand it." Also, she said, there "was not enough space" for other questions in the poll's format.[31]

U.N. Secretary-General Boutros Boutros-Ghali chided the media about its participatory behavior and for breaking the first commandment of media objectivity, remarking that the media had made itself part of the war coverage:

> "Today, the media do not simply report the news. Television has become a part of the events it covers. It has changed the way the world reacts to crisis."[32]

---

27. Interview with the author on April, 30, 1993.
28. *Newsweek/Gallup Organization* poll, August 6-7, 1992; *Newsweek* poll, April 29-30, 1993; *Time/CNN* poll, April 28-29, 1993.)
29. *Associated Press*, April 1, 1993.
30. Peter Maas, "Setting the Record Straight," *Esquire Magazine*, May 1993.
31. Interview by the author, August, 1993.
32. Address by U.N. Secretary-General Boutros Boutros-Ghali at *CNN's* Fourth World Report Contributors Conference in Atlanta, May 5, 1993.

Boutros-Ghali accurately described the routine and consequence of the media rule and habit of reporting in the Yugoslav civil wars that became part of the public's daily news:

> "Repeated scenes of misery can stir compassion. But they can also create fatigue and indifference. ...Public emotion becomes so intense that United Nations work is undermined. On television, the problem may become simplified, and exaggerated."[33]

In the Yugoslav wars, the media anointed itself as both "opinion leaders" and guardians of "world opinion."

Clothes Make The Interview

One of the most blatant incidents of media misbehavior for Lt. General Sir Michael Rose, the former UNPROFOR commander in Sarajevo, was a series of interviews by *ABC's* Peter Jennings for a television special, "The Peacekeepers—How the U.N. Failed in Bosnia" which aired on April 24, 1995.

Jennings hacked and slashed at Rose in an interview which was actually edited from multiple interviews over several hours, according to Rose—as evidenced, if by nothing else than Jennings' change of clothes!—until compiling enough footage to edit into what Jennings wanted to say and what he wanted to construe from Rose's answers. Among the most grievous omissions was Jennings' avoidance of context in the battles involving the "safe havens" of Gorazde and Bihac. The two predominantly Muslim towns became "safe havens" only after thousands of Serbs were brutally expelled.

But in 1995 Jennings bought the propagandistic line handed out from the Bosnian government, portraying the thousands of supposed casualties in both towns, but excluding earlier provocations against Serb civilians who were cleansed by Bosnian government troops before the Bosnian Serb military countered with equal force. Jennings used nothing from any Serbian side of the episode—except some second-hand audio recording from Jovan Zametica, an advisor to Bosnian Serb President Radovan Karadzic in an earlier angry exchange with Rose about U.N. threats to use NATO air attacks. Jennings featured Bosnian Prime Minister Haris Silajdcic with his condescendingly cynical explanation that the U.N. wanted to sacrifice Bosnia and that Rose was obeying orders to sacrifice Gorazde, Bihac and the rest of Bosnia.

The recording of Zametica was making the rounds of the foreign press, courtesy of the Bosnian government, and was used in a different factual context on the popular *British Broadcasting Corporation's* television program Panorama.[34] Silajdzic, whose government bugged Rose's telephone and personal living quarters in Sarajevo, was clearly angry and embarrassed in a devastating confrontation by correspondent John Simpson that left the Bosnian prime minister hostile and refusing to respond to U.N. estimates that only 1,000 deaths, mostly soldiers, had occurred at Bihac—not 70,000 which had blared over television newscasts and was never corrected!

Rose had obviously run out of patience and became the latest in the succession of Sarajevo's UNPROFOR commanders to declare that the Bosnian government repeatedly provoked Serb artillery attacks on its civilian population at critical diplomatic junctures. Jennings never used any of the information about Rose's telephones and living quarters being wire-tapped or, as Rose demonstrated on-camera to Simpson, that the buggings

---

33. Boutros-Ghali, *ibid.*
34. "Rose's War," *BBC*, January 23, 1995.

were also made available almost instantly by the Bosnian government to the Bosnian Serbs!

Jennings' hatchet job on Rose failed to spawn any new waves of public outrage and, probably, had only reinforced a passive public revulsion and intuition about the media's war reporting in Yugoslavia.

"He did not like the program that we did," Jennings recalled later, acknowledging he could remember at least two interviews he did with Rose, one of which was done in London. Jennings dryly conceded it was "quite possible" that the changes of clothes would indicate different interviews occurred with Rose, adding that the tight editing of his virtual cross-examinations of Rose for the hour-long special was necessary in order to include interviews from others recruited to flail Rose and the U.N. *ABC's* case, with Jennings as prosecutor, lined up several dissident U.N. officials, weaving together the circumstantial rhetoric from a familiar cast of interventionists, including Silajdzic, Admiral Leighton Smith, Senator Bob Dole, U.N. Ambassador Madeleine Albright, British Colonel Larry Hollingworth and Aryeh Neier, who headed billionaire philanthropist George Soros "humanitarian" schemes in the Balkans.

Peter Bean, a British Embassy official in Washington, said he was amazed that there were no angry telephone calls received the next day by embassy personnel after the Jennings tirade as there were during previous media outbursts that focused on complaints toward U.N. and British peacekeepers in the Yugoslav wars.[35]

Jennings' April 24th program had aired after a single-day's flurry of "news" that accused Serb war criminal, Dusan Tadic, was extradited from Germany to The Hague. Also, Bosnian Serb President Radovan Karadzic and General Ratko Mladic were officially targeted as probable war criminals by the chief prosecutor at The Hague. The coincidence of all three news events in a single day was not unusual in the Yugoslav war coverage.

The public was still numb and susceptible from the media aftershocks of the Oklahoma City bombing.

---

35. Author's interview with Peter Bean, April 26, 1995.

Chapter 11

'Journalism's Finest Hour? I Beg to Differ'

"What does he conceal from the reader?
What does he conceal from himself?"[1]
—**W.H. Auden**

"The matters I relate
Are true lies."[2]
—**Jean Cocteau**

Lewis MacKenzie, the retired Canadian general and first commander of U.N. peacekeepers in Sarajevo, returned to Etobicoke, Ontario, in late 1992. His retirement began with a busy round of speeches and numerous media interviews. But MacKenzie was always circumspect in his public statements about diplomatic, press and other political personalities, steadfastly sensitive about interpretations or manipulations of remarks that could cause reprisals for U.N. personnel, especially the large number of Canadian troops still in Yugoslavia.

The one complaint he received about his discreet memoirs[3] was that he avoided colorful critiques or insightful anecdotes about the politicians, generals and journalists he'd encountered, realizing the potential for retribution from all three.

He expected journalists to call him frequently in Etobicoke, but what he didn't expect were the kinds of questions they asked.

"What's interesting is that most of the calls now deal more with: 'Could you tell us again what happened on such and such a time because we're taking a look at the way we covered it in our reporting,'" said MacKenzie, paraphrasing. "And my message to them when they start wallowing in their anguish is, 'Don't feel too guilty about all of this—because you only reported what you saw, and what you saw was only 150 meters on either side of the Holiday Inn.'"[4]

---

1. "The Dyer's Hand," Part II.

2. *The Journals of Jean Cocteau*, 1956.

3. *Peacekeeper: The Road to Sarajevo*, Vancouver/Toronto: Douglas & McIntyre, 1993.

4. Interview with by author, October 1993.

Dubbed the "Pack Shack" by critics who felt the close living quarters, scrounging, supping and the regular late-night boozy roundtables, the not-so subtle peer-pressure for pro-Muslim, pro-Bosnian government bias that fostered pack-journalism, the Holiday Inn at Sarajevo was home to over 200 journalists in August 1993. With notably sparse nostalgia, they later recalled their stays at the hotel:

> "Sarajevo's Holiday Inn was often a merry refuge throughout 3½ years of bombardment."[5]"

> ...The basement garage of Sarajevo's Holiday Inn was packed with ungainly steel-plated white Land Rovers with the logos of news organizations stenciled on the doors."[6]

> "...Five years later, I walked into Sarajevo's Holiday Inn, which has been restored and now looks just as ugly as it did before the war. I had remembered it as a cold and grubby place filled with weary journalists."[7]

Rather, they were openly envied and detested by native journalists in Sarajevo—and even dissident colleagues in Belgrade in 1994:

> "The battered and extremely expensive Holiday Inn is full of foreigners: nervous and cynical journalists from the world's biggest newspapers—and nothing is happening these days; Sarajevo is just going on with its life. Humanitarian workers, diplomats, international bureaucrats, military officers, wheeler-dealers and one or two dumbfounded intellectual-humanists. Armed men guard them—there's a police station in front of the lobby. It's the Saigon 'Inter Continental' of the late sixties revisited: an air-conditioned island with an armed guard. They drive around town in armored white Land-Rovers with air-conditioning. Even then they are in radio-contact with some-body back at the Holiday Inn. The citizens of Sarajevo look on them with a mixture of scorn and disappointment. 'Those journalists, well there's some use in them, but the others, it's not that they don't spend money, they do; it's just that they don't understand and they never will.'"[8]

When MacKenzie spoke with journalists who were reassessing their Sarajevo war reporting, he was graciously sympathetic as he consoled the reporters who were having trouble with their consciences:

> "There was so little that we actually saw. And then I started to realize that a lot of what I was seeing was orchestrated and

5. Carol Williams, "Letter from Baghdad: Fear and Reporting," *The Los Angeles Times*, September 19, 2003.

6. John Kifner, "Correspondence/Dangerous Stories: Doing Your Best to Gauge the Risks Where Reporting Isn't Too Safe, *The New York Times*, February 24, 2002.

7. Peter Maass, "Back to Bosnia: A War Correspondent Returns," *The New Republic*, October 12, 1998.

8. *Vreme News Digest*, No. 154, September 5, 1994.

didn't happen naturally. And that began to bother me because I wasn't sure what conclusions I should draw, because these particular events perhaps were being done more for the benefit of the media than anybody else."[9]

But if journalists were having second doubts about what they saw or didn't see, they kept questions about that—and about what they wrote to each other—away from the public.

The reason is likely close to what was penned by British journalist Gregory Copley, who had the Yugoslav war reporting clearly in mind in early 1994:

> "At present, more than ever, facts are interfering with 'truths' as perceived and espoused by leaders and writers. Accepting 'truths' enables editors and politicians to have a continuity of policy and, perhaps more important for their careers, continuity of perceived opinion and attitude. For an editor or a politician to say 'I was wrong', or 'I have changed my opinion based on later and better information,' is a recipe for job loss. ...Facing up to facts, and embracing them, may mean initial public embarrassment, but will mean in the medium—and long-term that policy and policy-influencing journalism will be more constructive."[10]

All The News That's Fit To Censor

Enough facts interfered with what was reported as the "truth" behind the Markale market bombing on February 5, 1994, when the media ignored the fact that Bosnian Serbs had already commenced the withdrawal of heavy artillery and troops from around Sarajevo.

Unmentioned was that the pullback had been previously achieved through persuasion by Russian negotiators, and all parties in the war were on the brink of signing a peace agreement because disgruntled British and French leaders were threatening to pull out their large U.N. peacekeeping units.

Suddenly, the market explosion was touched off. The Serbs had nothing to gain but were blamed anyway. Munitions experts from Israel, France, Russia, the U.S., and elsewhere said the supposed explosion from a single mortar round could not have occurred as the headlines and news stories described. Even the Pentagon had "argued that it came from the Muslims, who fired on their own people to provoke Western air strikes."[11]

In one of the most controversial episodes of outright censorship in the war coverage, editors at *The New York Times* sat on the story researched and written by respected correspondent David Binder who said official blame for the market bombing was aimed at Bosnian government troops. The unpublished article and the latest censorship of Binder's reporting were the hot items in the Washington, D.C., rumor mill. The longer the story languished, the more infamous the censorship became. The day before the June 7, 1994, debate with Binder, the author, and British journalist Ed Vulliamy at the Carnegie Endowment for International Peace, *The New Republic's*

---

9. MacKenzie, *ibid.*

10. "When to Lie, When to Lead," *Defense & Foreign Affairs Strategic Policy*, February-March 1994.

11. "Washington Whispers," *U.S. News & World Report*, March 7, 1994.

Charles Lane rushed into print with a panicky challenge[12] to Binder's unpublished scoop that concluded U.N. and European Community officials "are convinced even in the absence of compelling evidence that a Muslim unit fired the mortar." But, unknown to Lane, *Times* editors had decided to block Binder's story from publication.

At the Carnegie debate, Binder confronted Lane about phoning him previously to see if the *Times* indeed was about to publish the damning story.

Lane was forced to grudgingly concede:

> "Of course, you can never rule out a Muslim setup or accident;
> they have committed abuses elsewhere."[13]

By November 1994, the U.N. was going public with the long-known fact that Bosnian Muslim troops were shelling their own civilians to evoke international sympathy and intervention. *The Associated Press, The New York Times* and others reluctantly reported that the Sarajevo government had carried out mortar attacks on the Kosevsko Brdo neighborhood, injuring at least one child. Bosnian Serbs were blamed for killing two other children in the exchange:

> "But the evidence that at least one of the Bosnians' recent wounds was self-inflicted seemed certain to harden the resistance of U.N. military officials here, who have been complaining *for months* that the Bosnian government is trying to draw the peacekeeping force and NATO into what would amount to a support role for the government. 'We're not going to get sucked into fighting their war for them,' said a senior U.N. military officer."[14] (Italics added)

Readers of *The New York Times* never saw Binder's article about the Markale market bombing, but it finally appeared in a subsequent issue of *Die Weltwoche*, the Swiss news weekly in Zurich. Later, Binder wrote a similar report for *Foreign Policy*.[15] It would not be the last time Binder experienced censorship of his Yugoslav war reports by the *Times*.

Sarajevo's foreign press corps had also generally ignored, except for insider talk, General Rose's threat to Bosnian government leaders that he would release information about the Markale explosion after they balked at attending the previously scheduled negotiating session in Sarajevo right after the February 5th blast. Rose indeed had proof that the fatal mortar was fired by Bosnian Muslim troops a short distance from the market. A U.N. observation post was set up inside an armored personnel carrier atop a summit overlooking Sarajevo five months earlier. The site was the location of an old Turkish fortress, and the vehicle used artillery-tracking sensors to pinpoint the source of mortars and heavier shells. A U.N soldier who manned the post said the accuracy of the Cymbeline mortar-tracking radar could pinpoint the spot where the weapon's "base plate" stood when the mortar was fired, using two intersecting beams that plotted the arc of the projectile. The mortar that fell on the marketplace had a nearly vertical trajectory, meaning that it had been launched very close to the vendors and their customers.

---

12. Charles Lane, "Shot Down," *The New Republic*, June 6, 1994.

13. Lane, *ibid.*

14. *The New York Times*, November 10, 1994.

15. Binder, "Anatomy of a Massacre," *Foreign Policy*, No. 97, Winter 1994-95.

Also the "flower pattern" signature of the mortar when it detonated on the pavement showed its source was no more than a couple of streets away.

The timing of the tragedy was suspiciously close to the departure of President Izetbegovic who forty-eight hours later was on his way to plead again to the United Nations to lift the arms embargo.

Instead, the Sarajevo reporters awaited their opportunity for more feverish headlines and television reports which would be provided by the upcoming propaganda theater at Gorazde. As Alexander Cockburn wrote concerning the Markale bombing:

> "This was the finale of a set-up by the Bosnian Muslims.
> ...(The) Bosnian Muslims and their U.S. public-relations firm
> have been successful in manipulating opinion here."[16]

Like Gorazde, the Merkale disaster bit deeply into the collective journalistic conscience about past obsessions with Muslim victimologies. Several correspondents were introspectively troubled over the sagging ethics in the media's hawkish attack against Serbs. The trickle of disillusionment had already set in for some foreign journalists in Belgrade by early 1993.

"The reporters here have had their own wars with their editors," confided Cedric Thornberry, director of Civilian Affairs for UNPROFOR in Belgrade. "It was driving one literally crazy until she demanded to be transferred."[17]

Other journalists were privately troubled.

"I was schocked when a relative read a story to me over the telephone," said Laura Silber, an American correspondent for *The Financial Times*, who replaced Judy Dempsey after the latter was transferred to Berlin. "My byline was on top of the story, but I couldn't recognize anything else."[18] Silber echoed the growing complaint from numerous journalists that desk editors thousands of miles away wanted stories about the war kept "black and white. There was no room for nuance."[19]

"I've done the same story fifty times!" said a frustrated Timothy Judah, of *The Times* (London), in Belgrade in January 1994.

A *BBC* correspondent angrily recalled how in May 1992 she had been in Belgrade when she received an important tip.[20] More than 1,000 Serb civilians—including men, women, children and many elderly—from villages around the southwestern Bosnian town of Bradina were imprisoned by Muslims and Croats in a partly destroyed railroad tunnel at Konjic, southwest of Sarajevo.

"My editors said they were interested in the story," she recalled. But they balked when she said it would take at least a week to make the round trip to get the story. Months later, she was near Konjic on another story and managed to verify details of the earlier report although the Serb prisoners were no longer there.

"The story was true, but several months had passed," she recalled. "I did the story anyway, but it wasn't played very well because of the late timing."[21]

The *Reuters* bureau chief in Belgrade, Don Forbes, agreed that the media had failed to make readers and viewers "sufficiently aware" of legitimate territorial claims of

---

16. *Los Angeles Times*, April 12, 1994.

17. Interview with author in Belgrade, February 10, 1993.

18. Laura Silber, an American correspondent for *The Financial Times*, who replaced Judy Dempsey after the latter was transferred to Berlin.

19. Interview with author in Belgrade, February 15, 1993. Silber was referring to her report that was picked up by *The Washington Post*.

20. Interview with author in Belgrade, February 13, 1993.

21. Interview in Belgrade, February 13, 1993

Serbs in Bosnia. However, the Bosnian government's PR machine was running full-speed with Foreign Minister Haris Silajdzic screeching his claims about mass rape. By February 1993, Forbes was blunt:

> "The problem with the rapes is that this guy Silajdzic is a total idiot in terms of the case he presents. It's just hype, hype, hype. He talks about 30,000 women being raped. Well, shit! We don't carry the stuff anymore. This guy has given us so many bum steers, playing on the fact that he's the Foreign Minister so people have to accept what the representative of the government says."[22]

Yet *Reuters'* correspondent in Sarajevo, Kurt Schork, a Muslim sympathizer judging from his reports aired on *National Public Radio* throughout the war, still considered Silajdzic a source for credible commentary in an *NPR* broadcast through April 5, 1995.

National Public Radio—'Radio Free Sarajevo'

There are two stories about what happened at Srebrenica—both equally hideous. Receiving enormous coverage was the story after July 1995 when thousands of Muslim combatants, along with some civilians, supposedly were slaughtered or turned up missing after Bosian Serb attacks and a chaotic, short-lived fifty-mile escape attempt toward Tuzla.

Then there was the "story" before July 1995—which was strangely kept out of the headlines. More than 1,000 Serbs in nearly 100 villages in the Srebrenica area were believed to have been slaughtered by Bosnian Muslim soldiers in the weeks and months before the final Serb onslaught of Srebrenica and the media melee that followed.

National Public Radio—or "Radio Free Sarajevo" as some called it—reached reporting extremes during late spring of 1993 with its packed menu of one-sided commentary about the besieged Srebrenica enclave, including one laughably paradoxical reference to the Vance-Owen peace plan as a "war plan," which it was (and as its nearly identical Dayton successor or any other "plan" would be).

NPR, subsidized in part with tax-exempt private funds and airing over numerous publicly-funded radio stations, had a vast amount of commercially uncluttered time for airing the best explanatory journalism. So, it is particularly deserving of criticism for extreme advocacy reporting, omissions and errors when it set up its media beachhead at Srebrenica during the week of April 12, 1993, when *NPR* lobbed a succession of journalistic bricks:

> •That the U.N. Security Council was meeting "to consider tightening sanctions gainst Bosnian Serbs," said *NPR's* Karl Kassell. There were never sanctions against Bosnian Serbs.

> •That the Vance-Owen plan had been signed by Bosnian Muslims, Croats and "Croatian Serbs"—the latter a glaring misnomer. When reporter Trevor Rowe was asked about the statement, he rasped: "You didn't call me up just to tell me that, did you?" No correction resulted. Moreover, through repeated use of the politically-biased term, the Serbs in the breakaway Republic of

22. Forbes interview with author in Belgrade, February 14, 1993.

Serbian Krajina were routinely called "Croatian Serbs" through 1995, through deliberate coinage of the misleading term.

•That Srebrenica had been under an artillery siege by Serbs the previous year. Actually, *NPR's* Jean Cochran was correct but omitted that the Bosnian government army's artillery and horrific attacks had been loosed against civilians in numerous Serb villages around Srebrenica for months. The later calamity at Srebrenica in July 1995 eventually resulted from the chaotic retreat by the government army and a final counterattack by indignant Serbs against Bosnian military forces which had used the town and the huge population of Muslim refugees as a shield. "I was just flat in error," admitted the *NPR's* Jean Cochran later. But again, no public correction. Nor was there any similar context provided during the final onslaught and fall of the Srebrenica "safe area" in mid-summer of 1995.[23]

•That a doctor at Srebrenica had performed over a thousand operations during the previous ten-month period before April 1993. But unreported was that most of the surgery was for Bosnian government troops from the preceding campaign of attacks and atrocities against Bosnian Serb civilians and villages.

There were other minimized accounts about what was really happening in Srebrenica and elsewhere, such as one surprising report that appeared in early 1993 and which, though available, was ignored by *NPR*:

> "Amid one of the biggest enemy offensives of the Bosnian war, a popular former officer is urging a government probe of the military and its commander. Armin Pohara, who became a hero for leading resistance to Serb attacks in northern Bosnia at the start of the year old war, says a special commission should be formed to examine such issues as why the army had not managed to break the siege of Sarajevo or prevent Serbs from overrunning villages in eastern Bosnia earlier this month."[24]

There was no follow-up.

But within a month another story appeared, likewise ignored, giving a clearer perspective about the suspicious carnage at Srebrenica and hinting at an overall pattern that was easily visible for any reporters who wanted to look.

The story written by a Bosnian Muslim journalist in Tuzla. Haris Nezirovic report in *The Observer* provocatively began with a chilling suggestion:

---

23. *NPR* and others omitted reporting that Srebrenica had never been a "safe area" under the terms of the 1993 cease fire brokered by UNPROFOR commander General Morillon. Under U.N. requirements, "safe areas" were not to be occupied and used as staging areas for raids by combat units of the Bosnian government army, which had violated the condition continuously since 1993 not only at Srebrenica but also at Gorazde and other U.N.-designated safe areas.
24. David Crary, *Associated Press*, March 20, 1993.

"The most horrifying thing about the siege of Srebrenica was neither starvation, nor epidemics, nor shelling, nor the 2,000 deaths they caused. The most horrifying thing was the fact that the town didn't have to be under siege at all. At the end of January, the Bosnian army needed to advance only three miles to break the encirclement of the town, but political chicanery plus some hefty bribes put a stop to their progress. Parts of the Bosnian command did not want Srebrenica to be liberated, as a combination of cash, power and orders persuaded them to acquiesce in the continuation of the siege."[25]

Renate Flottau, Belgrade correspondent for *Der Spiegel*, described her concerns about reporting bias in the Yugoslav wars and why some reporters preferred, as they did during the Srebrenica fighting, to look the other way:

"We had a big problem with all the newspapers from the very beginning. We said the good ones are the Croatians and the Slovenes, and the bad ones are the Serbs. And sometimes it was dangerous or difficult to say the Serbs are not as bad and the Croatians are not as good. And I think there was a long period when nobody had the courage to do it. It was always easier to say something good about the Croatians and something worse about the Serbs. I think it is still true."[26]

'Shady Strategems' And Risky Dissent

American writer Bella Stumbo said she "went through hell" and had to threaten editors at *Vanity Fair* with legal action while trying to salvage any "fairness" for her story about Serbian President Slobodan Milosevic and his wife, Mira.[27]

Julijana Mojsilovic, an *Associated Press* reporter in Belgrade, was angry with the revision of her story distributed in the U.S. in late 1991 about a village near the front lines in eastern Croatia. The fighting had subsided, and the story was about Serb and Croat neighbors who were repairing each others houses. But the story's lead was changed to focus on a bullet from a Croatian sniper that zinged past Mojsilovic. "I didn't think that was the most important thing in the story, and they led the story with that." The original version of the story ran in German newspapers, she said.[28]

Strangely, media outrage about the killing of its own, as when *ABC* producer David Kaplan was murdered in 1992 by a sniper in Sarajevo, fell silent as soon as it became apparent the shot could not have been fired by Bosnian Serbs who were originally blamed.

Media silence also shrouded the murder of British photojournalist Paul Jenks who died on January 17, 1992, in eastern Croatia. Predictably, a shot from a "Serb sniper" more than 900 meters away, was officially blamed, according to Sandra Balsells' story in *Barcelona's La Fotografia* after her twenty-two month investigation:

---

25. Haris Nezirovic, *The Observer*, April 20, 1993.
26. Interview with author in Belgrade, February 1993.
27. "Slobo and Dr. Mira," *Vanity Fair*, June 1994.
28. Interview with author in Belgrade, February 1993.

"The Croatian authorities took profit out of their position as victims of the Yugoslav conflict to carry out shady stratagems against the foreign press. In that way, in the summer of 1991, a shameful process of intrigues, misinformation, manipulations and threats was started, making our job even more difficult. ...The international recognition of Croatia was at stake and the Croatian leaders were not ready to allow any foreign journalist to spoil their plans."[29]

Croatia was internationally recognized two days before Jenks was killed. But Balsells said Jenks had written an article four months earlier under the headline "High Risk, Low Return" for the *Daily Telegraph,* describing "the risky game of conspiracy against foreign journalists. The article meant a great reverse for the sophisticated propagandistic machinery of Zagreb."

Jenks was twenty-nine when he died, and newspapers and magazines which had used his photos but did nothing to investigate his murder, said Balsells, included the *International Herald Tribune, The New York Times, The Times* (London), Liberation, *The Guardian, Time, Newsweek* and others.

By mid-1995, sixty-eight journalists had died in the Yugoslav wars,[30] lowering the incentive to produce any but continuing—and safer—stories from Sarajevo or Zagreb about non-Serb victims.

Venturing beyond the safety of Sarajevo or Zagreb hotel rooms continued to be hazardous as late as August 9, 1995, when *BBC* journalist John Schofield was killed by a single gunshot wound in the neck which was suspiciously fired, said U.N. spokesman Chris Gunness, "from quite close range." Before the shooting, Schofield and his cameraman, accompanying a relief convoy, had been "filming houses" in burned-out Serb villages in Krajina. "Croatian officials blamed rebel Serbs for the attack," said a brief *Associated Press* report, quoting Gunness further that Croatian soldiers "actually apologized for the killing."[31]

Said *NPR's* Sylvia Poggioli:

"In June 1993, two American reporters who had been covering the region for some time were discussing the disastrous role the international community had played in this tragedy. One of the reporters then said, 'but it has been journalism's finest hour.' I beg to differ. There have been innumerable instances where these conflicts have fallen into the disinformation trap. One of the most insidious was the numbers game—number of dead, number of refugees and, especially, number of rape victims."[32]

American reporters especially seemed addicted to shallow episodes about refugees and human interest stories, avoiding all but half-hearted probing into the suspiciously prolonged agony of Sarajevo. But, as noted by Poggioli, it hadn't started in Sarajevo:

---

29. "Low Return: The Dangers of Covering the Balkan War," *La Fotografia,* Spring 1994.

30. *Associated Press,* May 3, 1995.

31. *Associated Press*, August 10, 1995; see also Raymond Bonner, *The New York Times*, August 12, 1995.

32. Poggioli, *ibid.*

> "Starting with the ten-day war in Slovenia in June and July of 1991, one of the most difficult tasks for reporters has been to protect themselves from the propaganda offensive. The Slovenia Information Ministry organized a media center in a modern underground conference hall in Ljubljana. Here troops of young multi-lingual Slovenes constantly churned out reams of war bulletins. I sat through numerous bunker press conferences held by Defense Minister Janez Jansa while a dozen militiamen pointed Kalashnikovs at the reporters. The reason given was that they believed Serbian 'terrorists' had infiltrated the press corps. The effect was to create an atmosphere of extreme tension and alarm. Press conferences were often called as late as 7 p.m. We were supplied with excruciatingly detailed accounts of battles too far away to check personally before deadline. Often we learned the next day that the battles had never taken place. ...The Croats soon learned from the Slovenes' use of propaganda."[33]

Disturbed by the media's fixation with siege-mongering, one wire service editor in Europe had become concerned by late 1993 and wanted to divert from the profuse coverage about victims in Sarajevo and elsewhere in Bosnia. A meeting was held with top management.

"We wanted to talk about where they saw the Bosnia story going and where we see it going," said Alison Smale, who managed the *Associated Press'* bureau in Vienna.[34] Smale's bureau was the distribution center for all reports arriving from *AP* correspondents and stringers in the Yugoslav wars. Smale candidly acknowledged the more than three-year-old media blackout against coverage of the Serbian side of the conflict, stating spontaneously that "the Serbs have a case."

Still unresolved—Smale said because the media had ignored it—"is the whole argument about why the right of self-determination for the Croats in Croatia should be greater than for the Serb minority or the Serbs in the then-Yugoslavia."

The case for change put before Bill Ahearn, *Associated Press* vice president and executive editor, urging a shift to coverage of the "things that we think are important and the deeper issues that one has to cover sometimes. It's hard to get people interested in that because they want, you know, the winter, the cold, the guns, the stuff that's easy to understand about this terrible tragedy which, of course, should be reported anyway. And we also sort of said we just frankly don't know but we see the interest going down. And he said, 'No, no. This is a big human story. We stay with it completely.' No question in his mind whatsoever."[35] Also captive to the daily grind of reporting the carnage from Bosnia was *The Washington Post's* Mary Battiata, who said:

> "You have this raging-out-of-control story that you have to do. And then you've got all these other ones, and you think: 'I've got to go to Belgrade and do that story.' And, of course, you can't do every one. ...It appears to you and to a lot of other people that the end of the world is occurring in Bosnia, and you write all these stories."[36]

---

33. Poggioli, *ibid.*
34. Smale interview with author in Vienna, January 10, 1994.
35. Smale, *ibid.*
36. Battiata, American University panel discussion, October 5, 1993.

One of the most memorably skewed "victim" stories to come out of the Bosnian war was reported by John F. Burns in *The New York Times* on January 5, 1993, describing the tragic death of ten residents of a Sarajevo nursing home. They had frozen to death. But Burns omitted that some of the victims were Serbs, implying instead that they were all Muslims. Witnesses said bodies were taken for burial to a Serbian cemetery—an action which should have raised some question about all the victims being Muslims. What made the incident even more bizarre was the appearance seventeen months later of the George Soros/DePaul University project's results in the U.N.'s Final Report of the Commission of Experts to the Security Council about the control of food and water as weapons of war at Sarajevo:

> "The tendency of both sides to control food, water and electricity for publicity purposes...and *the fact that no one appears to have died during the siege from starvation, dehydration or freezing*, combine to make difficult the establishment of a solid case that starvation is being used as a method of warfare."[37] (Italics added)

Aside from contradicting the cause of deaths at the nursing home, this revelation was a baffling reversal after headline harangues for two years about starvation in Sarajevo.

The U.N. report was never publicly disputed as the Western media persisted in its coverage of the Yugoslav wars, decrying continued episodes of mass starvation nevertheless.

Ever so rare were even private regrets, such as came with admission about excesses when the media eagerly pounced on a statement from an unnamed FBI source who said Serbs were targeted as suspects in the World Trade Center bombing in New York City on February 26, 1993.

But *The Economist* of London on March 6, 1993, outdid all others with a photo that appeared in its story on the bombing. The picture showed an investigator running his gloved fingers through the rubble, and the caption read: "Looks like Serbs to me."

The author wrote a letter to *The Economist* some weeks later after the arrests of members of an Islamic terrorist ring who were charged for the crime, asking about the caption and the absence of a correction. Ann Wroe, the magazine's American editor, replied:

> "I must say I regret that caption. At the time we went to press, it was Serb organizations who had been most eager to claim credit for the bombing. The very next day, an Arab was arrested. Once the Arabs came into the picture, everyone forgot that for some days Serbs had been the principal suspects. The caption made sense for about a day, and after that looked both strange and gratuitously insulting. It does not often happen that the news overtakes us like that; if we think it may, we generally don't give hostages to fortune. I hope this answers your query; and I hope we don't give cause for puzzlement (or offense) again."[38]

There was never any proof that "Serb organizations" ever claimed responsibility for the bombing.

---

37. U.N. document No. S/1994/674, May 27, 1994, p. 48.
38. Ann Wroe, correspondence to the author, May 1993.

'I Hate The News. The News Is Evil'

With unusual candor, *The Washington Post's* Mary Battiata offered a poignant explanation for the news-reporting melee and confusion in the Yugoslav civil wars:
"I think that this war is the war of our post-Cold War disorientation because everyone seems to be floundering and struggling to understand and explain—and we, too, in the press, I think."[39]

Contrast Battiata's introspection to the callous reporting by *CNN* correspondent Christiane Amanpour.

Amanpour was the most recognizable face of war reporting to the public. The native Iranian was part of *CNN* boss Ted Turner's intentions to conquer the global news market. There is no doubt the martyrdom of Sarajevo was exploited by *CNN* and the ever-glowering Amanpour, his surly correspondent in Sarajevo.

Quality and objective news coverage were not part of the *CNN* mission:

> "Ted Turner's vision was always more technological than anything else. In 1976, the same year he pioneered cable by taking local Atlanta station *WTBS* nationwide via satellite, he replaced the anchor on his news show with a German shepherd. 'I hate the news. News is evil,' he explained. Four years later when he launched *CNN*, Turner talked about a news organization as an engine for world peace and global understanding. But this vision, too, was mostly technological. As he explained in 1990, 'I want to look to the future, not the past. We need more cultural exchanges, scientific exchanges, satellite exchanges. The impact of Turner's vision first flowered in the mid-1980s when *CNN* began making its signal available to broadcasters in exchange for video footage. Rather than creating harmony, however, the effect was to accelerate the pace with which international events would turn, and to give voice to political leaders who otherwise lacked political standing. Turner's intent was to help *CNN* have foreign bureaus on the cheap. ...But most of the foreign broadcasters it was signing deals with were government-run. Effectively, if somewhat accidentally, *CNN* was building a worldwide web of foreign ministries. That web soon made *CNN* a pulpit for foreign politicians who lacked traditional diplomatic standing, especially fading despots and sponsors of terrorism. Before long, the channel television critics once dismissed as Chicken Noodle Network was becoming a new force in foreign affairs."[40]

Amanpour, with her upbringing in Tehran's Muslim culture, graduated with a journalism degree from the University of Rhode Island in 1983 at about the time that questions arose about *CNN*:

---

39. Battiata, *ibid.*
40. Tom Rosenstiel, "The Myth of CNN: Why Ted Turner's revolution is bad news," *The New Republic*, August 22-29, 1994.

"By the mid-1980s *CNN* was having a significant if unintentional role in the press's loss of control over its own professional standards."[41]

Building her career and television image for unequaled biased reporting in the Balkan wars, Amanpour eventually became CNN's "foreign ministry" in Sarajevo where her news "reporting" at least rivaled the rhetoric and bias coming from the information specialists on the payroll of the Bosnian Muslim government. In a profile of Amanpour by *The New York Times*' Stephen Kinzer, she was judged as having stepped beyond the bounds of even advocacy journalism:

> "Amanpour is not simply a news reporter, but a television personality who performs in a news context, the first to emerge from the upstart Atlanta-based network. Because *CNN* is correspondent-driven, not only allowing reporters to shape their own coverage but often allowing them to choose what they cover, she has exercised more influence over what viewers see than almost any reporter in television. 'She pushed *CNN* to cover the Bosnia story when there really wasn't much interest in it,' said one network insider who requested anonymity. 'She just insisted on going there, and the impact of her coverage forced the other networks to follow. It was another example of her great news instincts.' But this same insider has doubts about Amanpour's commitment to objective journalism. 'I have winced at some of what she's done, at what used to be called advocacy journalism,' he said. 'She was sitting in Belgrade when the marketplace massacre happened, and she went on the air to say that the Serbs had probably done it. There was no way she could have known that. She was assuming an omniscience which no journalist has.'"[42]

An earlier assessment of Amanpour opened in much the same way that she would begin one of her own commentaries with the backdrop of deep snow in Sarajevo. Amanpour and her crew are crusing the city in their armored car, looking over the wreckage and skeletal apartment buildings searching for something to film. Amanpour suddenly notices an old man watching over his dairy cow which is grasing in a small patch of grass. Her imagination ignites and she orders her driver to stop, letting out the crew and Amanpour who shouts, "let's do the cow." Amanpour lively asks the man if he intends to sell the cow in the market of "the beseiged capital of Bosnia-Herzegovina, where people are starving and food prices are exorbident." His stiff response is that he'll "be selling cheese, not beef."[43]

The article cites the comment she made about her family's move from Tehran to London in 1978 and Amanpour's first yearnings "to be in the middle of things, with all the movers and shakers" as a "foreign correspondent."

Five years later she started out at *CNN* when, recalled one of her first supervisors, her post-collegiate ambitions had changed:

---

41. Rosenstiel, *ibid.*

42. Kinzer, "Where There's War There's Amanpour," *The New York Times Magazine*, October 9, 1994.

43. Ron Arias, "CNN's Woman at the Front," People Magazine, December 20, 1993.

"She said she wanted to be a star."[44]

The *People* narrative was accompanied by a photo spread. The last picture showed an uncharacteristically beaming Amanpour and her crew off-camera, toasting each other across an ample table at the Sarajevo Holiday Inn. There was no mistaking her self-image and reporting style as the undisputed "star" of Sarajevo amidst starvation and astronomical food costs. And there was no mistaking the presumption of immunity—from combate or professional conscience for her sneering dislike of the Serbs—she shared with her media peers in the coverage of the Yugoslav wars as winter approaches when "a lot of people are going to die." She crassly remarks she is there only to "report it." It's up to others to "do something about it,"[45]

And, after another five years, Amanpour wrote in *The New York Times* ("The Myth of the Cavalier Correspondent," July 17, 1998): "The bottom line is that a television correspondent's most important contract is with the public... Trust and credibility are the commodities we trade in; without them we are worthless."

Noticeably, she risked omitting the "commodities" of objectivity and truthfulness—concepts absent from the occupation of the professional performer.

---

44. Arias, *ibid.*
45. Arias, *ibid*

Chapter 12

The Hague:
Experiment In Orwellian Justice

O eyes, no eyes, but fountains fraught with tears;
O life, no life, but lively form of death;
O world, no world, but mass of public wrongs,
Confused and filled with murder and misdeeds.[1]
—**Thomas Kyd**

Summum ius summa iniuria
(Extreme justice is extreme injustice).[2]
—**Cicero**

As of late 2002, the killing fields in Bosnia were still being selectively excavated by forensic teams from the United Nations who sifted the remains for evidence to be used in the selective prosecution of alleged war criminals at The Hague. Since mass graves were dug up, beginning in 1996, about 3,500 corpses, in varying degrees of decay and unidentifiability, were stacked in body bags, seven-tiers deep, in a warehouse at Tuzla as of late 2002.

But, in an apparent unexplained surge of forensic zeal, nearly half again as many were apparently unearthed by late summer 2003—less than a year later!—as the *Associated Press* reported "5,000 bodies have been recovered from areas near Srebrenica. Of those, 1,083 had been identified using DNA."[3]

And, curiously, by the end of the decade, cadavers from various regions of Bosnia were being quietly transported around the country and, U.N. officials and others suspected, were being lumped together as "Srebrenica victims"! The explanation from Bosnian officials was that bodies were retrieved in other graves where they were first buried to hide their identification as victims from the July 1995 "massacre" at Srebrenica. But, the grisly inventory at Tuzla likely included other corpses that

---

1. *The Spanish Tragedy*, Act III, 1594.
2. *De Officiis*, I, 10, 33.
3. *Associated Press*, September 20, 2003.

pre-dated the July 1995 killings and bore enough signs that they were not Muslims —but local Serbs murdered earlier by Bosnian Muslim troops and mercenaries!

On the eve of the trial of indicted Bosnian Muslim commander Nasir Oric, forensic scientists from The Hague were noticeably silent about any exhumations of the nearly 1,000 Serb civilians killed at Bratunac and at nearby Serb villages that provoked the retaliation and killings of Muslims at Srebrenica.

Challenges persisted about the July 1995 Srebrenica episode. In early 1996, Linda Ryan questioned the toll of 8,000 dead in the Bosnian Muslim "massacre" (Missing Evidence," Linda Ryan, *NOVO* magazine, March/April 1996):

> "Whence the data on the alleged massacres at Srebenica? They are primarily based on a wrong interpretation of ...information of the International Committee of the Red Cross (ICRC). On 13 September 1995 it distributed a press release. It said that the ICRC had received about 10,000 reports (from) refugees in Tuzla who lost contact with family members after their flight from Srebrenica. About 2,000 of these reports were filed by various members of one family searching the same relative. It was then communicated that a careful investigation of the remaining 8,000 cases had shown that they were divided in two categories: 5,000 of those disappeared were the persons that had left the enclave even before its fall. The remaining 3,000 persons were captured by Bosnian Serbs. (ICRC News, No. 37). Accordingly, by the ICRC statement, at most 3,000 Muslims were killed. Despite this fact, the media toyed with the figure of 8,000.

> "The International Committee of the Red Cross came out with the assumption that between 5,000 to 8,000 refugees from Srebrenica had arrived to the Bosnian territory, but that their families had not been advised thereof. It was only when the ICRC began to make determined inquiries in Sarajevo (a) few months later (that) the Bosnian Government conceded that thousands of soldiers that had fled Srebrenica were re-assigned to other units of its armed forces. The fact that family members were not informed of it was justified by the obligation to keep it a military secret. However, the media did not attach much attention to this information."

And, a few days after the attack, *The New York Times* (on July 18, 1995) and The Times of London (August 2, 1995) had reported:

> "Some 3,000 to 4,000 Bosnian Muslims who were considered by UN officials to be missing after the fall of Srebrenica have made their way through enemy lines to Bosnian government territory. The group, which included wounded refugees, sneaked past Serb lines under fire and crossed some 30 miles through forests to safety." (*The New York Times*)

> "Thousands of the 'missing' Bosnian Muslim soldiers from Srebrenica who have been at the center of reports of possible

mass executions by the Serbs, are believed to be safe to the northeast of Tuzla.

"Monitoring the safe escape of Muslim soldiers and civilians from the captured enclaves of Srebrenica and Zepa has proved a nightmare for the United Nations and the International Committee of the Red Cross. For the first time yesterday, however, the Red Cross in Geneva said it had heard from sources in Bosnia that up to 2,000 Bosnian Government troops were in an area north of Tuzla.

"They had made their way there from Srebrenica "without their families being informed," a spokesman said, adding that it had not been possible to verify the reports because the Bosnian Government refused to allow the Red Cross into the area." (*The Times* of London)

Similarly, George Pumphrey called attention to a later report in *The Washington Post*, describing that:

"'The men set off at dawn on Tuesday, July 11, in two columns that stretched back seven or eight miles.' Even if the Red Cross did not know that they left Srebrenica in 2 columns, they at least knew that 2,000 were safe. And UN officials knew of the 3,000-4,000 that had arrived earlier. Yet the communiqué given in September failed to report that the 5,000 that 'simply disappeared,' simply disappeared back into the ranks of the Bosnian military." ("Srebrenica 'Massacre': Is The Hague Hyping a Hoax?"—posted online, May 8, 2000)

Pumphrey also pointed to a pair of remarkable discoveries by Professor Milivoje Ivanisevic, of the University of Belgrade in late 1996:

"(Ivanisevic) ...took a close look at the Red Cross list, he discovered it contained the names of 500 people who were already deceased before Bosnian-Serb troops entered Srebrenica." ("Faux electeurs... ou faux cadavers," *Balkans Infos*, Paris; Oct. 1996, No. 6)

"Even more interesting, when comparing the Red Cross' list with the electoral list for the 1996 fall elections (at Srebrenica), he also found that 3,016 people listed by the Red Cross as 'missing' were on the electoral lists the following year. This leads to one of two possibilities: either the Muslims were having their dead vote, meaning that the voters were bogus, and the election a fraud; or the voters were in fact alive, in which case, here is an additional piece of evidence that the massacre is a fraud." See Milivoje Ivanisevic, Milivoje, "Un Dossier qui pose bien des Questions," *Balkans Infos*, Paris; Dec. 1996 (No.8).

Whether exhumations of more mass graves eventually yield thousands, or mere hundreds or dozens, becomes a tangle of speculation and manipulation of evidence. Whether the remains on hand fit the prosecution schemes at The Hague, advocates for a provocative concoction of new international justice fall back on the myth of future deterrence. But, as if by devilish design, the seeds of resumed Balkan chaos will remain buried until, predictably, the next hideous harvest is reaped by future Balkan generations.

The Serbs 'More Guilty'

The International Tribunal to Adjudicate War Crimes Committed in the Former Yugoslavia (ICTY) was anointed as the descendant of Nuremberg. But after a decade, it was Orwellian caricature in concert with presumptions that, yes, all sides in the Yugoslav conflagration are guilty—but the Serbs are "more guilty" than others.

Certainly, the ICTY never intended to completely exhume all graves in Bosnia, Croatia and Kosovo. That was tacitly understood as being left up to the individual republics.

In early 1993, Venezuelan jurist Ramon Escovar-Salom took a quick look around the borrowed offices and sparse furnishings at The Hague when he first visited the Tribunal—and promptly resigned.

Escovar-Salom was hired to lead prosecutions against war criminals when it was created in February 1993. Its first eleven justices were seated ceremonially three months later.

There were no prisoners in custody. There was no prison. There were suspects, including presidents, generals, politicians, even journalists. The list would grow. And there were scores of thousands of victims, claims of hundreds of thousands —and the numbers were increasing because the two-year-old Balkan wars were still raging. Also, there was no relevant law to follow.

"A brave experiment in justice of a new kind is underway at The Hague. Too brave for a world of sovereign states?" asked editors of The Economist. "Rules of procedure had to be written from scratch. Different legal traditions have had to be reconciled."[4]

At The Hague, a wing of twenty-four cells at nearby Scheveningen prison was being remodeled. "There are already a number of guards who are waiting anxiously, I would say, with impatience until they can receive the first inmate," said Theo Van Boven, the tribunal registrar, with almost morbid anticipation.[5]

But despite being propped up as a descendant of the Nuremberg war crimes trials, the legacy was nurtured most from naive agitations by the Western media. The Tribunal at The Hague would not be the sequel to the expeditious proceedings of victor's justice that followed World War II.

In fact, the extreme narrow focus on the handful of Nazi defendants at Nuremberg five decades earlier had sowed many of the seeds that led to the breakup and nationalist inferno in Yugoslavia.

At Nuremberg, even with the magnitude of the horrors of the Holocaust recounted in hideous testimony and evidence, it was a generally simplistic performance. Nazi leaders were put on trial and after eleven months the court ordered a dozen executions and handed out seven prison sentences and three acquittals. Although

---

4. "Justice Without Victors," The Economist, January 7, 1995.
5. Van Boven, during a December 19, 1994, press conference at The Hague on his own resignation and departure from the Tribunal.

genocide was catastrophically carried out against Serbs and Jews by Nazi troops and their Croatian and Muslim collaborators during the war, international justice was locked out of communist Yugoslavia. The Allies watched indifferently as Josip Broz Tito, a Croat, practiced his own brand of ruthless internal justice before dying in 1980. After all, it was communists killing communists—until ten years later when Tito's legacy of political prosecutions were resurrected at The Hague.

The Hague 'Experiment'

Since 1993, it was conceded that "the Hague experiment" would not produce any victor's justice as at Nuremberg. Nor would it be prompt—or just. It was experimental because its intended role was that of midwife to the birth of a permanent International Criminal Court (ICC). The latter is what excited the small club of international law scholars and their scant following of legal specialists. The success or failure of the ad hoc Yugoslav tribunal would mean the success or failure of the ICC.

There is hardly any public awareness about and even less notice of the skepticism from law scholars toward the kind of "justice" resulting from a permanent international court or its predecessor, the current U.N. Tribunal at The Hague with its alchemy of rules and procedures borrowed ad hoc from varying national judicial systems. For those concerned about the forfeiture of sovereignty and the sole accountability of an ICC to the United Nations, the Yugoslav Tribunal raises high alarm.

"If the U.N. takes on the powers to arrest, prosecute, sentence and imprison individuals, it is taking on sovereign powers hitherto reserved to states," said C. Douglas Lummis, co-president of the Pacific-Asia Resource Center and instructor of political philosophy at Tsuda College in Tokyo. "What we are seeing, in short, is the founding, albeit gradual and half-hidden, of a political entity unprecedented in history... Where does the U.N. get the power to prosecute individuals?... The legal fiction is that the power comes from Chapter VII of the U.N. Charter."[6]

Lummis and others, such as Dutch scholar Peter Baehr, insist that Chapter VII authorizes the U.N. to deploy the armed forces of member states in peacekeeping operations only.[7]

> "Stretch the words as you will, you cannot make them say that the U.N. has the power to put people in jail under criminal charges. ...But what is being proposed this time is to give the U.N. power to prosecute individuals from states that still retain their sovereign independence. The legal and practical problems this presents are enormous."[8]

By the end of 1994, exiting registrar Van Boven proudly pointed out that the Tribunal had compiled nearly 130 rules of evidence and procedure, compared to a scant ten used during the Nuremberg trials. [9]

Senior American prosecutor Minna Schrag, who was briefly on loan to The Hague from a New York law firm, told international law scholars it was a novel experience to be deciding precedent on rules of evidence and procedure during impromptu

---

6. Lummis, *The Nation*, September 26, 1994.
7. Baehr, interview with the author at the University of Utrecht, December 1994.
8. Lummis, *ibid.*
9. Van Boven, *ibid.*

conversations in hallways at the Yugoslav Tribunal![10]

"The Tribunal itself is making the law and ...the document will not have to be submitted to any other U.N. organ for approval," said Lummis. "They write it, and it's law. Just like that."[11]

But if there was no applicable law for the Yugoslav tribunal to follow, there was a semblance of evidence presented to the Tribunal in the form of the DePaul University war crimes "data-base," which was authorized—but not paid for—by the U.N. in 1993 under the Commission of Experts on the Former Yugoslavia. The rushed construction of the data-base by a group of "volunteers" at the DePaul University Law School in Chicago was overseen by Mahmoud Cherif Bassiouni, an Egyptian-born Muslim and specialist in international law. It was paid for by billionaire George Soros. Bassiouni was originally a member of the Commission of Experts who later succeeded Dutch law scholar Frits Kalshoven as chairman.

Bassiouni, who authored books and essays on Islam and the Palestine Liberation Organization, energetically promoted the Yugoslav Tribunal and the primary thrust of the DePaul project which predominantly compiled alleged crimes by Serb perpetrators.

Kalshoven, a prominent professor of international law at the University of Leiden, had exited the Commission of Experts after publicly criticizing the legal veracity of "evidence" of 20,000 alleged mass rapes gathered by the European Parliament's Warburton Commission in early 1993. Much of the same so-called evidence, derived from Bosnian government sources in Sarajevo and continuously embellished and recycled by journalists and humanitarian organizations, found its way to the final report from the Commission of Experts to the U.N. Security Council and was forwarded to The Hague in May 1994—minus any completed annexes with statistics or specific data to back up the report's allegations! Bassiouni's resurrection of rape estimates and numerical extrapolations were deceptions, said Kalshoven, in the campaign to exact "justice" against the Serbs using the biased research from DePaul.

"It was just a number, just guesswork," said Kalshoven.[12]

Bassiouni described the frenzied Serbo-centric exertions of his mostly volunteer researchers at DePaul to compile, as one worker called it, the "road map" that Bassiouni wanted the Yugoslav Tribunal to follow.

"We worked seven days a week, two shifts a day," Bassiouni said, claiming data was developed from Bosnian, Croat and Serb sources, "and finally amassed a sum total of about 65,000 documents. ...All of the reports were prepared on the basis of information which we received and which our lawyers and analysts put together and produced. ...Quite obviously, we did not have the resources in order to obtain *firsthand* information. We had to work out a *multiplier effect*."[13] (Italics added)

The DePaul project's yield of "65,000 documents" produced, using Bassiouni's "multiplier effect," a comparatively modest roster of 5,000 incidents of murder, rape, torture, kidnapping, mass graves and prison camps.[14]

Expected to produce evidence to support earlier claims of 50,000 rapes against Muslim women from Bosnian government propagandists, the DePaul research ranged uncertainly between 500 to 1,673 alleged victims, but eventually fell back on the

---

10. Schrag, speech at University of Virginia international law symposium, Charlottesville, March 1995.

11. Lummis, *ibid.*

12. Kalshoven interview with the author in Geneva, December 1994.

13. Bassiouni speech during international law symposium at the University of Virginia, Charlottesville, March 1995.

14. *Associated Press*, April 24, 1994.

earlier investigation by the Commission of Experts which documented only 105 cases of rape.[15]

Kalshoven remained skeptical about what was reported by the DePaul project to The Hague—and what was not reported.

"There is no way to check that he handed over all of it," said Kalshoven, who added Bassiouni clashed with other members of the Commission and that there was an obvious motive behind the biased conclusions in the report.

"He can only work with subordinates, slaves," said Kalshoven, concluding with a general observation about the prosecutorial significance of the data-base. "The data-base itself is passive."[16]

As of December 1994, the DePaul data-base was sitting virtually unused on the floor of the prosecutor's vault at The Hague, according to one investigator[17] who reflected doubts about the information, its affidavits and large quantities of data received from Zagreb, Croatia, and the Croatian Information Centre (CIC), a propaganda arm of the Croatian government.

Not surprisingly, the Commission of Experts' final report to the Security Council ignored its mandate and virtually ignored Bosnian and Croat incidents of atrocities and human rights abuses, offering simple denial as the absurd basis for excuse: "The Commission has ...ascertained that the Government of Bosnia and Herzegovina has expressed its opposition to these individual violations."[18]

U.N. Security Council 'Guilty' Of Double Standards

Notably, even supporters of the concept of a permanent International Criminal Court were wary of the Yugoslav Tribunal.

"Unfortunately, experience has shown that ad hoc judicial tribunals are too often created and manipulated to serve political interests of particular states. Ad hoc tribunals tend to lack real independence and impartiality and there is a serious risk that they will fail the basic tests of justice and fairness which are well established in international law," warned Amnesty International.[19] Amnesty International recognized at the outset that the Yugoslav Tribunal at The Hague was a selective creation which had evaded previous genocides and crimes against humanity in Cambodia, The Sudan, the Indonesian army's rampage in East Timor, Turkish and Iraqi persecutions of Kurds and others. Amnesty International was dubious:

> "Even if this ad hoc tribunal is fair, the Security Council is still guilty of double standards by setting up a tribunal only for this conflict."[20]

Likewise, two months after the Tribunal was summoned into existence on May 3, 1993, a special task force of the American Bar Association *(ABA)* produced an insightful booklet, entitled *Report on the International Tribunal to Adjudicate War Crimes Committed in the Former Yugoslavia*. The *ABA* cordially supported the

---

15. "Final Report of the Commission of Experts to the U.N. Security Council," May 27, 1994.
16. Kalshoven, *ibid.*
17. Author's interview at The Hague, December 1994.
18. "Final Report of the Commission of Experts to the U.N. Security Council," May 27, 1994.
19. Statement by the Amnesty International Secretariat, February 26, 1993, London.
20. Amnesty International, *ibid*

concept of prosecuting war crimes, but its skepticism was visible in citing nearly 150 general and specific concerns, suggestions, and recommendations applicable to numerous sections of the Statute of the International Tribunal.

Understandably, the *ABA* emphasized its reluctance about Rules of Evidence and Procedure to the use of exparte testimony and evidence and limitations for allowing the accused to confront accusers. The *ABA* was also uncomfortable about allowing appeals by prosecutors.

There was no mention about the issue of statute of limitations, which would open up a legal nightmare about unprosecuted war crimes before and since the institution of the Geneva Conventions in 1949.

Apparently, there were more than enough justifiable fears lurking in the collective conscience of the U.S., British and French that amazingly had survived after seven decades of "mythology" about the conduct of the Allies in World War II, according to Richard Drayton, a senior lecturer in history at Cambridge University, writing in *The Guardian*, as late as May 10, 2005, under the headline "An Ethical Blank Cheque: British and U.S. mythology about the Second World War":

> "In 1945, as at the end of all wars, the victor powers spun the conflict's history to serve the interests of their elites. War time propaganda thus achieved an extraordinary afterlife. ...In Britain and the U.S. ...a certain idea of the Second World War is enthusiastically kept alive and less flattering memories suppressed.

> "Five years ago, (Dr. J.) Robert Lilly, a distinguished American sociologist, prepared a book based on military archives. Taken by Force is a study of the rapes committed by American soldiers in Europe between 1942 and 1945. He submitted his manuscript in 2001. But after September 11, its U.S. publisher suppressed it, and it first appeared in 2003 in a French translation."

French publication of Lilly's book was in remarkable irony to that country's own guilt-beset, post-World War II conscience, as it is recalled by German historians that it was General Charles DeGaulle who was accorded the honor of "liberating" Stuttgart, unleashing his mobs of Algerian/Moroccan marauders and sadists that plundered, murdered and raped their way through the city. Continued Drayton:

> "...(W)e prefer not to know about mass rape committed by American and British troops. Lilly suggests a minimum of 10,000 American rapes. Contemporaries described a much wider scale of unpunished sex crime. *Time* Magazine reported in September 1945: 'Our own army and the British army along with ours have done their share of looting and raping ... we too are considered an army of rapists.'

> "The British and American publics share a sunny view of the Second World War. The evil of Auschwitz and Dachau, turned inside out, clothes the conflict in a shiny virtue. Movies, popular histories and political speeches frame the war as a symbol of Anglo-American courage ...This was, we believe, 'a war for democracy.' Americans believe that they fought the war to rescue the world...

"All this seems innocent fun, but patriotic myths have sharp edges. The 'good war' against Hitler has underwritten 60 years of warmaking. It has become an ethical blank cheque for British and US power. We claim the right to bomb, to maim, to imprison without trial on the basis of direct and implicit appeals to the war against fascism.

"When we fall out with such tyrant friends as Noriega, Milosevic or Saddam we rebrand them as 'Hitler.' In the 'good war' against them, all bad things become forgettable 'collateral damage.' The devastation of civilian targets in Serbia or Iraq, torture at Abu Ghraib and Guantánamo, the war crime of collective punishment in Faluja, fade to oblivion as the 'price of democracy...'"

A "report was issued by the German police chief of Stuttgart in August 1945 in which he stated that local police had verified 1,198 cases of rape. The ages of the victims ranged from 14 to 74 and most of them were attacked in their homes by turbaned Moroccans who broke down the doors in looting forays. Four of the women were killed by their attackers, and four others committed suicide. One of the victims was killed by her husband who then killed himself."[21]

More from Drayton:

"We forget ...that British and U.S. elites gave aid to the fascists. President Bush's grandfather, prosecuted for 'trading with the enemy' in 1942, was one of many powerful Anglo-Americans who liked Mussolini and Hitler and did what they could to help. Appeasement as a state policy was only the tip of an iceberg of practical aid to these dictatorships. Capital and technology flowed freely, and fascist despots received dignified treatment in Washington and London. Henry Ford made Hitler birthday gifts of 50,000 marks.

"We least like to remember that our side also committed war crimes in the 1940s. The destruction of Dresden, a city filled with women, children, the elderly and the wounded, and with no military significance, is only the best known of the atrocities committed by our bombers against civilian populations. We know about the notorious Japanese abuse of prisoners of war, but do not remember the torture and murder of captured Japanese. Edgar Jones, an 'embedded' Pacific war correspondent, wrote in 1946: 'We shot prisoners in cold blood, wiped out hospitals, strafed lifeboats, killed or mistreated enemy civilians, finished off the enemy wounded, tossed the dying into a hole with the dead, and in the Pacific boiled flesh off enemy skulls to make table ornaments.'"

With such skeletons still rattling persistently in Western closets, the Yugoslav Tribunal prudently was limited to offenses committed since January 1991.

Monroe Leigh, a Washington attorney and *ABA's* Task Force chairman, said the Tribunal's response was "cloudy" about the Commission of Experts final report. In

---

21. "Rape Story Dispute Grows in Stuttgart," *New York Times*, August 11, 1945.

view of the subsequent guidelines adopted by the Tribunal, Leigh's observation was profound understatement.

But two months before the creation of the Tribunal, there was at least one other set of recommendations submitted to the Tribunal. The Organization of the Islamic Conference (OIC) set forth a brief series of forty-two recommendations. The difference between this document and the *ABA* task force report is extraordinary if comparing only the sizes of the two documents. The *OIC's* six pages indicated it was very enthusiastic about the Tribunal's procedures headed for final adoption, including the right of appeals by prosecutors and provisions that defendants were liable to double jeopardy. The *ABA* task force report was seventy-one pages long with 150 concerns and, effectively, would be brushed aside.

Among the seven signatories to the OIC recommendations were representatives of Malaysia and Pakistan, each of which landed a judge on the original eleven-member Yugoslav Tribunal—Pakistani Rustam Sidhwa and Malaysian Lal Chand Vohrah. The rest of the original Tribunal included Gabrielle Kirk McDonald, an American; Adolphus Godwin Karibi-Whyte, of Nigeria; Germain Le Foyer de Costil, of France; Elizabeth Odio Benito, of Costa Rica; Antonio Cassese, of Italy; Georges Michel Abi-Saab, of Egypt; Jules Deschenes, of Canada; Li Haopei, of China; and Sir Ninian Stephen, of Australia.

Glaringly absent were representatives from nations with recognized reputations for neutrality, such as Sweden, Norway, Finland and Switzerland. Also omitted was any Tribunal member whose homeland contained a sizable Orthodox Christian population, while Roman Catholic/Islamic presence on the Tribunal was more than abundant. The Tribunal's composition was the more incredulous in light of the decision that sentences would conform to punishment, excepting the death penalty. Accusations that it was a "stacked" court could not be—but were—ignored.

When several new justices were hired in 1997, the same discriminatory—i.e. non-Slavic representation—pattern resulted. A footnote in the *ABA* task force report contained mention of the cloud that nagged the conscience of Western promoters of an international law collective since the end of World War II but never inspired any criticism from the bench of the Yugoslav Tribunal. Referring to the Tokyo War Crimes trials: "The French judge at the Tokyo Trials dissented from the Tribunal's decision as a whole on the ground that procedures were *inherently flawed*." (Italics added.)

As it applied to war crimes in the ashes of Yugoslavia, whatever "justice" served up at The Hague was selective and historically unjust.

Clearly, the investigators and prosecutors at The Hague were synchronized to look primarily for Serbian offenses. Escovar-Salom's successor admitted in private correspondence that serious investigations against suspects connected to atrocities and war crimes against Serb victims did not begin until 1995.[22]

Richard Goldstone, a former South African judge and runner-up successor to Escovar-Salom as chief prosecutor at The Hague, indicated his investigators had taken a passive posture, admitting that they had received initial information about Croat and Muslim abuses but had received no responses to a series of "requests" and "correspondence" for additional information or evidence through use of "the usual diplomatic channels" with the Federal Republic of Yugoslavia. The priorities at The Hague clearly aimed at prosecutions against Serbs for genocide.[23]

By March 1996, investigators were compelled to follow up on the existence of a Muslim-run detention camp which had held up to 600 male and female Serb civilians

---

22. Justice Richard Goldstone in private correspondence related to the Tarcin crimes by Bosnian Muslims, December 1995.
23. Goldstone correspondence, *ibid.*

in an empty wheat silo at Tarcin near Sarajevo. Torture, abuse and starvation were suffered by civilian inmates of all ages since the Tarcin silo began operating as a prison camp in May 1992—a month after the Bosnian war began and three months before the media hysterically announced the discovery of Serb-run detention camps in Bosnia.[24] By mid-1996—and nearly eight months after signing of the Dayton peace accords that called for immediate release of all prisoners—Tarcin remained in full operation! Though plentifully documented as existing as early as 1992 by the International Red Cross, the Tarcin silo investigation dragged forward through 1997.

By June 1997, blind Lady Justice was keeping one eye opened at The Hague with indictments against fifty-four Serbs, eighteen Croats and three Muslims. By design, justice at The Hague moved slowly for some and rapidly for others.

"Out of indignation at the war in Bosnia, the world has at last agreed to a workable legal framework, and in remarkably short time," *The Economist* editorialized naievely.[25]

Along with the *ABA's* reservations, it appeared that the mainstream of Western and American lawyers especially were vulnerable and vexed by the media and political indignation driving the five year old Yugoslav wars. Also, it was predictable they would be gullibly sucked along in the stampede to inflict justice upon the handful of defendants destined for trial at The Hague.

However, it was remarkable that the rush to judgment was detoured through unthinkable shortcuts in comparison with the American judicial system, such as:

- Allowing substantial forfeiture of defense rights to cross-examine witnesses.

- Disallowing the rights of accused to confront their accusers.

- Permitting liberal use of hearsay and minimized requirements for production of forensic evidence if not allowing its outright absence.

- Depreciation of guarantees as equal protection under the law.

- And more repugnant to American thinking, the Tribunal with its selective oversight could bring defendants to trial again after acquittals or token convictions and light sentences from national courts, thus eliminating protection from double-jeopardy.

"It's very important for us to resist the judicial romanticism that infects American lawyers, a belief that if we just create a court and set it up somewhere, it will begin to bring about changes *ipso facto* by its existence," warned Michael Reisman, professor of international law at the Yale University School of Law. "...Indignation can also lead to impetuous, destructive action. In some cases (war crimes tribunals) are likely to increase the costs of suspending violations under way, for violators will conclude that if they do not prevail they will be tried and punished... If the elite and substantial parts of the rank and file of one side anticipate that a consequence of a peace agreement will be their prosecution and punishment for their acts in the course of the conflict, they will hardly be disposed to lay down their arms."[26]

---

24. Internal investigative documents, dated April 1995, on file with the Tribunal at The Hague.

25. *The Economist, ibid.*

26. Reisman, speech at University of Virginia international law symposium, Charlottesville, March 1995.

Such potential was clear in the political creation of the Tribunal before the end of Yugoslav hostilities in weighing the double-edged effects of the its dubious creation —and its life span. Reisman was struck by the peculiar mission and longevity of the Yugoslav Tribunal set up by the U.N. Security Council:

> "Curiously, the manifest purpose of the establishment...of the Yugoslav Tribunal was not to punish serious violators but to secure compliance with obligations under international law and to press the parties to a peace agreement...Thus, the moment a peace agreement was secured between the warring factions the life of the Tribunal would end. In the ordinary course of events it is precisely at the end of a conflict that an international Tribunal kicks into operation... (W)e should be quite candid: at least at the moment of creation, the purpose and essential design of the Tribunal was to use it to accomplish goals unsuited to its structure and to terminate it as soon as those goals were secured."[27]

Without doubt the Tribunal was intended less for justice than for political leverage— primarily by the U.S.—to extort concessions primarily from Serb leaders with the threat of redoubled sanctions against innocent and primarily Serb civilians.

Racist Justice For Rwanda

Suddenly, in the midst of the Bosnian fighting, genocidal slaughter broke out in Rwanda and forced the awkward creation of a companion Tribunal in 1994. But highly publicized indignation, along with some initial dedication to equally apply international justice to alleged genocides in Yugoslavia and Rwanda, evolved into lopsided results through mid-1996 and suggested a latent racism and pacifism about African war crimes.

In Yugoslavia and Bosnia, white Europeans fought each other. Slovenians, Croats, Muslims and Serbs were ethnically indistinguishable in the mayhem that yielded propaganda-inflated fatalities of 200,000 or more when hostilities ceased by mid-1995. The Rwandan Tribunal was a face-saving, public-relations maneuver thrown together with little hope for justice after the much more savage rampages among blacks in Rwanda where up to one million were slaughtered!

Optimism for the Tribunal as the panacea equally suited to Rwanda as Yugoslavia was misplaced despite such expectations voiced in an early editorial: "Rwanda should be the easier case in practical terms because evidence is plentiful and the perpetrators more accessible."

But the Rwanda exercise eventually languished with ineptness by The Hague's investigators—most of whom were non-black and strangers to Africa.

One human rights worker recalled how she sent a list of possible witnesses at two massacres to the Tribunal's investigators:

> "'They sent me back a form to fill with spaces for name, street address and telephone number,' she said. There are no telephones and no streets in rural Rwanda."[28]

---

27. Reisman, *ibid.*
28. Editorial, *The Independent*, November 2, 1994.

Prosecutor Richard Goldstone, though celebrated more as a "reformer" by non-South Africans, displayed exactly the kind of imperialist behavior that gratified skeptics elsewhere in Africa who had questioned whether he could fairly and comprehensively sort out Rwandan war crimes. Goldstone, a white jurist, exhibited a presence that was ambitious, ethical, and energetic, vowing he would play no favorites nor would he be restrained or intimidated by politics. But with Goldstone as the Tribunal's figurehead, prospects for justice with Rwanda were unsettling for most African nations because no matter how seriously Goldstone was perceived as a sincere reformer, he derived from the South African judicial system lately emerged from apartheid.

Most Ruwandan war crimes suspects were hiding in Zaire and Kenya. Calling a bluff by Kenyan President Daniel arap Moi, who had "threatened to arrest any member of the Tribunal who set foot in his country," Goldstone barged into Nairobi a week later and announced he would "rather investigate senior people even if we're not likely to get them."[29] The quickly pliant Kenyan president could not mistake the message as applying to those who harbored suspected war criminals.

On the issue of Tribunal impartiality, the distribution of investigators was disproportionate to alleged war crimes. After perhaps as many as a million deaths, only thirty investigators were sent to Rwanda[30] while fifty investigators[31] were probing the more accessible claims of 20,000 to 30,000 killings in Bosnia[32]—and not the wildly inflated claims of 200,000 to 350,000 dead or missing.

By early 1996, only a feeble handful of token indictments resulted against Hutu war criminals from the Rwanda Tribunal based in Arusha, Tanzania. And any "justice" was not expected soon.[33]

Escovar-Salom's premonitions at The Hague proved correct when he quietly backed away from judicial caricature that inevitably doomed southeastern Europe to renewals of maelstrom for the next generation and which may well engulf more than the whole of Europe and Africa.

War Crimes Prosecutions: 'Selective' And 'Symbolic'

By 1994, operations at The Hague remained dubious. "When I was at The Hague in July, 20 assistant prosecutors and investigators had to share, for reasons of economy, a single telephone that could call outside the Netherlands," said Thomas S. Warrick, a Washington attorney and past senior counsel to the chairman of the U.N. Commission of Experts on the Former Yugoslavia.[34]

By mid-1996, and after more than three years since it was formed, the Tribunal prosecutors had indicted fifty-eight suspects and trial had commenced against Dusko Tadic, an alleged guard at the Serb-run detention camp at Omarska in Bosnia. But Tadic was far from being one of the "big fish" alleged masterminds or political leaders behind the five-year-old Yugoslav civil wars.

---

29. Lindsey Hilsum, *London Observer Service*, November 13, 1995.
30. Hilsum, *ibid.*
31. Hilsum, *ibid.*
32. Jane Perlez, *The New York Times*, January 27, 1996.
33. *Washington Monthly*, March 1995; *The New York Times*, January 9, 1993. The figure of 200,000 dead in Bosnia was being recited by Bosnian government officials in early 1993 when, except for the coming flare-up in Kosovo, most hostilities had ceased. The claim of 8,000 Muslims who died during the taking of Srebrenica in July 1995 was not initially confirmed, despite exhumations of supposed mass graves by U.N. forensic through 2000.
34. Barbara Crossette, *The New York Times*, February 22, 1996.

Goldstone astonishingly conceded barely four months after taking the job that prosecution would be both "selective" and "symbolic" and, using the same occasion to complain about inadequate funds, began a series of unofficial threats about quitting if obstructions continued against getting the budget he wanted from the financially strapped U.N.[35] Just previous to the U.N. officially going broke in April 1996,[36] Goldstone grimly announced that he would quit by October.

"Justice Goldstone could have played the budget game of asking for 2X in the hopes of getting X. This is not his way, though," said Warrick.[37] The U.N. had originally budgeted The Tribunal at $28.6 million. Goldstone said he was quitting after being turned down in his request for a 1996 budget of $40.3 million.

From the beginning, Goldstone furiously defied critics who were concerned about the Tribunal's political misuse.

"I can give you the assurance that we won't respond to the political consequences either in what we do or in its timing," Goldstone vowed.[38] However, the largest single batch of indictments against twenty-one Serbs occurred on February 13, 1995, and "coincided with this week's budget discussions for the Tribunal at the United Nations."[39]

Goldstone's politicking was second only to the drum-beating in 1994 by Germans, as Germany's Chief Prosecutor Kay Nehm announced they were independently investigating fifty-one Serbs for war crimes and expediting a law to allow for extradition to The Hague.[40] Unnamed "Bosnian human rights activists presented the German government with a list of about 1,300 people they accused of war crimes."[41] The German dragnet was as thorough as it was indifferent to arresting the innocent and ignoring basic methods of establishing correct identities of alleged suspects.

Goran Lajic, a Bosnian Serb arrested in Germany for murder and torture was jailed for over three months until released after authorities in Germany and The Hague decided he had only the same name and birth date of a real war crimes suspect.[42]

"The reversal also underscored one of the Tribunal's major hurdles—identifying the often obscure perpetrators of atrocities committed several years ago. The Tribunal does not even have photos of some of its suspects... Lajic said he repeatedly told German judges when he was first arrested that they had the wrong man. The German jurists replied they had no jurisdiction in the case."[43]

This cross-jurisdictional chaos was what chilled Tribunal critics who generally "regarded it as a sop to public opinion or a surrender to naive American moralism."[44]

Needless to say, the Yugoslav Tribunal was not in business to prove defendants innocent. And, although given oversight of national courts, the Tribunal did not intervene in a series of judicial mockeries, including:

> •A Danish court convicted Refic Saric, a Muslim, for helping his Croat captors kill fellow inmates in 1993. After a three-week trial, Saric was sentenced to eight years in a psychiatric wing of a Danish prison. "The man has said he is a victim of mistaken

35. Warrick in an op-ed column, *The Washington Post*, December 20, 1994.
36. Christoph Driessen, *Deutsche Presse Agentur,* November 6, 1994.
37. Robert Reid, *Associated Press*, April 30, 1996.
38. Warrick, *ibid.*
39. *The New York Times*, April 24, 1996.
40. *Associated Press*, February 13, 1995.
41. *Associated Press*, quoting from the German magazine *Stern*, November 1, 1994.
42. *Associated Press*, February 14, 1995.
43. Jennifer Chao, *Associated Press*, June 17, 1996.
44. Editorial in *The Independent*, November 2, 1994.

identity, and he has been declared mentally ill by a Danish medical examiner."[45]

•Dusko Cvjetkovic, a Bosnian Serb, was accused of murdering one detention camp inmate and with the disappearance and presumed murder of two others. Austrian prosecutors charged Cvjetkovic with genocide in two jury trials in Salzburg which ended in acquittals. Cvjetkovic remained in custody while prosecutors appealed the not-guilty verdict and was eventually released. Cvjetkovic's case—applying genocide to a single case of murder and possible complicity in a pair of disappearances —struck several as ludicrous. "That's pretty steep. It shocks my sensibilities," said former Commission of Experts chairman Kalshoven.[46]

•The Hague Tribunal, along with the Western media, ignored what appeared to be several serious trials of accused war criminals in Serbia and in Bosnian Serb courts. For instance, a former member of a Serb paramilitary unit was prosecuted in Sabac (Serbia) during November 1994. Dusan Vuckovic was convicted and sentenced to death for killing sixteen Muslim civilians near Zvornik in 1992![47]

•Prosecutors at The Hague declined to extradite Borislav Herak, the infamous Bosnian Serb soldier who was captured in early 1993 and who had falsely confessed to raping ten Muslim women and killing twenty civilians. Herak became an international sensation and took the spotlight in the Bosnian government's propaganda onslaught to convince world opinion about mass rape. In a show-trial in Sarajevo, Herak was convicted and sentenced to death solely on the basis of a "confession." There were no actual witnesses or evidence. Herak, the focus of a Pulitzer Prize-winning package of stories in *The New York Times*, later claimed his confession was beaten out of him and asked for a new trial at The Hague. The plea was ignored —even after some of the murder victims later turned up alive in Sarajevo.[48]

•Through February 1995, Croatian courts (without required monitors from The Hague) had convicted more than 100 Serbs in absentia[49] and continued to stage token trials against Croat war crimes defendants, making it less likely for the Yugoslav Tribunal to retry suspects in light of sensitivities about double jeopardy. The token trials against Croats actually shielded them from extradition to The Hague.

---

45. Mike Corder, *Associated Press*, November 7, 1994; Jan M. Olsen, *Associated Press*, November 23, 1994.

46. Kalshoven, *ibid*.

47. *Associated Press*, *ibid*.

48. Olsen, *ibid*.

49. Kit Roane, *The New York Times*, January 30, 1996

•After deciding there was no evidence to hold Bosnian Serb Col. Aleksa Krsmanovic for mass killings around Sarajevo, the Tribunal unconscionably returned Krsmanovic to his Bosnian government captors who had kidnapped Krsmanovic in January 1996 and claimed after his return from The Hague and re-imprisonment that "new evidence" had developed.[50] The Tribunal declined to reconsider, and Krsmanovic became a pawn of double jeopardy— one of the American Bar Association Task Force's main concerns in 1993—and a trumped-up trial in Sarajevo by a judiciary which, ironically, was lavishly praised for its supposed ethics and self-styled Western impartiality by the American Bar Association in March 1996![51]

•Though clearly within its jurisdiction, the Tribunal refused to investigate the conspiracy between the White House and Saudi Arabia in smuggling $300 million worth of weapons to the Bosnian government over a three-year period. The illicit arms trafficking was in direct violation of the U.N. arms embargo and took place with U.N. peacekeeping troops on the ground in Bosnia.

•Unanswered omissions by Tribunal prosecutors and investigators include the blatant ethnic cleansing of tens of thousands of Serbs from Sarajevo suburbs, verified by U.N. officials on the scene, in early 1996 and in direct violation of the Dayton accords.[52]

•The Tribunal and its investigators turned a blind eye after the theft of four "computerfuls" of war crimes evidence from the U.N. Center for Human Rights in Zagreb on January 12, 1996. "There were no backup files for the data stored in two of the computers, almost exclusively allegations of widespread human rights abuses by Croatian troops during their offensive against rebel Serbs last summer."[53] The "rebel Serbs" were in fact the hundreds of thousands of original occupants of the Krajina region which were ruthlessly cleansed as 22,000 homes were "looted and torched" and at least 230 mostly elderly Serbs "were found with throats cut, or a bullet in the back of their head."[54] The stolen data probably included damning information about "mass graves that U.N. officials say contain 750 bodies (of Serbs)."[55] Croats refused to permit exhumation of the mass graves, again in defiance of the Dayton treaty.

---

50. *Associated Press*, February 28, 1995.
51. *Associated Press,* March 29, 1996; *American Bar Association Journal,* March 1996.
52. *Associated Press*, March 15, 1996.
53. Jasmina Kuzmanovic, *Associated Press*, January 31, 1996.
54. *Associated Press, ibid.*
55. *Associated Press, ibid.*

'Justice For Serbia ...From Cliche To Cliche'

In March 1996, popular German novelist Peter Handke was beginning his speaking tour throughout Germany, Austria and Slovenia to promote his controversial new essays, entitled "Justice for Serbia: A Winter Trip to the Danube, Sava, Moravia and Drina." Handke had long been troubled by five years of demonizing the Serbs, which he blamed on a "conspiracy of lazy and mendacious journalists who surf 'from cliche to cliche'."[56]

During the same month, an echo of Handke's criticisms of press bias came from an unlikely source who was nearing the end of his Bosnian tour. Admiral Leighton W. "Snuffy" Smith, commander of the U.S.-led NATO forces occupying Bosnia, loudly announced that American troops would protect Tribunal investigators arriving to begin inspection of suspected mass graves. Smith noted the Tribunal's personnel were not receiving cooperation from Bosnian Serb troops around Srebrenica. Smith said he urged Serb commanders to cooperate "because right now your country is the one that has been sort of indicted *by world opinion*."[57] (Author's emphasis)

By July 1996, the Yugoslav Tribunal at The Hague had succumbed to the ranting from the American-led media in its macabre portrayal of Bosnian Serb President Radovan Karadzic.

After a series of inflammatory hearings at The Hague, the Tribunal issued international arrest warrants for Karadzic, stemming from alleged mass killings a year earlier in Srebrenica, a small town in eastern Bosnia which had a pre-war population of less than 10,000—around two-thirds being Muslims and the rest Serbs. Srebrenica achieved notoriety in mid-1993 after it became a U.N. safe haven for a deluge of about 30,000 Muslim soldiers, refugees, and mercenaries. Nobody wanted to explain what happened to Srebrenica's vanished Serbian population in the town and surrounding villages—as with Mostar's pre-war 25,000 Serb population and huge numbers of Serbs who had vanished from Gorazde, Sarajevo and elsewhere in Bosnia!

In violation of its safe-haven status, Srebrenica had also become a staging center, like Gorazde, for Bosnian government troops who marauded through Serb villages during the previous year—a fact ignored or minimized by war correspondents and the Yugoslav Tribunal until the belated arrest of local warlord Naser Oric nearly a *decade* later.

Arrest warrants for Karadzic came on July 11th—the same day a new judicial fiat rippled out from the World Court in The Hague, announcing its intentions to take parallel jurisdiction on crimes of genocide in the vortex of Balkan cataclysm. The Yugoslav Tribunal was restricted to individuals; the separate World Court with its fifteen sitting judges adjudicated state disputes and had been weighing arguments for three years from legal representatives of the Bosnia Muslim government that Serbia had instigated and sustained the Bosnian war. The Bosnian Muslim leadership gloated as the World Court's ruling increased pressure immediately on Serbian President Slobodan Milosevic to hand over Karadzic or face prosecution for war crimes.[58]

As the war crimes sweepstakes commenced at The Hague, there was an increasing probability that Karadzic was being politically set up for abduction similar to the kidnapping of former Panamanian President Manuel Noriega by U.S. troops. Certainly, such a plan existed at the Pentagon and at the NATO headquarters in Brussels. Not

---

56. *Associated Press, ibid.*
57. *The New York Times*, March 31, 1996.
58. *Associated Press*, July 11, 1996.

insignificantly, it was also an election year, and the reelection hopes of President Clinton needed a "home run."

Journalists at a press conference in Zagreb could not mistake the bait dangled by U.S. Defense Secretary William Perry—and which he later had to eat:

> "'I do not expect to see either one of them in a position of authority in (Bosnia) at the end of the year.' Asked whether special forces might be sent in to get (Bosnian Serb General Ratko) Mladic, instead of using the NATO peacekeepers, Perry replied that he does not comment on future operations – 'either ones we really have plans for or ones were just thinking about.' Perry added that he believes the issue of Mladic and Karadzic will be 'resolved well before this one year is up.'"[59]

Political intrigue intensified, but nowhere was war-crime politicking more obvious than among the Tribunal itself.

Impatient that his chief prosecutor had not landed the "big fish," Tribunal Chief Judge Cassese successfully campaigned for indictments against the Bosnian Serb president which resulted at last on July 25, 1995.

Surprisingly, senior Tribunal prosecutor Schrag had said three months earlier that investigators at The Hague had "no evidence" to indict Bosnian Serb leaders![60] But within thirty days, Karadzic was branded officially as a war crimes suspect—a stigma that successfully prevented Karadzic from travel to sites of peace negotiations where arrests could occur at any moment. Journalists sniffed the ploy but sidestepped "the legal maneuver that could further damage U.N. relief and truce efforts in Bosnia."

Cassese was restless over Goldstone's too methodical investigations and berated Goldstone in a press release, ordering the prosecutor to produce indictments against "big fish" to satisfy the clamor whipped up by the mainstream Western media. The press release came a month before Schrag would state there was no evidence to justify such indictments![61]

At the same time, the Muslim-dominated Bosnian government schemed to stampede indictments by The Hague Tribunal against Karadzic, saying Bosnian courts in Sarajevo were ready to prosecute Karadzic and Mladic in absentia in its own courts with the unwritten threat Muslim troops would be amassed for one last "go-for-broke" manhunt and were even willing to trample peace agreements. After all, it had happened before. And so far, Sarajevo-style justice was willing to go as far as to execute Mladic and Karadzic, and convict them later.

Faced with at least the blemish of double jeopardy in the Tribunal's most important case, Goldstone knew his hand was forced on all sides to head off the Bosnian courts:

---

59. *Associated Press*, March 30, 1996. Actually, in mid-July 1997, British soldiers raided a restaurant in Prijedor in northern Bosnia, killing the police chief who had been named in a sealed indictment for alleged war crimes. British soldiers, feigning delivery of an International Red Cross relief package, kidnapped a Serb doctor who was also under sealed indictment at The Hague. The mission was planned, largely with White House direction, to coincide with the formal realignment of NATO, which occurred just hours earlier in Madrid. The raid no doubt pleased President Clinton in that widely televised senate hearings in Washington on potentially illegal campaign contributions to Clinton and the Democratic National Committee had just started and were preempted for NATO-saturated programming.

60. Schrag, *ibid.*

61. *Associated Press*, April 24, 1995.

"The names of Karadzic and Mladic will appear in a written request from the United Nations Tribunal to the Bosnian government that it defer its own judicial investigations of the two men to the Tribunal in the Hague. The officials said this 'formal request for deferral' amounted to a statement that the U.N. court is preparing to bring charges against Karadzic and Mladic, and therefore wants to avoid the possibility that the two men could be tried twice for the same crimes."[62]

Srebrenica: Self-Fulfilling Media Prophecies

World opinion was sculpted to portray Karadzic and Mladic as Nazi-like reincarnations. The Yugoslav Tribunal's hearings that preceded international arrest warrants for Karadzic and Mladic were publicly perceived as explicit justification in hopes of, at least, political assassination:

"For all its lofty purpose, the conduct of the Bosnian war crimes probe has become intertwined with expedience. As the biggest supplier of money and information to the Tribunal, the U.S. has secured invaluable leverage over the region's power-brokers. Crudely put, it can blackmail them by threatening to share the huge amount of intelligence it has gathered in the war."[63]

Karadzic had consistently stated his intentions to deal with possible war criminals in his ranks.

"We will shoot some people. We will execute them," Karadzic calmly repeated over lunch in modulated tones that were as much his trademark as the floppy lock of thick hair across his forehead. "But not now. After the war."[64]

The Bosnian Serb president was not talking about executing political rivals or traitors or enemies. He was talking about the severity of consequences he intended to impose after the war, a topic that obviously sat uneasily in the back of his mind as did the realization that justice was a luxury only during peacetime. "We are going to try anyone if you give us any evidence."[65]

With a series of unusual and inflammatory hearings, the Yugoslav Tribunal paraded witnesses and testimony before issuing the warrants against Karadzic and Mladic. Specifically, allegations would focus on the episode of the eventual Serb takeover of Srebrenica. It was typically minimized that Srebrenica's Serb population was expelled or eliminated before it was recreated in the media as a besieged Muslim town and U.N.-declared safe haven in 1993.

A series of news reports suggested a daunting range of facts about the episode of Srebrenica, including brief and cryptic hints about whether thousands of Bosnian Muslim men were murdered and disposed of in mass graves or whether, as Serbs claimed to scoffing reporters and officials, Muslims had fought desperately among themselves about whether to fight or surrender or to attempt a breakout and escape to the nearest areas controlled by Bosnian government troops.

---

62. *Balkan War Report*, May 1995.
63. Editorial in *The Financial Times*, February 13, 1996.
64. Karadzic interview with author in Belgrade, December 1994.
65. Associatede Press, February 13, 1995.

To remain "officially missing" for as long as their actual whereabouts were not officially substantiated eventually buttressed the accepted belief that thousands were executed by Serbs although nothing near the oft-quoted 8,000 who were killed and hid in mass graves was provably produced.

The actual numbers remained aggravatingly elusive—no matter the increase in insistence from officials, media and frustrated Bosnian Muslim groups which manipulated "missing" and "death" ratios incessantly.

Also indirectly aiding the varying reports, the Tribunal six months later demonstrated it was never interested in exhuming all the war-dead, a naievely utopian assumption and expectation that was subtly mocked in dry responses to "new" Bosnian mass-grave discoveries by spokesman Christian Chartier who said the Tribunal would be "interested in participating in exhumations 'if graves are related to ongoing investigations or indictments.'"

Spanning nearly a decade, the trend of foreign media samplings included:

> "...Exhumation of suspected mass grave sites is considered crucial to determining what happened to the 27,000 people reported missing in Bosnia's war."[66]

Seven years later:

> "...The exhumation (at Crni Vrh, or Black Peak), some 50 miles northeast of Sarajevo is expected to reveal the fate of at least some of the more than 20,000 people still missing in the former Yugoslav republic, nearly eight years after the conclusion of the war, thought to have left about 250,000 people dead."[67]

Eight years later:

> "...Nearly 3,500 people went missing from Prijedor alone, and about 1,000 are still unaccounted for. ...About 29,000 people, mostly Muslims, are still missing from the war. The remains of around 18,000 have been found in mass graves—including about 5,000 of up to 8,000 Muslims killed by Serb forces in Srebrenica in 1995—and 10,000 have been identified."[68]

One month later:

> "...Over the years, UN and local forensics experts in Bosnia have exhumed 16,500 bodies from more than 300 mass graves. Thousands of people remain missing following the war. About 260,000 people were killed and 1.8 million driven from their homes during the conflict, which pitted Bosnia's Muslims, Croats and Serbs against each other."[69]

---

66. "New Mass Grave Found in Northwest Bosnia Cave," *BosNet News* online, March 21, 1996.

67. Muslim American Society/MASNET, August 6, 2003

68. Miran Jelenek, *Reuters*, September 24, 2004

69. *The Australian*, October 29, 2004.

One day later:

> "...About 18,000 bodies have been exhumed from more than 300 mass graves throughout the country (Bosnia), most of them Muslims, according to forensic teams. About 16,000 people, including 3,200 from the Prijedor area, are still listed as missing. Bosnia's war claimed more than 200,000 lives and spawned 2.2 million refugees, more than half the Balkan country's population."[70]

Three days later:

> "...Since the end of Bosnia's war, some 18,000 bodies, mostly Muslims, have been exhumed from over 300 mass graves throughout the Balkan country. Some 16,000 people, including 3,200 from the Prijedor area, where Keraterm, Omarska and Trnopolje are located, are still listed as missing. Bosnia's war claimed more than 200,000 lives and left 2.2 million refugees, more than half the country's population."[71]

A similar chaotic chronology raised more questions than answers surrounding the Srebrenica episode in July 1995:

> •**July 15**—"The Bosnian government deliberately increased the suffering of Muslim refugees fleeing Srebrenica to put pressure on the international community, according to documents made available to *The Daily Telegraph*. The papers include instructions to the United Nations from the government of Alija Izetbegovic in Sarajevo that the refugees must be taken in their thousands to a single location rather than being spread around numerous available centers. The resulting television pictures—including initially preposterous *CNN* footage showing supposed refugees clad in heavy coats against a winter background with snow (!)—and media reports of chaos among aid workers overwhelmed when the refugees arrived at the U.N. base at Tuzla—were intended to bring about a decisive international response. *It is not the first time the Bosnians have manipulated events...*"[72] (Italics added)

> •**July 16**—Thousands of Muslim women and children refugees began arriving at Tuzla from Srebrenica hours after Serb takeover. "They said that most of the men among them had fled into forests in the hope of making their way to Muslim-held territory... U.N. officials in Tuzla said that they knew of no effort yet to interview refugees by investigators from The Hague... 'It's going to be a very difficult job to separate the crimes that people *heard about or may be imagining* from the ones they can really prove,' said Lars Morkholt, a European Union observer based

---

70. *Al-Jezeera.net Global News*, October 30 2004.
71. *Agence France-Presse*, November 2, 2004.
72. *The Daily Telegraph*, July 15, 1995.

in Tuzla."[73] (Italics added)

•**July 24**—In the absence of a single retrieved or verified Muslim body from Srebrenica, a report from Tuzla said that "(a)fter five days of interviews the United Nations chief investigator into alleged human rights abuses during the fall of Srebrenica *has not found any first-hand witnesses of atrocities.*"[74] (Italics added)

•**July 26**—U.S. spy satellites and unmanned Predator "drone" aircraft—with around-the-clock, night vision and infrared capabilities—had scanned Srebrenica for days, *searching without results* for evidence of mass killings and other atrocities since the mid-July fall of the enclave. ...Unidentified State Department official, citing reported "eyewitness" accounts of executions at Srebrenica: "There are ways to confirm what eyewitnesses say, he added. If massacres were large enough 'and if the timing is right, the birds can take a picture,' he said, referring to spy satellites. But so far, the official said, satellites have produced nothing."[75] (Italics added)

•**July 27**—The stories of mass Muslim atrocities at Srebrenica were inconsistent with accounts from Muslim refugees who arrived from nearby Zepa a few days later: "They brought tales of two weeks of living in caves in the wooded hills during the heavy bombardment of the U.N.-designated 'safe haven,' but did not recount atrocities like those people brought out of Srebrenica after the Serbs overran that 'safe area' on July 11... 'We were treated well,' by the Serbian soldiers,' said Ms. (Ramiza) Kolovac, a law student in Sarajevo who was visiting her parents in Zepa..." The surprising reports from refugees and aid agencies about "no evidence of systematic abuses of the Zepa civilians" was desperately disputed by Bosnian government officials in Sarajevo who decided to bar journalists from camps holding Zepa refugees. U.N. officials rebutted that it was part of Sarajevo's "propaganda line."[76] U.N. chief human rights investigator Tadeusz Mazowiecki resigns in protest that nothing is being done after 2,000 Muslim men were massacred at Srebrenica, reports the *Associated Press.*

•**August 1**—Assistant Secretary of State for Human Rights John Shattuck said he interviewed a dozen refugees at Tuzla, *including survivors of firing squads,* and that 7,000 people are missing from Srebrenica.[77] (Italics added)

---

73. *The New York Times,* July 16, 1995.
74. *The Daily Telegraph,* July 24, 1995.
75. Paul Quinn-Judge, *Boston Globe,* July 26, 1995.
76. Raymond Bonner, *The New York Times,* July 27, 1995.
77. *Associated Press,* July 27, 1995.

•**August 4**—A Dutch peacekeeper reports seeing a "'row of shoes and backpacks belonging to about 100 people on a football field'... The owners *presumably* had been massacred."[78] (Italics added)

•**August 9**—U.S. spy satellite and U-2 aerial photos, "coupled with interviews with Muslim refugees," provide "the most compelling circumstantial evidence that Serbian troops *executed at least several hundred military-age men and boys* as part of an ethnic cleansing campaign (at Srebrenica), Clinton administration officials said." The International Committee for the Red Cross said "6,000 people are unaccounted for since the fall of Srebrenica... It is unclear how many of the remainder are in hiding, dead or living in refugee camps"... CIA deputy director for intelligence John Gannon, told a senate hearing that "a CIA analysis shows that more than 3,000 settlements, mainly in Serb-controlled areas of Bosnia, have been burned or destroyed in a campaign of ethnic cleansing so that up to 90 percent of non-Serbs will have no homes to return to."[79] "Serbs had shot Muslims in a soccer stadium in *retaliation for Muslim killings of Serbs in past conflicts.*"[80] (Italics added)

•**August 10**—Madeleine Albright showed spy photos to the U.N. Security Council and claimed 2,000 to 2,700 missing Bosnians from Srebrenica may have been shot by Bosnian Serbs.[81] An unidentified "63-year-old Bosnian refugee told a team led by U.S. Assistant Secretary of State John Shattuck that Gen. Ratko Mladic... had promised safety to a group of refugees being held at a soccer field, a U.S. official said,[82] speaking on condition of anonymity. But men and boys were later loaded onto trucks and driven to a site half-mile *(sic)* from the soccer field, where they were lined up in groups of 20 to 25 and machine-gunned, the official said." Secretary of State Warren Christopher's daily intelligence briefings have not disclosed "*any* intelligence

78. *Associated Press*, August 4, 1995.
79. *The New York Times*, August 9, 1995. This was the controversial CIA report that juxtaposed successive news reports that quoted the CIA as saying Bosnian Serbs were responsible for ninety-percent of the atrocities during the Bosnian war.
80. *The Boston Globe*, August 9, 1995. This briefly alluded to the systematic murders of Serbs by Bosnian government troops in numerous villages around Srebrenica that preceded the Serb takeover of Srebrenica, which was used as a launching pad for government attacks on civilians in direct violation of U.N. rules that established demilitarized safe havens. Certainly, some of the Muslims feared detection by Serbs as war criminals if Srebrenica fell.
81. *The New York Times*, August 10, 1995. The photos supposedly showed large dirt mounds—not piles of bodies. Interestingly, the photos were not widely printed in U.S. newspapers. Also, compared to original claims that 6,000 Bosnian soldiers were missing, the lower number suggested what was later discovered in that some Bosnian government soldiers were not "missing" but had escaped and fled cross-country and later were quietly absorbed into other units.
82. *Associated Press*, August 10, 1995.

imagery that could confirm massacres." But within a week after the Croat government unleashed a vicious campaign to cleanse hundreds of thousands of Serbs from the Krajina, Madeleine Albright diverted media attention by waving eight satellite photos of mounds of dirt which, she said, were mass graves containing Muslims at Srebrenica.[83] (Italics added)

• **August 15**—The International Committee of the Red Cross reports that 5,000 Muslim soldiers escaped and were secretly assigned to other units. Family members were not even notified about the reassignments by the Bosnian government, said ICRC Report No. 37.

• **October 7**—On July 11-12, "Bosnian Serbs marched into Srebrenica and captured it *without firing a shot.*" ... "As peacekeepers saw the bodies of freshly killed Muslims in Srebrenica, they raised no alarm," according to Bert Kreemers, Dutch Defense Ministry spokesman... "On July 17, as Dutch peacekeepers were preparing to leave Srebrenica, one of their senior officers, Maj. Robert Franken, signed an agreement with Bosnian Serb authorities certifying that 'the evacuation was carried out by the Serb side *correctly.*' Later that week, as the peacekeepers were arriving in Zagreb, Croatia, the commander of the Dutch ground forces, Lt. Gen. Hans Couzy, who had flown from Amsterdam to meet them, said he knew of *no evidence* suggesting that the Bosnian Serbs in Srebrenica had committed crimes akin to genocide. At a news conference the next day in Zagreb, Lt. Col. Tom Karremans, who had commanded the Dutch battalion in Srebrenica, asserted that the Bosnian Serbs' "*militarily correct* operation" had been carried out "in the right way."[84] (Italics added)

• **November 7**—The Tribunal's Chief Prosecutor Richard Goldstone complained to the U.S. Embassy at The Hague about the "*quality and timeliness*" of U.S. information given to Tribunal investigators.[85] This was in general reference to reports about the Srebrenica incident. "'There's certain types of intelligence

information that our government *cannot* share with the international community,' said White House spokesman Michael McCurry when asked about Goldstone's complaints. 'McCurry cited "national security reasons" as the reason the United States

---

83. Louis Meixler, *Associated Press*, August 10, 1995.
84. Stephen Kinzer, *The New York Times*, October 7, 1995. The inaction by the Dutch, although later chastised by Dutch politicians who were embarrassed because of the contradictory deluge of media reports about massive slaughter, appeared to give credence to the Bosnian Serb claims that a number of opposing Muslim factions had shot it out with each other over disagreement on whether to fight or run. Muslims fighting Muslims, after all, was no Balkan phenomenon when compared to the conflicts among Muslims at Bihac and elsewhere.
85. *Associated Press*, November 7, 1995.

would withhold some evidence, and criticized the complaints by the prosecutor, Judge Richard Goldstone of South Africa, as 'unfortunate.' during Dayton negotiations. Goldstone calls U.S. intelligence provided so far as *'disappointing.'* He complained about the *failure to hand over spy photos* that he said could help the U.N.-sponsored Tribunal identify mass graves that appeared after the fall of Srebrenica in July." "...Some press reports have said that U.S. and other intelligence agencies monitored radio conversations in which Gen. Momcilo Perisic, the head of the Yugoslav army, gave military advice to Mladic during the Serbian campaign to overrun Srebrenica. Senior U.S. intelligence officials contacted Tuesday *again insisted that they were unaware of the existence of such reports.*"[86] (Italics added)

•**November 8**—"(McCurry) said today the limitation will not keep *important evidence* out of the hands of the Tribunal. 'If there is information in the possession of the United States government that could lead to a successful prosecution of war crimes, we'll figure out a way to share it.'... 'We have spent an enormous amount of time and resources and, frankly, a great deal of courageous work by embassy officials in the field to develop eye-witness material, interview transcripts which we have *always quickly shared with the commission.*"[87] "Shattuck has turned over volumes of his findings already to the War Crimes Tribunal," (State Department spokesman Nicholas) Burns said.[88] (Italics added)

•**November 29**—The U.N. "pointed to undeniable evidence" that Bosnian Serbs carried out "summary executions" after taking (Srebrenica). "Estimates of the number of missing civilians previously ran as high as 8,000, but the 'best current estimate' is between 3,500 and 5,500."[89]

•**November 30**—A Dutch "government report in October cleared the 300 Dutch peacekeepers of blame, saying they were over-whelmed by a Bosnian Serb armored unit that took the safe haven July 11."[90] (Italics added)

•**December 18**—Serbs were blamed for the "butchery of an estimated 5,000 men" in Srebrenica.[91]

•**December 19**—The U.N. rejected Serb explanations that Muslims fought and killed Muslims at Srebrenica... "There were 'disorders and conflicts within the Bosnian Muslim army... In the clashes that ensued, those units which wanted to continue fighting

86. *Associated Press*, November 7, 1995.
87. *Associated Press*, November 8, 1996.
88. *The New York Times*, November 8, 1995.
89. *Associated Press*, November 29, 1995.
90. *Associated Press*, November 30, 1995.
91. *London Observer* Service, December 18, 1995.

were mercilessly killing those who wanted to surrender and were in favor of a cease-fire.' Madeleine Albright, the U.S. representative called this account of events in Srebrenica 'the big lie.'"[92]

•**January 15**—"The problem is a *lack of first-hand evidence.* Yes, the world has been exposed to television footage of camps and freight cars during the deportations of 1992, to reports that thousands of young men have simply disappeared..."[93] (Italics added)

•**January 17**—"Among the 20,000 people the (Bosnian) government lists as missing at least some 3,000 men were believed captured after the Serbs took the eastern enclave (of Srebrenica)."[94]

•**January 21**—Shattuck and Tribunal investigators visited six sites near Srebrenica, finding "debris and human remains" and taking photographs of the suspected grave sites... '*The Muslims made a lot of attacks in these areas,* and a lot of them died in the combat,' an angry Serb police official said. 'What about the 40 Serbs the Muslims slaughtered in this village (Glogova)? Why doesn't anyone look into what happened to them?'"[95] (Italics added)

•**January 22**—"'Srebrenica was the worst war crime, the worst crime against humanity committed in Europe since 1945, and we are going to pursue it,' Shattuck said in *Jerusalem.*"[96] (Italics added)

•**January 27**—"But a Washington official who has access to the administration's intelligence on Bosnia and who visited The Hague this month said that promises by the CIA in December to provide more satellite imagery and intercepts 'still had a way to go to make it work.'"[97] (Italics added)

•**February 5**—Elizabeth Rehn, the U.N. Human Rights Commission special investigator viewed the discovery of *four* rotting corpses on hilltop at Kravica (near Srebrenica).[98] Shattuck described his visit in late January to six mass grave sites: "First, I interviewed refugees as they came out of Srebrenica in late July (when Serbs overran the former U.N. safe area); I received firsthand accounts from survivors of (attempted) executions but had *no way to corroborate them.* What I saw (in late January) corroborated them in far more detail than I

---

92. *The New York Times*, December 19, 1995.
93. Chris Hedges, *The New York Times*, January 15, 1996.
94. *Associated Press*, January 17, 1996.
95. *The New York Times*, January 21, 1996.
96. *Associated Press*, January 22, 1996.
97. *The New York Times*, January 27, 1996.
98. *Associated Press*, February 5, 1996.

thought would be possible. I saw places where people were held, blood on the ceiling of a warehouse, a large hole in the warehouse where a bulldozer had gone in to get the bodies. These were things eyewitnesses had told me about. ...We went to every site we wanted... One major conclusion from my trip is that I saw *no evidence* whatsoever of tampering... I believe there are 12 to 15 (mass graves) throughout Bosnia."[99] (Italics added)

•**February 11**—Karadzic: "We did not commit a single crime... We had prisoners of war, but we didn't kill them... (The Hague) is a political body that was created to blame the Serbs... We have discovered more than 50 mass graves of Serbs killed by Muslims around Srebrenica in 1993. There are 10 to 50 people in each of those graves."[100]

•**February 13**—"The International Committee of the Red Cross estimates that some 3,000 Bosnian Muslims were rounded up by Bosnian Serbs at Srebrenica and massacred."[101]

•**March 20**—*Eight months after the takeover of Srebrenica*, U-2 aerial photographs (taken on July 17, or six days after Serbs took Srebrenica) show "more than 100 bodies scattered in a mass grave, military sources say."[102] (Italics added)

•**April 2**—Lt. Col. John Batiste, a U.S. battalion commander in Tuzla, said satellite surveillance of mass graves showed "they had *not* been tampered with."[103] (Italics added)

Apparently, the Bosnian government was not confronted about or the media did not report whether there were any requests for verifiable records concerning Bosnian Army troop strengths, individual names, identity of their units and dates of deployment, the previous and subsequent locations of these units with comparative strengths before and after the mid-July 1995 Srebrenica episode to determine possible troop absorptions by other units, comparative casualty tallies of all units before and after the Srebrenica takeover to establish or disprove allegations of massacre.

Certainly, the Bosnian government should have been eager enough to produce such statistics. But instead, according from wire service reports, there was only silence from Sarajevo. The reason came in a remarkably lucid though belated account about Srebrenica in a 2001 report by *Radio Netherlands*:[104]

"Six years after the fall of the Bosnian Muslim enclave of Srebrenica, there's still no clarity about the events that led to the tragedy, nor about the precise death toll. Sensitive files remain closed, despite the installation of a democratic government

99. *The New York Times*, February 5, 1996.
100. *Newsweek*, February 11, 1996.
101. *The New York Times*, February 13, 1996.
102. *The New York Times* report with Sarajevo dateline, March 20, 1996.
103. *Associated Press*, April 2, 1996.
104. "Srebrenica: the Questions that Remain," *Radio Netherlands*, July 13, 2001.

in Belgrade and recent Bosnian-Serb cooperation with the war crimes tribunal in The Hague. The Netherlands Institute for War Documentation has yet to publish the findings of its investigation.

"Since the fall of the UN safe haven of Srebrenica, there've been extensive discussions about what went wrong.

"...The 1993 accord on disarmament called for the demilitarization of the entire enclave. But the UN failed to enforce compliance with the accord and Bosnian government forces continued their numerous attacks from the enclave, providing the perfect excuse for the Bosnian Serbs to launch their all-out attack on the enclave.

"The Bosnian troops were known as the government army's 28th Mountain Division, thought to number up to 8,000 troops. They were under the command of the Tuzla-based Second Army Corps, which in turn was led by Commander-in-Chief Rezim Delic. On the eve of the fall of Srebrenica, the 28th Mountain Division received orders to withdraw to Tuzla, moving through the Serbian lines.

"According to the then army chief of staff, General Sefer Halilovic, some 6,000 troops arrived in Tuzla. A Red Cross official told *Radio Netherlands* at the time that he had seen 'a few thousand troops from Srebrenica near Tuzla, with whom he wasn't allowed to talk. *In August 1995, a month after the enclave's fall, Commander in Chief Delic reported to parliament in Sarajevo that 'the withdrawal of the 28th Division had been largely successful.'*

"The upshot was that in July 1995, an advance party of Serb troops found Muslim positions at Srebrenica deserted, after which the Bosnian Serbs launched their final attack. The UN protection force then left the enclave. The suggestion that just over 400 Dutch blue-helmets could have put up any meaningful resistance to an advancing Serbian brigade of some 3,000 troops is simply absurd. The government in Sarajevo had given up the enclave..." (Italics added)

Halilovic was indicted in September 2001 and turned over to The Hague for murder and loss of command and control of his troops during a late 1993 massacre of sixty-two Croat villagers at Uzdol and Grabovica about ninety miles west of Sarajevo.

The Western media, vexed and embarrassed by the eruption of fighting between its favored Muslims and Croats, minimally reported the massacre or Halilovic's arrest. Similarly ignored were two other major stories in 2003 that clouded the mainstream media reporting about the episode of Srebrenica.

First was the indictment and arrest for war crimes on March 28, 2003, of some-time Muslim hero and warlord Naser Oric who commanded Bosnian government troops in Srebrenica. During the ten-month period from May 1992 through February 1993, Oric's units rampaged through eastern Bosnia and in the "municipalities of Bratunac, Srebrenica and Skelani, burned and otherwise destroyed and plundered a minimum of fifty predominantly Serb villages and hamlets…," according to prosecutors at The Hague. As a result, thousands of Serb individuals fled the area. Oric used Srebrenica as a staging area for his raids until provoking the July 1995 Serb onslaught.

Then, six months later, a million-dollar monument to Srebrenica's dead—financed by American taxpayers—was dedicated as new criticisms were leveled about the infamous "massacre":

> "Former *BBC* journalist Jonathan Rooper, who has researched the events in Srebrenica since 1995, says that the region was a graveyard for Serbs as well as Muslims and that a monument to inflated casualties on one side 'serves neither truth nor the goal of reconciliation.'

> "Phillip Corwin, former UN Civilian Affairs Coordinator in Bosnia during the 1990s, said: 'What happened in Srebrenica was not a single large massacre of Muslims by Serbs, but rather a series of very bloody attacks and counterattacks over a three-year period which reached a crescendo in July of 1995. …I was the United Nations' chief political officer in Bosnia the day that Srebrenica fell. Coincidentally, it was the same day that the Bosnian government tried to assassinate me as I drove over Mount Igman on the way to Sarajevo.'

> "Intelligence expert and strategist Gregory Copley, President of the International Strategic Studies Association and the ISSA's Balkan & Eastern Mediterranean Policy Council, accused US Ambassador Donald Hays, who serves as Deputy High Representative of Bosnia-Herzegovina, of using the power of the Office of the High Representative (OHR) governing Bosnia 'to force Bosnian Serb elected officials to sign a fraudulent document accepting the official version of events in Srebrenica. The leaders of Republika Srpska [the predominantly Serbian province of Bosnia-Herzegovina] invited the office of the High Representative to join their investigation of the events in Srebrenica. Instead they were told to sign a statement drafted by OHR endorsing casualty figures they publicly disagreed with.' Copley added: 'It is significant in that the former US Clinton Administration fought this war unquestioningly supporting only the Croat and Muslim factions and disregarding the historic alliance of the Serbian peoples with the US. Then, after the war, the Clinton Administration failed to follow US tradition in helping to heal the wounds of war, but, rather, perpetuated ethnic divisions and hatreds. This differs from the US role in all other wars.'

> "'Unfortunately, all of the policies and officials put in place in the region by the Clinton Administration remain. The current Bush Administration has neglected the Balkans and has, instead, allowed the Clinton policies to continue, which has meant that divisive politics continue. This, then, requires the ongoing commitment of US peacekeeping forces in both Bosnia and in the Kosovo province of Serbia.'

"Copley added that, according to intelligence obtained from Islamist sources, that the monument was intended to become a shrine for radical Islamists in Europe and site for annual pilgrimages. He added: 'Deputy High Representative Donald Hays forced the Republika Srpska government to issue a statement which accepted the radical Islamist version of the Srebrenica affair, despite the fact that the Office of High Representative does not have any investigative capability of its own to make a valid assumption on the matter. As well, the International Criminal Tribunal on Yugoslavia (ICTY) in The Hague "no friend of the Serbs" has itself not completed its investigation of Srebrenica, and nor has the office of the Government of *Republika Srpska* which has been working with the ICTY.'

"Ambassador Hays and OHR chief Paddy Ashdown forced the Republika Srpska statement merely to ensure that the opening of the 'shrine' to be attended by Clinton 'would vindicate Clinton Administration policies of support for the radical Islamists.' Yossef Bodansky, who has written several books on the war in Yugoslavia and also serves as Research Director of ISSA, *calls the 7,000 figure 'disinformation' and notes that 'all independent forensic evidence points to Muslim casualties in the hundreds, possibly the low hundreds.* Continued emphasis on such allegedly high numbers of Muslim deaths at Srebrenica obfuscates the Muslim in that city, earlier, of Serb civilians.' Bodansky also wrote extensively on the link between Osama bin Laden and the Bosnian Islamists in numerous articles and special reports and three books...

"Rooper says that at least 1,000 Serbs, mostly civilians, were killed by forces led by Oric who did not bother to hide his crimes, even showing videotapes of slaughtered Serbs to Western journalists. Meanwhile a group of academic experts and journalists from the United States, Canada, Germany, France, Serbia, and the United Kingdom has been organized by Professor Edward S. Herman of the University of Pennsylvania to examine the evidence regarding events at Srebrenica in July 1995 and earlier, how the media reported these events, and the political role of claims about Srebrenica. It is expected that a report from this group will be available in June 2004. *Rooper points out that the 40,000 inhabitants the UN used in July of 1995 before the capture of Srebrenica roughly matches the number of former residents accounted for in the aftermath.* A commander of the Muslim-dominated Army of BiH (Bosnia-Herzegovina) later confirmed to parliament in Sarajevo that *5,000 BiH troops escaped largely intact to Tuzla while the UN registered some 35,632 civilian survivors.*

"While the capture of Srebrenica was reported in July 1995, as it unfolded, an international outcry only took place a month later, after Madeleine Albright, then US representative to the UN, held up a photo which she said provided evidence that thousands of Muslim victims had been buried at field near Nova Kasaba, 19 kilometers from Srebrenica. Excavations which took place following the war, however, yielded 33 bodies at Nova Kasaba. Two years after the event, a total of 400 bodies had been found at 20 sites near Srebrenica, an area which had seen bloody fighting over a three year period. Instead of acknowledging that there was no support for the original figures, Rooper says various means were used to prop up the official story.

"Spokesmen for the Clinton Administration suggested that Serbs might have moved the bodies to other locations. Rooper points out that excavating, transporting and reburying 7,000 bodies was 'not only beyond the capabilities of the thinly stretched, petrol-starved Bosnian Serb Army, but would have been easily detected under intense surveillance from satellites and geostationary drones.'

"By 1998, thousands of bodies excavated from all across Bosnia were stored at the Tuzla airport. Despite state of the art DNA testing, only 200 bodies have been linked to Srebrenica. Around 3,000 names on a list of Srebrenica victims compiled by the Red Cross matched voters in the Bosnian election in 1996. 'I pointed out to the OSCE (Organization of Security and Cooperation) *that there had either been massive election fraud or almost half the people on the ICRC missing list were still alive,'* says Rooper. *'The OSCE finally responded that the voting lists had been locked away in warehouses and it would not be possible for them to investigate.'*"[105] (Italics added)

Exhuming 'Enough' Proof

By mid-summer 1996, Tribunal forensic teams began the gruesome excavations of selected mass graves which began to yield the dead from Srebrenica, while suspected mass graves containing Serb victims appeared untouched. At Cerska, about ninety corpses were unearthed after six days of digging. Forensic experts had their assignments from Tribunal prosecutors.

"There seems to be some assertions that these are battlefield casualties," said William D. Haglund, the team's head scientist, adding that corpses had hands tied behind them and that they had been shot from close range. "I'm here to dispel that."[106]

Prosecutor Goldstone knew that proof of genocide must be painstakingly exhumed—slowly by scores, then hundreds. As to the "thousands" alleged by the Bosnian and Croat governments? That would cost millions, and never mind the Bosnian and Croat silence about mass graves its troops had filled with Serb civilians. Goldstone requested a sizable increase in the Tribunal's budget for forensic work before his scheduled departure in October 1996.

---

105. Gregory Copley, "Srebrenica Casualty Numbers Challenged by Experts as Politicized and Ethnically Divisive," *International Strategic Studies Association*, September 18, 2003.

106. *Associated Press*, July 12, 1996.

But, strangely, it fell to lesser-celebrated Canadian Louise Arbor to pursue a comprehensive gathering of evidence from mass graves in the former Yugoslavia. She was on a leave of absence from the Ontario Court of Appeal when hired by The Hague and was "a vice president of the Canadian Civil Liberties Union before her appointment to the bench in 1995."[107] There was no public explanation by the U.N. for snubbing Bassiouni—other than the too blatant selection of a Muslim who was without judicial experience—and the selection of Arbor whose experience amounted to only a single year as a sitting judge!

But the most bizarre legal twist in the prosecution of Yugoslav war crimes came with the U.S. Supreme Court's ruling on June 17, 1996, upholding a 2nd U.S. Circuit Court of Appeals decision to allow two women to seek monetary damages in a civil lawsuit against Karadzic in U.S. District Court. Human rights groups in New York originally filed two lawsuits in 1993 "on behalf of thousands of Bosnian Muslim and Croat women. He is accused of ordering a campaign of murder, rape and other forms of torture to destroy non-Serbian people."[108] Since it was not likely—aside from the possibility of abduction or an extraordinary occurrence of voluntary extradition —that Karadzic would surface to face whatever judgment resulted, his assets, if any, would be seized.

The basis of the suit is a two-century-old law allowing foreign citizens in the U.S. to sue foreigners outside the country for violating the "law of nations." But the most interesting potential in such a case was that the stiffer American rules of evidence and procedure would have to be used in a U.S. court. Conceivably, the exercise of greater demands of proof, vigorous cross examination and witness credibility, would have cast the more lenient rules of procedure and evidence at The Hague in the light of judicial parody.

However, Karadzic would also be taking on the entire might of the U.S. Department of Justice and State Department since the American government, at taxpayer expense, joined the plaintiffs in the two suits. "A State Department memorandum sent to Secretary of State Warren Christopher urging his approval ...argued that it would be an opportunity for the Clinton administration to distinguish itself from its Republican predecessors in the field of human rights."[109]

The American lawsuits and judicial charades in other national courts—along with the politics, selective prosecutions and legal calumny at The Hague—for the most part has so far lived up to the expectations of critics. The Yugoslav Tribunal briskly shrugged off the expected challenges of jurisdiction and allowed nothing to impede its momentum, while critics observed proceedings with casual fatalism. Professor Alfred Rubin, an international law scholar at Tufts University, said:

> "The international war crimes Tribunals are 'unworkable' under most circumstances. No state or group of states can make law for another nation... That's neither good nor bad. It's inevitable. It's the way the legal order is structured."[110]

The structure of the causes of the Balkan civil wars was featured in the testimony by a history expert before the Tribunal in May 1996 at the outset of the trial of Dusan Tadic, who was a minor figure accused and subsequently convicted of murder and genocide. Historical competence has always been conceded as having preeminence

---

107. *New York Times*, February 22, 1996.
108. *Associated Press*, June 17, 1996.
109. *The New York Times*, September 26, 1995.
110. Kenneth Jost, *Congressional Quarterly,* July 17, 1995.

when considering causes, let alone solutions, to the legacy of European upheavals. The Tribunal justices had no acknowledged expertise in the historical tapestry of the Balkans or Yugoslavia. In fact, as of 1996 there were indications of less than even the minimum of the most basic European orientation:

> "On the bench in The Hague, (American Justice Gabrielle Kirk) McDonald displays a breezy Texas style that mixes directness with humor... At a recent evidence hearing, a witness described a Bosnian village as being 'a few clicks up the road'. The Swedish soldier paused. 'Do you know what a click is, Ma'am?... It's a kilometer.' 'Sir, I haven't been in Europe too long,' McDonald answered. 'I don't even know what a kilometer is.'"[111]

---

111. *Assocaited Press,* May 6, 1996.

Chapter 13

The Frog, The Snake
And Chicken-Wire Stalags

*"Bomb the Serbs, said George Kenney. Arm the Bosnian
Muslims. So unlike official Washington, the realm of cool,
cordial schemers. A city-state that plans wars but does not fight
them, and where policy positions are shown off on Sunday
talk shows but shed long before they threaten a career,
much less cost a job. ...Who was George Kenney?"*[1]
—**Mary Battiata**

*"I've often been asked at what point I changed my mind.
But it wasn't ever so simple—I had no conversion.
Rather, it was a cumulative process."*[2]
—**George Kenney**

In-mid 1996, Mary Battiata of the *Washington Post* wrote "Time would
diminish the act, and the actor..." She had herself studied acting since the
previous November.

It was only fitting, then, that she first met George Kenney under the lights three
years earlier, in front of cameras and in front of an eager audience. He was thirty-six-
years-old and, as a State Department defector since 1992, a much sought-after media
commentator, columnist and analyst of American foreign policy in the Balkans.

Their encounter, first as passionate interventionists and consoling acquaintances,
and then as antagonists with Battiata's eventually public betrayal of Kenney's
confidence and friendship as his perception of the Bosnian conflict changed, is
worth a closer look at the "personal side" of Yugoslav-war journalism behind the
headlines.

"We meet soon enough, by chance, at a panel discussion at American University's
School of Communication," recalled Battiata.[3]

---

1. Battiata, "War of the Worlds," *The Washington Post Magazine*,
June 30, 1996.
2. Kenney, "Steering Clear of Balkan Shoals," *The Nation*, January 8-15 1996.
3. Battiata, *ibid.*

Media Cleansing: Dirty Reporting

That was October 5, 1993. The forum was entitled "Making Sense Out of Chaos: Reporting the War in Bosnia." Battiata, at thirty-seven, had returned after four years abroad, reporting for *The Washington Post*. She was a self-described "castoff from a crumbling war zone, ordered home to salvage my crumbling physical self."[4]

"In Washington in the winter of 1993, Bosnia is urgent," said Battiata. "Bosnia is horrific. Bosnia is chic, a romantic cause, a moral compass. It will be our Spanish civil war."[5]

As for Kenney? It could presumably pose as a platonically fatal, Bergman-Cooper liaison to an interested observer.

She arrived in Europe in 1989 after trekking through the institutional misery of Africa. She was steeped in suffering, filtered almost resentfully through the eye of her camera or from her reporter's notebook. She began reporting on the demises of Communism and, like everyone else, idealizing romantically over the budding democracies in Poland, Czechoslovakia and Romania, Bulgaria, Hungary and Albania:

> "...It is historic, thrilling and interesting. And somehow, coming from Africa, it feels like more of the same. Only worse."[6]

Before Bosnia, her writings evoked seismic spasms of journalistic melancholy. She was ideally suited for tragedy, an ultimate victim's victim:

> "...In Ethiopia, Sudan and Malawi, journalists followed the trail of drought, hunger and Kalashnikovs, pushing our way into stifling hospital tents and dark huts sooty with smoke and grease, to ask the walking skeletons where they had come from, where they were going. ...In southern Sudan, I lie on my belly in the dust to photograph dozens of children, toddlers, some younger, sitting with bloated bellies on the ground. Patient, doomed little Buddhas, waiting for food that is not coming."[7]

An easy supposition, if one believed what she wrote in 1997, was that her ethereal schooling on another planet, called a Prince Georges County "inner suburb" of Washington, D.C., possibly skipped over the cliche "war is hell"—much less the reporting about it.

> "...The job of a journalist in these settings is clear. Shine a spotlight. Direct the attention, if only for a few moments, of a busy world.

> "The responsibilities of a human being are less clear. What is the proper, what is the possible, human response to a bombardment of suffering?

> "The superficial drumbeat of deadlines and the soothing static of plane schedules and car rentals only partly obscure the fact

---

4. Battiata, "On the Healing Power of Wild Places," *The Washington Post Magazine,* November 23, 1997.
5. Battiata, "War...," *ibid.*
6. Battiata, *ibid.*
7. Battiata, *ibid.*

that you are wading through a sea of misery, but doing little to help.

"The tide of the misery rises slowly, ever so slowly, around you, weighing down your feet, silting in the space around your knees.

"You must detach, or you will drown.

"You must do something or you will die.

"But what?

"Motion. Keep moving.

"And when that stops working?

"Some journalists slip a fifty here, a hundred there, to people dying for lack of medicine, food, transport or water. Some adopt children. Become aid workers. Write books.

"Your colleagues do not talk about these things and neither do you. There are eminently good reasons for this.

"First and perhaps foremost, such questions and qualms seem self-indulgent and irrelevant in the face of the suffering of the people around you, the ones with real problems.

"You are just an observer. And on one level you are completely untouched. If you are fortunate enough to be working for a prosperous Western newspaper or television network, more often than not, at the end of the day you will catch a dilapidated street taxi back to your hotel, where, unless you are in the middle of a war zone, and sometimes even if you are, you may get a hot shower, certainly a meal. And then, if your luck and the electricity hold, you will get to sit in your comparatively quiet room to compose your thoughts and your story.

"Dwelling on your feelings in these situations—your grief, your helplessness, your guilt, your powerlessness—does not help you get your job done, and the job is difficult enough.

"Further, it is futile. It is weak. It calls attention to oneself, a violation of the reporter's goal of impartiality and invisibility. For all these reasons, admitting a story has begun to scour out your insides is tacitly forbidden by the steel-plated code of the foreign correspondent.

"But a code is not a code without cracks.

"Late at night at the hotel bar, your frayed packmates restore

their nerve endings with alcohol and opinion, talk and high spirits. In these sessions, indignation and outrage, grief and amazement seep through the professional armor like light.

"There is a fine gallows humor and a grim self-awareness of the kind that inspired the classic correspondent's memoir Anyone Here Been Raped and Speak English?

"These sessions are a release of sorts. Who was the hack who first called foreign corresponding 'summer camp with whiskey'?

"But they are all you get and they are not quite enough. For anyone. The questions haven't really been answered, nor the powerful griefs lanced. Not for any of the ink-stained lords and ladies of the long bar. The night ends and the next day begins and you are all still very much on your own.

"(In Yugoslavia) I have become efficient and expert at drawing out the details of massacres and other mayhem from shattered, frightened people. No, keep them talking, try to look sympathetic, but not so horrified that they become self-conscious and clam up. It's for the story. Keep going. Keep going. Deadline in two hours? Next!

"I spend my days listening to the unbelievable from the inconsolable. My stories are filled with things that I can't seem to shake out of my head at the end of the day. Far from washing out, they seem to be accumulating.

"...I am a blotter, a reluctant collector of sights and smells and physical sensations.

"...You keep the people talking. And then you go on to the next. And you tell yourself that your stories may help them."[8]

After four years as a correspondent for *The Washington Post*, mainly in northwestern Bosnia, mainly covering the "side" of Muslim victimologies, she was forced to return to Washington due to fatigue and a malady which, she said, severely impeded the use of her hands. She was also in substantial doubt about what she had seen and written—and what had gone unwritten.

A borrowed phrase from novelist John LeCarre kept falling from her stammering lips.

"And I think this war is the war of our 'post Cold War disorientation' because everyone seems to be floundering and struggling to understand and explain, and we, too, in the press, I think."[9]

---

8. Battiata, *ibid.*
9. Battiata, American University panel discussion. October 5, 1993.

When she met Kenney, she had shelved her newspaper career in order to deal with her physical debilitation which prevented use of the keyboard.

She was taking walks at all hours through the suburb-encased woods beside Cabin John Creek in southern Montgomery County. Her mood was mostly, deeply introspective, sometimes manic or emotionally volatile.

> *"...I have taken to walking in these woods for hours every day, at all hours. By moonlight and in the bright, leaf-steam glare of noon ...It's well after sunset, and long after supper. Early October. The woods are blue and black... I am not gliding through the woods like an Iroquois tonight. Not at all. In fact, I am venting, crying, raging. At a new doctor, the latest in a series..."* [10]

Her walks, self-taunts and soul-searching continued three years later:

> *"...Early 1996. I sing in the woods. Every song I know, at the top of my lungs. 'The Queen of the Silver Dollar,' 'Jolene,' and sometimes, just for the hell of it, a belligerent little number in Serbo-Croatian, the anthem of Serbian nationalists: 'Who says Serbia is small? It's not small. It's not small. It won three wars!'"* [11]

Kenney, an aspiring young State Department officer on the Yugoslav desk, created a stir in August 1992 when he abruptly walked out in very public protest of the Bush administration's failure to devise any realistic policy in the heat of the Yugoslav maelstrom.

Kenney arrived in Battiata's life a year later and in time to offer compassion and personal affirmation. Wronged idealists both, vulnerable to re-illusion:

> *"...In Washington in the winter of 1993, Bosnia is urgent. Bosnia is horrific. Bosnia is chic, a romantic cause, a moral compass. It will be our Spanish Civil War. Susan Sontag is going to Bosnia to direct 'Waiting for Godot.' There are panel discussions at the Holocaust Museum, photo exhibits, bumper stickers. Bosnia is the main course at Georgetown dinner parties, and recent returnees are on the A list. Television's talking heads, having boned up on Bosnia and its complicated roster of combatants, are crafting sound bites. Bosnia! In or out? Worth risking the lives of American boys? What's the strategic interest? Quickly!"* [12]

The pair seemed to be in exquisite harmony, overshadowing the other side of the panel at American University. Their chemistry was hard to mistake. Battiata said she was "amazed at the level of sophistication and understanding" about the Bosnia story since it was "a really difficult and complicated story both to write and to explain and to understand..." Her amazement would devolve to contradiction.

---

10. Battiata, "On the Healing Power...," *ibid.*
11. Battiata, *ibid.*
12. Battiata, "War...," *ibid.*

Gradually, Kenney was beginning to zero in on the gaps in the war reporting, alluding to tightening editorial controls:

> "There is a very interesting discontinuity between reporting from the field and reporting from Washington or Geneva or from London. And I kind of wish they would trade places every now and then because the reporters in the field have done a superb job of covering the issues. But the reporters in Washington draw a line somewhere and say, 'Well, we're not really going to press the State Department or the White House. We're not going to jeopardize our relationships in talking with these guys on background. When they say things that are preposterous and absurd, we're not going to point that out publicly.'
>
> "So, why hasn't the Washington press corps been going after the administration and bracing them and saying, 'What you're saying just doesn't make sense...'?"[13]

Battiata, though unintentionally, likewise displayed the war-time media's Achilles heel:

> "...We were being forced to write these impossible stories. I can remember sitting at the keyboard just defeated. How do you explain this in three paragraphs and still have room left in the story to explain what's actually going on?
>
> "The difference in this story, I think, is that you have to be very well-informed as a reporter to ask the right questions and to see what they are doing. And the other thing is that you have to have been with the story for a year or two. It's not a story that lends itself to coming in every three or four months because it changes all the time. It's always tearing off in a different direction. And there are important threads, and you lose them if you're just coming in. We saw it in Bosnia all the time. And I think it must be much worse if you're sitting in Washington. Someone new comes in and you can't believe what they don't know. It's just a very, very complicated story."[14]

Battiata answered the stirring voices of critics about media bias:

> "Advocacy journalism? Only in the sense that struggling every day to be objective when very well-intentioned people were lying to you. In some ways it was very easy to cover this story because you had incredible mobility until a few months ago. You could travel anywhere on every side... There was incredible access. People were very open on all sides...
>
> "It was an incredible experience because on all sides at least once a day you met somebody who made you cry. And it's not

---

13. Kenney, American University panel discussion. October 5, 1993.
14. Battiata, American University panel discussion. October 5, 1993.

that hard to figure out who's lying to you and who's telling the truth…

"When you were talking to mostly Bosnian Muslims who had been brutalized, you did have to keep reminding yourself. I mean it was hard. Sometimes you would be talking to someone who had terrible things happen to them and you had to press them to make sure they were telling you accurately and you were getting the right story.

"But it wasn't that hard because even on the Serb side I knew a lot of Serbs and I felt a responsibility to try to be truthful on behalf of everyone. And the minute you stop doing that, obviously, you don't belong there anymore…

"You can write a story with a lot of background in it in October, and in February not even your own parents remember it… And you just can't keep writing the same story, and that's a great frustration…"[15]

Battiata didn't go far enough with her response about "advocacy journalism," trailing off into silence with: "I don't think that we as journalists should be presenting ideas and opinions."

On that October evening at American University and seated together, they passed notes to each other. She appeared to draw strength from him—against her journalism instincts that would win out later. Her skills and tactics of war reporting would work on him, too:

> "…Not especially eager for publicity, he nonetheless agrees to meet for coffee. At the Java House, a neighborhood joint near Dupont Circle, he is open, guileless."[16]

Kenney could be characterized as vulnerable, though chivalrous, sympathetic and transparently genuine. But she remained like a butterfly in regression, being tragically sucked back into her cocoon. The imagery remained long after the abrupt end of their relationship:

> "…The caterpillars are falling down, crawling down, even as you read this, inching their way down the plant stems toward the autumn ground, to wrap themselves like origami inside their tiny leaf sleeping bags and wait for spring."[17]

Quite another intention would emerge from the origami and administer a cruel sting to Kenney.

Their relationship continued over four years—long enough for her to earn a payoff from the 1996 Sigma Delta Chi Awards for Excellence in Journalism in Magazine

---

15. Battiata, *ibid.*
16. Battiata, "War…, *ibid.*
17. Battiata, "A Perilous Beauty," *The Washington Post Magazine,* September 12, 1999.

Reporting. Her twenty-page cover story, "War of the Worlds," appeared in *The Washington Post Magazine's* June 30, 1996 edition.

The *SDX* judges were kind in describing a classic hatchet job:

> "Battiata, who covered the grotesque and murderous early stages of the war, frames this story around George Kenney, the obscure State Department official who resigned in protest over the Bush administration's failure to act in the summer of 1992. 'The War of the Worlds is a powerful piece of writing delivered from the gut,' the judges wrote. 'The scenes from Bosnia read like that "visceral video" playing in the writer's head upon her return to the unnerving, abstract debate in Washington. Ms. Battiata deserves this award, ultimately, for writing an *honest story*—honesty that is reflected in her careful choice of word, her illuminating metaphors, her compelling portrait of George Kenney, and her deeply revealing personal observations.'"[18] (Italics added)

Some would say it was George Kenney's honesty that rewarded Battiata.

> "In three years, we had around 20 lunches together. She was very clever. I thought I was helping her to come around."[19]

Few journalists, who immersed themselves in the war reporting from Yugoslavia, talk at length about their personal pathologies. Answers to direct questions are at first waved away with irritable, spluttering, angry denials.

Newsday's Roy Gutman bulwarked himself behind a facade of adamant, too profuse insistence that holes in his reporting did not exist. It was impossible for them to exist. After all, he won half a Pulitzer Prize.

The New York Times' John F. Burns spoke only at safe podiums, shielded by his editors in New York, his hospitable Bosnian government "owners" in Sarajevo and, finally, the safely distant redoubts of India. After all, he won the other half of Gutman's Pulitzer.

Christiane Amanpour, at *CNN*, was unapproachable. Anyone who wanted to ask her anything would need an inexhaustible bank account and a fistful of frequent-flyer cards to catch up with her. Besides, what kind of questions could be asked about a sneer, a squint, arrogance, demagoguery? Once she married James Rubin, Madeleine Albright's spokesman at the U.S. State Department, all the answers became evident!

Among their colleagues in the Balkans, there was some early attempt at answering the newsroom credo: Who? What? When? Where? Why? How?

How? This sixth fundamental became the quicksand of reporting inside the blood-stained triangle of Zagreb, Belgrade and Sarajevo. "How" became a mutation of advocacy, interpretation and outright surrealism.

Selling the Yugoslav wars exceeded even tabloidism.

Numerous war time journalists later retraced their steps with long thoughtful articles, displaying their own human woundedness, or they wrote books to try to amend the earlier excesses, negligence and that of their nameless editors. But these

---

18. Announcement by *Sigma Delta Chi* for 1996 awards.
19. Kenney interview with the author, September 1996.

volumes were wearisome efforts, pretenses of analyses on diplomacy, corrections for "the record" but falling short of candor and real confession. The books, though historically repetitive, attempted to explain, to rationalize, to condemn again. Reporters playing at historical novela, trying again to "get it right." No matter if the first truths were edited, rewritten, shortened—or spiked.

Kenney was not trained as a journalist. But he eventually demonstrated more passion for journalistic accuracy and moral diplomacy at the cost of his martyred career at the State Department.

But Kenney also became the catalyst for Battiata's self-revelations and profuse exhibitions of journalistic obsession, if not self-traumatizing delusion, in the Yugoslav catastrophe. At first, he confirmed Battiata's own misty doubts, though he was beginning to become quietly suspicious that the sensational body counts—that illusory foundation behind cries of "genocide"—were being hyped overall.

> "All told, how many people have died in Bosnia? ...As long as the world tosses around words like 'genocide' so loosely, the present tragedy will revolve endlessly," wrote Kenney later, finally rejecting unverified, if not unverifiable, tallies of the dead. "Counts count."[20]

Kenney's shot was heard round the world of journalism—and echoed embarrassingly for Battiata in the comfortable second year of their friendship. Why?

> "In 1995, lacking the bodies, the charge of Genocide has worn thin. It seems to have almost become sensationalism for its own sake. Apart from any question of the number of fatalities, journalists have begun a hot little debate about how 'objective' coverage of Bosnia has been, about whether it has tended to favor the Muslims. Several journalists with whom I spoke expressed the uneasy feeling that something was obviously wrong..."[21]

He also offered a more plausible surmise about the devotion to exaggeration, negligence and naivete brought to the Yugoslav wars by Western journalists who had other ambitions:

> "...(T)oo many journalists dreamed self-aggrandizing dreams of becoming Hemingway."[22]

At first, Battiata and others thrilled after Kenney, as an interventionist, went public with his sensational resignation from the State Department in August 1992:

> *"...'I can no longer in clear conscience support the administration's ineffective, indeed counterproductive, handling of the Yugoslav crisis... I am therefore resigning in order to help a stronger public consensus that the U.S. must act immediately to stop the genocide in Bosnia and prevent this conflict from spreading throughout the Balkans.'*

20. Kenney, "The Bosnia Calculation," *The New York Times Magazine.* April 23, 1995.
21. Kenney, *ibid.*
22. Kenney, *ibid.*

"Genocide. There, he had said it. In plain English. Genocide. Not 'casualties,' not 'combatants,' not 'participants,' not 'the parties' to 'the conflict.' None of the bloodless, diplomatic language the State Department had been using to describe the mayhem that had broken out four months earlier...

"Genocide. The soft, insinuating 'g.' 'Gen' from the Greek genos for race, a people. Or as in genuflect, as in kneeling, as in humiliation, as in doing what you are told, at gunpoint, waiting to die...

"Reporters gathered to inspect the bureaucratic curiosity. Photographers snapped his picture. Bureaucrats all over Washington, and especially inside the State Department, speculated on his motives. Who was George Kenney? This minor State Department figure emblazoned on the front pages, taking the Bush administration to task. And what was he up to anyway? Was he grandstanding? Or worse, for an aspiring Washington player, was he naive?

"It didn't matter at first.

"Kenney was greeted as a hero by those who believed the United States had a moral responsibility and a strategic interest in bombing the Serb Army's gun positions and stopping the killing. In the brief flare of celebrity, he personalized what to many Americans was still an incomprehensible war in a distant corner of Europe. If his resignation did not change U.S. foreign policy, it turned up the heat, and ripped a hole in the Bush administration's facade of policy unity.

"His decisiveness, his nerve, was a mocking counterpoint to the traveling circus of diplomats, Eurocrats and United Nations pooh-bahs gathering in London that August on the first round of what would become a two-year mobile peace conference on Yugoslavia." [23]

But by 1995, Kenney's ideological defection and betrayal of intervention in Bosnia was unforgivable, though uniquely, opportunistically exploitable by Battiata:

"...In the fall of 1995, I have my own disorientation to deal with. Three years later, the memories of what I saw covering the war for this newspaper are still strong enough to derail me. Place names, photographs, a certain kind of rain, a particular sky, send me back there. Questions about my own decisiveness, my own analysis, still entangle me. So I have come calling this afternoon to ask about the man who briefly seemed one of its most heroic actors, whose impatience with a passive policy and disingenuous doublespeak drove him to act when Washington failed to.

---

23. Battiata, "War...," *ibid.*

"George Kenney, whose policy prescription, had it been followed when he made it, might have stopped the war in its tracks. Crisscrossing Bosnia in a balky Russian jeep in the fall of 1992, I had heard stories about George Kenney. So I am surprised to find that the once high regard has curdled. That Kenney is now dismissed by many former admirers in Washington as a puzzle, a disappointment, and worse, by colleagues who once applauded him."[24]

During 1993-96, she was also told stories *by* him. But, she was more interested in publicly degrading Kenny, betraying his candor if not his confidence. Given the near incapacity of her hands to take notes, she apparently used a tape-recorder. But, the astonishing devotion she gave to her first-person task of "getting Kenney" is apparent from manually transcribing her notes despite the severe painfulness in her hands. Her condition preceded meeting Kenney by a year:

"...Sometime in the past few months I have started to cradle my arms on my belt buckle whenever I can. They burn and ache all the time, from my wrists all the way up to my shoulders... I have a laundry list of related arm and hand injuries. (Among them, I later learn, are 'bilateral repetitive strain injury with chronic forearm myofascitis, bilateral medial and lateral epicondylitis, bilateral cubical tunnel syndrome, right radial tunnel syndrome,' and 'thoracic outlet syndrome appearing to involve the upper and lower trunk and lateral cord.') I should be hospitalized immediately for six weeks, (a London specialist) says. I may need traction. If I don't stop using my arms immediately, he warns, my fingertips could blacken. Amputation in these circumstances is not unheard of...

"...June 1994. A disastrous trip to the Eastern shore. As I sit in my mother's car, my arms burn from the exertion of packing a suitcase. As we drive, they begin to be irritated by the vibration. I can't find a place to put them that doesn't hurt. Fold my hands on my lap. Try and fail to compose myself. Burst into tears ...Intense disappointment. It is more than a year after my return, but my arms seem to be getting no better..."[25]

She and Kenney by this time had known each other for eight months.

"...September 1995. Everything hurts. My hands, my arms, my heart. Back at work, I struggle to use a voice-activated computer program. It is slow, balky and makes four or five mistakes a sentence. Correcting each of those mistakes requires six or seven voice commands."[26]

When Battiata met Kenney, it was the same month that she had a defining encounter during a painful, surreal walk in the woods along Cabin John Creek:

---

24. Battiata, "War...," *ibid.*
25. Battiata, "On the Healing Power...," *ibid.*
26. Battiata, *ibid.*

"So, yeah, I think of this as a kind of fairy tale. A fractured one.

"It has most of the elements. There is a beautiful forest. A sort-of happy ending.

"No princess.

"But it does have a frog.

"But this frog, an olive-green pickerel frog the size of a nectarine is in dire trouble when the dog and I spot it in the fall of 1993. ...(L)ocking eyes with this frog stops me cold. It brings me down and messes me way up, and as I stand riveted, I can't figure out why.

"Things take their time in fairy tales. It will be three more years and a lot more walking before I suddenly understand what the frog was all about. Three years in the forest, trying to outwalk the past.

"...It is a frog. A damp green beauty, damp-skinned and streaked with yellow.

"We come close, but it remains frozen on a pad of dead leaves. The only things moving are its eyes, which blink frantically, and its little flanks, which balloon in and out like a small bellows.

"I don't understand this. I crouch closer. And then I see the problem: The frog's left hind leg is buried to the second joint in the mouth of a small snake.

"It is a common garter snake... Its jaws gape grotesquely, its mouth stuffed with pulsating frog muscle. The rest of its body trails loosely on the forest floor, as delicate and refined as a tendril of a woman's hair

"Now we are frozen too, the dog and I. We stand there for I don't know how long, two giant mammals gazing down at an amphibian and a reptile. The forest seems to have gone completely quiet. The snake, interrupted in its slow assault on a living supper, does not move or give any sign of being disturbed. But the frog is frantic. Blinking. Staring up at me. Breathing hard.

"I know there is nothing special in this drama. It is a common-place event repeated many times each day as part of the forest food chain.

"But its violence is shocking, embarrassing, weirdly intimate. It is as if we have stumbled on a pair of lovers having sex in the middle of the trail. And as we watch, I am overpowered by *an intense and completely bewildering feeling that I have been here before.*

"...The snake is entitled to its supper. The predations of snakes keep the frog population healthy. ...So why do I imagine that the frog's stare is beseeching me? Why do I feel so depressed and helpless at having to move on?

"...I have been home barely eight months after many years away. In this awful autumn of 1993, everything around me seems to be wounded and dying. Even in the woods, the world seems surreal and out of control." [27]

The metaphor could apply to much she had gone through and was going through. But it appears that only George Kenney was vulnerable, as Battiata—in the self-described throes of physical pain, mental depression and journalistic vendetta—set her sights on Kenney. She mustered remarkable energy, as a supposed near-invalid, in recruiting "the score of diplomats for this story (who) will not be quoted by name" and who eagerly, generously, jealously lambasted Kenney. Battiata described one of them:

"...The analyst has kicked around in a few jobs since 1992, when he, like dozens of other Balkan area specialists at State, backed away from Bosnia in frustration and protest. It was either that, or quit. Lots of people wanted to quit, he says, would have, except for the kids, the mortgage and other responsibilities of middle-aged life. He was part of a behind-the-scenes rebellion in the State Department by those who believe the United States allowed genocide in Bosnia in 1992. Tempers flared, careers buckled, friendships sundered..." [28]

Likely, Kenney knew them all—and even provided Battiata with a roster. She quoted or paraphrased ten of them anonymously:

"'George is a man of principle. I'm just not sure what the principle is,' says one former colleague...

"'There were people in his own bureau who wanted to go after him,' says a former colleague. 'He made them look like monkeys.'...

"'I think he's vile,' one former colleague will say, echoing the view of others.'...

"'Kenney had a fine moment—not without guile, but it was guile constructively applied,' one says. 'But now he's a guy roaming around Washington without perspective or prospects, revising his positions every five minutes.'...

27. Battiata, *ibid.*
28. Battiata, "War...," *ibid.*

"'He's irrelevant,' says another testily.'"[29]

What was Kenney's crime, in Battiata's words?

> *"...April 1995. ...I have checked in with Kenney on and off for two years. I still tend to think of him as an underdog, the hero of a running saga titled 'The Price of Principle.'*

> *"But lately, the more I see of him, the more I wonder. Because for the past two years, the country's most influential interventionist has been energetically arguing against the position that made his name.*

> *"In one of the stranger intellectual odysseys in Washington, the man who once was passionately in favor of U.S. military intervention in Bosnia is now dead set against it. Since leaving the State Department, Kenney has tracked U.S. policy in an inverse arc. The closer the United States moved to air strikes, the farther away George Kenney went. And in the process, he has made a new name for himself—as a curiosity, a pariah, an outcast from the community he once inspired...*

> *"Now ...Kenney is talking enthusiastically about his next article. It will be the ultimate recantation.*

> *"The piece, which will appear shortly in the New York Times Magazine, will assert that there was no genocide in Bosnia after all. It will accuse the Bosnian government, the Western news media and the United Nations, of grossly exaggerating the numbers of dead and missing.*

> *"Citing official but anonymous sources at the Pentagon, the State Department's bureau of intelligence and research and European military officers with extensive experience in Bosnia, and analyzing and 'extrapolating' from estimates by the International Committee of the Red Cross, the piece will set the number of Bosnian war dead, on all sides, at somewhere between 25,000 and 60,000—far short of the 200,000 figure used by most media at that time.*

> *"He will accuse the Bosnian government of deliberately exaggerating the numbers in a cynical ploy to win international sympathy and force allied military intervention."[30]*

The article appeared, as Kenney said, a few days later on April 23, 1995. Interventionists, media included, cringed and bombarded Kenney with criticism and slander.

Battiata hobbled for the exit in their relationship. Better to minimize any blowback:

---

29. Battiata, *ibid.*
30. Battiata, *ibid.*

"...It is an interesting idea. War time casualty figures are notoriously unreliable, and in the Balkans maybe even more so...

"...I look at Kenney and I suddenly feel dizzy and nauseated. Yes, we are juggling death counts... Become a pundit, teach yourself to juggle.

"And respected analysts will dispute the piece's numbers and its central argument...

"Kenney's figure of 25,000 to 60,000 dead is absurdly low, they will say, because there are 10,000 graves in Sarajevo alone...

"And above all, Kenney's critics will ask, what is the point of doing hard analysis of death counts in the middle of a war? Fifty thousand or 200,000 dead doesn't change the basic fact that tens of thousands of unarmed civilians have been slaughtered in the middle of Europe in the last decade of the 20th century, 50 years after the war that was supposed to have taught us never again." [31]

In character, Battiata's monologue moves her from side-to-side, as though on a stage.

"...On the other hand, though his central argument—that the inflated numbers might lure us into the war—has proved wrong, his narrower point is valid. The numbers did jump implausibly. Reporters, myself included, did use Bosnian government and U.N. casualty counts. And after his piece appears, the number used in boilerplate will drop. The use of the 200,000 figure will tail off...

"With his bright blue eyes and insistent skepticism, Kenney has waded into an area that no one else had the stomach to touch. He is annoying, he is irritating—but he has a point. I don't think his numbers are right, either, and I am even less sure that they matter. But I have a grudging admiration for his willingness to take on an odious task...

"A few thousand dead in Kozarac. A few thousand at Brcko. But what are a few thousand deaths, or tens of thousands? One mass grave does not a Holocaust make. Does that justify U.S. intervention, putting American troops at risk? Bosnia, up or down? Quickly?...

"At State, a desk officer in the region finds Kenney's changing views 'helpful and interesting,' his analysis 'cautious and thorough'—and more honest than those whose position on the war stayed frozen at intervention...

---

31. Battiata, *ibid*

> *"Others, who disagree with his conclusions, nonetheless admire his persistence. His stubbornness...*
>
> *"But to many former colleagues and others who consistently pushed for U.S. action to stop the war, George Kenney is a man who has focused on the details and lost the larger picture. They disagree with his facts and disdain his analysis."[32]*

At the time, Kenney applied the same scrutiny to the massacre at Srebrenica, which Battiata found inexcusable – even in the absence of "what we know factually":

> *"...I look at Kenney and it is as if I am looking at him through the wrong end of a telescope. He is sitting at the table, but he has gotten very, very small..."[33]*

Eighteen months after their first meeting, Battiata was still physically unable to drive, continuing to sort out her jumbled, angry, impatient subsistence. She seemed grateful for his company. Although, he was an attentive, intellectual sounding board, she disliked his irritability over improperly prepared oatmeal:

> *"...He is a type, I decide tentatively. A whistle-blower type. Truculent. Self-confident. Demanding. A bit arrogant. And stubborn."[34]*

Battiata also had open access to the home of his parents in Chevy Chase where Kenney lived in the basement that also serves as his office.

> *"...His 'quarters,' as he calls them, are two white-walled rooms. Spartan, monkish. ...On the floor by the bed, there is a book on teaching yourself to juggle."[35]*

Kenney's coming-out article in *The New York Times Magazine* in April 1995— "The Bosnia Calculation: How many have died? Not nearly as many as some would have you think"—generally silenced critics who thought he could be cowed in his persistence to force the government, diplomatic and media rail-birds to own up to realistic and factual statistics in the Yugoslav wars.[36]

Far from the myopic rap from his go-along, get-along former colleagues of having "lost the larger picture" and "focused on the details," Kenney had a clear view of the Balkan panorama. Their disagreement "with his facts and disdain (for) his analysis" only exposed their compartmental ineptness to comprehend the conflict of the 1990s as rooted in the ever-present Balkan past:

> "The question of how many fatalities there have been in Bosnia is far from academic. Many wars, maybe all—but this war especially—are fought for prestige and honor, not rational reasons. Many atrocities in the former Yugoslavia have been justified as revenge for killings during World War II. Yet the number

---

32. Battiata, *ibid.*
33. Battiata, *ibid.*
34. Battiata, *ibid*
35. Battiata, *ibid*
36. Kenney, *The New York Times Magazine*, April 23, 1995.

of fatalities in Yugoslavia during World War II was also never documented. In fact, interpreting those numbers today defines your brand of ethnic nationalism. Thus, people in the Balkans think the number of fatalities makes a difference—and since they do, so should we. The difference could be between getting a settlement in our lifetime and waiting generations. Not to break the cycle is a gratuitous, even immoral error."[37]

Kenney's echoing salvo in 1999 about casualties in Kosovo sharply contradicted the State Department's shrill claim seven months earlier that "225,000 ethnic Albanian men aged between 14 and 59" were missing:

"On September 23 *El Pais*, a mainstream Madrid paper, reported that Spanish forensic investigators sent to Kosovo had found no proof of genocide. The team, which had experience in Rwanda, had been told to expect to perform more than 2,000 autopsies in one of the areas worst hit by fighting, but it found only 187 bodies to examine. No mass graves and, for the most part, no signs of torture. ...Given the number of ICTY (International Criminal Tribunal for Yugoslavia) identified sites and the tribunal's findings so far, a reasonable guess of the Albanian dead lies somewhere between 2,000 and 4,000."[38]

Unlike his critics and those in the media who refused to revise casualty counts downward in the face of obvious forensic contradiction—the *Associated Press* would even note without any corroboration that there were 300,000 war dead(!) during Tribunal proceedings at The Hague in 2002—Kenney was intellectually honest enough when it came to accuracy:

"After the war, I did some (unpublished) research that suggests the total killed during the war was roughly 70,000 to 90,000, and that the percentage of each population base killed was roughly identical. A cross check of my range could be done for purposes of rough confirmation: Take the numbers provided by the Stockholm International Research Institute for military deaths during the war, published in its annual yearbook by Oxford University Press. Add known civilian deaths. Add those officially declared missing to the International Committee of the Red Cross (assume they are dead), subtract some for double-counting and people who fled the region, and it's hard to get a reasonable range higher than 70,000 to 90,000.

"Do these numbers matter? You bet! It seems, looking at interventionist rhetoric regarding crises around the world, that 200,000 is a kind of magic number. Almost every Kosovo interventionist talks about genocide and glibly rattles off the high number for Bosnia, as if there were 20 or 30 as-yet-undiscovered Srebrenica massacres—as if the Serbs had butchered everyone they could

---

37. Kenney, *ibid.*
38. Kenney, "Kosovo: On Ends and Means" (a book review of Noam Chomsky's *The New Military Humanism: Lessons From Kosovo*), *The Nation*, December, 27, 1999.

get their hands on."[39]

It is interesting to speculate how many times amidst the woods on Cabin John Creek that, gazing narcissistically into pools of quiet water, there was only a shimmering likeness of Kenney's face.

In response to Battiata's "highly emotional" profile of Kenney in "War of the Worlds," different letter-writers instead sensed Kenney's veracity in Battiata's attack out of her "own cold war disorientation":

> "Battiata misses the true lesson of Bosnia for American foreign policy: that the United States has become handcuffed by a media and public that are unwilling to accept sacrifice as the price for a higher cause..."[40]

> "Kenney's virtue, Battiata makes clear, is that he honestly, if oddly, has been thinking for himself. The eccentricity of this maverick analyst illuminates the collective cowardice of the policy herd and brings out what is unique in the Bosnian horror..."[41]

> "Regarding the profile of my son, I would like to describe him in my own way. George did have a very promising career in the Foreign Service. ...His guiding principle is that good policy must be based on reality. ...His constant forward-looking approach and his willingness to question the established consensus are valuable qualities in any organization, but they should be given significant weight by the foreign policy establishment." [42]

"We never spoke again," said Kenney about Mary Grace Battiata in 1998, who became the lead-singer and songwriter of the local country-rock group "Little Pink," her self-described singing style being "part garage, part girl, and violet—a sound like the weird colors and feelings that you get at dusk."

Of course, in the real-life allegory of Cabin John Woods, the frog could have been saved—if Battiata had killed the snake!

Battiata won awards from the Overseas Press Club, Sigma Delta Chi, and others, along with being a two-time nominee for the Pulitzer Prize.

Judging from her self-revealing narrative in 1997, her four years of solitary treks through the woods gave her more than a casual recognition for botanical and zoological minutia:

> "...There are two dozen kinds of ferns and mosses. There are more than 80 species of fungi: death angels and sulfur top, deer mushroom and chicken of the woods. ...There are bullfrogs and salamanders, corn snakes and king snakes, three kinds of turtles. ...And there are wildflowers, more than 320 kinds,

---

39. Kenny, "Kosovo Talk—Genocide." *MOJO Wire (Mother Jones Magazine* online), pre-dates 1998.

40. Letters to the Editor, *The Washington Post*, September 22, 1996.

41. Letters, *ibid.*

42. Letter from George R. Kenney to *The Washington Post*, September, 22, 1996.

everything from partridge pea and evening primrose to stinging nettle and pussytoes. ...Sometimes I come across traces of the land's earlier uses: rusted and toppled barbed-wire pasture fencing that now flows through the middle of the tree trunks that have grown up around it."[43]

In hindsight, all the more strange that in her October 11, 1992, piece about her visit to the "Trnopolje detention camp," two months after sensational news reports about "concentration camps" were roaring through the Western media, that with her fine appreciation for detail she had mentioned no notice of barbed wire—nor chicken-wire!

---

43. Battiata, "On the Healing Power...," *ibid.*

Chapter 14

Welcome To The 'Brave New' Journalism

"There was no barbed wire fence around the (Trnopolje) camp area, which also included a school, a community center, and a large open area with a sports field. This was verified by international institutions such as the International Criminal Tribunal in The Hague and the International Red Cross in Geneva. The fact that it was the reporters that were surrounded by barbed wire can be seen in the other film material that was not edited or broadcast."[1]
—Thomas Deichmann

"Never let the facts get in the way of a good story."[2]

It seemed odd that *Washington Post* correspondent Mary Battiata thought it important enough to say that barbed wire was used to enclose 6,500 Muslim civilians at nearby Kotor Varos when she wrote her subsequent story from nearby Trnopolje where 3,500 civilians were gathered in October 1992—just two months later! [3]

Odd only because she made no previous mention of barbed wire—or chicken-wire—at the camp outside the village of Trnopolje.

Trnopolje is sixty or so miles southeast of Kotor Varos.

Normally, Battiata might be forgiven for the omission. In the same story she described Banja Luka as a town of "200,000 people, mostly Muslims..." Banja Luka's predominate population was always Serbian.

But, the omission about what, if anything, was used to enclose or merely stood intermittently on the Trnopolje school grounds was inconsistent with repeated reports

---

1. Deichmann, "Photos Never Lie—Or Do They?" *Berliner Morgenpost*, September 1997.

2. Newsroom sarcasm, anonymous.

3. Battiata, *The Washington Post*, October 11, 1992.

that barbed wire was prominently used to isolate civilians—a feature Battiata should have grasped with journalistic gusto.

Battiata was typically susceptible to emotional allegory, even overkill:

> "A tour of the camp revealed the Muslims to be living in con-
> ditions of *medieval squalor*... Most of the camp's residents live
> ...in *Dickensian squalor*..."[4] (Italics added)

More than four years later, the issue of barbed wire and chicken-wire at Trnopolje exploded across Europe in a bedlam of media controversy. Journalism in the U.S. largely looked the other way, strangely unfazed.

German and British reporters and news commentators fired accusing salvos at each other, reputations were besmirched and bitterly defamed, lawsuits were filed, retractions were made and, when the snarling and bloodied combatants returned to their introspective corners, at least one crusading newsmagazine was destroyed.

A raw nerve was touched in the world's second oldest profession.

Two months before Battiata's report in *The Washington Post*, sensational images taken by a British television cameraman horrified the world showing several malnourished and supposedly brutalized men reaching through barbed wire at Trnopolje, shaking hands with three reporters on August 5, 1992.

Apparently, there could be no doubt that the notorious Nazi concentration camps of a half-century earlier were resurrected in Bosnia. All too graphic, close-up and wide-angle television shots would not lie. The proof was, it seemed, indisputable.

Within forty-eight hours, screaming headlines and telecasts worldwide sent government leaders and policy-makers scurrying:

"BELSEN '92"
"THE PROOF! Behind the barbed wire, the brutal truth about the suffering in Bosnia"
"Evidence mounts of executions and beatings in Serb-run camps"
"HORROR OF THE NEW HOLOCAUST"
"THE PICTURE THAT SHAMES THE WORLD"

It was "the picture" that played the news for days to come. Front pages. Margin-to-margin. Top-to-bottom. The dominant American news-weeklies, *Time* and *Newsweek*, had passed deadlines and did not have time to re-plate for upcoming editions, deciding to wait until August 17th to give Trnopolje the splashy treatment. Meanwhile, the U.S. dailies and television networks were churning it out.

Time and *Newsweek* lunged into the free-for-all ten days later.

Time went with five large photos, including the cover, showing "the picture" with the young Bosnian Muslim man, the skeletal Fekrit Alic, his washboard rib-cage, grotesquely thin limbs and a jack-o'lantern grin that was more a grimace leering out of an open grave.

Newsweek laid out fifteen large photos, including the cover and another unidentified but equally emaciated, shirtless man from the same footage from Trnopolje.

Even though the Trnopolje event had sparked the sudden, frenzied coverage, both *Time* and *Newsweek* buttressed the breaking video effect with less recent photos from Sarajevo.

---

4. Battiata, *ibid.*

Essays, graphics, opinion polls, red ink and gore filled the text columns—first from Time headlines and insets:

> "...These Muslim prisoners stare out from behind the barbed wire of their camp. That such cruelty could still happen in Europe mocked the new world order. ...ATROCITY And Outrage ...Specters of barbarism in Bosnia compel the U.S. and Europe to ponder: Is it time to intervene? ...HATRED Ten Times Over"

Under J.F.O. McAllister's byline, *Time's* lurid narrative began with:

> "The shock of recognition is acute. Skeletal figures behind barbed wire. Murdered babies in a bus. Two and a half million people driven from their homes in an orgy of 'ethnic cleansing.' Detention camps, maybe even concentration camps. Surely these pictures and stories come from another time—the Dark Ages, the Thirty Years' War, Hitler's heyday."

Several hundred words into his text, McAllister belatedly inserted:

> "...So far, there is *no evidence* of genocide or systematic extermination; *actual proof of individual murders is still rare.* But there are numerous accounts of starvation, beatings, interrogation and miserable sanitation. Western diplomats think many of the camps will turn out to be similar to the few they have been allowed to see: harsh but not murderous detention sites where enemies, civilian and military, are warehoused before expulsion or exchange

> "...(A)s the images of atrocity flicker across the world's television screens, the U.S. and its allies find themselves forced to mull over the unattractive military options available that might put a crimp in Serbian aggression—or at least send a message of retribution to Belgrade. In the long run, the international community must develop a new ethic, and institutions to match, concerned less with the sanctity of borders than with the rights of people..." (Italics added)

While McAllister, along with three contributing writers, reached an impotent conclusion, Time editors even inserted "A Lexicon of Horrors" and explained why:

> "Newspapers screamed of death camps. President Bush warned of Nazi-style genocide. But these emotionally freighted words obscured the fact that such phrases have precise historical meanings, and their misuse is often an act of propaganda..."

Time concluded with a question-and-answer sidebar from "outgoing" UNPROFOR commander General Lewis MacKenzie, highlighting one of MacKenzie's answers in larger type in the center of the eighth and last page of its spread: "Even if only 10% of what each side accuses the other of doing is true, in the minds of the people it has grown to horrendous proportions."

Newsweek's cover package went on for twelve pages, including headlines and photo captions:

> "'Ethnic Cleansing' (sic) Bosnia's Cry for Help ...Shocking images from battered Bosnia put pressure on Bush to decide what America should do—or can do—to stop the nightmare ...A defining event: British television shows emaciated prisoners at a Serbian camp in Trnopolje ...Horror stories: A distraught mother holds her son in northern Bosnia, a Sarajevo morgue receives the bodies of Bosnian soldiers ...Life and Death in the Camps(,) Inmates tell of starvation and beatings inflicted by their former neighbors ...In the Pediatric ward at Kosovo (sic) Hospital, a boy lies swathed in bandages—treatment for burns and lacerations suffered in a mortar attack; a woman says her last goodbye during a funeral at Lion Cemetery, once a popular park; young men make a run for it through 'Sniper Alley,' the most dangerous intersection in the city."

Groping for some pose of "balance," *Newsweek* featured essays with opposing viewpoints from interventionist Charles Lane and the more cautious columnist Col. David Hackworth. Hackworth, writing under the headline "It's All Too Easy to Get Sucked Into War," was circumspect:

> "So far, no one is talking seriously about committing U.S. ground troops; the idea is that we can deal with Serbia from the air. The plan, if it comes to that, would be to replay the gulf war with all its laser and stealth wonder toys: totally antiseptic, almost bloodless and oh, by the way, a boon for the depressed U.S. defense industry, which is a heavy-duty political contributor. ...To help prevent starvation, for example, the U.S. military could fly well above harm's way and airdrop bundles of food and water to the poor people who are trapped in the quagmire below. But this time it should be their quagmire, not ours."

The last-page and rallying last-word was given to Lane—"When Is It Genocide?" ending with his trademark, breathless foot-stamping:

> "...The whole subject is a minefield of moral equivalence. Those who invoke the Hitler analogy must be prepared to stand by it. ...Bosnia may not be Buchenwald, but it's bad enough..."

The *Time* cover photo of Fikret Alic was used a year later in *The Washington Post Magazine's* cover story, "In the Shadow of the Holocaust," by Steve Coll. The fourteen-page piece with its sixteen photos included a large, two-page photo of the Bergen-Belsen concentration camp, provided by the United States Holocaust Memorial Museum. Another prominent photo showed Herman Goering, Rudolf Hess and Joachim von Ribbentrop in the war crimes court in 1945.

Coll attempted to gauge the veracity of a cumbersome international court to deal with alleged war crimes in Yugoslavia, beginning with a complete version of its official title—"The International Tribunal for the Prosecution of Persons Responsible for Serious Violations of International Humanitarian Law Committed in the Territory of

Former Yugoslavia Since 1991":

> "Only bureaucrats at the United Nations could have invented
> this title... Note, for starters, the absence of the phrase 'war
> crimes'..."[5]

Readers were relieved to see Alic, two years after his haggard photo was taken at Trnopolje, looking fit, calmly smoking a cigaret and reflecting in front of the customary camera about his role, according to Coll, as "the poster boy of Serbian war camps."[6]

Coll peppered his lengthy article with references to the Holocaust, concentration camps, Nazi Party, the SS, the Gestapo, Hitler, "Schindler's List," and calls for "a second Nuremberg."

And, Alic again told his story for Coll about his August 5 meeting with British reporters at Trnopolje:

> "Galvanized, reporters and television crews raced across
> Bosnia toward Prijedor. Britain's Independent Television News
> broadcast the first pictures on August 6, showing emaciated, shirt-
> less, frightened men *trapped* behind barbed wire. A bone-thin
> Fikret Alic ...stood at the fore in these pictures and became,
> inadvertently, the poster boy of Serbian war camps. 'It was a
> big group, big microphones,' he recalls of his encounter with
> the Western media. Still imprisoned by the Serbs, he worried
> about what would happen when the journalists had gone. 'I
> was thinking, this is a big problem. I looked at the cameras and the
> microphones. I thought, 'This is no good. We might be killed.'
>
> "The prisoners managed strong hints to the journalists about
> atrocities in the camps. The information from these pressured,
> fragmented interviews was scanty, but the visual images were
> overwhelming. Washington called an emergency session of the
> U.N. Human Rights Commission. When the U.S. government
> first knew of the camps, and what it knew, remain controversial
> topics; some published reports have alleged that American
> intelligence agencies were aware of the camps well before
> August..."[7] (Italics added)

Reuter's Belgrade bureau chief, Don Forbes, said the existence of the camps was known by Western reporters and the International Committee for the Red Cross practically as soon as the Bosnian war began.[8]

Two-and-a-half years later, Alic described again details about his first meeting with reporters at Trnopolje:

> "Fikret then explained what really happened on August 5,
> 1992: *'We were 100 percent behind that barbed wire. There*

---

5. Coll, "In the Shadow of the Holocaust," *The Washington Post Magazine*, September 25, 1994.

6. Coll, *ibid.*

7. Coll, *ibid.*

8. Forbes interview with the author in Belgrade, February 1993.

was wire all around us. They took some of it down on August 8, 1992, when Serb television crews arrived from Belgrade and Banja Luka...' He gulped a couple of painkillers for his irreparably damaged kidneys..."[9] (Italics added)

But, Serbian television crews were on hand on August 5 and filmed the interviews by *International Television News (ITN)* with Alic and others. *ITN* and the Serb cameras never showed Alic and his companions "surrounded" by any barbed wire. Instead, *ITN* filmed between four top strands of rusted, sagging barbed wire strung haphazardly between posts—with a thin "chicken-wire" mesh hanging underneath.

By contrast, heavy-gauge, woven and electrified barbed wire is seen in the stark, black-and-white, double-page photo of Bergen-Belsen in *The Washington Post Magazine's* article. But contrasted with the small inset color photo of Alic at Trnopolje, the comparison was an obvious mismatch—even with several bare-chested companions of Alic's who'd intentionally removed their shirts to show some weight-loss. But contrasted to Alic and a few others who were similarly gaunt and shirtless, more than several—especially those who kept their shirts on—appeared comparatively well-fed. The equally reasonable explanation was that the visibly undernourished men were just released from the Keraterm detention camp, while the others arrived from areas with conditions of less privation.

The difference between the photograph of Bergen-Belsen and Trnopolje was that there was no chicken-wire at Bergen-Belsen.

But, cameramen and layout editors cropped the photos of Alic so that the three or four strands of old barbed wire were emphasized. Tellingly, the chicken-wire was plainly visible in all the publications and telecasts of "the picture" on August 6th and 7th, and thereafter.

No, "the picture" didn't lie!

Nor did Serbian television footage of the August 5th encounter at Trnopolje, which filmed the *ITN* crew during its visit and interviews with the men on the other side of the fence. *ITN* cameraman Jeremy Irvin hyped the shot.

'As Any Gardener Knows...'

German journalist Thomas Deichmann testified in 1996 at The Hague about German press coverage in the northwest or Prijedor-area of Bosnia and about Dusan "Dusko" Tadic, a Bosnian Serb who was later sentenced to twenty years in prison for war crimes committed at the nearby Omarska and Keraterm camps.

Deichmann became interested in the barbed wire at Trnopolje as it figured in the perjured testimony of a prosecution witness. He obtained copies of "out-takes," or unused film footage, from *ITN's* first August 6, 1992, telecast about Trnopolje:

> "One night, while I was going through the pictures again at home, my wife pointed out an odd little detail. If Fikret Alic and the other Bosnian Muslims were imprisoned inside a barbed wire fence, why was this wire fixed to poles on the side of the fence where they were standing? As any gardener knows, fences are, as a rule fixed to the poles from outside, so that the area to be enclosed is fenced-in. It occurred to me then that perhaps it was not the people in the camp who were

---

9. Luke Harding, "A Shot that is Still Ringing," *The Guardian*, March 12, 1997.

fenced-in behind the barbed wire, but the team of British journalists." Deichmann, after talking with Tadic's defense lawyer, was convinced enough to return to Trnopolje to have a look:[10] "I decided to go back to Bosnia, and to review the British news team's coverage of Trnopolje, in order to unravel the real story about how those pictures had come about."[11]

In an effort to prove what many of his critics would call trivial and incidental to the tragedy and alleged barbarity of the refugee camp itself, Deichmann methodically recreated the physical structure at Trnopolje, interviewed locals and others in the Prijedor area who were familiar with the details of what he said was "no internment or prisoner camp; it was a collecting camp for exiled Muslims. Everybody I spoke to confirmed that the refugees could leave the camp area at almost any time."

Deichmann's fixation did not minimize tragedy and misery at Trnopolje; he was safeguarding journalistic accuracy and professionalism.

Although Deichmann reported that *ITN's* Penny Marshall, the *Guardian's* Ed Vulliamy, and *British Channel 4* reporter Ian Williams never intended that *ITN* camera-man Jeremy Irvin's initial footage of Trnopolje be construed as depicting a "concentration camp," the international public and political uproar shrieked otherwise:

"For many, this picture has become a symbol of the horrors of the Bosnian war ...But that image is misleading.

"The fact is that Fikret Alic and his fellow Bosnian Muslims were not imprisoned behind a barbed wire fence. There was no barbed wire fence surrounding Trnopolje camp. It was not a prison, and certainly not a 'concentration camp', but a collection centre for refugees, many of whom went there seeking safety and could leave again if they wished.

"The barbed wire in the picture is not around the Bosnian Muslims; it is around the cameraman and the journalists. It formed part of a broken-down barbed wire fence encircling a small compound that was next to the Trnopolje camp. The British news team filmed from inside this compound, shooting pictures of the refugees and the camp through the compound fence. In the eyes of many who saw them, the resulting pictures left the false impression that the Bosnian Muslims were caged behind barbed wire.

"Whatever the British news team's intentions may have been, their pictures were seen around the world as the first hard evidence of concentration camps in Bosnia.

"...Penny Marshall, Ian Williams and Ed Vulliamy have never called Trnopolje a concentration camp. They have criticized the way that others tried to use their reports and pictures as 'proof' of a Nazi-style Holocaust in Bosnia. Yet over the past four and a half years, none of them has told the full story about

---

10. Deichmann, "The Picture That Fooled The World," *LM97* magazine, February 1997.
11. Deichmann, *ibid*.

that barbed wire fence which made such an impact on world opinion."[12]

To any journalist, the scenario provided by Deichmann showed unethical license was taken to hype the photo because *Newsday's* "scoop" on August 2 about the Omarska "death camp" had put pressure on other Western reporters in the region to file similar reports:

> "When Marshall, Williams and Vulliamy arrived in Bosnia at the end of July 1992, they were under intense pressure to get the story of the camps... After her return Penny Marshall told how she and Williams had received orders from the managing editors of *ITN* and Channel 4 to do nothing else before they had the camps story in the bag: 'They had set Ian Williams and myself loose with an open-ended brief to find and visit the detention camps, and with orders to file nothing until we had come up with the story.' (*Sunday Times*, 16 August 1992)

> "As the end of their trip approached, however, the British news team had been unable to find the camps story they were after. Their final stop was to be the refugee camp at Trnopolje, next to the village of Kozarac which had been overrun by Bosnian Serb units a few months earlier in May 1992. This was to be their last chance to get the story which their editors wanted.

> "The pictures they shot at Trnopolje camp on 5 August were edited in Budapest the next day, then sent to London and broadcast the same night. The broadcast centered on shots of the journalists talking to Fikret Alic and the group of Bosnian Muslims through the barbed wire. These were the pictures which were widely interpreted as evidence that the Muslims were penned behind a barbed wire fence, and which the international media seized upon to make a symbolic link to the Nazi camps..."[13]

Examining the out-takes, Deichmann reconstructed the movements of the reporters in obtaining their barbed wire shots at Trnopolje:

> "But how did the British team get them?

> "I have looked through the rest of the team's film from Trnopolje, at the pictures which were not broadcast. They reveal a lot more about the story.

> "The camp at Trnopolje consisted of buildings that had previously been a school, and a community centre and a public hall, alongside a large open area that had been a sports ground. The only fences around parts of the camp were little more than a metre high, of the kind you might find around any school

---

12. Deichmann, *ibid.*
13. Deichmann, *ibid.*

or public building. The British news team were (sic) able to enter all areas of the refugee camp. They shot some pictures in the buildings. Their attention, however focused on a group of Muslims who had just been brought from the camps in Keraterm close to Prijedor, who were waiting in the open air to be registered and given food and somewhere to sleep.

"To film these refugees, Marshall and her cameraman Irvin entered a compound next to the camp area. Inside this small compound were a kind of garage shed, an electricity transformer station, and a brick barn. Before the war, horticultural products could be brought there and tractors and construction machinery had been housed in the barn. To protect this from thieves, the compound area of approximately 500 square metres had been fenced-in with barbed wire a couple of years before. The erection of the barbed wire fence had nothing to do with the refugees, the camp or the war. The poles to which this barbed wire was attached are still standing today, and traces of the wire can be found on the west side of the compound.

"When Marshall, Williams and Vulliamy entered the compound next to the camp the barbed wire was already torn in several places. They did not use the open gate, but entered from the south through a gap in the fence. They approached the fence on the north side, where curious refugees quickly gathered inside the camp, but on the outside of the area fenced-in by barbed wire. It was through the barbed wire fence at this point that the famous shots of Fikret Alic were taken.

"The unused footage shows how cameraman Irvin zoomed through the compound's barbed wire fence from various angles, apparently searching for the most dramatic shot. Most of the refugees in the camp were marked by their experience of the war, but few looked as emaciated as Fikret Alic. Yet he captured the camera's attention…

"The other pictures, which were not broadcast, show clearly that the large area on which the refugees were standing was not fenced-in with barbed wire. You can see that the people are free to move on the road and on the open area, and have already erected a few protective tents. Within the compound next door that is surrounded with barbed wire, you can see about 15 people, including women and children, sitting under the shade of a tree…

"Another unpublished sequence on the tape shows Fikret Alic and the other refugees who had just arrived from a different angle. The cameraman is no longer inside the barbed wire area, but about 20 metres to the west of it. From here it is obvious that the refugees are not caged behind the barbed wire. While they wait to be registered and told where to go, they are standing

behind an ordinary wire mesh fence which is a little more than
a metre high, adjacent to the barbed wire..."[14] (Italics added)

Footage from the Serbian television team, shadowing the British reporters and cameramen, corroborated Deichmann's account, and immediately caused a firestorm of outrage from reporters across Europe and, to a lesser degree, in America.

The reactionary attacks from pack-journalism's interventionists commenced with fury and gusto, attempting to belittle Deichmann—and to destroy the magazine which had not yet published his article! Six months later, the harangue was picked up by Eric Alterman, in "Bosnian Camps: A Barbed Tale," published in *The Nation*, July 28/August 4, 1997 issue. The journalistic bloodbath in Britain attracted only criticism against Deichmann's transgression of supposedly minimizing the suffering of the Bosnian Muslims at Trnopolje and for challenging journalistic ethics:

> "Deichmann was so excited by his scoop that he did not bother
> to call any of the journalists whose deception, he says, 'fooled
> the world.' Nor did he seek out any of the Bosnian Muslims
> who had lived through the Trnopolje experience. Instead, he
> rushed his story into print in *Novo*, a small-circulation Trotskyist
> publication in Germany. The article was then republished in
> the February 1997 issue of *Living Marxism*, a rather glossy
> publication of the pro-Serb Revolutionary Communist party in
> England."[15]

Having seen Deichmann's first printing of the story in the small German magazine *NOVO*, which was published on January 13, 1997, *ITN's* lawyers immediately demanded *LM97* spike the story scheduled for publication in Britain on January 30 and pay damages for libel along with legal costs! The demand, which came the day after *LM97* issued a press release announcing the upcoming January 30 publication, was received from the Biddle & Company law firm—which noted by Deichmann and others as Prime Minister John Major's law firm.

British newspapers, news organizations and press pundits internationally were quick to join the frenzy:

> "The article was picked up and syndicated by the British Press
> Association and reported uncritically by *The Independent* on
> Sunday. From there it made its way across the Continent, and
> suddenly the *LM* attack on the three journalists became an
> international cause celebre. The *BBC* invited the journalists
> to debate Deichmann on television and asked for a copy of
> the *ITN* outtakes. ...(The) the article was reported and debated
> in Germany in *Frankfurter Allegemeine Zeitung, Suddeutsche
> Zeitung, Der Tagesspiegel, Freitag, Die Welt, Berliner Morgenpost,
> Die Tageszeitung, Leipziger Volkszeitung* and *Konkret*; in Italy
> in *Il Corriere della Sera, L'Unita and Il Sole* ; in Switzerland
> in *Weltwoche*; and in Austria, Sweden and the Netherlands as
> well. The result was that, after five years after their discovery,
> the reality of the Serb concentration camps—indeed, the entire

---

14. Deichmann, *ibid*.
15. Eric Alterman, "Bosnian Camps: A Barbed Tale," *The Nation*,
July 28/August4, 1997.

question of ethnic cleansing in Bosnia—became contested again."[16]

Fearing the voracious British libel laws, the *British Press Association* and its subsidiary syndicate *Two-Ten* Communications jettisoned Deichmann's report, abruptly calling it "completely untrue" and the original reports by Marshall, Vulliamy and Williams as "accurate and impartial almost to a fault":

> "*The Independent* also followed with a quick retraction, refusing at the last minute to run a pro-*LM* story by the journalist Philip Knightly, later published in *Novo*. *LM*, seeing itself as an aggrieved David up against a bullying Goliath, launched an international campaign denouncing this 'unprecedented attack by a media giant on press freedom.'

> "The free speech argument is what led Noam Chomsky to sign a letter in support of *LM*, where he was joined by a politically contentious mix, including Knightly and the right-wing libertarian Auberon Waugh. Random House editor Harold Evans also criticized the suit on these grounds..."[17]

The issue of manipulated camera angles and positions to show the most suggestive angle of the barbed wire remained taboo, except that Alterman contradicted Alic's contention that the men he was with outside the barbed wire were "surrounded" by it. Alterman offered up yet a new description of how the barbed wire was placed, saying nothing directly about the obvious chicken-wire:

> "It was not a four-sided barbed-wire fence, though no one ever asserted that it was. The barbed-wire made two sides; the other sides were a wall and a non-barbed-wire fence guarded by heavily armed Serbs, ready to shoot to kill."[18] (Italics added)

Alterman apparently had not seen the Serbian television footage, which showed Alic being shoved to the front for the *ITN* television cameraman. No armed guards are visible anywhere. At first self-conscious and trying to squat on the ground, Alic was prodded to stand and display his emaciated condition.

The few dissenting voices among British journalism seemed shaded more toward the effects of the legal aftershocks than supportive of the essence of Deichmann's reporting:

> "I don't know enough the truth of the allegation, but I do think journalists might be humble enough to admit they might be wrong, and discuss it sensibly rather than hysterically."—Jake Ecclestone, general secretary, National Union of Journalists[19]

> "We encourage all journalists to support LM against the libel writ and defend a free press and open debate."—letter signed

---

16. Alterman, *ibid.*
17. Alterman, *ibid.*
18. Alterman, *ibid*
19. Ecclestone, quoted in *Journalist* magazine, May/June 1997.

by sixteen "respected" journalists, published in *UK Press Gazette* weekly[20]

"So long as this matter proceeds, the waters are bound to be muddied in a way that will hardly be to the benefit of the broadcaster."—Stephen Glover, media columnist, *The Spectator*[21]

"It is a shame that (ITN) did not choose to seek redress against Living Marxism in a television confrontation... rather than by issuing writs and apparently silencing discussion of a complex situation."—Harold Evans, former editor of *The (London) Times*[22]

Inevitably, *LM* lost the suit and was forced to close its doors.

Meanwhile, the best explanation of why *The Washington Post's* Mary Battiata made no mention of the barbed wire at Trnopolje when she wrote about the camp in October 1992—two months after *ITN/Guardian* reporters made their sensational visit on the previous August 5—came from Alic himself: "They (Serbs) took some of it down on August 8, 1992..."[23]

The broken-down barbed wire around the small shed and electrical transformer —which the media symbolically hyped as the resurrection of Nazi-style concentration camps—was removed.

'Like A Kafka Figure...'

Western journalists did a double-take in 1996 when novelist Peter Handke published a short volume based on his scathing observations about the media coverage of the Yugoslav wars.[24] Such criticism from a popular writer in Germany, a country and society still stigmatized at least in popular American thinking to eternal guilt and condemnation for the Holocaust, was particularly offensive and unforgivable.

Handke, whose fame was that of being probably one of the most important postmodern writers since Becket in Europe and praised among academics in the U.S., —was inspired to examine the war in Bosnia, "but not as most journalists.

They always came via the West. I wanted to get to Bosnia from the other side, from the East, through Serbia and over the Drina..."

But most threatening to journalists about Handke's remarkable book was his reputation for "terrifying" honesty:[25]

"Peter Handke is a terrifying writer, because he is so honest. Many writers claim to be honest, and their claims are blatant fictions. They lie about their motives, their incomes, their

20. *UK Press Gazette* weekly, letter signed by sixteen "respected" journalists, May 9, 1997.

21. Stephen Glover, media columnist, *The Spectator*, May 17, 1997.

22. Harold Evans, former editor of *The (London) Times*, writing in *The Guardian*, June 2, 1997.

23. Harding, *ibid.*

24. *Eine winterliche Reise zu den Flussen Donau, Save, Morawa und Drina oder Gerechtigkeit fur Serbien (A Winter Journey to the Rivers Danube, Sava, Morava and Drina, or Justice for Serbia)*, Frankfurt/M.: Suhrkamp, 1996.

25. Handke, 1996 interview in Paris, copyrighted translation by J.P. Maher.

politics, their sexuality, their sex lives, and all the other things that human beings like or need to lie about. Peter Handke probably lies about these things too, but, in his writing, he is frighteningly honest..."[26]

Handke, a Catholic of Slovenian heritage on his maternal side, pulled no punches in his criticism about infamous media performances in the Yugoslav wars, which was detailed in an interview that appeared a few weeks after his book was published in 1996:

"...(A)ll the stories that I read about the war were written, as if in front of a mirror. I wanted to get behind that mirror. Nothing had ever been written about the country of Serbia (during this war). Once in a while there was something about Belgrade, but it was always just full of cliches: 'everything is grey, nobody is willing to speak, the opposition is weak, the war wounded have nothing to come home to,' etc. etc. Every report was the same, and it was always Belgrade. ...At first I believed the reporting, but felt the balance was wrong. I kept seeing the same turn of phrase, the same twist of grammar and choice of words ...I felt that just can't be, or if it is so, then everyone, whether journalist or author, at least has the duty to consider the other side, without passing judgement..."[27]

Handke sounded an angry foreboding about the implications of the Yugoslav wars:

"Yugoslavia, however fragmented it might have been was a model for a future Europe. Not Europe as it is now, our somewhat artificial Europe, with its free trade zones, but a place with different nationalities living among each other, especially as it affected young people in Yugoslavia after Tito's death. That, I thought, is how I would like Europe to be. So, for me the vision of Europe was destroyed with the destruction of Yugoslavia."[28]

He rejected suppositions about positive perceptions of a "multi-cultural, multi-ethnic" Bosnia.

"...I can't stand hearing the word 'multi-cultural' anymore. That was a dishonest excuse to conjure up a Muslim state of Bosnia out of nowhere. I can't take it when the word is applied to Sarajevo. But when you apply it to the old Yugoslavia, where the nationalities lived together with one another, naturally separately, then I can accept the words 'multi-ethnic' and 'multi-cultural.' Not, however, when it's applied to Bosnia. For me it was a lie to make a state out of a region that was formerly a mere administrative unit. That's what Bosnia was in Yugoslavia. Bosnia had never been a sovereign state. For me, creating sovereign states

---

26. Josh Lacey, review of Peter Handke's *A Sorrow Beyond Dreams*, Hyde Park Review of Books, Vol. 1 No. 3; 2002.
27. Handke interview, *ibid.*
28. Handke interview, *ibid.*

out of Slovenia, Croatia and Bosnia-Herzegovina was also just concocting historical fakes. In the beginning, I too believed all the talk about freedom and freedom fighters battling against 'panzer' communism for multi-ethnicity. In the beginning, I believed it. But now I don't believe a word of it."

Handke discounted popular secessionist origins for Slovene and Croatian independence at the outset of 1991:

"It was the opportune moment. I'm not a political commentator and I never will be. It was the favorable moment, after the death of Tito, for everyone to make a run for it, to grab something for himself.

"Much too little has been written about what Hitler, together with Catholicism, inflicted on the Balkans. Catholicism, too, was a horribly pernicious force in Croatia, where it was utterly fundamental and destructive, perhaps a bit less so in Slovenia. [Much too little has been written about] the crimes committed in Croatia during the Second World War by Catholicism and Nazism, and nationalism. There was the concentration camp *Jasenovac*, where between six- and eight-hundred thousand Serbs and Jews were annihilated, and Muslims, too...

"The breeding ground for the collapse of Yugoslavia was Croatia, with its unchecked Nazi-Catholic history in the Second World War, and even earlier. We Europeans, and the whole world, know far too little about all this. But just as the history of the Jews before and during the Second World War has been examined and clarified, as I have said in my book, it is now necessary to bring to light everything that facism did during World War II in Yugoslavia, as well as its holocaust of the Jews.

"(The present wars are) a metamorphosis, or better said, a metastasis, as we say of cancer. It is a continuation of the Second World War. It is significant that when the Croats overran the area of Jasenovac [in May 1, 1995], they destroyed every monument to the victims killed there. The Jasenovac camp was destroyed—as a monument—again this year by the Croats. This is significant. This is what inspired me to write."

In his book, Handke probed into the effects upon the West of news reports from Yugoslavia:

"It tells of problems. It tells of problems, the newspaper reader's problems in thinking. It tells about the history reader's problems. It talks about the viewing problems of someone looking at a photo, the problems of a television viewer. It speaks continuously about problems of how a distant reader sees, how I, how we, almost all, read the war reports. Criticism deals with structures. One criticizes esthetic forms of camera technique, of grammar, of the art of war reporting..."

On claims and complaints that Handke's positions were biased and "pro-Serb":

"...Naturally I have my opinions and convictions, but what I have written has nothing to do with opinions. It has to do exclusively with basic questions. My best expression for this is, it is a question of telling a story, as it is, as I always have done in my literature since I began writing. I never let it be known what my opinion is. That's why it's so amazing that all this hate and aggression has erupted against my little book, especially in Germany."

On perceiving the war through the Western media and correspondents sent to Yugoslavia to cover the wars:

"Even if you go there, you go with interpreters, so I don't necessarily believe in the evidentiary value of simply having been there. Many journalists can remedy this when using interpreters, but it's a rarity when they succeed. Most journalists from the West take an interpreter who speaks English or German. Where do they get this interpreter? What does the interpreter tell you? Where does he take you, etc.? First of all, the journalists usually do not understand the language of the country. They can't decipher the Cyrillic alphabet and have no idea, much less any real knowledge, about Yugoslavia before the war broke out. They are always taken to where the victims are, as per arrangement, or according to news reports, They always come to Sarajevo. This was always, as far as history goes, suspicious to me. ...Many journalists, whose good will I do not doubt, were *nutzliche idioten* ('useful idiots') in the hands of the two regimes that claimed to be the chief victims, the Croats and the Muslim Bosniacs."

On his personal knowledge about Serbs, their supposed intolerance and disinterest "in other cultures":

"That is one of the worst and most monstrous lies. Almost worthy of Goebbels. What has been spread about the Serbs is a lie. I believe that is not must my personal story, but everybody's who has dealt with Serb culture and the Serb people. If there is any people in the Balkans open to the East, the West, the South, or simply has any sensitivity to the rest of the world —that is in Serbia, not in Croatia or Slovenia. Where do you find books of the whole world, today and yesterday, published and read in translation? In Serbia. Far less in Croatia, and even less in Slovenia. Serbia, I can enthusiastically recommend to everyone who thinks about what a country can be—a land of rivers. What can a country be that is far from the sea? Naturally, Serbia is disadvantaged in the media landscape, as compared to Croatia (with) Dubrovnik, Split, or Zadar. But apart from these fabulous cities on the Adriatic, Croatia is totally a land of the interior and almost unknown to the traveler or the tourist. ...But Serbia, I would say, is a warm-hearted land... In its history Serbia was always tolerant. In World War II, if there was any land that accepted Jews, sheltered Jews, that took Jews into their houses, that was not Croatia, not Slovenia —but Serbia. Serbia was the only philosemitic country in the Balkans, together with Greece—though Greece, strictly speaking, isn't Balkan. What has been done to the Serbian people and the lands of the Serbs in the last five years is an enormous injustice. It's an injustice that cries to high heaven to compare Serbia with Nazi Germany..."

On the "right of national self-determination" for all but Serbs:

"That is the height of absurdity. The Serb nation in Croatia and the 35% of Serbs in Bosnia-Hercegovina—no one recognized any right of self-determination for them. Where is the justice in that? That is a lot of sanctimonious talk about the right of national self-determination. But these nations, the Croats and Slovenes, I believe, were well off in the Yugoslav state. Especially in the ten years following Tito's death they never once made a complaint that they were mistreated or disadvantaged under the federal government in Belgrade. Their (recent) claims of such are a historical lie. The Croats and Slovenes, on the contrary, were given preferential treatment, economically, in trade on the Mediterranean and in tourism, and much more."

Astonishingly, Handke predicted that "Yugoslavia" and its now-severed fellow republics would reconcile in some future form of federation:

"I believe it can't be otherwise. It will resurrect. It is the only sensible thing. Look at the economics, the geography, the rivers, the mountain ranges. The common history after 1918 was not so bad. There was the Kingdom of Yugoslavia and there was Tito's partisan communist Yugoslavia. By the 1980s there was no more communism. For me that was a near religious event. Compared to many European states, Yugoslavia was a model for Europe. It cannot remain fragmented..."

Inevitably, Handke earned the wrath of European interventionist media for his published views:

"...There have been insults and outbursts of hate against me in the media, specially the German, Austrian, and Swiss, and French and Spanish, too. It affected me. But like a Kafka figure, you accept it, as if it belongs to history."

Fellow artists and academics more clearly understood Handke's intrusion into media stereotype of the Balkan war reporting:

"The storm of disapproval that arose in the press following the publication of Justice for Serbia ...can only be understood if one keeps in mind the really audacious provocation that the poet was undertaking, legitimized by nothing other than the artist's sheer self will. The poet is not only seeking to criticize the predominant media practices and place a question mark over them. He wants to counterpose his poetic experience, his poet's eye, to the picture of the Serbs that the media paints world-wide. Against the superior power of media opinions about this war, he counters with his poetic voice. A single individual opposes the world's entire press: the poet, in and for himself. And he has the nerve to pose the question anew: Which side bears the guilt for the Yugoslavian war of secession?"[29]

But, the lesser guilt resided inside the borders of the former Yugoslavia—before deliberate Western dismemberment in 1991.

Voices Of Silence

For daring to reprint *Foreign Policy's* "Dateline Yugoslavia: The Partisan Press" with its controversial condemnation of the Western media's Yugoslav war reporting in early 1994, Boris Groendahl got a threatening phone call from K Street's Hill & Knowlton. "They said if we don't publish a retraction immediately, they will sue," said Editor Boris Groendahl, calling from his Hamburg office a few days after the next issue was published that March. Groendahl and *Konkret*, with its modest circulation, were viciously broadsided as a Trotsky-style journal.

But when U.S. Justice Department documents were produced that backed up the Washington PR Goliath's involvements in Yugoslavia—the bluff withered.

However, it was with conscious certainty that reprisal awaited any publication that dared to stray into published skepticism and question the veracity of the overall war reporting in the West. Equally certain were recriminations from superiors whose corporate boards as well as executives of competing media reacted to articles about the pack-reporting dereliction.

Foreign Editor Hanspeter Born, of the popular and respected Zurich news weekly *Die Weltwoche*, was no newcomer to following threads of unraveled misconceptions on volatile subjects.

Before toppling under scandal and disgrace, former Austrian president Kurt Waldheim had filed criminal charges against Born for revelations in his book *(Fur die Richtigkeit: Kurt Waldheim)* which Waldheim later withdrew. Born's range of expertise extended even to probing abstract myths about the origins of controversial works by Vincent van Gogh ("Fake! The history of a van Gogh") and in providing authentication of 700 sketches drawn by a young Pablo Picasso.[30]

For reprinting "Partisan Press..." Born endured an onslaught of criticism and was regaled by his editor and the owners of *Die Weltwoche*, and colleagues in the Swiss press.

"One day there appeared about forty Bosnian refugees, organized by Swiss activists, who began demonstrating in front of our building," said Born, gesturing toward the

---

29. Sigrid Loffler, *"Peter Handke und die Kontroverse um seine Streitschrift, Gerechtigkeit fur Serbien,"* Goethe-Institut InterNationes, 2002.
30. Hansjoerg Derx, "My own Story," *On-line Picasso Project,* 2003.

front of the offices on Edenstrasse on a bleak, rainy day in Zurich.[31] "And they came back every afternoon for some weeks. They had signs denouncing me and the newspaper. But we noticed that they stayed only until a certain hour and then they calmly went away, like leaving their jobs. They were not very sincere as soon as the television reporters stopped filming them. After several days, my colleagues here were no longer amused. And, neither was my boss."

But more stinging to Born was when representatives from the Union of Swiss Journalists met later in Berne.

"They held a small trial, and at the end, there were about sixteen journalists who signed a document that condemned me and the newspaper," said Born. "But it was harmless—it meant nothing."

Born reflected on how he had long been "suspicious" of the "pack-reporting of journalists in Yugoslavia."

But, an explosion of accusation and debate had been set off by Born and *Die Weltwoche:*

> "*Die Weltwoche* has unleashed a fierce controversy with waves reaching beyond the state boundaries."[32]

Within a few months, Born revealed how attacks against him intensified— personally and professionally:

> "...When the *Neue Zurcher Zeitung* published an attack against me, the editor-in-chief also made an appearance and phoned the editor-in-chief of *Die Weltwoche* to ask him what was actually going on. Even earlier the representatives of our managing board were questioned by a member of the managing board of the Munich daily *Die Suddeutsche Zeitung* about whether they intended to ruin their paper by publishing (such a text). My superiors suggested it would be best if I did not go on writing about Bosnia... I found myself quite alone... Later I learned that the management had been considering the possibility of relieving me of my post as editor of the foreign column because of this controversy...

> "Croatia, and Bosnia and Herzegovina, are more multi-layered and since many events cannot at all be understood without knowing their historical background, many (Western) correspondents found themselves in a situation they were not up to. Many found it easier to take over the thesis spread by certain press bellwethers about the Serb-communist aggression against the peoples of Slovenia, Croatia and Bosnia craving freedom. The obstinacy shown by Milosevic's regime and war crimes committed by Serb irregulars enhanced the diffusion of this thesis among journalists and turned it into a dogma. It is difficult for a journalist not to take sides in war conflicts, while advocating the cause of the weaker is looked upon as some kind of moral obligation. Since the Serbs were superior in the war in Croatia and Bosnia, and thereby a majority of the victims were Muslims and Croats,

---

31. Born interview with the author in Zurich, December 9, 1994.

32. Thomas Fleiner, member of the Commission on Security and Cooperation in Europe, "People Must Not Be Pilloried," *Die Weltwoche*, April 14, 1994.

many correspondents considered it their moral obligation to be against the Serbs.

"How could a journalist reporting from Sarajevo remain impartial when constantly confronted with the sufferings of its inhabitants? No one reproaches a journalist for advocating a clear stand. But what is incompatible with journalistic ethics is the distortion of facts. ...(I)n the Yugoslav conflict journalists, correspondents and people from editorial boards, were continuously swallowing propaganda. False news was often given as the absolute truth. Occasionally, journalists and editors made an additional contribution by embroidering unverified reports on atrocities or commenting on them as being the preconceived war tactics of the Serbs who had been demonized in the meantime. A typical example of harnessing the press to a propaganda campaign, in which *Die Weltwoche* had one of the leading roles, was the unbelievable hysteria about systematic mass rapes and rape camps.

"No one denies that in the conflicts in Bosnia, much as in all other wars, rapes took place, and that the majority of those rapes could be blamed on the militarily superior Serb; but it goes beyond the limits of permissible speculations when known rape cases are used by the press to establish a theory on rapes as a war strategy..."[33]

More than any other writer for a major European newspaper, Born vividly substantiated the isolated echoes from a handful of disillusioned correspondents who clearly sensed, sometimes self-consciously and apologetically, that Western journalism was already fatally off course shortly after the Croatian war started, becoming progressively negligent and biased:

Phil Davison, *The Independent*—"...For one reason or another, and I'm not quite sure what it is, the (Croatian war) very quickly got split into a two-sided affair. There were journalists who always went to Zagreb, and there were journalists, much fewer, who always went to Belgrade. To be honest, I'm not quite sure why it is. I mean Zagreb is nearer, and there are more international flights from pleasant places where you can have lunch in Vienna and champagne on the planes to get there. I may be exaggerating but that perhaps had something to do with it..."[34]

Alex Mitchell, *The Sydney Sun-Herald*—"You had the Croatian forces who took them on guided tours, took them out on the road, introduced them to one atrocity story after another... They couldn't believe their luck. They were just turning out stories every day. There was just a new kind of dimension of horror to this story. But of course it colored then the overall picture. In any single conflict there are two sides—at least two. This one actually has three and perhaps more. But, that's what the

33. Born, "Serbia Must Die," *Deutsche Welle* (Cologne), October 1, 1994.
34. Phil Davison, *Free for All*, Britain's Channel 4, August 24, 1993.

nature of civil conflict is. It's like going to Ireland and spending your day with the Orange, and coming out and thinking that you know about the problems of Ireland. And then, of course, once you come under siege by those people, the other side, they become the enemy. They are no longer a feature of an internal conflict that you've got to understand. They're the enemy because they're throwing things at you."[35]

Martin Bell, *BBC World Service*—"I've had one criticism of the press since the beginning of this (Croatian) war. I don't think we have paid sufficient attention to the Serbs. I think there has been a tendency to be holed up in the Holiday Inn in Sarajevo as the Serbs bombard the city, and say 'Oh, those terrible Serbs—why are they doing it?' Having said that, can I say in the defense of the press, this is the most difficult war ever to cover in the sense that it's the most dangerous. You just can't kind of roll around and cross front lines because you'll be killed if you do."[36]

Maggie O'Kane, *The Guardian*—"We knew what was happening on the Serb side. We knew that it was a military campaign... What I'm more interested in really is to write about what happens to people in war. Of course, there were Serb victims. But I believe the scale of that was smaller. And, in a sense, you gravitate to where the bigger story was or where the most events were. You have to be selective... I think that I could have seen more of the Serb side. But, I didn't deliberately ignore what was happening to the Serbs... I'm satisfied that I tried to find out what was happening and that, in my view, what was happening, the greatest number of victims was on the Muslim side."[37]

Misha Glenny, *BBC*—"Regarding the matter of what happened in Srebrenica earlier this year (1993), the media ignored entirely that in a large degree this was due to a response from a very big Muslim offensive in the area in December when Muslims pushed the Serbs back and destroyed quite a few Serbian civilians on the way in one or two very nasty massacres. And so, the attack on Srebrenica was essentially a response to that Muslim offensive. But, of course, we didn't hear anything about that offensive when it was happening. And, we certainly didn't hear anything about it when Srebrenica was having the shit bombed out of it. ...The essential thing that was missing out of the coverage was: Why did the Serbs behave like this? And, the result and general perception we have of why the Serbs behaved like this now is because they are stark, raving mad, vicious, mean bastards—and that's the be-all and the end-all of it. But, it's not the be-all and end-all of it. There are very deep, serious reasons why they have behaved like that and indeed why the Croats and the Muslims have behaved in the ways that they have."[38]

---

35. Alex Mitchell, *Free for All, ibid.*
36. Martin Bell, *BBC World Service, Free for All, ibid.*
37. Maggie O'Kane, *Free For all, ibid.*
38. Misha Glenny, *Free for All, ibid.*

'Never Again' ...Again

One of several curious reactions in the journalism profession was the near silence to the Jack Kelley scandal at *USA TODAY* that broke in January 2004 with revelations about fabrication and plagiarism. The public was unmoved by all the breast-beating, lament and vows by editors to launch an in-house investigation. War correspondents sensed danger.

Kelley, bemoaned his newsroom superiors at Tysons Corners across the Potomac River from the Capital, resigned after he was threatened with dismissal for attempting to obstruct an investigation of his sensational front-page story on July 14, 1999, from Belgrade. Kelley reported about a "direct order" that had surfaced in writing, linking ethnic cleansing in Kosovo to the "government of Yugoslav President Slobodan Milosevic."

But, whatever Kelley described was not the actual document that supposedly ordered the cleansing of a village and was in the hands of U.N. war crimes investigators.

Fraudulent reporting was not why Kelley was being terminated. He was forced to resign for attempting an elaborate cover-up attempt:

> "*USA TODAY* had chosen to treat the issue as a confidential personnel matter, but because Kelley made it public and because some published accounts have contained inaccurate information, we are providing a summary of the central events that led editors to end Kelley's employment... "The reason for ending Kelley's employment was that he engaged in an elaborate deception during an investigation into his work. He admitted that he engaged in conduct designed to deceive the investigation..."[39]

Editor Karen Jurgensen's tedious chronology of the investigation droned on for 2,204 words about how another reporter had tipped off Executive Editor Brian Gallagher the previous May that Kelley "was fabricating or embellishing stories." The *Washington Post's* media critic Howard Kurtz piled on:

> "Some staff members staunchly defended Kelley as a risk-taking foreign correspondent who they believe has been badly treated, while others said management looked the other way for too long while questions mounted about his exclusives that others seemed unable to match... In nearly 20 interviews, *USA Today* staff members described a 'culture of fear,' as several put it, in which many employees are afraid to speak out and there is widespread talk of personal vendettas by editors."[40]

> "The probe began with a June 26 anonymous letter, apparently from a fellow staffer, to Gallagher, calling Kelley 'a golden boy' and 'star reporter' who 'is paid far more than the rest of us.' Likening Kelley to Jayson Blair, the *New York Times* reporter who admitted to fabrication and plagiarism, the letter said Kelley used quotes that 'are obviously fake' because they do not 'sound

---

39. Karen Jurgensen, "*USA TODAY* statement on Jack Kelley," *USA TODAY*, January 13, 2004.
40. Kurtz, "Fear and Lying at *USA TODAY*: Writer Says Panic Led to Deception, Then Resignation," *The Washington Post*, January 11, 2004.

like the way people talk,' and questioned his ability to 'arrive in virtually any foreign land, not speak a word of the language, and within an hour or two come up with pithy quotes.'"[41]

USA TODAY's online archive showed Kelley reported or co-reported thirty-eight reports from March to August 1999 with datelines in the Yugoslav war zone.

"Still to be resolved was what the newspaper would do about correcting its record," wrote Jurgensen introspectively. "*USA TODAY* policy requires correcting or clarifying stories that are incorrect or misleading."

But, in sifting the 720 stories by Kelley during the decade after 1993, the newspaper launched an unprecedented effort that eventually flagged "about 100" stories uncovering "evidence that found Kelley's journalistic sins were sweeping and substantial."[42]

For seven weeks, editors and writers assigned to damage-control seemed to muster every imaginable tool available to ferret out the truths and fables in Kelley's repertoire.

"...The reporters read about 720 stories Kelley filed from 1993 to 2003. Each of the stories was read and discussed by at least two members of the team. Hundreds were relatively routine news reports. But about 150 stories stood out to the group for a variety of reasons.

"At least 56 were based on exclusive, eyewitness reports, usually reported overseas. Dozens cited anonymous intelligence officials. Others were human-interest stories that offered poignant details about the suffering of war, illness and oppression. In at least 10 cases, Kelley wrote that he watched someone die."[43]

Editors and reporters backfilled with interviews of people connected to Kelley, said lead *USA TODAY* reporter Blake Morrison:

"To verify the stories, members of the team interviewed dozens of people; reviewed scores of Kelley's expense reports; traveled to Cuba, Israel and Jordan; scoured records from Kelley's hotel, mobile and office phones; reread transcripts of speeches Kelley gave; ran at least 150 stories through plagiarism-detection software; and examined the contents of the laptop computer Kelley was issued by the company. Phone records were incomplete, and most of the documents on the laptop had been deleted before Kelley left the newspaper in January...

"...A story was considered fabricated if expense reports, phone records, official documents or witnesses clearly contradicted all or parts of what was published, and if Kelley's explanations failed to reconcile those contradictions."

---

41. Kurtz, "*USA TODAY* Found Hoax Before Writer Confessed," *The Washington Post*, January 13, 2004.
42. Blake Morrison, "Ex-*USA TODAY* reporter faked major stories," *USA TODAY*, March 19, 2004.
43. Morrison, *ibid.*

Even Cuban weather reports were scrutinized to discredit a story Kelley wrote about refugees whose boat capsized and drowned while trying to flee to the U.S. Weather communiqués from ships in the area were examined to determine whether a storm was at fault, but the seas and winds were officially reported as calm. A mention by Kelley about how refugees used "the dim light of a crescent moon" to make their way, wrote Morrison, was refuted by U.S. Naval Observatory records, showing the moon had not risen on the date in question.

Finally, Kelley flunked twenty hours of grilling by editors who additionally confronted him with charges that he "wrote scripts to help at least three people mislead *USA TODAY* reporters to verify his work." Also, all of Kelley's submissions as a five-time Pulitzer Prize nominee were retrieved by *USA TODAY*, which washed its hands of the ordeal with an eight-story self-expose on March 19, 2004.

Only two of Kelley's reports about Croat and Kosovo war victims were determined to be factual, while Jurgensen explained the "notebook" story written from Belgrade in 1999 that set off the whole conflagration was undecided! "In this case, the investigation was unable to resolve what had actually occurred," she said. "As to other stories examined during the investigation, the editors either concluded they were accurate or that the passage of time and the difficulty of retracing events in distant war torn countries made verification impossible."

The preposterous apology unmistakably indicated Kelley's remaining Yugoslav reports were being taken for granted even though being the most fertile ground for uncovering other journalistic misdeeds. These stories contained the usual quotes in too telltale perfect English from anonymous "victims" and other personalities plugged into the familiar formula reporting and anti-Serbian slant. Also, the eleven reporters/editors involved with the in-house investigation of Kelley were not recognizable as "on-the-ground" correspondents during the Yugoslav wars.

Morrison brushed it all aside,[44] echoing *USA TODAY's* publisher Craig Moon's earlier dubious guarantees: "As an institution, we failed our readers by not recognizing Jack Kelley's problems. For that I apologize. In the future, we will make certain that an environment is created in which abuses will never again occur."[45]

The eerie hush from fellow Balkan war correspondents of other news organizations about Kelley was predictable as many were understandably "hunkered down." The post-Kelley amends, according to a few scattered opinion pieces, called only for the profession to tighten its monitoring systems over reporters and to beef up editing checks.

Strangest of all was the silence and absence of any efforts to interview others who were part of the pack-reporting in the coverage of the Yugoslav wars.

The equally obvious question went unasked, profession-wide: Was Kelley alone?

---

44. Morisson's e-mail response to author, March 22, 2004.
45. Morrison, "Ex-*USA TODAY* reporter...," *ibid.*

Chapter 15

'Everything Is Soothed By Oil'

"Lost in the barrage of images and self-serving analyses are the economic and social causes of the conflict. The deep-seated economic crisis which preceded the civil war is long forgotten. The strategic interests of Germany and the US in laying the groundwork for the disintegration of Yugoslavia go unmentioned, as does the role of external creditors and international financial institutions. In the eyes of the global media, Western powers bear no responsibility for the impoverishment and destruction of a nation of 24 million people."[1]
—Michel Chossudovsky

"All hope abandon, ye who enter here!"[2]
—Dante Alighieri

It was just before New Year's Eve in 1992 when Dick Arnold, a Slavic specialist and Fulbright Scholar, telephoned from Florida. I first met him in San Diego. He took a long trip through the Balkans earlier that year and innocently provoked his own arrest in Belgrade with an impromptu and unwelcome discussion about firearms on a street corner with an unimaginative, nervous police officer. Arnold was an Army Special Forces veteran. Later, during the same trip, he was the victim of a savage beating by Croat extremists in a confrontation at the train station in Varazdin.

Arnold was an academic swashbuckler, a one-time Princeton lecturer with a depth of firsthand knowledge about Yugoslavia, a "Scottish mountaineer" by heritage and "humble-as-hell" beginnings in Buncombe County, North Carolina, as he liked to tell it.

Between the Belgrade and Varazdin episodes, Arnold had lunch and conversation with then-Yugoslav President Dobrica Cosic who made an impression on him with a prediction about the potential contagion of Balkan wars.

---

1. Michel Chossudovsky, "Dismantling Yugoslavia, Colonizing Bosnia,"
Covert Action Quarterly, Number 56, Spring 1996.
2. *The Divine Comedy, Inferno*, Canto III, l.9.

"He looked at me gravely and said it could all become psychically more explosive," said Arnold. "It could light up everything from the Bosporus to Kamchatka."

In fact, the international media rarely explained the larger stakes behind the Yugoslav "fratricide" except to despair vaguely about the possibilities for wider humanitarian disaster.

"Pack journalism" required almost a voluntary cessation of independent thinking while collectively cheerleading. But the phenomenon was void of any admission by the media about its own schemes. The "pack journalism" became more than a ploy to cover up the bad job of reporting the Yugoslav wars, especially among the American media.

In late April 1993, *Newsweek's* Tom Post divulged that the magazine was about to "run a story about Bosnia hawks ...*a kind of informal, loose coalition of journalists*, some government people, consultants, other advocates, who want to keep and have been keeping the Bosnia story before the American public and believe the West, in particular the Clinton administration, is not doing enough in the way of forceful intervention."

Post named prominent journalists, including *New York Times* columnists Anthony Lewis and Leslie Gelb (who later took a post with the elite and secretive Council on Foreign Relations), *ABC News* anchor Peter Jennings and others. But the short-lived story was spiked, said Post a month later, because *Newsweek* opted to run "an American policy-type story ...I should probably write thank-you notes to everybody or letters of apology," said Post.[3]

The disclosure went far to explain why there was such a conscious unanimity throughout the war with nearly identical patterns of reporting from certain leading news publications, networks, prominent journalists and their imitators.

When asked in December 1993 if he was a "coalition" member, Charles Lane denied it. But he indicated he knew about it.

Newsday's Roy Gutman, *Newsweek/New Republic's* Lane, *NPR's* Tom Gjelton, *MacNeil-Lehrer's* Charlene Hunter Galt, and John F. Burns, Anthony Lewis and Michael Gordon of *The New York Times*, and others had variously attempted, individually and together, publicly and behind the scenes to intimidate, ridicule, harass, denounce and discredit the journalists who raised the issue of unfair and biased reporting in Yugoslavia.

Avoiding the realities and ignoring the huge consequences of the media's role as co-combatants, it was easier to harp against the Serbs and the United Nations and to replay the episodes of carnage from Sarajevo, being careful to minimize or omit any of the ethical annoyances that suggested tell-tale flaws in the pack reporting. Who, again, had competently reported the "ethnic cleansing" of the Serbian community at Sarajevo? at Mostar? at Gorazde? at Dubrovnik? at Srebrenica?

On February 7, 1994, came another—though not the last—condemnation from a U.N. commander against a series of deceptions in Sarajevo. This time it was from Belgian General Francis Briquemont, who had been recently relieved from command of UNPROFOR troops in Bosnia. Reporters weren't all that interested, and it was buried at the bottom of a story which quoted from Briquemont's report in January to the civilian head of the U.N. in the former Yugoslavia, Yasushi Akashi. Briquemont was furious about how "safe areas established by the U.N. were being compromised and undermined":

> "In Sarajevo the Bosnian army provokes the Serbs on a daily basis.
> Since the middle of December, the Bosnian army jumped another

---

3. *Post* interview with the author, April 16, 1993.

step by launching heavy infantry attacks from Sarajevo to the Serb-held suburbs of the city. The Bosnian army attacks the Serbs from a safe area, the Serbs retaliate, mainly on the confrontation line, and the Bosnian presidency accuses UNPROFOR of not protecting them against Serb aggression and appeals for air strikes against the Serb gun positions."[4]

It was the identical choreography at Gorazde, Srebrenica, Bihac and elsewhere. But prominently reporting a story with that kind of message, which was ignored overall by the pack, ran the danger of vehement scourging for the messenger. Reprisal was the rule, and some among Post's "coalition" fired off letters "not for publication" to editors (and their publishers and board presidents) about the occasional reporter who broke ranks with the media hawks.[5] The fact that there was so little unbiased reporting in the Yugoslav wars only made the rare voice of informed objectivity stand out, as in the case of widely read British "correspondent" Kenneth Roberts, who in early 1994 wrote:

> "Almost two years into the Bosnian war, there is no discernible sign of German influence preventing Croatian atrocities. The uncomfortable truth appears to be that Germany is siding with Croatia, at least tacitly, to avoid domestic pressure from those who feel emotional ties with their former partners in tourism and genocide. On the American side, there are none so blind as those who will not see Swastikas, black uniforms, rape and pillage fade into insignificance beside the demonic image which the State Department has built for the Serbs. To talk to a U.S. official about Serbia in 1994 is to hear powerful echoes of Iran in 1989. As in Vietnam and Central America, the enemy of America's enemy is America's friend, no matter how reprehensible."[6]

It was long believed that "Kenneth Roberts" was the pen name for an anonymous, high-ranking U.N. official, who chose to do some press commentary of his own because the pack journalists, due to their own self-censoring paralysis as well as enormous pressures from their distant editors, could not or would not report about Croatian atrocities against Muslims and Serbs through the end of 1993.

"Several correspondents told me outright about these obstructions," said Cedric Thornberry, deputy UNPROFOR chief in Belgrade. "One especially, from *The Financial Times*, who went nearly crazy trying to get *The Financial Times* to print other than stories that demonized the Serbs."[7]

---

4. Ian Black, *The Guardian*, February 7, 1994.
5. *New York Times* columnist Anthony Lewis fired off a complaint to *Foreign Policy* editor Bill Maynes, attacking publication of the author's "Dateline Yugoslavia: The Partisan Press." Lewis accused the author of being a "holocaust denier." Likewise, *The New Republic's* Charles Lane and *NPR's* Tom Gjelton wrote private letters of condemnation, including racist nuances about the author's family, to Maynes and Morton Abramowitz, chairman of the board at the Carnegie Endowment for International Peace.
6. Kenneth Roberts, *The Spectator*, March 19, 1994.
7. Cedric Thornberry interview with author in Belgrade, February 1993.

Did Thornberry, who questioned the "hostility" and "intellectual honesty" of the media especially in its harangue against United Nations officials in the Balkans, believe the media was co-belligerent in the Yugoslav wars?

"In Bosnia, yes. I think that (*The New York Times'*) John Burns, for example, who was given vast quantities, acres of space all the time, had become so. I think Blaine Harden of *The Washington Post* became so. ...Blaine and I had a few knock-down, drag-out's because he didn't observe the rules. And there were enough complaints to bring out some of his editors to find out exactly what was going on."

Simon Jenkins reflected on history and applied the correct perspective for the eccentric, hawkish media behavior about Yugoslavia:

> "'You furnish the pictures and I'll furnish the war,' William Randolph Hearst cabled his bemused staff in Havana in 1898. ...The techniques used by the modern press to drive politicians to war are, I believe, hardly less insidious. ...Press analysts have mocked the United Nations' humanitarian mandate, ignored the fate of the relief convoys and pressed, overtly or covertly, for military aid to the Bosnian side. The Bosnian Serb case, such as it is, has gone by the board, as has Croatia's since the Croats were shown to be less than angels. Equally neglected is the argument for no intervention. ...The non-intervener is not just a spoil-sport, he is immoral, blind, an accomplice to unilateral evil."[8]

Jenkins was talking about the pseudo-humanitarian egos of the militant media, like columnist Anthony Lewis who hurled his ultimatums at NATO leaders. The latter were carefully planning air strikes around Sarajevo while not wanting to upset negotiations or undermine Bosnian Serb promises to pull back heavy artillery:

> "To be effective, in my view, the ultimatum to the Serbs would have to be more explicit: Stop firing within twenty-four hours or we bomb artillery positions. On day two we take out (Bosnian Serb General Ratko) Mladic's headquarters in Pale. On day three we attack military targets in the privileged sanctuary of Belgrade."[9]

Too coincidentally, on the same day, Lewis' co-columnist William Safire at *The New York Times* laid out his own battle plan to goad hesitant NATO generals into air attacks:

> "1. Tell the U.N. to assemble its forces in a defensible position, hunker down and get out of the way. This is known as sending the Serbs a signal.

> "2. Tell the Bosnian Serbs they have until Friday noon to cease firing everywhere, to withdraw all forces from within fifty miles of Sarajevo, and not to interfere with any relief supplies anywhere —or else. This is known as an ultimatum.

---

8. Simon Jenkins, "We Should Beware the Laptop Bombardiers,"
The Times (London), April 23, 1994.
9. Anthony Lewis, *The New York Times*, August 8, 1993.

"3. Inform our European allies that if NATO is not empowered to make good on this ultimatum, the United States will accelerate its drawdown of forces in Europe to 20,000 monthly until no U.S. troops remain. This is known as coercive diplomacy."[10]

The Serbian Example – Of What?

Frequently, a columnist or politician would insist that Serbia should be made an "example." But what kind of example? To whom? By whom? For whom? Were the Yugoslav civil wars—and the surreal image of Serbian aggression —perceived as the advent of some larger, mysterious menace?

A vile likelihood was that the heinous U.N. sanctions against Serbia could be repeated against any upstart in the region who balked against designs by the West —notably American schemes for oil and minerals in former Soviet republics in central Asia.

But the media was routinely uninterested in reporting with any wider insight about the immediate and long-range results of the apocalyptic economic sanctions against ten million civilian "victims" in Serbia and the half-million-plus Bosnian Serb, Muslim and even Croat refugees who had fled there. There was only shallow and infrequent inquiry about the plight of all of the Balkan republics which were languishing in post-communist economic doldrums because the world community —with the United States and Germany as the main instigators—had broken the back of the Serbian economy. And as the historic hub of Balkan commerce, Serbia was being pushed down into its sentenced, long-term economic "black hole," as one State Department official observed in March 1994.

The entire region, which had arrived at the threshold of democratic free-market capitalism, was left shivering on the doorsteps of the New World Order. Convulsing with lethal spasms of Western-induced ultra-nationalism, the Balkans and their neighbors would be allowed entry to the European Community's "promised land" only in a state of crippled dependency—which not accidentally was the ideal prescribed condition for exploitation by the West.

It was one of the bigger stories being snubbed as long as Muslim "genocide" victims could be conjured by the boxcarfuls onto television screens.

But carefully concealed was the story about the genocide carried out insidiously with U.N. sanctions against Serbian and Montenegrin populations, including the West's contradictory indifference toward ethnic Albanian Muslims in Kosovo—who despite U.S. favoritism suffered more under the same sanctions!

During some of the quiet interludes in the Bosnian wars, the Western media and politicians espoused with endless hand-wringing the two million deprived and impoverished Albanian Muslims in the Serbian heartland who were denied nationhood. Downplayed was that the crushing U.N. sanctions were denying food and medicine to them as well, and resulting in worse afflictions upon the Albanian-Muslim citizens of Serbian Kosovo. Smothering the economy and cultures within the maverick Balkan republic was intended to be visible and felt by all in the region —including the restless Central Asian republics.

It was clear that the U.S. and Euro-German community intended for the staggering post-communist societies to be watching, listening and tasting at least a measure of the bitter experience of stubborn outcast Serbia.

Meanwhile, media consumers in the West were shielded from seeing the twilight

10. William Safire, *The New York Times*, August 8, 1993.

descent of a New Dark Age, complete with dramatic increases in medieval diseases and maladies that settled malignantly upon the Serbs.

"From the break-up of the trading system and the consequent loss of markets (due) to the effects of the war, there is no doubt that the economic blockage brought about by the imposition of sanctions has dealt the final blow to a once prosperous society and economy," said a shocking UNICEF report from Belgrade in August 1993, which added:

> • After the first year of sanctions, three-percent of the population of Serbia had become enormously rich through the flourishing black market and other profiteering. The plague of inflation proceeded at one-percent per hour or a billion-percent annually. The bottom was ruthlessly cut out from under the once envied standard of living enjoyed by Serbs.

> • Malnutrition and disease were taking hold across Serbia because basic chemicals for pharmaceuticals were denied by the sanctions. Daily food consumption and caloric intake per family had dropped by a third while the nutrient value of all foods was twenty-eight-percent less than in 1990. Less than seven-percent of the children in pre-school institutions or elementary schools received the two to three daily meals that were previously provided to all children. The rates of low weights at birth and numbers of prematurely born babies were rapidly growing, and anemia was named among the top ten leading health disorders for the first time in decades. Infant deaths due to infectious and parasitic diseases showed sharp increases.

> • Infections that were normally treated with routine antibiotics (which had practically disappeared because of sanctions) were now untreated and were advancing to a threatened epidemic of heart disorders.

> • Patients requiring other than emergency surgery were required to bring their own anesthetics, bandages and drugs to hospitals.

> • The children's cardiac clinic in Belgrade was forced to reduce by half its schedule for heart surgery, and medical authorities even reported that heart pacemakers were retrieved from exhumed cadavers for implants into new recipients.

> • Tens of thousands of patients with chronic diseases—such as diabetes, kidney disorders, leukemia and hypertension—were denied medication and treatments due to the economic blockade of spare parts for worn out equipment. Also, due to lack of proper diagnostic materials, there were alarming increases of incorrect medical diagnoses because necessary chemicals and reagents were not available for clinical and microbiological laboratories.

•Some mental disorders had increased by 600-percent, and psychiatric asylums and hospitals were forced to resort to the ancient inhuman practice of restraining patients with chains in the absence of tranquilizers.

•The denial of imported chemicals threatened public water supplies and sewage treatment.

•Rates of tuberculosis were skyrocketing.

•Children with vision and hearing impairments were imprisoned in darkness and silence because of the embargo on imported batteries, braille paper and special equipment.

"As heavily-armed US and NATO troops enforce the peace in Bosnia, the press and politicians alike portray Western intervention in the former Yugoslavia as a noble, if agonizingly belated, response to an outbreak of ethnic massacres and human rights violations," wrote Canadian economist Michel Chossudovsky in early 1996.[11] "In the wake of the November 1995 Dayton peace accords, the West is eager to touch up its self-portrait as savior of the Southern Slavs and get on with 'the work of rebuilding' the newly sovereign states..."

Chossudovsky's revelations were irrefutable:

"But following a pattern set early on, Western public opinion has been misled. The conventional wisdom holds that the plight of the Balkans is the outcome of an 'aggressive nationalism,' the inevitable result of deep-seated ethnic and religious tensions rooted in history. Likewise, commentators cite 'Balkans power-plays' and the clash of political personalities to explain the conflicts...

"...(T)hrough (German and U.S.) domination of the global financial system, the Western powers, in pursuit of national and collective strategic interests, helped bring the Yugoslav economy to its knees and stirred its simmering ethnic and social conflicts. Now it is the turn of Yugoslavia's war-ravaged successor states to feel the tender mercies of the international financial community.

"Multiethnic, socialist Yugoslavia was once a regional industrial power and economic success. In the two decades before 1980, annual gross domestic product (GDP) growth averaged 6.1 percent, medical care was free, the literacy rate was 91 percent, and life expectancy was 72 years. But after a decade of Western economic ministrations and five years of disintegration, war, boycott, and embargo, the economies of the former Yugoslavia are prostrate, their industrial sectors dismantled.

"...The US had earlier joined Belgrade's other international creditors in imposing a first round of macroeconomic reform

11. Michel Chossudovsky, "Dismantling Yugoslavia...," *ibid.*

in 1980, shortly before the death of Marshall Tito. That initial round of restructuring set the pattern. Throughout the 1980s, the (International Monetary Fund) and World Bank periodically prescribed further doses of their bitter economic medicine as the Yugoslav economy slowly lapsed into a coma.

"From the beginning, successive IMF-sponsored programs hastened the disintegration of the Yugoslav industrial sector—industrial production declined to a negative 10 percent growth rate by 1990— and the piecemeal dismantling of its welfare state, with all the predictable consequences. Debt restructuring agreements, meanwhile, increased foreign debt, and a mandated currency devaluation also hit hard at Yugoslavs' standard of living.

"...'Shock therapy' began in January 1990. Although inflation had eaten away at earnings, the IMF ordered that wages be frozen at their mid-November 1989 levels. Prices continued to rise unabated, and real wages collapsed by 41 percent in the first six months of 1990.

"The IMF also effectively controlled the Yugoslav central bank. Its tight money policy further crippled the country's ability to finance its economic and social programs. State revenues that should have gone as transfer payments to the republics and provinces went instead to service Belgrade's debt with the Paris and London clubs. The republics were largely left to their own devices.

"In one fell swoop, the reformers engineered the final collapse of Yugoslavia's fiscal structure and mortally wounded its federal political institutions. By cutting the financial arteries between Belgrade and the republics, the reforms fueled secessionist tendencies that fed on economic factors as well as ethnic divisions, virtually ensuring the de facto secession of the republics."

The inferno was ignited. But prospects for greater and more permanent devastation awaited the population which was already paralyzed by a growing syndrome of physical and psychological despondency. The potential for worse humanitarian abuses remained hidden about the belief that members of European Community governments, aided by giant German and U.S. interests, had more sinister designs on some of the war-ravaged areas of the former Yugoslavia. These included, but not exclusively, the sites of destroyed Serb villages and districts in the Krajina and other parts of Croatia that had been cleansed of Serb populations who had fled or were driven away.

At least two locations in the Pupak region of eastern Slavonia, and in the area of twenty-four former Serb villages west of the Pozega commune, were reportedly designated for development as dumps for chemical and radioactive wastes from Germany including illegally exported nuclear wastes, according to documents filed on March 21 and April 6, 1994, with the U.N. Commission of Experts. These dumps were precariously positioned on the watersheds of the Orljana River, which feeds directly downstream into the Sava and Danube rivers in Serbia and would inter much of Germany's million-plus metric tons of lethal industrial, hazardous, toxic and radioactive wastes produced annually.

The New York Times' Chuck Sudetic apparently knew more than he wrote about the maneuvers to create new waste dumps in Serb regions of Yugoslavia. Before Sudetic went to cover the war, he wrote a large section of a publication for the U.S. government and the Department of the Army on Yugoslavia and intended only for a selected readership among federal agency, diplomatic, military and international relations specialists. Sudetic tersely described only that radioactive wastes were piling up at the nuclear power plant which provided electricity to both Slovenia and Croatia, echoing similar sparse reports:

> "Nuclear waste from Yugoslavia's only nuclear electric plant,
> at Krsko in Slovenia...had almost filled its subterranean nuclear
> waste storage facilities in 1990."[12]

The huge Krsko plant was built under joint Westinghouse-German direction and had not obtained additional waste storage space by the outbreak of the war, according to officials at the International Atomic Energy Agency in Vienna.[13] Although housed in an opulent, modern office building, the IAEA exerts only passive, advisory influence—through its banal international conventions—and only solicits governments for voluntary information about use, storage and international movement of nuclear fuel and wastes. As of early 1995, there was no mechanism for monitoring dangerous transport and storage of nuclear wastes throughout the Balkans. IAEA officials relied only upon information "volunteered" to them from the Croatian government which, of course, was reluctant to expose the lucrative importation and planned waste storage at suspected sites in the Krajina and eastern Slavonia regions that were cleansed of Serb populations.

Oddly, there was little interest by the international press in 1988 when the first mass demonstration of workers occurred in the downstream Danubian city of Backa Palanka in Serbia located barely outside the western border of Croatia.

Workers marched on the nearby parliament in Novi Sad, Vojvodina, and stoned the buildings, breaking windows and damaging offices and furniture of legislators and other officials, demanding the ouster of its leaders.

The demonstration was glibly passed off as due only to frustration with the sinking Yugoslav economy. However, the thrust of the crowd's anger stemmed from recent discovery and notoriety that engineers and surveyors were marking out plots for nuclear waste facilities. This occurred in the immediate aftermath of the Chernobyl disaster, and fears of radioactive contamination were causing panic throughout eastern Europe.

These disclosures about rumored radioactive waste storage plans incited the protests in Backa Palanka. When Krajina and Papuk regions of Bosnia and Croatia were being cleansed of Serb settlements, the nuclear waste designs were occurring under the noses of the largest news organizations in the world and at the height of media concern, if not hysteria, about environmental and ecological abuses!

---

12. See Steve Coll's "Global Economy Faces the Global Dump,"
The Washington Post/International Herald Tribune, March 24, 1994.
13. IAEA records and officials interviewed by the author in Vienna,
December 1, 1994.

Serbia Was Always The 'Prize'

Ibriefly set aside these gloomy preoccupations as I sat in the comfortable breakfast room of the same small hotel in Vienna where I stayed several times since my first exit from Yugoslavia in January 1976.
I let my reflections wander, available for casual distraction.

It was the same kind of gray wintry morning in December 1994, and I savored the aroma of hot coffee, cheeses and sliced meats. It was a sort of personal tradition to stay at the Prinz Eugene for a day or so after arriving at the *Sudbahnhof* on the overnight train from Yugoslavia. The arduous ordeal of Balkan travel usually left me in a crumpled condition, physically depleted and mentally exhausted. And I had gratefully lugged my bag out of the station and across the sluice of traffic on *Margaretengurtel Wiedner*. I enjoyed barging through the front doors of the Prinz Eugene, attracting skeptical glances from the prim Viennese desk clerks who noticed the beard stubble, bleary eyes and wrinkled shirt and trousers from the journey. Stuffed into my bag were clothes which bore sufficient amounts of Yugoslav grime and countryside.

"I brought gifts," I joked, signing the guest card, "for the laundry."

The flash of a credit card dispelled their doubts, and I was given the key to my room with its deep bathtub, large towels, pleasant smelling shampoo and soap. Then, a short search on the radio for something ideally Straussian with which to descend into a long nap. Later, it would be a long stroll to the *Karlsplatz*, sampling a couple of coffees along the way. "The Tales from Hoffman" was sold out at the grand old Vienna State Opera. Anyway, I preferred something lighter and instead ate a quiet supper at the Café Gloria before my return trek up *Argentinastrasse* to the hotel.

I put off calling Edwin, an acquaintance who had roots and family in Sarajevo but apparently never bothered nor wanted to contact them. That had troubled me. But I liked Edwin, who was a petroleum engineer and probably had access to a lot of information about the logistics of transporting immense volumes of crude oil to satiate Europe's industrial and commercial gluttony. He was quiet and thoughtful, always listening with wide-eyed interest about my Balkan journeys through the years. But, for him ...maybe some other time.

Still wide awake and ready for some conversation, I decided it was time after several years absence for a reunion at the seedy Little Dusseldorf with its proprietor, his two large Boxers and working-class clientele.

Sure enough, said Kurt, the dogs had died from old age in the interim, but he was surprised I remembered them. After a couple bottles of beer and a weary discussion using remnants of my scant German, I went back to the hotel.

Idling over breakfast the next day, I began to arrange my schedule and a visit to the International Atomic Energy Agency. I was going in cold but with a list of questions for someone. I already had the answers.

As I swirled the black coffee at the bottom of my cup, I looked up and suddenly noticed the large mural on the wall. Until now I had never noticed it nor studied its prophetic message veiled in a traditional scene of one of the many bloody battles centuries ago between Austro-Hungarian royalist armies against the Ottoman Turks at the gates of Vienna. Hacked apart or impaled bodies of men and horses were strewn about the scene with varieties of anguish on the faces of those who were dying. Plumes of smoke from distant burning buildings in the city were in the background of the mural. The Danube was not blue or green or gray, but black, like its growing condition as the murky flume of poisonous sewage being dumped throughout the Balkans.

But the sky, hills and other scenery in the mural were in shades of gold. The men and mayhem were in black.

The symbolism of centuries past and future was accurate. What descended the Danube in black torrents and ended at the Black Sea would first ascend the great river as "gold," passing through the short, historically contested span that ran through northern Serbia with its legacy as "the gate" between the Orient and the Occident, East and West. Among the many descriptions of Serbia as "the gate" was in a speech by the late British Prime Minister David Lloyd George on August 8, 1917.[14] Yes, a gate which the Ottoman hordes were historically unable to seize and which the West now seemed desperate to dominate once and for all.

It was no secret what was envisioned to pass through that gate to Europe and the West from Kazakstan, Uzbekistan, Turkmenistan, Azerbaijan and other former Soviet republics in huge volumes of petroleum and minerals. These "republics" were barely emerging from pre-communist tribalism while being promoted in the West as "new democracies" so as to require "protection" and, therefore, invasion, subjugation and occupation.

Throughout these latest Yugoslav wars, the giant Western petroleum conglomerates were silent—but busy. So, to a degree, were the Arab oil states, except in promoting holy war against the Serb enemies of their Caucasus-Illyrian-European Muslim kinsmen in Bosnia-Herzegovina and Kosovo. The new "democratic" tribes of central Asia were seen as squatters atop the petro-chemical treasure house of the 21st Century, wholly incompetent to exert "free-market" management over foreign exploitation of incalculable, untouched resources of chemicals, petroleum, uranium, cobalt, iron, sulphur, zinc, gold, silver, coal, chromium, copper, lead nickel—all the necessary and vulnerable consumables to be mined and devoured by affluent societies and cities in the rapacious New World Order.

The political sovereignties of these new Central Asian republics and ancient Balkan domains were, at best, negotiable if not perishable or, ideally, corruptible:

> "The deputy U.S. energy secretary (Bill White) used a recent seven-nation tour of former Soviet republics to stake his country's claim to a share in the development of the vast gas and oil resources of the Caspian Sea region, which has already attracted nearly $30 billion in promised investment from western companies. ...The purpose of White's tour, along with members of the national Security Council and the State Department, was to galvanize the southern republics of the former Soviet Union into standing up for themselves. ...He said he was urging all the republics he visited 'to think of themselves as future major oil-producing nations, and of Russia and Iran as competitors.' White is blunt on how the world's growing demand for oil should be satisfied in the coming decades. 'World demand is growing at one million barrels a day per year, and where that new oil comes from will be a function of policy as much as geology.'"[15]

---

14. R.G.D. Laffan, *The Serbs: The Guardians of the Gate*, New York: Dorset Press, 1989.

15. Steve LeVine, "Who Will Control the Caspian Sea Oil?" *The Financial Times*, May 4, 1995.

Getting it out of the ground was easy. Getting it to the West was the harder task. It was clear that a northern "gate" had Russian obstacles:

> "Washington is already involved in the other row over energy in Kazakstan, which focuses on the Tengiz gas field where Chevron has pledged to invest more than $20 billion over forty years but recently froze its plans because of concerns about a lack of agreement on an export pipeline. A struggle is underway for control and financing of a proposed $1.2 billion pipeline which would transport the output of the Tengiz field to the Russian Black Sea port of Novorossisk.[16]

A southern "gate," of course, was unthinkable as it would pass through the competition which wielded the Arab oil embargo in the 1970s. Public revulsion and horrific fears of lines at American gas stations, after all, led to the appeasing posture of Western nations with Muslim Bosnia. Central Asia's promising petroleum and mineral fields were the leverage against the repugnant and humiliating exercise in the 1970s of squeezing oil shale from America's pristine Rocky Mountains ever again.

And an eastern "gate" through China, Japan and Indonesia was realistically prohibitive.

There was only the westward conduit and up through the ancient but enforceable Danube, through the Balkans and Serbia, the crossroads of the Balkans. And, barges are the cheapest form of transporting large volumes of raw petroleum, minerals and chemicals.

To the ancient Romans and Germans, the Danube was worshiped as a god with the name "Danuvius" and "Donau," respectively. Its 1,786-mile length is long-proven as a commercial transit, passing through Germany, Austria, Slovakia, Hungary, Croatia, Serbia, Romania, Moldavia, and the Ukraine, and the four capitals of Vienna, Bratislava, Budapest and Belgrade. It is called Donau, Dunaj, Duna, Dunare, Dunav and Dunai. In 1992, its commercial value was vastly increased when it was joined with the Rhine-Main-Danube Canal which was completed after construction (interrupted by World War II) during most of the 20th Century and at a cost of more than six billion Deutschmarks. The extension provided a theoretically continuous waterway for large barges and other sea-going vessels from the Black Sea to the North Sea. "Theoretical" only in that regional armed conflicts may interrupt this giant transportation conduit across the heart of the European continent, despite the numerous treaties designed to safeguard its operation.

The planned development of South Central Asia's huge petroleum and mineral fields and delivery to refineries in Europe, the United States and elsewhere would logically occur via the Danube. A single barge could carry the equivalent volume of 100 tank trucks or 100 railroad tank cars, and prior to the Yugoslav civil wars more than 10,000 barges—at 20,000-tons individual capacity—had transited the Danube.

Oil pipeline construction projects were planned before 1990, including one which would be able to move nearly thirty million gallons per year westward from the Black Sea/Caspian Sea regions. But the inevitable pipelines will take years to construct and to navigate through international red-tape. The U.S. Geological Survey estimated Caspian Sea oil reserves alone at 200 billion barrels with proven natural gas reserves up to ten trillion cubic meters. Meanwhile, Danube transportation was more promising and apt to weather economic and political instability in the immediate regions if not throughout the world. But, operated under numerous treaties, the Danube waterway

---

16. LeVine, *ibid.*

was historically vulnerable to conflict, and the river's commerce through a 368-mile stretch of Serb lands slowed to a trickle after 1991. But the Dunav was still open and navigable until American bombs destroyed bridges and left the shipping channels blocked in 1999.

Estimates of initial phases of clean-up of the Dunav in Serbia ranged into the billions of dollars.

By 1997, a socially and economically pulverized Serbia seemed imminent as the corporate strategist "sharks" sensed the time was ripe to complete the westward links from the south central Asian oil fields:

> "In donating $300,000 to Democratic Party organizations during the 1996 campaign, an ambitious businessman named Roger Tamraz sought access to President Clinton and other senior officials so he could ask them to support his project for a new oil pipeline from the Caspian Sea.

> "...Tamraz's efforts to buy access to the White House emerged as a key issue in Washington's campaign finance investigations. But in the drama now unfolding around the Caspian, Tamraz is a bit player and $300,000 a laughably small sum. The big players are nations including Russia, Iran and the United States, companies like Amoco, Pennzoil and Exxon and lobbyists with names like Kissinger, Haig, Baker and Brzezinski. They and every shark east of Suez have recognized that over the next decades, the greatest of games will be played around the Caspian.

> "Forget mutual funds, commodity futures and corporate mergers. Forget South African diamonds, European currencies and Thai stocks. The most concentrated mass of untapped wealth known to exist anywhere is in the oil and gas fields beneath the Caspian and the lands around it, regions at best dimly familiar to even the most assiduous newspaper readers.

> "The stakes are enormous; the value of the vast reserve, capable of fueling the industrial world for years to come, is measured in trillions of dollars, and foreign companies are expected to invest $50 billion or more merely to extract it.

> "The strategic implications of this bonanza hypnotize Western security planners as completely as the finances transfix oil executives. Once Caspian oil begins flowing, they dare to dream, they will never again have to kowtow to OPEC or maneuver to prevent oil-thirsty nations from dealing with Iran and Iraq.

> "With that relief, however, will undoubtedly come new troubles, for the competition involves not only governments and oil companies, but also warlords and clan chiefs who control or move through the remote regions where the pipelines needed to bring the treasure to market might be built..."[17]

17. Stephen Kinzer, "A Perilous New Contest for the Next Oil Prize," *The New York Times*, September 28, 1997.

The deeper explanations behind the Russian conflicts in Chechnya and Afghanistan can be intuited, along with American obsessions against Iran and Iraq. Add to this all the other concealed strategies involving multi-national alignments and tanker/pipeline schemes of Georgia, Turkey, Bulgaria, Romania, Greece, Armenia—and even the more adventurous possibility to run a pipeline from Turkmenistan south to the Indian Ocean through Afghanistan where the ruling Taliban faction was previously receptive to pipeline talks with the giant U.S. company (Unocal) before the war!

Among the stratagems:

"The first flow of oil is to be sent through an existing pipeline that runs north from Baku through Chechnya to the Russian port of Novorossisk on the Black Sea. Russian leaders would like to expand this line so it can be used for the far larger flows to come, but to do so they must cooperate with Chechnya's secessionist rebels.

"Russian and Chechen leaders finally reached an accord this month on splitting the transit fees, but reflecting their mistrust, the Russians immediately announced that they want to build a new alternative route through North Ossetia, a region that is marginally more stable politically.

"The only existing alternative pipeline does not run through Russia at all, but westward from Baku to the Black Sea port of Supsa in Georgia. It passes through potentially explosive regions of Georgia, but Georgian officials say they can guarantee its security.

"Once the oil reaches Supsa, however, what should be done with it? One option is to ship it in tankers across the Black Sea, through the Bosporus into the Mediterranean. But Turkish officials strenuously object to such heavy tanker traffic because of the environment risks.

"The Turks propose to build a 650-mile pipeline from Supsa across eastern Turkey to their port of Ceyhan on the Mediterranean. But some oil executives worry about the time and expense of building such a pipeline, and they cannot ignore the risk that Kurdish guerillas in eastern Turkey might try to attack it.

"Another possibility would be to ship or pipe oil from Supsa across the Black Sea to Bulgaria or Romania, sending it by pipeline from there to a Greek port. Azerbaijan's president, Heydar Aliyev, has even suggested that he would consider a pipeline through Armenia if the two countries can settle their dispute over the occupied Nagorno-Karabakh region.

"When oil planners look at maps, however, they cast their eyes on a tantalizing alternative: simply tie Baku to the existing pipeline network in neighboring Iran and send the oil south to the Persian Gulf.

"This proven route leads to ports already equipped for shipping oil and avoids the baffling range of political, ethnic, national and religious conflicts bubbling across the Caucasus. But the United States, which rejects virtually all cooperation with Iran, strongly opposes it. Some influential figures in Washington are quietly suggesting that it may be time to reappraise policy toward Iran, ...but they have not had any visible success.

"An even more daring possibility is to run a pipeline from Turkmenistan south to the open sea through Afghanistan, where the ruthlessly fundamentalist and anti-Western Taliban movement is in control. At least one U.S. company, Unocal, has reportedly held pipeline talks with Taliban officials..."[18]

Thus, the roster of potentially desperate and international combatants in the region.

Before, during and after NATO bombs fell on Belgrade and Danube River crossings in Serbia in 1999, in pseudo-sympathy for ethnically-cleansed but marauding Kosovo Muslims, the oil money was flowing.

"Everything," prophesied Pliny the Elder, and classical naturalist, twenty centuries ago at Rome, "is soothed by oil."[19]

Serbia—not whole but diseased, impoverished, politically feudal and at last dispirited—always loomed as the real prize in the new Balkan wars, and not pluralistic democracies in Slovenia, Croatia, Macedonia, Kosovo and Bosnia. In the minds of Germany, Europe and the United States, the goal was a pliant Serbia—either democratically submissive or depleted and decimated by Dark-Age desolation.

This side of the story was always fairly easy to dig out. But telling it was overlooked or deliberately distorted, manipulated and suppressed.

None of it is surprising to those who remember the ancient Balkan admonition— "Never dare to judge till you've heard the other side."[20]

The story about the Western media's obsession and downfall is a tragic enough epitaph to the bigger story of what happened to the proud profession of Western and, especially, American journalism in the Yugoslav wars—where it lost its soul.

18. Kinzer, *ibid.*
19. *Natural History*, Bk. II, 234.
20. Euripides, from *Heraclidae*, 428 B.C.

The War 'Literature'

> *"(General Lewis MacKenzie) expected journalists to call*
> *him frequently in Etobicoke, but what he didn't expect were*
> *the kinds of questions they asked. 'What's interesting is that*
> *most of the calls now deal more with: "Could you tell us again*
> *what happened on such and such a time because we're taking*
> *a look at the way we covered it in our reporting,"' said MacKenzie,*
> *paraphrasing. And my message to them when they start*
> *wallowing in their anguish is, 'Don't feel too guilty about all of*
> *this because you only reported what you saw, and what you*
> *saw was only 150 meters on either side of the Holiday Inn.'"*[1]
> **—Lewis MacKenzie**

> *"C'est avec de beaux sentiments qu'on fait de la mauvaise litterature."*
> ("It is with noble sentiments that bad literature gets written.")[2]
> **—Andre Gide**

The Yugoslav war correspondents and reporters came marching home again with a dilemma. Toting bundles and boxes full of notebooks and scrawl and clippings and cassette-tapes, they long before decided to write their memoirs, their books and their volumes. But, how to write it? Non-fiction? Fiction? Confession? Surrealism? Synthesis? Screenplays? Musical lyric?

Why not all?!

And, the appreciably sparse though varied published works so far yield a remarkable insight about motives, ambitions, and personal reflections of individual journalists and the collective Western media. But, understandably, the precise writing about the "war reporting" itself is rarely divulged. But, it can be glimpsed!

Not surprisingly, many former Balkan correspondents chose not to write at all, perhaps awaiting a better time or a better war. Some rushed into print and quickly rushed back to make necessary revisions and corrections for new editions. Some moved on. Some got promoted or were hired by other news organizations. Others were forced into retirement, quit or got fired. Some died.

All of that colored the post-war writings.

Of course, martyred Sarajevo would be eulogized and canonized in the post-war writings of the war correspondents who had lived for months inside the 300-room Holiday Inn, a smudged, pock-marked, thirteen-story bunker that offered comfort,

---

1. Interview with the author, October 1993.
2. Andre Gide, *Letter to Francois Mauriac* (1928).

cuisine and camaraderie a few steps from the Bosnian Parliament. In the heart of the business district, the hotel was built for the 1984 Olympic games.

But, by the time Western reporters began streaming into its 300 or so rooms in the early 1990s, the war's most notorious innkeeper was having an profoundly institutional effect on its guests/inmates who daily churned out the victim idolatries of exploited tragedy obtained from government propagandists or overheard in its dining room and hallways. It was, in fact, the Bosnian government's *defacto* public relations annex that provided endless grist of misery and ready access to media-ready misery.

National Public Radio's Tom Gjelten became fixated upon the serialized human wretchedness of the city's remaining daily newspaper and its obsessed employees and the political actors outside its doors who were recreated by the fantasized notion of harmonious Balkan pluralism and propped up by the morbid idealism demanded among the outside media.[3]

When his tale ended, the trumpet cry of martyrdom instead blew flat about *Oslobodjenje* that had managed to publish for "thirty terrible months" with a steady supply of newsprint that was suspiciously cut off from Sarajevo's other papers.

The dirge, taken up by Gjelten and others, was unceasing throughout the Bosnian war that Sarajevo was a global centerpiece displaying "the spirit of pluralism and tolerance that has been the principal casualty of the Bosnian war" no matter that "the world was indifferent to their struggle" and the cadre of the paper's journalists who showed "that *right-minded Serbs*, Muslims, and Croats could work together no matter the assault on their community."[4] (Italics added)

Some might disagree and offer that it was more a picture of how misperceived pluralism by a diminishing free press—inside the Holiday Inn and outside Bosnia—failed to "save" multi-ethnic Sarajevo or the susceptible romance of journalism with Balkan wars.

"This *was to be*," said Gjelten, using curiously futurist tense he divined behind the first shots that were rattled off, "a war over the way people identified themselves and defined their city..."[5] (Italics added)

Notoriously neglected in the Western reporting was that bullets were fired into a Serbian wedding party the day before "spontaneous" busloads of crowds were unloaded outside the Holiday Inn to be fired on from inside.

Gjelten correctly demonstrated the pattern of biased reporting practiced by most international journalists who overstayed assignments "in besieged Sarajevo" and sympathized "instinctively" with citizens. "I know I did." They wrote, apparently, in unison for "an enlightened Western world..."

Years later, "enlightened Western" journalism still refused to acknowledge the flight of tens of thousands of Sarajevo's Serbs along with its entire Jewish community—both with palpable memories from World War II atrocities—on the eve of the recognition of Bosnian "independence" in early 1992. Gjelten grudgingly conceded that "the Serb exodus" eventually forced foreign journalists "to reconsider their initial judgment" about Sarajevo's harmoniousness.[6]

Apparently, at some time before the end of 1993 Gjelten left Sarajevo, returning in June 1994 to note the abdication of pluralism and the now-total predominance of newly-urban Muslim hardliners in control of the government and the black market

3. Tom Gjelten, *Sarajevo Daily: A City and Its Newspaper Under Siege,*
New York: HarperCollins, 1995; p. 1.
4. *Sarajevo Daily...*, pp. 194, 199.
5. *Sarajevo Daily...*, pp. 3,4.
6. *Sarajevo Daily...*, p. 12.

controlled economy. It was "the" story that belatedly received minimal context or concern from the Western media – and only as they were checking out of the Holiday Inn and exiting past Sarajevo's "front-line defenders …and local military commanders became rich as war profiteers…"[7]

Oslobodjenje did its own carefully considered war-reporting at virtual gunpoint, the victimologies fitting neatly into the profiteering scheme. Indeed, the story went "largely untold"—period! The suffering brought in mountains of food, clothing and other essential relief supplies that went mostly into the hands of the warlords and their illicit commercial and government operatives.

Gjelten, along with others, was reluctantly forced to chart the unraveling of journalistic wish-dreams for Sarajevo by Western correspondents and their routine of "romanticizing prewar life in Sarajevo and 'demonizing' the Serb nationalist side."[8]

Bowie, Maryland—1992

Professor Alex Dragnich, the retired Vanderbilt University political scientist and former American Embassy official in Belgrade, was troubled by the increasing trends of what he saw among journalists in the last two decades of the 20th Century:

> "I was led to write this book primarily by the realization that the journalism produced in the wake of the collapse of Communist regimes in Eastern Europe, including Yugoslavia's, has been not only inadequate, but also often incorrect. Errors of fact and highly misleading interpretations were owing, I believe, mainly to a lack of knowledge of European history, especially that of the Balkans. Other writers, equally ignorant of this history, repeated misinformation and questionable interpretations, and thus added to the confusion.

> "My aim here is to help clarify and correct the background for the average interested reader who is often impatient with lengthy books, countless footnotes, and endless quotations."[9]

Dragnich's *Serbs and Croats: The Struggle in Yugoslavia* was a deliberate labor to urgently inform and educate the deteriorating journalism which was paralyzed and unwilling to minimally inform the average interested reader.

Credits on the front and back covers said it best:

> "Concise, lucid …a *floodlight* on the tragic drama unfolding in Yugoslavia." —*Publishers Weekly* (Italics aded)

> "[Dragnich's] narrative has a *clear and concise historical knowledge.*"—*Wall Street Journal* (Italics added)

> "The *necessary context* in which the reader who is unfamiliar with Yugoslavia may *begin to understand* who's fighting and

---

7. *Sarajevo Daily...*, pp. 194.
8. *Sarajevo Daily...*, p. 17.
9   Alex N. Dragnich, *Serbs and Croats: The Struggle in Yugoslavia*,
New York: Harcourt Brace & Company, 1992; p. x.

why, and to make sense of the horrific scenes of destruction."
—*Booklist* (Italics added)

The war reporters and correspondents declared themselves, apparently, exempt from the invaluable benefits of Dragnich's primer, judging by the results of a decade's worth of informed "coverage" from the Yugoslav civil wars.

Ottawa, Quebec—May 1993

The Yugoslav wars made writers and journalists out of generals, such as General Lewis MacKenzie who made several discreet but telling references about the performance of the local and international media in Sarajevo when he was its first UNPROFOR commander.

His diary-style reflections made up the record of his Yugoslav experiences:

> **"MAY 23 (1992) ...** Watching the TV news (*BBC* and *CNN*), one gets the impression Serbs are 100 percent to blame. Some of the reports are unbalanced, based on what we know. Serbs bear majority of responsibility, but Izetbegovic has done an excellent job of mobilizing world opinion on his side, which covers up his hidden agenda..."

Especially, during the siege of Sarajevo, manipulation of the Western media—in one case for MacKenzie specifically involving a story in *The New York Times*—instigated savage reprisals, as when MacKenzie cautiously related a too coincidental mortar barrage that occurred precisely at the time and location of his scheduled arrival for a meeting at the Bosnian Presidency.

MacKenzie, who wrote down his account for publication within a few months after leaving Sarajevo and UNPROFOR, was always careful to not say anything that could still result in reprisals against U.N. troops.

However, less than two months before his exit in August 1992, he displayed a more than cynical disbelief in the innocence of Bosnian officials who habitually wire-tapped and bugged locations used by UNPROFOR commanders. It was the occasion of the too suspicious mortar attack at the main entrance on June 22, 1992, to keep an eleven o'clock appointment. Arriving two minutes late, MacKenzie saw that a barrage had targeted his usual parking area a minute earlier and killed fourteen people, including elderly and children. Pre-positioned ambulances routinely arrived moments later to sort through the gore. Cynically, MacKenzie offered his sympathies to President Izetbegovic along with the sarcasm that there was nothing to indicate it was not caused by Bosnian-Serbs.

MacKenzie then tore into Izetbegovic about the "particularly damning article" in *The New York Times*, attributed to statements from Defense Minister Jerko Doko containing "a number of outright fabrications that placed UNPROFOR in a bad light."

Doko tried to apologize, saying he had been misinformed by his deputy commander who stood nearby but just stared away from MacKenzie.

MacKenzie's cryptic account heavily inferred the mortar attack originated not from Bosnian Serbs but from the government's own troops. It was not the first or the last time that the Bosnian army—given the green light by news accounts in the Western media—took opportunity to inflict carnage on its own people.

A month later on July 21, MacKenzie was the featured entrée at a news gathering at the international press centre where he was castigated for supposedly saying there was equal "blame" for an overnight mortar bombardment. MacKenzie denied the quote, offering that his accurate statement was that there was "plenty of blame to go around." A government interpreter had been obtained for non-English-speaking reporters and was soon at odds with reporters for "misrepresenting my words," he said.

Goteborg, Sweden—December 1994

Roy Gutman seemed to crave the role of international, influence-wielding diplomat and policy-maker instead of a working reporter.

Diplomats, journalists, European government officials and academics seemed to reach a point of anguish in the last session of the two-day International Balkan Conference at the University of Goteborg in 1994.

During a tedious harangue of retired Swedish General Lars Wahlgren, a former UNPROFOR commander in Sarajevo, and others on a final panel, author/journalist Misha Glenny finally could not tolerate any longer Gutman's anti-climactic diatribes from the audience and interrupted his chastisements of the five-nation Contact Group for sacrificing "principles" and shunning military enforcement of a re-mapped Bosnia in the latest attempt to coax a comprehensive Balkan peace agreement.

From the audience, Gutman was inserting his breathless soliloquys about whether "this is a conventional war" or whether "it is not a war at all, in a rational sense, that it is a genocide with the aim of genocide ...exterminating populations," questioning "conventional diplomatic approach ...They don't have any back-up for their plan. There's no coercion. It's just simply a plan," Gutman rattled on, oblivious to the shaking heads around him. "...I don't see where the Contact Group is going to go here, except to back down. And if it starts backing down from a position that didn't seem to have much principle in the first place, that had no principle in the first place, then how is the public internationally going to have any understanding of what could be done, what should be done, and how to stabilize Europe? In other words, when once you abandon your principles—what is left?..."

"The point is, Roy," interjected Glenny instantly, spinning in his seat with obvious annoyance toward Gutman and reciting with rhythmic impatience, as though to a disruptive pupil, the chronology of frustration over manipulative incitements by Germany, Britain and the U.S. "...We've not used principles from the very beginning of this conflict! ...We are dealing with realpolitik from the very beginning, from the original response to the Yugoslav crisis. And because we have been utterly unprincipled from the very beginning, we're in the situation we're in now—which is there is no decent solution for anybody. So, the Contact Group peace proposal ...is the only way out! "

Gutman fell silent as when he was similarly hushed the previous day from his tiresome "defense" of the "Western press," continuously squirming and clearing his throat, repeating rhetorically the "dangers" for journalists in armed conflicts and, it seemed to his listeners, insinuating that the media "on the ground" were therefore allowed more latitude with factual reporting and responsible journalism, more immunity from first-hand reporting. It was the standard Gutman defense not of the Western press—but of the license for hearsay and other of his "reporting methods" that earned him half of the 1993 Pulitzer Prize. *Helsingborgs Dagblad* editor Soren Sommelius was unimpressed and flatly accused the Western media of biased coverage, "distortions and distractions" in the war reporting of the Yugoslav conflicts.

"That kind of journalism has made the big politicians react to use our 'good violence' to get rid of the bad people's 'bad violence'. And that is creating a world which can be very, very dangerous for all of us," said Sommelius.

The room filled with about seventy mostly European journalists broke out with enthusiastic applause for Sommelius' criticisms.

"In the case of this war, the (Western) media have left behind all the ethics of their profession," continued Sommelius.

Undaunted, Gutman flailed about. "The problem is getting your orientation," he insisted. "It's trying to figure out who is doing what to whom and why. Is it a civil war? Is it an ethnic war? Is it a religious war? Is it an ideological war? And then trying to figure out a way to explain it to our readers. Because if we can't explain it in some way that is straightforward that fits the facts, then we shouldn't be out there. But it takes a tremendous effort and it takes a lot of risks. And, as it's been pointed out, the numbers of reporters who've been killed or wounded or roughed up or robbed or mistreated is staggering. I'm not saying that this should influence us in reporting the right from the wrong. Because the question at the end of the day is, did we get the story right? At the end of the day, the question is what happened? And I think the Bosnian war has been easier to report."

"Is this a question? Excuse me, is this a question?" interrupted Sommelius whose patience was exhausted.

"No, I'm making a comment," stammered Gutman, admonishing the seasoned professionals in the room that "the hardest thing, as a working journalist in this process is to get your compass. And we have nowhere to look... because we're in a different era right now. This is not the war of a conventional variety. This is not something we've seen in Europe before."

More moans, embarrassed whispers and sighs.

"Now we simply can't rely on anybody but ourselves to get our orientation. And, I don't think we've done so bad, personally," Gutman concluded in nearly a whisper.

Several years later Gutman was *Newsweek's* "international security reporter" as well as director of American University's altruistic "Crimes of War Project." He was also a senior fellow at the United States Institute of Peace, pursuing studies of the Geneva Conventions. He co-edited, with David Rieff, *Crimes of War: What the Public Should Know*, a tedious anthology of 140 articles on aspects of international humanitarian law written by ninety journalists/jurists.

Despite the rush to publish his *A Witness to Genocide,* Gutman received credit for "exposing" the various detention and refugee camps in Bosnia—a distinction given partly by his being the first published work of any kind on the subject and partly by default in the general absence of any clear definitions by early 1993 of what reporters and others were or were not seeing.

Gutman made several curious statements, alleging incorrectly that "the Serbs *invented* the euphemism 'ethnic cleansing,'" while again padding his excuses for non-firsthand reporting and that "the only way to reconstruct events was to question refugees who were flooding out of Bosnia."[10] (Italics added)

Other reporters, such as Mary Battiata, disagreed about movement restrictions until late in the fighting. But judging from his material, Gutman habitually obtained much of whatever information he decided was credible through the filtered layers of interpreters, Bosnian government operatives, and anonymous second and third

---

10. *A Witness...*, p. vii; see Chapter XI "Where, One Might Ask, Are The Bodies?"; the phrase "ethnic cleansing" was used earlier by Croat Ustashe extremists towards ridding themselves of Serb populations early in World War II.

parties. He even offered that his "theory ...about the events and those responsible should be potentially falsifiable—that is, structured in a way that if it was wrong, it could be so proven.

He departed from "such lofty standards" and "*immediately* made an exception and wrote about the Omarska camp, which I had *not* visited, based on the second-hand witness account." But, Gutman got the woman's account not directly but from notes produced by Muslim officials in Banja Luka.[11] (Italics added)

Of the more notable "theories" from Gutman that were factually disproved were his notions that "Bosnian leader Alija Izetbegovic had followed to the letter a plan prescribed by the United States and its European partners."[12] Also, Gutman's flat denial that *mujahedin* mercenaries were involved in the Bosnian war was exposed as false when the U.S. government ordered Izetbegovic and the Sarajevo regime to get them out of the country.[13]

Gutman persisted with his original, conspiratorial hunches when weaving his spooky conclusions in Bosnia that "the world reaction did not sit right" and questioning how journalists' "scoops" on the ground were inconsistent "in the age of spy satellites" and that "U.S. intelligence or UN organizations must have had some information" about the presumed "practices" in detention "camps weeks if not months earlier."[14]

Say what you will, Gutman mesmerized almost everyone and enough of the rest —with no little help from 360 journalists who were stampeded through northern Bosnia in the summer of 1992!—and closed more or less all but the vile Muslim and Croat camps which he failed to report about with equal zeal. Also, U.S. intelligence and U.N. organizations knew about them as well.

On an unusually warm night in December 1994, I sat in a small pub along the *Kungsportsavenyn* promenade, mulling over the concluding revelations from the International Balkan Conference in Goteborg.

What did the old gentleman mean who'd reacted earlier that day with surprise to see Gutman and rushed to greet him? Gutman gave him a copy of his book, as the white-haired, jovial fellow leaned close to Gutman's ear and hissed loud enough for anyone nearby to hear: "You're full of secrets!"

Gutman smiled though he was visibly embarrassed.

One such "secret" persists, even after all his detailed study of the Geneva conventions and humanitarian law: There is still no documented proof to even suggest that there were "tens of thousands" of war criminals at large in the former Yugoslavia, as Gutman reported eight months earlier.[15]

Roy Gutman came closest to influencing the mainstream war reporting in Bosnia and to fitting what *New York Times* reporter Chris Hedges detailed later in *Nieman Reports* published in 1999. Although Hedges clearly had in mind the Serb and Bosnian Serb leadership, he pulled the curtain back far enough on other provocateurs inside the Balkans and in the West.

> "How does one cover such a story, one that because of its implications, both real and perceived, erodes the beleaguered forces struggling to prevent a slide to intolerance and war? What does one do when the stories one writes become grist for

---

11. *A Witness...*, p. xii.
12. *A Witness...*, p. xxvii; see Chapter VII "'A Partial Story' and Half a Pulitzer"; also David Binder, *The New York Times*, August 29, 1993.
13. *A Witness...*, p. xxvii
14. *A Witness...*, p.xiii.
15. Gutman, *Newsday*, April 16, 1994.

the Serb propaganda effort, *or any effort, to foment conflict? What moral obligations do we, as journalists, have to those we are writing about? It is one of the hallmarks of our trade that stories we report can assist, in the short term, those we would least like to empower.*"[16] (Italics added)

New York City—February 1994

David Rieff was lauded as "perhaps America's most acclaimed chronicler of displaced people, of lives in flux."

He had returned to New York right after Sarajevo the market massacre when television was still reverberating with "the sights and sounds of that explosion."

He received "a call from an ex-lover, a decent, apolitical woman with no very great interest in Bosnia." The caller said she felt "terrible," leaving Rieff questioning why "ordinary people" were moved to tears while "the powerful" vowed action.[17]

Rieff was the sort of parachutist literary itinerant you'd expect to arrive in bleeding Bosnia—sooner or later.

He is self-portrayed as the moral voice of martyred Sarajevo, the wronged Bosnian government, the Western pack journalism, accuser of failed international diplomacy and the United Nations, and the best Serb-hater among the Gjelten-Gutman-Rieff trilogy of tragedy and victimhood. The most prolific user of the personal pronoun "I" in the early war literature, he took the phrase "ethnic cleansing" at face value as soon as he arrived, congratulating Gutman and a few others for their "heroic efforts... but most people in the West seemed unable to confront the bad news..."

Devoting himself "to write as frankly *incendiary* a narrative" drawn from his days in Bosnia in early 1992, Rieff resolved that if the "the bad news" about Bosnia could be laid before people back home then the "slaughter" would end. Also, people back home could understand better "why I and many other foreign writers, photographers, and television journalists *kept choosing, often over the objections of friends and superiors*, to spend time on the Bosnian side."[18] (Italics added)

In practically the same breath—and on the next page—Rieff admits his abrupt disillusionment in the Bosnian paradise-lost and his re-illusionment! In the cauldron of war, his "darkest suspicions" about "the heroic defenders of Sarajevo" were short-lived because of their co-loyalty with defending the racketeering and black market enterprises.[19]

Rieff's introspective odyssey found space for debunking Bosnian-Muslim and Croat images as the forces of innocence and good and assessing, apologetically, the media's vulnerability for exaggeration and superficiality. He could, however briefly, acknowledge at least some legitimacy in premonitions of World War II-style genocide in Croatia against Serbs and Jews.

Prior to his first trip to wartime Yugoslavia, he along with hundreds of millions in a gullible global audience, including journalists, was subjected to the hype from *CNN, Antenne 2, Britain's Sky News* and Germany's *ZDF* and the orchestrated coverage

---

16. Chris Hedges, "War Crimes, Human Rights and Press Freedom: The Journalist's Job—In Yugoslavia, the Consequences of Not Reporting the Truth," *Nieman Reports*, Vol. 53 No. 2, Summer 1999. Hedges was Balkan Bureau Chief for the *Times* from, 1995-1998.

17. David Rieff, *Slaughterhouse: Bosnia and the Failure of the West*, New York: Simon & Schuster, 1995, p. 18.

18. *Slaughterhouse...*, p. 9.

19. *Slaughterhouse...*, p. 11.

of the orchestrated "siege of Vukovar" and the manufactured "bombardment" of Dubrovnik. Rookies in Bosnia had been steeped with information about what they thought was happening in crumbling Yugoslavia, all "televised down to the last detail."

More essentially, Rieff was confident that he "knew already that in order to get from the airport to the Holiday Inn, where the journalists stayed" required a series of vehicles, some armored, some not, and a stealthy route to avoid snipers once setting out from the city's communications center. After all, the route was vouchsafed "because I had seen these roads on *CNN*." Sarajevo had plenty of shocks for Rieff "when I finally began to spend time there" most of his expectations were correct. "And yet I knew *nothing* (Rieff's emphasis)."[20]

Rieff joined in berating UNPROFOR, and then offered anticlimactically not a completely unintentional disclosure of the obvious co-belligerency between the Western press and the Bosnian government, indelibly throbbing with chest-beating lament and sentiment. After all, in desperation the Sarajevo government plied their schemes and media mischief on the reporters billeted at the Holiday Inn who could be counted on to sensationalize "one more picture, or one more story, or one more correspondent's stand-up taped in front of a shelled, smoldering building" and force the United Nations to "stop blaming the victims."[21]

Bandying about rationalizations about fairness and impartiality, what the press and Rieff did not understand was the extent of their license to be "more" than "fair" and "impartial" which became the inevitably surreal excess and distortion and disillusionment that it was. The natives had a clearer view of Western insistence that Sarajevo and Bosnia live up to the outsiders' mirage of life there that "was as pitted with dreams as it was with shellfire."

Sarajevans and Bosnians generally were tired of the reporters and disillusioned about the media as the vehicle for influencing international solutions about anything. The war correspondents who were once hailed as saviors had become irrelevant in the movement outside of Yugoslavia to "save" the city and the countryside. A friend greeted Rieff and asked, "Another safari?" when he returned late in 1993. Pressed to answer if he was looking only for more bodies and more mayhem, his friend suggested Rieff ought to pay for "admission."[22]

Sarajevo—1994

In his last column from the collection that would appear in his book, Bosnian columnist/essayist Zlatko Dizdarevic used a curious alignment of "those 'up there' in the hills," "they," "we" and "us." It was a codified, literary device for deliberately and derisively identifying who he was writing about by denying nationalist labels.

"Those 'up there' in the hills" and "they" were given nationalistic non-person status although they were obviously Bosnian Serbs who for several years rained down some artillery shells on Sarajevo—i.e. the city's Bosnian Muslim, Croat and the handful of remaining Serb inhabitants. The latter three were the idyllic "we" and "us" of the non-hyphenated conglomerate long-iconized by the Western media.

Dizdarevic's scorn and despair slides into a concluding diminuendo of dark-tabloid cynicism in that it is "kind of tragic being an inhabitant of this planet, at the end of the Twentieth Century."[23]

20. *Slaughterhouse...*, p. 41.
21. *Slaughterhouse...*, pp. 222, 223.
22. *Slaughterhouse...*, pp. 223, 224.
23. Zlatko Dizdarevic, *Sarajevo—A War Journal*, New York: Henry Holt and Company, 1994; p. 199.

The War Literature

There is no mention in the sixty-three essays about artillery attacks by Bosnian government troops inside Sarajevo that killed Sarajevans. Likewise absent are any accounts of organized crime with connections to the Bosnian presidency that infected Sarajevo. Nor the mujahedin mercenaries. Nor the Bosnian government-operated prison dens where non-Muslim women were held for recreational rape. Nor the Bosnian-operated detention camps converted from grain silos and railroad tunnels.

Nor was there any nuance suggesting that war profiteers and the Sarajevo mafia were looking threateningly over shoulders of *Oslobodenje's* editors and writers.

There are a few sullen, sneering references to as many as 50,000 Serbs who abandoned Sarajevo, impelled by memories of Serb slaughters from fifty years before. The Western media, too, become "they." After all, they were supposed to have lured NATO reprisals against the Bosnian Serbs. Now, in 1994, Dizdarevic's morose anthology is one man's last attempt, a final jungle scream from the mayhem. NATO's F-16s shrieked in over the hills around Gorazde the following year—AFTER a nearly predictable second solo mortar round fell on the marketplace on August 28, 1995, killing thirty-seven shoppers and stall-tenders.

Dizdarevic's evolved and varied resentments for "foreign" journalists are easily seen, beginning in June 1992 when responding to foreign journalists in Sarajevo who are incredulous at *Oslobodenje's* reporting styles that fail to name belligerents or parties in the conflict.

A month later, he distinguishes between Western journalists "who have come to honor their obligation to truth and their profession, and those who came to make a pile of money out of our misery."[24]

Dizdarevic's acrimony for Western journalists in their comfortable accommodations at the Holiday Inn, brushing elbows with Sarajevo racketeers, was seething when he arrived for a UNHCR event in July 1992 to discover that the plush interior of the restaurant looked the same as before the war with "immaculate white tablecloths" with polished silver utensils and wine glasses, and a substantial menu of "steaks, french fries, beef stew, crepes with chocolate sauce."[25]

At the end of 1992, he attacks—almost with relish—the international prize awarded him by Reporters Without Borders from Paris, scolding his benefactors that, as a "prisoner" of "Camp Sarajevo, Prison Sarajevo," he may never get to Paris again and that it was not the season for "prizes."

Belgrade, Serbia—February 1993

The streets and broad sidewalks glistened in the bright winter sun. The air was biting, as several people were strolling early. For days it was oppressively cloudy and windy, finally whipping up into the brief snowfall the night before. On one side of Lole Ribara Avenue, steam rose from the melt, while on the other side the frozen glaze under the Sunday morning shadows was still hard and slippery.

I was early for my meeting with *The Financial Times* (of London) and a Fulbright Scholar. Turning down the side street across from the *Politika* building, I was thinking about another Fulbright Scholar Dick Arnold, who a few weeks earlier and on the other side of the world sat across from me, eagerly sampling his Mexican food.

He had an easy answer.

"The synchronic American mind can't understand European history, and it sure can't understand Serb history," said Arnold, a Slavic specialist recently returned from Yugoslav battlefields. "It is ancient and present."

---

24. *Sarajevo...*, p. 73.
25. *Sarajevo...*, p. 104.

"They don't hate Americans yet because they're not ready to," he said. "God knows for the last fifty years we've given them reason to, stabbing them in the back every chance we get. What we don't understand is that you push a Serb, and he'll give. You can push him again and again, and he'll give and give. But somewhere down the line, he won't give anymore. And, brother, that's when they finish you off. They even lick up the grease spots."

Arnold scoffed at notions by the Western media that "ancient animosities" played no role in the Yugoslav wars.

"When they finally nailed the Turks after a half millennium of brutal occupation, they weren't ready to write it all off. These damned reporters with their synchronic little minds can't handle that in their nice, neat little world of ideal good and evil. The Serbs are not ready to give up hating the 'Turks.' Sure, the Muslims in Sarajevo want them to, but nobody tells you how to think about your own history. Nobody tells the Serbs when to stop hating."

The slush squished underfoot.

The restaurant was cold inside. Silber and I were the only ones there other than a couple of employees who were cleaning up from the night before. They kept up a steady racket, banging around, hosing down the floor, yelling at each other above the radio.

She was young, sniffling from a cold. I counted at least two sweaters under her coat, as she hunched forward when the coffee was served.

I told her that UNPROFOR's Cedric Thornberry recommended I talk with her. We shared summaries of our backgrounds.

Well, yes, the media was doing a one-sided job. And, yes, the ancient hatreds were partly to blame. Yes, all these Balkan players are bastards. Germany shouldn't have pushed the Yugoslav breakup. They knew America would follow along. Well, yes, there was hell to pay in Bosnia.

The "synchronic American mind"?

"This friend of mine says that's the reason why we—especially American journalists—won't accept that nationalistic or ethnic hatreds had a hand in these wars," I explained. "I think what he meant was that our American thinking goes no further than the present moment. We don't have enough of a past to call 'ancient.' We have no reference to compare it with."

She smiled.

It is odd that two statements stood out in the introduction of her book, hailed as the first competent history about the conflict, written with Britisher Allan Little in 1995. Surprisingly, both sought to dispel the two most significant elements that drove the Yugoslav wars.

First, the offhand acknowledgment that historical animosity, though masked by brooding and ancient ethnic restraints, played no role in the eruption of current or future conflicts, as ethnic and cultural "grievances" were not erased by Yugoslavia's Communist interlude.

Second, that the co-belligerence of the media would not be examined because the book " it is not a book about journalism or journalists; it is not a 'we were there and it was horrible' account of life on the front line."[26]

The excision of these issues thus deprived this new "history" of any deeper credibility—perhaps because their effort was first conceived as a six-hour television documentary which disqualified any historical discussion because of the nature of the medium. Television is for the immediate, sensual manipulation of images. Perhaps the book retained the defect.

---

26. *Yugoslavia: Death of a Nation,* TV Books Inc./Penguin, 1996; p. 27.

The narrative was more or less an obvious exercise in connecting the anecdotal dots to indict Serbian President Slobodan Milosevic at The Hague, although some of authors' original reporting was captivating.

Mainly American journalists insist there were no ancient animosities or passions in the Yugoslav wars. But, the point is, the Yugoslavs believed otherwise! Silber and Little as much as stated it in a chapter entitled "Tsar Lazar's Choice," recording Milosevic's finest hour on June 28, 1989 when a million imported Serbs gathered to hear Milosevic on the 600th anniversary of their legendary defeat by Ottoman Turks at the battle of Kosovo.

Silber and Little portrayed the memorial as a parallel urged by Milosevic to spurn the "foreign oppressor" and to embrace the course of Serbian nationalism.

Regarding the media's role at least previous to secession and war, Silber and Little noted the round-robin of rebellion, reaction, expose, arrests and political trials in Slovene newspapers and journals, including Nova Revija, Mladina, Delo and official retorts in Narodna Armija.

Yugoslavia: Death of a Nation, though widely acknowledged as the first important historic volume to come out of the Yugoslav wars, including a treasure trove of one-liners, noting the diminutive writer Dobrica Cosic's ascent to the presidency of the rump Yugoslavia in 1992 when he "rode in a battered taxi to his own presidential inauguration."

Silber left *The Financial Times* and appeared on numerous panels and at public presentations on the issue of Yugoslavia. She also became a "senior policy adviser" for George Soros' Open Society Institute.

Nova Kasaba, Bosnia-Hercegovina—August 1995

David Rohde stumbled around for more than two hours in overgrown fields he believed were areas depicted on a photo from a U.S. spy satellite as sites of suspicious soil disturbances. He found a scrap of paper, a pair of discarded sneakers, two empty ammunition boxes, a primary school diploma, snapshot photos with Muslim names on the backs, two mounds of excavated earth, a pile of clothing and a string of Muslim prayer beads and some shell casings.

Heading back to his parked car—his Serb driver and an interpreter he left nameless—Rohde said he came upon a pair of white bones that he judged to be a bare human femur and tibia, jutting out of the ground along with shreds of cloth.

In a prefacing note to a August 25, 1995, follow-up article, Rohde, who was the southeastern Europe correspondent for *The Christian Science Monitor,* said the report stemmed from his original August 18th story about his initial arrival at the plot. In December, Rohde testified four months later before a hearing of the U.S. House Permanent Select Committee on Intelligence that the exact date of his discovery was August 16th.[27]

By the time of the congressional hearing, Rohde eagerly filled in a few more blanks about his experiences that included his arrest the previous October 29 by Bosnian Serbs on charges of spying during a return trip to eastern Bosnia.

He told the hearing that he agreed with an Helsinki Human Rights Watch official, linking accounts Rohde heard from three Bosnian Muslim men who were part of group of 10,000 "military-aged men..." on foot and on the move preceding "an ambush" in eastern Bosnia.

---

27. Hearing of the U.S. House Permanent Select Committee on Intelligence, Washington, D.C., December 6, 1995.

Rohde later won the 1996 Pulitzer Prize for International Reporting and joined *The New York Times*. He also became another "Open Society Institute Individual Project Fellow" in George Soros' stable.

When he gave his congressional testimony, he was emphatic about having discovered "a decomposed human leg" the previous August—about a month after a controversial series of massacres of Muslim civilians and soldiers in and around the eastern Bosnian town of Srebrenica.

Writing in the *Monitor* on August 25, 1995, Rohde said he became convinced one of the bones he saw on August 16th was a human femur because he examined "pictures from friends' medical books and x-rays of my own once-broken femur..."[28] He also said he had looked at bone samples of cows, horses, pigs, bears, dogs, deer, and other animals at the Belgrade University veterinarian school, staring at the femurs and tibias of cows, horses, pigs, bears, dogs, deer, and other animals, and that the bone he saw protruding from the ground earlier was "too thin" for an animal.

His impromptu orthopedic study was conceivably undertaken in case of any future doubts—say, during a congressional hearing—about the unusual bareness of the bone, which presumably was attached to a human buried in haste just one month earlier. He did not volunteer to tell hearing officials that between 1992 and 1993, a Bosnian government warlord, black-marketeer, gun-runner and later-accused war criminal, and his Bosnian government "troops" had razed almost a hundred Serb villages around Srebrenica. Estimates placed the Serb civilian deaths at almost 3,300 that were murdered by the self-styled Bosnian Muslim "commander" Naser Oric who left a scorched, bloody swath of atrocities in Rupovo Brdo, Ratkovici, Bradjevina, Ducici, Gornji Ratkovici, Jezestica, Bozici, Fakovici, Radijevici, Divovici, Bjelovac, Sikirici, Kravica, Jezestica, Siljkovici and scores of other Serb villages.

Before joining the *Times*, Rohde hastily compiled a book in a premature attempt to "reconstruct" the final days from July 6th through 16th in 1995 that led up to the deaths of an unknown number of people at Srebrenica. Although self-admittedly not able to understand Serbo-Croatian and with no known ability to speak Dutch, Rohde wove his tale together with exact quotes from local Muslims and interviews quoting former Dutch U.N. peacekeepers. He gave an unusual amount of narrative about Oric, but overall minimized Oric's butchery that provoked however large a slaughter at Srebrenica in 1995.

In an October 2, 1995, sequel to his original articles, Rohde included a curiously terse statement in the thirty-fourth paragraph of his report from Tuzla and that the supposed Srebrenica "massacre" appeared to have been in response to revenge for murders of civilians and torched Serb villages by Oric and his men, as he had learned the previous August.

His unusually casual reporting was apparently used to fill in the cracks of the Srebrenica story about murders and rapes of local Serbs in their villages before 1995. This awkward fact impeded designs to indict only Serbs for war crimes in and around the eastern Bosnia enclave and safe haven used by Oric and other Bosnian government troops as a staging area for their raids on nearby Serb hamlets.

So, it was evidently not hard to find bleached human bones—Muslim or Serb—sticking out of the ground around Srebrenica.

Writing about Rohde's return to the area that October and suspected mass-grave sites and his abrupt arrest by Bosnian Serbs, *Christian Science Monitor* writer Peter Grier described the three-part series of articles about Rohde's excursion to locate

---

28. Rohde, "Monitor reporter eluded soldiers and discovered evidence of Serb atrocities," *The Christian Science Monitor*, August 25, 1995.

more "evidence" to verify "the worst massacre in Europe since the Holocaust" by supposedly Bosnian Serb soldiers. But, Grier's description of Rohde's motives was inadvertently revealing, calling Rohde's "full story, related in a four-hour monologue, ...one of ambition and moral choice, comedy and danger, paranoia and obsession" and that "(t)o reporters, the Balkans conflict is this generation's Vietnam. That means it is an assignment of great danger and *correspondingly great opportunity*... Pressure and proximity have made the international press corps in the Balkans close-knit, yet competitive."[29] (Italics added)

But the claim was false in his August 18 report that Rohde was the first Western reporter at Srebrenica after the mid-July killings.

"The visit by this reporter was the first by a Western journalist to the sites of the alleged atrocities near the former safe areas of Srebrenica and Zepa," wrote the *Times'* noted correspondent David Binder who checked the story out.

Rohde's first visit to the Srebrenica area came long after the arrival of other journalists:

> "...(T)he fact, supported by detailed Republika Srpska documents, (was) that in the latter half of August, less than a month after Srebrenica was conquered by the Serbs, twenty-two foreign journalists from six countries, including Mike Wallace of *CBS*, toured the Srebrenica area carrying CIA reconnaissance photographs of purported mass grave sites, searching for evidence of war crimes. Some reported what they saw (no mass graves). Some did not (notably Mike Wallace). So much for the claims of exclusivity of a young *Christian Science Monitor* reporter, David Rohde, who entered the region nearly two months later without permission of the Bosnian Serb authorities and 'discovered' what he alleged was a mass grave site. He was arrested the second time he headed in looking for scenes of atrocities."[30]

Rohde's 1997 volume, *Endgame: The Betrayal and Fall of Srebrenica, Europe's Worse Massacre Since World War II*, was among the first of the "victim epics" published in 1998. He first qualified the idea of "truth in the former Yugoslavia" as "a nebulous concept." He continued that distortion and twisting "the facts are well-accepted tools for survival and propaganda is the norm."

But, the remarkable feature of his account were the experiences of a mere seven individuals to buttress and verify accounts of the notorious "massacre" in eastern Bosnia. Rohde astonishingly said he allowed the three Muslims, two Dutch, a Croat and a Serb to give their detailed experiences, even inviting them to peruse drafts containing their "detailed thoughts and recollections." (But, was it incredulous that Bosnian Muslim, ex-Dutch peacekeepers or others, including interpreters, could examine English texts and comprehend Rohde's slant and nuance?) Rohde himself said at the outset that "(s)urvivors and people from Srebrenica exaggerated, openly lied or presented a sanitized version of their actions and decision making." And, he urged that his book should be taken only as a beginning account of the Srebrenica incident and "not the final word."

---

29. Peter Grier, "Into Bosnia's Killing Fields," *The Christian Science Monitor,* November 17, 1995.

30. David Binder, "Beyond the Pale: Perspectives from the Two Serbias," *Mediterranean Quarterly*, Spring 1996

The volume was very obviously a hurried re-assembly of some of the events and episodes selected in order to guide U.N. war crimes investigators toward supposed Serb perpetrators.

Rohde's transparent blame-game redundantly added to the interventionist mantra and bashing of the U.N. and NATO for hesitating to unleash air attacks to protect the "safe" areas. His patchwork of theories behind war criminal Naser Oric and his Sarajevo superiors, and sleuthing for conspiracies in the "sacrifice" of Srebrenica by the U.N. and by the Bosnian government and various U.S. and European internecine dealings, all fell hopelessly wide of the mark except as a chronicle advocating for war crimes indictments—complete with Rohde's pseudo-affidavits.

Although questions persist about hastily-imposed or presumed Muslim identities for the contents of some of the several thousand body bags cataloged by U.N. forensic teams—many containing only unidentifiable body parts—virtually absent are any public reports about even a handful of identified Serb victims from the mass killings that preceded the Srebrenica finale.

Almost a decade (!) after the carnage, the remains of a few thousand victims—Muslims possibly mixed with local Serbs or exhumed from other parts of Bosnia—were reportedly stored for further forensic examination in September 2003 when former President Bill Clinton commemorated a monument for 103 identified victims that were interred with much media fanfare.

Paris – March 1994

Roger Cohen sat pensively behind his desk, reminding his visitor somewhat of Lewis Carroll's caterpillar. A deliberate passiveness in his voice and tense expression conveyed that he really had better things to do, being in transit to or from Sarajevo within a few days, than to idle his time away with an obscure American reporter who interrupted his routine and wanted to ask some abstruse and absurd questions about "fair" and "objective" media coverage of the Yugoslav wars.

He was enviously ensconced in an upper floor office of *The New York Times'* bureau at the Royal St. George Bank building. It was sunny and cloudless and the morning sun liberally daubed the pale facades along Rue Scribe with its incomparable springtime Paris pastels.

He made the most of the distance across his desk, receding even further into his chair and contemplating the first few questions with no intention of giving any direct answers.

"What," he asked cooly, "do you think of John Burns and John Pomfret?"

The atmosphere was too menacing for humor—such as, "The poets or reporters?"—to break the ice.

Aside from *Washington Post* correspondent Pomfret's scattering of reports included in a tabulation on the factors of overwhelming pro-Croat, pro-Muslim media bias among Western reporters, I had not studied his total portfolio of war correspondence.

No, Cohen was not interested in seeing the tabulation.

"As for Burns," I answered, "he *is* the media bias."

This produced the only twinge in the Oxford-educated Cohen's demeanor before we shifted to a vapid discussion about the "future" and condescendingly conceded that Yugoslavia would recede into its own Balkan brand of Lebanon-ization.

Beyond a half-hour, any continuation was useless with the cagey, monotone journocrat (destined to become Foreign Editor at The *Times* on September 11, 2001) whose phone was, I thought, strangely silent for the entire session. For a reporter's phone, that is.

The encounter with Cohen was disappointing. I had been told by a respected Balkan correspondent that he "understood what was going on."

He declined an offer for lunch. I wanted to watch him eat.

The iconized victimhood of Bosnian war reporting, fixated upon the Western media itself in Sarajevo, was palpable when Cohen reverently conferred tribute to slain journalist Kurt Schork in remote Sierra Leone in May 2000:

> "Journalism, it is said, provides a first draft of history. It is a cliche, yet sometimes an unlikely combination of war and a witness illustrates the hallowed truth that lurks behind a hollow phrase. I write this sitting in Berlin, dreaming of Bosnia, and thinking of Kurt Schork, the *Reuters* correspondent whose dispatches from Sarajevo *helped shape the world's view* of a war that was as *morally indelible to my generation of correspondents as Vietnam was to another.*[31] (Italics added)

In fact, it took the better part of more than a decade for the American "journalism" to noisily reverse its course from the propaganda/coverage in the Vietnam war. But, after a decade of Western media bias in Yugoslavia, Cohen's "generation" of reporters were still peering down languidly from their smoky hookahs at any scribbler who strayed into their wonderland to question the unraveled Sarajevo media catechism.

In his zeal to canonize Sarajevo, Cohen's own dreamy reflections about Bosnia and the slain journalist were superimposed historically upon whatever were Schork's actual passions about war reporting:

> "...(A) deep moral conviction guided this unusual newsman, who came to journalism late after a career that included running Bill Bradley's first Senate campaign. It backed his stubborn belief that his words would ultimately count and perhaps even right wrong. The truth is, he changed things, and with his death an era has passed: that of a gradual awakening to the fact that distant war and genocide could not be ignored by America and its allies. When Yugoslavia began its protracted disintegration in 1991, precipitating the latest round of Balkan wars, the West's instincts were those of Neville Chamberlain on Czechoslovakia in 1938: these were conflicts 'in a faraway country' involving people 'of whom we know nothing.' Not knowing amounted to the best excuse for not acting, especially when the imperative to do something was accentuated by the daily Serb bombardment of Sarajevo that began in 1992 and by an archipelago of Serbian concentration camps for Bosnian Muslims uncovered that year. Mr. Schork was driven by a desire to ensure that nobody could claim ignorance.
>
> "In these days of databank journalism and infotainment as news, he wrote what the great war correspondent Martha Gellhorn famously called 'the view from the ground.' in so doing, he brought journalists back to the basics: to see, to listen, to

---

31. Cohen, "Correspondence/Slain Journalist," *The New York Times*, May 28, 2000.

remain, to reflect, to report. *His copy was so lapidary that the oft-repeated claims of muddle in Western capitals—the repetitive talk of 1,000 year old conflicts between indistinguishable Balkan tribes—became largely preposterous in the gleam of Mr. Schork's clear-eyed observation."*[32] (Italics added)

If, in Cohen's mind, Yugoslavia's "protracted disintegration" only began in 1991, it validated the chorus of insistent denials about the "ancient animosities" prevailing in the minds of Western journalism alone which ferociously rejected any view of histories other than its own!

Why else does the static argument and complaint persist in the Western versions of the Yugoslav war "literature"—except to re-insist, straddle and revise the history as the Western journalists wrote it? Cohen—like Gutman, Rieff, Gjelten, and the rest of the pack—protested too much, while Burns with his checkered reporting wisely abstained from any "literary" re-visitation since the crown-jewel of his Pulitzer-winning reporting was cracked.

Cohen, still caught up months later in emotional aftershocks from the destruction of the World Trade Center, provoked concern about the past Yugoslav war reporting and reflecting about his halcyon days of jetting in and out of the Balkans and "history-making" compared to the chores of editorship:

> "The *wonder* of foreign correspondence lies in the *freedom* it affords t*o give voice to your passions. Oh, the heady air* of some new place, the smells, the scenes, the signals ...*all yours to compose a canvas...* History, it has been said, happens, but only just."[33] (Italics added)

Cohen provided more ethereal, even erotic confessions about the soul of Western journalism:

> "When we come closest to the distillation of the truth we observe, we come closest to a journalism that has the resonance of artistic creation. Let me be clear: journalism deals in facts. Art selects facts, shapes them, changes them, in the quest for a higher truth. That distinction must never be blurred. So the term 'literary journalism' is problematic; it may even suggest an oxymoron to some. But its meaning to me resides in the notion of so marrying patient observation, the discipline of form and attention to the revelations of silence that the resultant journalism assumes the ineffable glow we associate with genuine creation. Journalism, like art, involves the refraction of life through the prism of a single human sensibility...

> "As a journalist, I have striven to set the truths down, but of course they are the truths that impressed me as most revelatory. Let us not fool ourselves about objectivity. Yes, we must strive for a balanced picture. But a sensibility is always at work in journalism and that is as it should be. In great journalism, a voice is

---

32. Cohen, "Correspondence...", *ibid.*
33. Cohen, "Substitute for Love," *The New York Times*, March 4, 2002.

ever discernible... In this light, foreign correspondence has never appeared more essential. *I believe it should be pursued in the same essential manner: going out, looking, listening, probing, feeling, analyzing, searching in present and past, in an attempt to paint in words the most truthful, the most profound, the most revealing pictures...*

"...Our profession, it seems, has become *more dangerous*. But if we shrink from it, the cost will be extremely high, *for the possibility of mutual understanding* will further recede...

"When we write, we explore: That is our challenge and our singular joy. Yes, a perfect sentence is an act of love, its satisfactions as complete and mysterious. I know that now more than ever.

"The wonder of foreign correspondence ...the freedom it affords to give voice to your passions. Oh, the heady air ... all yours to compose a canvas ...the distillation of the truth ...the resonance of artistic creation ...so marrying patient observation, the discipline of form and attention to the revelations of silence that the resultant journalism assumes the *ineffable glow* we associate *with genuine creation*. Journalism, like art, involves the refraction of life through the prism of a single human sensibility ...When we write, we explore: That is our challenge and our singular joy. Yes, a perfect sentence is an act of love, its satisfactions as complete and mysterious..."[34] (Italics added)

Thus, journalism and war reporting, and the Yugoslav correspondence as near aphrodisiac or, at least, a media mysticism?

But where, a reader of parallel history might ask, was there a Cohen or any of the other press corps among the inmate population at Sarajevo's mustard-yellow sanitarium with enough "heady air," to compile like aromatic volumes penned from Kigali in Rwanda—where up to a million were being simultaneously slaughtered?

Of course, Anglo Western journalism gave the shrug of consent to that little tick at having virtually ignored yet another of the authentic "genocide" where up to a million perished! Where were the "victim" chronicles? Where are the interventionist memoirs?

Alas, there was no Holiday Inn in Kigali, nor cocktails nor fine supper banter after filing stories—and there would be no *Sagas of Kigali*. Despite filing daily stories about the morass of suffering around them, the Western journalists seemed always receded into their own musings about themselves and their emotional pantomimes of inner woundedness which "in my own case, were not physical, but they were deep enough to prompt the writing of this book."[35]

Cohen and others insisted upon the banishment not only of ancient Balkan histories of ethnic hatreds but of Balkan historic facts themselves, seeing only through their own naïve idealism the dream-wishes of Western media alchemy, concluding that he could not put the Bosnian war between hard covers until overlaying it by presumptuously "writing the story of Yugoslavia."

Cohen thus succumbed to that most seductive and fatal of Balkan and Yugoslav

---

34. Cohen, "Substitute...", *ibid.*

35 . Cohen, *Hearts Grown Brutal—Sagas of Sarajevo*, New York: Random House, 1998 ; p. xv.

traps for Westerners at the outset—to comprehend the whole of the maelstrom in order to redeem it, driven by "anger" to understand.[36]

Soon thwarted, he selectively and conveniently found focus for his "anger"—using the late 20th Century pseudo-rationale of a Western journalist—toward the indictment of a race on the basis of its most aberrant, individual criminals. The vignette was almost as uniquely outrageous as it was obscenely manipulable, recounting—as Borislav Herak obediently intuited the answers John Burns wanted to hear —a concocted "Serb obsession with the sexuality, fertility, and promiscuity of the Muslims" from a Serb soldier who told Cohen that the Muslims "expelled us from Kosovo with their sexual organs."[37]

With a nearly national deviancy framed in his mind, reprisal was easily surmised with his consent, too, that "(t)housands of Muslim women were systematically raped by the Serbs in 1992."

No matter the unproven claim of mass systematic rape, even in what should have been his calmer, literary retrospect up to eight years later, Cohen too easily excised the long, agonizing subjugation of the Serbs beneath the half-millenium of Turkish occupation as easily as he rejected the minimal findings by the European Parliament and the U.N. Commission of Experts of mass rape by Serbs alone (see Chapter V: "Only Muslim Victims—Only Serb Perpetrators"). The solely Bosnian Muslim phenomenon of mass rape was a huge, though ultimately debunked, propaganda success.

Also, as the successor to *The Times*' John F. Burns in Sarajevo in early 1994, Cohen was understandably not about to jeopardize Burns' 1993 Pulitzer even in his memoirs and cause embarrassment for their employer—if not the legendary excesses of their former Sarajevo government hosts—for drawing attention to the insupportable claim by propagandists at the Bosnian presidency that 200,000 Bosnian Muslim troops had been killed by mid-1993. After all, it was Burns who first reported the uncorroborated claim by the Bosnian government of 200,000 fatalities by early 1993 when, except for Kosovo, most battlefield hostilities had ceased.

The most humane perspective on Cohen's book was from Yugoslav correspondent Tim Judah, who compared Cohen with fellow *New York Times* correspondent Chuck Sudetic's simultaneous publication in 1998 of *Blood and Vengeance—One Family's Story of the War in Bosnia*.

"Cohen's book is a more straightforward account. It is also a far more personal tale than Sudetic's," begins Judah's contrast of the two victim epics.

> "We learn for example that Cohen, twice a Pulitzer Prize nominee, was shattered by his experiences in Bosnia. 'There are things that simply have to be written down before they destroy you,' he explains. So Cohen writes everything down. Here we have finely observed reportage woven in with Yugoslav history woven in with lashings of moral outrage at the West's failure to act until it was too late, plus the life and times of four Bosnian families whose stories he uses in an attempt to give us the bigger picture. Lachrymose though their tales may be, sometimes it is unclear what the families are doing in the book, apparently wandering into and out of chapters at random.
>
> "While Sudetic is anything but emotional, Cohen's rage bursts from every page. For him, the war was: 'a labyrinth in which

---

36. Cohen, *Hearts...*, pp. xvi, xx.
37. Cohen, *Hearts...*, p. 222.

each clearing only led into the next maze. The dawn, I knew, would come, but would bring only the first, throaty burst of machine-gun fire followed by the flapping of pigeons scattering over deserted streets; the reek of plum brandy and international hypocrisy; and on some meaningless mountain, yet more unsung young lives blotted out like bugs on the windshield of a hurtling car.'

"...(I)t is really a book for people who did not follow the war, or a book for those in the years to come who want to read a lively history. Otherwise, there is an unfortunate sense of deja vu that pervades *Hearts Grown Brutal.*

"Cohen rakes over the same old arguments about intervention in Bosnia that raged from 1992 to the devastating NATO air raids of the summer of 1995..." [38]

In the "acknowledgments" of Cohen's book, the same old roster of interventionist journalists is followed by an affectionate and curious credit to Duska Anastasijevic, an editor on the staff of the dissident Belgrade journal *Vreme*: "I was helped beyond measure, by Dushka Anastasijevic in Belgrade..."

Apparently, she was the blonde Belgrade translator and Bosnian companion for Cohen—as she had been for *Newsday's* Roy Gutman, *The Times'* John F. Burns, and *The Chicago Tribune's* Thom Shanker.

An attractive common translator can subtly weld some impressions of three or four like-minded American journalists—especially with their limited or nonexistent abilities to speak and understand spontaneous Serbo-Croatian.

Belgrade, Serbia—February 13, 1993

The small rusty taxi tore down *Bulevar Kneza Milosa,* careening along the snow glaze that began to fall earlier that evening. The driver hunched over the steering wheel, squinting and puffing furiously on his cigarette. I wondered if there was enough tire-tread to hold the pavement, and I tried to concentrate on what I wanted to ask Chuck Sudetic.

At one time, he was the most controversial reporter among Americans of Yugoslav descent. So, I planned to ask him the routine questions about media bias in the war, and would probably earn a brittle response much the same as I heard from the rest of the Belgrade press corps that answered one of two ways. Like *Reuters* Don Forbes' cynical laugh: "So, what else is new?!" Or, Duska Anastasijevic's irritated rasp: "That's your problem!"

Maybe it was. I remembered her retort at Verdi's, the chic little restaurant on the *Terazije.* It was one of the few times she glanced up from her plateful of pasta, which she rapaciously consumed with gusto, wielding her fork and spoon to fix and twirl mouthfuls of noodles.

The air was warmer and more pungent with coal smoke in the lower Senjak neighborhood that rose above the banks of the Sava River.

Sudetic's background was Croatian; his wife Ljiljana was Serbian. I'd spoken earlier with a cab driver who was a Croat but now preferred to live in Belgrade.

---

38. Tim Judah, "Two books on Bosnia take a new approach to writing history," *The Family Angle*, November 1998.

Probably his previous career as a boxer had something to do with his longevity among the Serb hacks he joked and argued with while waiting for fares at the main train station. But I also met numerous other Croats and Muslims and Rumanians who were living agreeably in Belgrade and throughout Serbia.

Sudetic jerked the door open wide, grumbled something about not having "a lot of time" and left me to close the door myself, standing inside, hanging up my jacket as he brusquely disappeared into another room to "finish something."

His wife smiled, listening to him still muttering. She made an attempt to apologize.

"Oh, Chuck," she said musically, "he talks so much."

He stormed back into the room. "So, you said something about some questions?"

His opening opinions and varied dislikes came out in a torrent.

"I know what's going on because I can read the Belgrade papers and magazines. I know the language," he said.

John Burns? Bias? For awhile he was on the Serbs' side; now he favors Muslims. That implied balance in Sudetic's thinking.

Yes, he probably should get a Pulitzer, and deserves one, he said sarcastically. No, it's because of all the space *The New York Times* editors give Burns for his huge "epics" that crowd out Sudetic's own reports and those from other Times correspondents in the Balkans. It's the sheer volume of it. Sudetic was understandably envious.

Yes, he thinks *Reuters* is doing a better job than *The Associated Press*. His and *Reuters'* daily offerings are ahead of the *AP*. He likes to scoop the competition, sneering, "the *AP* takes our stuff and makes call-backs."

No, he doesn't like the transiting journalists who are "just passing through." Too much time to educate them.

He praises one reporter in Zagreb on a story about a "rape center," commenting cynically that she used two different sources, and in the next breath is condemning former Secretary of State Lawrence Eagleburger.

"There's not a deep enough hole to throw all those Kissinger people into!"

He thinks Roy Gutman did a good job uncovering the camps but disagrees about calling them "concentration camps."

He's full of vignettes, like the story about a Yugoslav ambassador to Israel who submitted his credentials "by FAX"! Such anecdotes must have filled his notebooks, awaiting compilation in a post-war memoir.

End of hospitality; the coffee is still warm in my cup.

The air smelled better when I left, deciding to walk back to my loaned flat near Lole Ribara. The snow was falling in large, feathery flakes, dissolving on the wet, glistening pavement next to the train station.

Turning up the *Terazije*, I recalled talking with the "ambassador," Budimir Kosutic, a couple of days before. Sudetic didn't believe Kosutic's claims about there being plans to locate nuclear dumps in areas of "cleansed" Serb villages in Croatia. Sudetic said Kosutic had lost family members who were killed in 1941 in the Croatian town of Glina. His relatives, among about 1,200 other local Serbs, were herded into a church and butchered before it was blown up. Kosutic, the former vice premier of Serbia and professor of law at Belgrade University, was still nursing revenge, but the present Serb leadership was not eager to re-ignite the Croatian war. According to *Vreme*, Kosutic was "quickly promoted into one of the most popular Serbian politicians. The consensus which has been reached concerning his nomination in Belgrade must have been prompted by the need to keep Kosutic as far as possible from Western Slavonia."[39]

Sudetic insisted there were no "ancient animosities" between Serbs, Croats and Muslims at the roots of the civil wars.

39. *Vreme News Digest*, February 24, 1992.

Kosutic insisted that two genocides against Serbs in two world wars in the 20th Century gave the opposite proof.

I instinctively liked Sudetic, a former Fulbright Scholar. I watched him grill U.N. officials and others at the press conferences at the International Press Centre, bantering incessantly until he got the answers he wanted. He had guts. And, he liked chasing "the story." It was "the story" that counted.

Sudetic's long-awaited *Blood and Vengeance*, published eight years after he arrived in Yugoslavia to cover the federation's demise and ensuing inferno, was everything his professional colleagues and acquaintances—and his critics—expected it to be. Included were glimpses of why and how he "covered" the wars.

Judah's praise for another insatiable chronicler of the addictive mayhem that seduces Western journalists into the Balkans was magnanimous, even though mechanically denying the role of ancient provocations that were discernible in *Blood and Vengeance* itself:

"Quite simply, Sudetic's work is brilliant. This is the book for all those people who have never understood why. It also nails shut once and for all that ridiculous debate about ancient ethnic hatreds. That is to say, were the Yugoslavs killing one another because they were genetically predisposed to do so every now and then or because their leaders were evil?

"It is a gripping book about real people. It shows how power-crazed politicians fanned the embers of hatred, how they breathed new life into conflicts that were almost, but not quite, forgotten. As Sudetic shows, these conflicts bound Bosnian Serbs and Muslims together in a bloody embrace, not just as nations but as families and neighbors. 'Memories have a long lifetime,' recalls one of his interviewees, 'and the evil memories have the longest lifetime of all.' Sudetic, from Cleveland, Ohio, had a long fascination with Yugoslavia. He has Croatian ancestry and a Serbian wife. At the end of the war, he embarked on an ambitious quest: he went to hunt for the Celiks, the Muslim family of his Serbian sister-in-law. In 1992, as the fighting started, the family fled the eastern Bosnia hamlet where they had lived for generations. They slept in the woods and in caves before finally ending up in Srebrenica.

"What makes this book stand out is that it reads *like a novel* —except, terrifyingly, every detail is true. It also answers the crucial question of motivation—but not in a dry, academic way...

"Sudetic's Bosnia is the real Bosnia, *not the paradise* it is some-times believed to have been by dewy-eyed Westerners who had never been there before the war. This is the land where grandfathers killed one another during World War II, where grandsons went to school together while their fathers muttered quietly that, one day, revenge would come.

"Although focused on one family's war, Sudetic's book comes to a chilling climax with his account of the fall of Srebrenica and the massacre of up to 8,000 of its men. Instead of simply laying out a chronology of what happened or trying to prove that Mladic supervised the slaughter, Sudetic strips the story bare, going straight to the heart of the matter.

"He visits the Serb village of Kravica, where during World War II Kravica Serbs had died at the hands of Muslim *ustasha* fascists. On 7 January 1993, on the Serbian Orthodox Christmas, thousands of Srebrenica's Muslim soldiers swooped on the village as its womenfolk roasted suckling pigs. More than two years later, Sudetic talked to one of Kravica's survivors, quoting him as saying:

'Revenge ...' [The Serbs] said, *'Kad tad. Kad tad*, sooner or later our five minutes will come.'

'And the opportunity finally came.'

'Yes.'

'Vengeance?'

'Yes, blood vengeance.'"[40]

Bloody. Grimy. Mercenary. On the front cover, the flipped, inside photo of the grieving Sanela Halilovic, nursing her infant son from an exposed breast and holding up a picture of her missing husband, Mohamed, for photographer Rachel L. Cobb, was typically exploitive. Yes, it was graphically correct according to the ethically inverted standards of media victimology.

Sudetic was lured back to Yugoslavia in 1990 after an earlier stint as a Fulbright scholar the previous decade.

He exchanged suburban life in Cleveland for a "mercenary, monomaniacal existence" earning "real money *only if I found stories that got into print...*" succumbing to the "addictive, groin-tingling excitement to working in Bosnia. I relished the hunt for stories and words that would show the horror and the scandalous injustice of the destruction of Bosnia and the war's primary victims, the Muslims..."[41] (Italics added)

No mask then of unbiased objectivity or reporting here. Sudetic raged through press conferences, roaring back and forth from Sarajevo and Belgrade and gutted villages, hamlets and towns like a Hemingway driven by, feeding on and being fed upon by that incendiary, schizophrenic Western journalism and the "method to presenting the reality of war in *Times* style ...leaving the common folk to exemplify trends, to serve as types: a fallen soldier, a screaming mother, a dead baby—literal symbols."

The "method" relied on "detachment, disinterestedness, dispassion, distancing, and others with negative prefixes engineered to obliterate any relationship between observer and observed."

He plunged through towns with bodies of men, women, and children, some dismembered and decapitated, accidentally killing a young man on a bike who strayed

---

40. Judah, "Two books...", *ibid.*
41. Chuck Sudetic, *Blood and Vengeance—One Family's Story of the War in Bosnia*, New York: Penguin Books, 1999, p. xxxi.

into the path of his car. He accompanied the man to a Sarajevo hospital, and then went to attempt to console his father before being towed back to his hotel where he sent his story to New York, calling his routine "my *addiction*, my *mania*."[42] (Italics added)

Sudetic wove the Celik saga in between anecdotes from his war coverage and his roster of the villainous officialdom of Milosevic, Tudjman, Izetbegovic, Karadzic and Mladic that sowed and reaped the federation's undoing.

On the eve of landing a reporting berth in Yugoslavia in 1990, Sudetic sneers at official journalism's tidy dearth of merely competent Balkan coverage, citing his own account about how he arrived to chronicle the Yugoslav mess after a brief pre-*Times* incubation and three sessions of orientations at the *Times* where he was given "a few tips about how to construct a newspaper story." He was never asked for references or to fill out an application or to provide copies of his work.[43]

Retrieved back to New York and given a regular reporting job in early 1995, he soon quit out of boredom and, by September 1995, Sudetic was back in Bosnia, picking up the pieces of the Srebrenica story first for *The Rolling Stone* and then a few months later quit the *Times* and returned to write of Srebrenica ...again.

London – 1999

As a would-be media-soldier-of-fortune and war "tourist" by his own definition, heroin addict Anthony Loyd wrote about parts of the Bosnian war the way most straight correspondents wished they could—with free-basing journalism.

As he tells it, Bosnia made a "war reporter" out of him.[44]

Educated at Eton and from a notable English military family and ancestry that distinguished themselves in the Boer War and World War II, Loyd was a platoon commander in the British army with benign tours in Northern Ireland and the Persian Gulf before he found himself adrift at twenty-six-years-old in West London, nurturing a sprouting death-wish.

A moment of passage apparently came in 1992 when he was "angered" by a picture in London newspapers of a Serb paramilitary fighter "kicking dead Muslims in Bijeljina" in northeastern Bosnia.

War reporting as an addiction? Who better to describe it than an admitted drug addict? After mustering out of the British army, Loyd added another craving to his list of addictions—a pseudo-career of journalism in the Balkans. Alcohol, suicidal depression and eventually psychotherapy attempted to rescue him, but could not save him from endless news reports in 1992 that eventually seduced him with "a revamped urge to go to war." With "no clue about journalism" he decided to take a cram course in photography.

Eight years and six wars later—Bosnia, Albania, Chechnya, Nigeria, Sierra Leone and Afghanistan—"Ant" Loyd was lecturing students in the World Room of Columbia University's School of Journalism on the finer points of getting started as a war correspondent. At the time he was on a $1,000 retainer as an on-call war correspondent with professional savvy in finding interpreters and body guards to get the necessary job done, advising listeners to "choose 'the right war'."[45]

His reviewers marveled at Loyd's heroin-laced observations and powerful

---

42. *Blood and Vengeance...*, pp. xxxii-xxxiii.

43. *Blood and Vengeance...*, p. 80

44. Anthony Loyd, *My War Gone By, I Miss It So*, New York: Penguin Putnam Inc., 1999.

45. Andrea McDaniels, "Notes from a Talk by Anthony Loyd," *Society of Professional Journalists*, December 18, 2000.

portraits of destruction and bloodshed and the "sexual release of blasting away with an automatic machine gun." Loyd's audience was appalled by his description of a bedridden, paralyzed stroke victim who was forced to watch the rape of his daughter. One reporter called Loyd's style "pure war reporting, free from the usual journalistic constraints that often give a false significance to suffering."[46]

He concludes a war correspondent cannot "operate without bias."[47] Loyd, who worked with *The Times* of London, was "contemptuous of the mainstream reporters" who stayed in Sarajevo and drove out of the Holiday Inn basement in their armored cars every morning to retrieve information from the U.N. as the backdrop for footage of locals and then "returned to their sanctuary to file their heartfelt vitriol with scarcely a hair out of place."[48]

Loyd, however, was the nearly lone reporter—drunk, stoned or sober—about the Western war correspondents he saw, knew, imitated—and exposed. When "away from the confines of the Holiday Inn they seemed like an affable clan of damaged children." Journalists had their own lives of "personal tragedy and misfortune" and even showed clear symptoms of Post-traumatic Stress Disorder. They brawled with each other or carried out their intimate sexual liaisons when the opportunity presented itself. They stuck together with an "altruistic camaraderie" and Loyd settled in effortlessly, fitting in "just fine."[49]

Near Vitez, Loyd recalls, the *Daily Telegraph's* Patrick Bishop was wounded when a claymore mine exploded. A short time later, Bishop left Bosnia after hurriedly anointing Loyd as his stand-in. Loyd didn't know if he could function as a reporter or whether he even had the tools to ask the routine questions or what "formula" to use in writing his dispatches.

His analysis of war reporters, especially print journalists, was that in Yugoslavia they "hamstrung themselves with a work ethic so empty and meaningless that its only benefit was one of physical security." They did not need to risk danger at the front when they could hang back at the press centers, hotels and conference rooms, quoting politicians or officials who had "a broader understanding of what is going on."[50]

The war-reporting calculus was that everyone in the Bosnian war lied some of the time or all of the time, and the "more authoritative a figure the bigger the lies; the more credible his position, the better the lies."

Their bureau chiefs and editors far away probably were more satisfied "with lies from names their readers recognized as power figures."[51] Chancing excursions to the front for the sights and sounds of death at close proximity made no sense.

In covering a battle at the Bosnian village of Stupni Do, Loyd was overawed by *Reuters* reporter Kurt Schork, his intensity and charisma, his toughness which derived from a previous forays into business and politics, and among the Bosnian war reporters had "fast assumed the high priest's mantle." Schork's ability to concentrate, Loyd observed, his quiet outrage and powerful objectivity would have made him "a fine killer."[52]

Vukovar, Croatia – 1996

---

46. Judith Coburn, "A jaded British correspondent feeds his smack habit in Bosnia and Chechnya," *Salon.com*, January 28, 2000.

47. Justin Brown, *Christian Science Monitor*, January 27, 2000.

48. Brown, *ibid.*

49. *My War...*, p. 82.

50. *My War...*, p. 91.

51. *My War...*, pp. 91, 92.

52. *My War...*, p. 142.

It was the second rain of the day, lighter this time but still miserable for the small group of spectators on the wooden platform and the handful of people working quietly inside the shallow excavation.

The odor seemed enhanced because of the dampness. Someone walked quickly off the back of the platform, took two steps and vomited, gagging loudly and gasping.

The workers, forensic scientists and others commissioned by the war crimes prosecutors at The Hague, looked up for a moment at the visitor who loudly cleared out his throat and mouth, continually spitting.

They wore bulky, smudged coveralls, protective gloves and rubber boots, and bent over or squatted as they methodically scraped the surface of the pit at Ovcara, a broken-down pre-war pig farm a few kilometers south of Vukovar. It was one of the "mass graves" in the area and was thought to contain the bodies of Croat patients, medical staff, malingering soldiers and civilians who were supposedly taken from the hospital and were executed by Serbs in November 1991 when the town fell to the JNA. Against international law, the hospital had been used as a shield by Croat soldiers firing mortars wildly toward nearby Serb militia and civilian enclaves while federal army units were massing. The Croats were oblivious about killing Serbs or Croats that were still hunkered down in cellars. Later, Serb "irregulars" took it out on the occupants of the hospital when it was overrun.

Five years later, the fetid smell of rotting corpses permeated the area and increasingly reeked as the van drove up the road and parked next to the site.

"What does it mean—Ovcara?" someone asked.

"Sheep," I answered over my shoulder. "It means something about 'sheep' or 'shepherd' in Serbo-Croatian."

The man in front of me snapped his head around, growling: "There is no 'Serbo-Croatian' here. We speak only Croatian!"

I noticed an attractive young woman moving gracefully around the floor of the grave, stepping carefully to not disturb markers and other objects. Ballet-like, she delicately paced her deliberate, measured strides, head down, watchful. What a contrast to the nauseating stench of human rot and decay that wafted up in thick sickening fumes!

Every now and then, a distant "whump" could be heard as unexploded artillery rounds, grenades or mines were detonated. Only the Westerners whirled around to try to see where the noise came from.

There were plenty of Serbs murdered around the region and dumped into the more dependable "mass grave" that flowed past Vukovar. The reliable Danube was eternally secretive.

Eight years later, Clea Koff wrote "The Bone Woman" about her five weeks in and around Ovcara as a twenty-three-year-old Stanford-educated forensic anthropologist.[53]

Earlier that year, she spent the previous two months in the Srebrenica area of Bosnia after a prior three months exhuming mass graves in Rwanda. In 2000, she would return to Kosovo for three months.

She subtitled her book: "A Forensic Anthropologist's Search for Truth in the Mass Graves of Rwanda, Bosnia, Croatia, and Kosovo."

She believed the forensic cliché "that bones can talk" would somehow deter mass murder and war crimes, and her narrative blithely focused on the ghoulish methods and techniques used in search remains for clues that would affix blame. But, strangely she said relatively little about the total numbers or the propaganda technique of multiplication and extrapolation used to arrive at the exaggerated and routinely inflated body counts throughout the Yugoslav conflict.

---

53. Clea Koff, *The Bone Woman*, New York: Random House, 2004

Koff started out hopefully with the modulated perspective on the fighting that she characterized as lasting for three years, "...and was marked by war crimes and crimes against humanity on all sides; detention camps, shelling of civilians, forced migrations of millions of people..." But, just as quickly, she lapsed into the convenient hearsay about the "systematic rape of 20,000 women, the deaths of 200,000 people, and the disappearances of tens of thousands of military-aged men."[54]

The latter threadbare statistic, of course, referred to Srebrenica—never mind the forced migrations of 350,000 (including many Serbs with Croat spouses) from Krajina, 50,000 Serbs from Sarajevo, 25,000 Serbs from Mostar, 4,000 Serbs from Dubrovnik, and elsewhere. Koff's colleagues only tentatively probed suspected mass graves containing Serbs at Gospic and Knin, as war crimes prosecutors aided the "cover-up" of a claimed 10,000 Serbs who mostly were dumped into the Danube and other non-exhumable mass graves when more than 500,000 Serbs were "ethnically cleansed" from Croatia.

> "During the interethnic war in the Republic of Croatia (1991-1996), Croatian armed forces liquidated more than ten thousand Serbs. In doing so, they tried, and in most cases succeeded, to remove and conceal their bodies. The most frequent practices for disposing of bodies included buring of victims in unmarked graves, incineration of bodies or throwing them into fish ponds or rivers." [55]

But before arriving at Vukovar and Ovcara, Koff and the other members of her forensic team spent most of July and August in the Srebrenica region and were over-confident they would succeed in their assignment to investigate the disappearance and suspected mass-killing of 8,000 men and boys who fled toward Tuzla before the arrival of the Bosnian Serb army. Koff and her colleagues "knew we would find the missing men."[56]

Koff and others stopped first at Cerska, a short distance northwest of Srebrenica, exhuming over 150 bodies from a mass grave at Cerska. Their movements were watched by international journalists throughout each day that stood guard over their previous stories.

Since by mid-July—or just one week after beginning to excavate the Cerska grave —they had uncovered more than 150 bodies, it seemed odd that in their remaining week at Cerska only about fifty more were found before they finished. It was far short of the number that was expected despite the skeptical glares from reporters who had to remain at a distance while photographers used large telephoto lenses from the second story of gutted buildings.

The excavation and exhumation at Nova Kasaba lasted apparently for about a week, and the refrigerated container was sent to Kalesija, just outside of Tuzla, and the makeshift morgue. Again, curiously, Koff never divulged the numbers of corpses found at Nova Kasaba, nor the numbers that were stored and examined at the morgue.

Then it was on to Vukovar and Ovcara. There was, according to Koff, no mention of any number of retrieved bodies close to the 10,000 men and boys "we knew we

---

54. *The Bone Woman*, p. 115.
55. See Vojin S. Dabic and Ksenija M. Lukic, "Crimes Without Punishment: Crimes Committed by Croatian Troops Against the Serbs in Eastern Slavonia and Western Sirmium In 1991," Dossier No. A-87, *Balkans Repository Project*, 1997. ("Sirmium" is the ancient Pannonian area adjacent to northwestern Serbia.)
56. *The Bone Woman*, p. 117.

would find."

Why Koff and others became passive apologists for the "ethnic cleansing" of 350,000 Serbs in the Croatian army's brutal sweep through western Slavonia and the Krajina in 1995 is disturbing[57] as she inexplicably minimized the event nine years later as involving "tens of thousands of Croatian Serbs."[58]

Her month at Vukovar/Ovcara yielded more of the gory intricacies of exhuming mass graves with inconsistencies about how many bodies were found, first recorded as "more than 260 people" and later as "more than two hundred and fifty bodies."[59]

"There are thousands of people missing from Vukovar," Koff summarized, nuancing the assumption that she was talking about "missing" Croats instead of the missing and/or ethnically cleansed 44,000 pre-war majority population of the city's Serbs and "Yugoslavs."

Returning four years later and commencing three months (April-July) of gathering supposed forensic evidence for the indictment of crimes against humanity and war crimes against President Slobodan Milosevic, Koff "estimated that the remains of several thousand people were in these various states of interment throughout Kosovo."[60]

Mass graves, it turned out, were rare in Kosovo after the "war" ended in 1999. Koff and her colleagues searched cemeteries for victims buried by family members in marked and unmarked graves. Her narrative winds down with more post-mortem minutiae—but nothing about the numbers of dead except rhetorically recalling an encounter with a young man who gave her the "Serbian nationalist salute" and wondering whether he knew in 2003 about "the corpses of a thousand Kosovar Albanians buried in Belgrade's suburbs, police stations, and military barracks?"[61]

Koff was referring to a spate of hysterical reports coming from Belgrade newspapers that claimed the bodies of between 800 and 900 missing Muslims from Kosovo had been transported by refrigerator trucks and were secretly buried at Batajnica, the location of a government anti-terrorism training facility just outside of Belgrade.

The murky and dubious "refrigerator truck" episode along with the propagandized disappearance of Kosovo Muslim bodies at the Trepca iron mine complex—where supposedly a thousand bodies were daily dumped into mine shafts, dissolved by hydrochloric acid or incinerated—were used to buttress dispelled earlier reports by the U.S. State Department that 100,000 to 500,000 Kosovar Albanians had been killed by Serb forces. Aside from reports that the FBI had located thirty sites containing a total of 200 bodies, and a Spanish team of investigators that found in one area only 187 bodies buried in individual graves, forensic scientists found comparatively little

---

57. See *The Washington Post*, May 16, 1997, which reported the exodus of 350,000 Serbs from the two regions.

58. By contrast, Roger Cohen, of *The New York Times*, wrote in 1996 that "(a)bout 750,000 Muslims were chased from their homes on a swath of land stretching from Prijedor ...in the northwest to Trebinje ...in the southeast." But, the departure of 350,000 Serbs from western Slavonia and the Krajina was minimized at the end of same report: "Successive military victories by the Croats over the Serbs in 1995 drove most of the Serbian minority out of Croatia..." Cohen's article, "Savage Atrocities Demand Vengeance In the Twisting Spiral of Madness," appeared in a special 1996 publication by the Times' "Atlas of War & Peace," a 50-page collection of maps and articles that attempted to present a simplified reference for the conflicts. The cover included a self-mocking subtitle: "Who What Where When Why How."

59. *The Bone Woman*, pp. 187, 193.

60. *The Bone Woman*, p. 212

61. *The Bone Woman*, p. 256.

work in Kosovo.

When Koff was on her way to Kosovo in 2000, she read the familiar article about relatives of an alleged "massacre" at Racak who were requesting forensic scientists to investigate whether bodies were victims of murder or killed in combat. She liked to read the article during her lectures to students at the University of Nebraska at Lincoln, underlining how people in Racak asked for "forensic investigation into the dead before reqesting humanitarian aid for the living."[62]

Six months later the substance of Koff's "article" about massacre victims was debunked by a report in the *Berliner Zeitung:*

> "The final report by the Finnish forensic scientists finds no evidence for the alleged massacre in the Kosovo village of Racak on 15 January 1999. A detailed report..., which will soon appear in the respected forensics journal, 'Forensic Science International,' will summarize the investigation of the 40 bodies found in Racak. The report, which was made available to the 'Berliner Zeitung' prior to publication, does not conclude that a group of peaceful Albanian villagers in Racak were executed by Serbian security forces.

> "In the spring of 1999, the Organisation for Security and Co-operation in Europe (OSCE) said there was proof of 'killings and mutilations of unarmed civilians, many shot at extremely close range.' The alleged Serbian massacre at Racak gave many politicians, especially in Germany, a justification for supporting Nato's war of aggression against Yugoslavia.

> "(But, the final report said) ...three experts explained that 'there were no signs of posthumous mutilation' by humans. In great detail, the report says that in the 40 bodies studied between 1 and 20 bullet wounds were discovered. Only in one case did the forensic experts find powder marks, which would hint at an execution.

> "The report ...confirmed the conclusion to which the 'Berliner Zeitung' had come to in March 2000 by analyzing classified autopsy protocols: There was no proof of a mass execution of Albanian civilians by Serbian security forces, contrary to claims at the time by the OSCE and many Western politicians. Completely ignored was the question of whether some of the dead in Racak were KLA fighters killed in battles with Yugoslav forces. Even after the publication of the Berliner Zeitung article, the UN Tribunal in the Hague said the starting assumption was that Albanian civilians were murdered in Racak..."[63]
> (Italics added)

The *Berliner Zeitung* continued that the European Union resumed the Racak investigation after the Kosovo war ended, and on June 21, 2000, submitted its completed

---

62. *The Bone Woman*, p. 200.
63. Bo Adam and Roland Heine, "Racak: Finnish pathologists find no massacre," *Berliner Zeitung*, January 17, 2001.

313

report to the Yugoslav Tribunal—that "was immediately marked secret"!

"In the meantime one international body had drawn inferences from the growing doubts: The Parliamentary Assembly of Nato ...set out its criticism of the war and above all of the crisis management that preceded it. In this context, the Nato assembly spoke of the 'the alleged massacre at Racak, which even today is still not fully explained.'"

Evidence was presented by the defense in the trial against Milosevic on April 27, 2005, that thirty of the forty "massacre victims" at Racak were members of the Kosovo Liberation Army. Also, the "massacre"on January 15, 1999, was instead an ambush set up by the KLA to provoke international intervention. Within a few weeks, bombs and missiles from NATO and American aircraft rained down on Belgrade, Novi Sad, Nis and other Serbian targets for seventy-eight straight days.

More bones would speak—but were never asked.

Afterword

Again, why would someone want to write a book about what happened in the "former" Yugoslavia in the last decade of the 20th Century? Better yet, why would someone write a book about what happened to the Western media in connection with the overt and criminal dismantling of Yugoslavia, a sovereign nation?

The answer is simple: Because there needs to be a ...record. And, because it's taken almost fifteen years.

Thirty years ago, when I probably couldn't find Yugoslavia on a map, I went there for the first time. I say "went." Rather, I had to be led there.

And, now, I've spent the last decade and a half lugging around documents, news stories, wire-service printouts, pamphlets, and books by other writers and reporters while trying to get it done.

The manuscript has accompanied me not like the bulging boxfuls of dog-eared piles of paper, but more like an arm or a leg. ...El Paso, Texas; Albuquerque, New Mexico; Monterrey, California; Rio Rico, Arizona; Creede, Colorado; Kensington, Maryland; Washington, D.C.; Geneva, Switzerland; Paris, France; Cambridge, England; The Hague, Netherlands; Goteborg, Sweden; Vienna, Austria; Budapest, Hungary; Trieste, Italy, and a host of other cities, towns and villages in Yugoslavia and the "former" Yugoslavia.

I have not gone the traditional route of imploring authors' agents and publishers who cannot and will not buck the bias or accepted trends in a journalism that has little of its soul left to sell. Nor have I used the dialectical idiosyncracies to attempt proper Slavic and Balkan word pronunciations for readers. If it is important to know that "river" is the Serbian word "reka" (pronounced rey-kah) and is the Croatian word "rijeka" (pronounced ree-yeh-kah), then they may find themselves curious enough to risk peeling back the first layer of the "Yugoslav" (South Slav) story to see what's underneath. Likewise, plenty of maps and photographs are available from other sources.

Of course, any flaws or errors are mine.

I am deeply grateful for the encouragement and tolerance of my family, friends, colleagues, scholars and acquaintances who offered much patience, understanding and shared wisdom. And even to my critics and attackers who afforded me their unwitting guidance. There simply are too many of the former to name—and not a few of the latter.

Afterword

It is difficult to select the right quotation from the great English writer Rebecca West, who set down her memoirs of several journeys to Yugoslavia during the mid-1930s, luring all of us later with the incomparable *Black Lamb and Grey Falcon: A Journey through Yugoslavia*. Likely, this one is appropriate:

> "Violence was, indeed, all I knew of the Balkans: all I knew of the South Slavs... But I must have been wholly mistaken in my acceptance of the popular legend regarding the Balkans, for if the South Slavs had been truly violent they would not have been hated first by the Austrians, who worshipped violence in an imperialist form, and later by the Fascists in a totalitarian form..."[64]

As of now, certainly the rest of us fall somewhere in between.

---

64. Rebecca West, *Black Lamb and Grey Falcon: A Journey Through Yugoslavia*, New York: Penguin Books, 1994; p. 21. (First published in the U.S. by The Viking Press, 1941).

Index

Rieff, David, 82, 290, 292.
Rohde, David, V., 296, 298.
Rolling Stone Magazine, 56.
Rohrabacher, Dana, 128.
Rooper, Jonathan, 219.
Rose, Sir Michael, 75, 175.
Rosenthal, Abe, 14.
Rosenstiel, Tom, 188.
Ruder-Finn, 117, 124, 126, 127, 128, 129, 130, 131, 133, 134, 140.

S

Safire, William, IV, 14, 272, 273.
Saints Cyril and Methodius, 144.
San Francisco Chronicle, The, 88.
Sarajevo Daily, 52, 121, 132, 286, 287.
Saric, Refic, 204.
Sawyer, John, 58.
Schork, Kurt, IX, 14, 182, 300, 309.
Schorr, Daniel, 58.
Schrag, Minna, 26, 195.
Senate Foreign Relations Committee, 57.
Serb-controlled, 21, 24, 78, 213.
Serbian Orthodox church, 11.
Serbo-Croatian, IX, 2, 36, 41, 44, 97, 229, 297, 304, 310.
Serdari , 96, 115.
Seventeen, 62.
Seward, Deborah, 21.
Shalikashvili, Gen. John, 32.
Shanker, Thom, 63, 304.
Shattuck, John, 17, 212, 213.
Shultz, George, P., 137.
Silajdzic, Haris, 59, 75, 131, 133, 156, 182.
Silber, Laura, 14, 181, 321.
Sisak, 43.
Sivac, Nusreta, 108.
Slaughterhouse, 82, 292, 293.
Slavonia, IX, XIII, 3, 26, 28, 148, 170, 276, 277, 305, 311, 312.
Smajlovic, Liljana, 14, 96.
Smale, Alison, 14, 44, 134, 165, 186.
Smith, Tony, 14, 151, 324.
Sniper Alley, 248.

Soloman Norman, 126.
Soros, George, 51, 66, 67, 70, 74, 98, 107, 108, 109, 134, 135, 136, 137, 138, 139, 140, 165, 176, 187, 196, 296, 297.
Spectator, The, 142, 256, 271.
Split, 259.
spy satellites, 26, 212, 291.
Srebrenica, 5, IV, VII, VIII, 23, 26, 27, 28, 74, 75, 119, 173, 182, 183, 184, 191, 192, 193, 203, 207, 209, 210, 211, 212, 213, 214, 215, 216, 217, 218, 219, 220, 221, 240, 241, 264, 270, 271, 297, 298, 299, 306, 307, 308, 310, 311.
Srecko, Latal, 23.
Sremski, Karlovac, 145.
Stampa, 152.
Stavrou, Nikolaos, A., 53.
Stumbo, Bella, 14, 184.
Stara, Lipa, 45.
Stefanovic, Ivan, 145.
Schwartz, Stephen, 130.
Stepinac, Alojzije, 143, 159, 160.
St. John, Robert, 18.
Stojanovic, Dusan, 14, 47.
Strossmayer, Bishop Josip, 144, 145, 148, 159.
Struga, 40, 42, 43, 44, 45.
Studio B TV, 139.
Suddeutsche Zeitung, 150, 254, 262, 323.
Sudetic, Chuck, 14, 41, 80, 123, 142, 277, 303, 304.
Suhopolje, 45.
Sullivan, Elizabeth, 71, 84.
Suponcic Joe, 1, 2.
Sydney Sun-Herald, 93, 263.

T

Tadic, Dusan, 107, 176, 222.
Tagliabue, John, 156, 157.
TANJUG, 89, 95.
Tatrow, Nick, 14.
Times of London, The, 14, 45, 75, 192, 193, 309.